BEST PRACTICE CASES IN BRANDING:

Lessons from the World's Strongest Brands

BEST PRACTICE CASES IN BRANDING:
Lessons from the World's Strongest Brands

Kevin Lane Keller
Dartmouth College

VP/Editorial Director: Jeff Shelstad
Project Manager: Melissa Pellerano
Associate Director, Manufacturing: Vincent Scelta
Production Editor & Buyer: Carol O'Rourke
Printer/Binder: R. R. Donnelley, Harrisonburg

10 9 8 7 6 5
ISBN-13: 978-0-13-188865-4
ISBN-10: 0-13-188865-X

Table of Contents

The brands and companies spotlighted in this book represent some of the world's most successful brands and companies over the last decade or so. The marketers behind these brands and companies have all made noteworthy additions to our understanding of the strategic brand management process and how to best build and manage brand equity. These cases highlight these achievements while also suggesting some of the opportunities and challenges they currently face.

The cases cover a broad spectrum of industries, geographies, and brand management issues. The cases range from fast-moving consumer goods to high-tech and online brands and from durables and business-to-business brands to service brands. The cases often provide detailed descriptions of the global landscape for the brand and how it has performed in different markets. In fact, two cases are primarily set in Europe (Nivea and Red Bull). Finally, a host of brand management topics are addressed in the cases that will help the reader understand how to:

1) Brand a new product (even if it is a commodity or ingredient);

2) Employ new marketing approaches to build brand equity and brand loyalty;

3) Expand a brand into new geographical markets and channels;

4) Establish a brand hierarchy and introduce brand extensions;

5) Establish a sub-brand;

6) Manage a brand across multiple categories and markets;

7) Manage a corporate brand;

8) Keep a brand strong over time;

9) Revitalize a brand that gets into trouble; and

10) Change a brand name or reposition a brand.

Collectively, these cases provide a comprehensive overview of the strategic brand management process and corresponding best practice guidelines. Each of the 15 cases also yields valuable specific lessons into how to build and manage brand equity.

As good as the marketers have been with these brands, however, marketing is never perfect. As these marketers themselves would probably readily admit, sometimes mistakes have been made and opportunities have been overlooked. If given another chance, they might have done some things differently. So as the reader studies these cases, it is important to do so with a critical eye to properly discern the key lessons in strategic brand management. What did these brands do well? What was their formula for success? What could they have improved on? What might you have done differently? Finally, in looking forward, what kinds of things should be done so that the brand flourishes?

Acknowledgements

I would like to acknowledge some of the many people that helped to create this casebook and develop associated teaching materials. First, many thanks to all the companies profiled here whom, directly or indirectly, provided valuable input or feedback. In particular, I would like to extend special thanks to the following individuals who provided important assistance when they were associated with companies that were studied: Scott Bedbury, Jerome Conlan, Howard Behar, Sheri Marzolf, and Oren Smith (Starbucks); Liz Dolan, Bill Zeitz, David Kottcamp, Steve Miller, Nelson Farris, and Trevor Edwards (Nike); Jamie Murray, Barbara Pandos, and Cheryl Gee (DuPont); Dennis Carter, Sally Fundakowski, Karen Alter, Ann Lewnes, and Ellen Konar (Intel); Rolf Kunisch, Norbert Krapp, Ann-Christin Wagemann and Franziska Schmiedebach (Beiersdorf); Steve Goldstein, Robert Hanson, James Capon, and Bobbi Silten (Levi-Strauss); Jeff Manning (CMPB); Jim Murphy, Teresa Poggenpohl, Charles Teeter, and Brian Harvey (Accenture); Michael Weinstein, Ken Gilbert, and Jack Belisto (Snapple); Norbert Kraihamer (Red Bull); and Anke Audenaert (Yahoo!).

At Prentice-Hall, Melissa Pellerano offered ample assistance, but a number of other people there provided guidance and help for which I am thankful, specifically, Carol O'Rourke, Jeff Shelstad, and Christine Ietto.

Finally, I would also like to thank my case writing assistants who helped to research and write these cases over the years: Leslie Kimerling, Sanjay Sood, Peter Gilmore, Greg Tusher, Emmanuelle Louis Hofer, and Eric Free. Jonathan Michaels and Lowey Sichol provided invaluable assistance in the preparation of this edition. I would like to express special thanks to my research assistant over the years, Keith Richey, who was involved in writing or updating every case in this book. An incredibly gifted writer and natural-born marketer, his contributions were immense.

Dedication

This book is dedicated to my wife, Punam Anand Keller and my two daughters, Carolyn and Allison with much love and appreciation.

Kevin Lane Keller
Hanover, NH
October 2006

BIOGRAPHY

Kevin Lane Keller is the E. B. Osborn Professor of Marketing at the Tuck School of Business at Dartmouth College. Professor Keller has degrees from Cornell, Carnegie-Mellon, and Duke universities. At Dartmouth, he teaches MBA courses on marketing management and strategic brand management and lectures in executive programs on that topic.

Previously, Professor Keller was on the faculty of the Graduate School of Business at Stanford University, where he also served as the head of the marketing group. Additionally, he has been on the marketing faculty at the University of California at Berkeley and the University of North Carolina at Chapel Hill, been a visiting professor at Duke University and the Australian Graduate School of Management, and has two years of industry experience as Marketing Consultant for Bank of America.

Professor Keller's general area of expertise lies in marketing strategy and planning. His specific research interest is in how understanding theories and concepts related to consumer behavior can improve marketing strategies. His research has been published in three of the major marketing journals -- the *Journal of Marketing*, the *Journal of Marketing Research*, and the *Journal of Consumer Research*. He also has served on the Editorial Review Boards of those journals. With over sixty published papers, his research has been widely cited and has received numerous awards.

Professor Keller is acknowledged as one of the international leaders in the study of brands, branding, and strategic brand management. Actively involved with industry, he has worked on a host of different types of marketing projects. He has served as a consultant and advisor to marketers for some of the world's most successful brands, including Accenture, American Express, Disney, Ford, Intel, Levi Strauss,

Procter & Gamble, and SAB Miller. Additional brand consulting activities have been with other top companies such as Allstate, Beiersdorf (Nivea), BlueCross BlueShield, Campbells, Eli Lilly, ExxonMobil, General Mills, Goodyear, Kodak, Mayo Clinic, Nordstrom, Shell Oil, Starbucks, Unilever, and Young & Rubicam. He has also served as an academic trustee for the Marketing Science Institute. A popular speaker, he has conducted marketing seminars to top executives in a variety of forums.

Professor Keller is currently conducting a variety of studies that address strategies to build, measure, and manage brand equity. His textbook on those subjects, *Strategic Brand Management*, has been adopted at top business schools and leading firms around the world and has been heralded as the "bible of branding." As of the 12th edition, he is also the co-author with Philip Kotler of the all-time best selling introductory marketing textbook, *Marketing Management*.

An avid sports, music, and film enthusiast, in his so-called spare time, he has served as executive producer for one of Australia's great rock and roll treasures, The Church, as well as American power-pop legends Dwight Twilley and Tommy Keene. He is also on the Board of Directors for The Doug Flutie, Jr. Foundation for Autism. Professor Keller lives in Etna, NH with his wife, Punam (also a Tuck marketing professor), and his two daughters, Carolyn and Allison.

INTEL:
BUILDING A TECHNOLOGY BRAND[1]

INTRODUCTION

Intel's corporate branding strategy, which many credit for the company's unparalleled success in the microprocessor industry during the 1990s, stemmed from a court decision. On March 1, 1991, U.S. District Judge William Ingram ruled that the "386" designation used by Intel for its microprocessor family was a generic description and could not be trademarked. Intel had been confident that the judge would rule in its favor, and the unexpected court decision effectively invalidated Intel's current branding strategy. This decision allowed competitors to use Intel's established naming scheme, which could have been disastrous.

Intel's response was to develop a trademark name for its processor family, the now-familiar "Pentium," and launch a corporate branding campaign designed to make Intel the first name in processors. Both moves proved to be enormously successful. Intel became one of the leading companies in the PC boom, enjoying virtually unchallenged market leadership through the 1990s. Problems arose, however, as the PC industry slowed in the early 2000s. Intel faced a future where the PC, which represented the core of the company's microprocessor business, was no longer the essential tool for the Information Age. Wireless telecommunications devices were becoming increasingly popular, and they required different types of processors.

The company had spent over three decades building the most recognizable brand in the PC microprocessor industry. Intel's challenge in the new century was to extend into innovative categories while maintaining the equity in the brand and its microprocessor leadership position. In response to this challenge, in 2006 Intel retooled its brand identity, restructured its brand architecture, and launched an entirely new branding campaign called "Intel. Leap Ahead."

COMPANY BACKGROUND

Intel Corporation was founded in 1968 by Robert Noyce and Gordon Moore. Soon thereafter, Andy Grove joined the firm and later became President and Chief Executive Officer. Intel's initial focus was the integration of large numbers of transistors into silicon chips to make semiconductor computer memory.

In 1978, Intel introduced the 16-bit 8086 processor followed by the 8088, the 8-bit bus version of the 8086 in 1979. These microprocessors were the first of the Intel "x86" line of microprocessors. At the time, Intel faced competition from a number of companies, the most serious being Motorola with its 68000 microprocessor. In response, Intel launched a campaign to make the 8086/8088 architecture the standard in the emerging microprocessor market. A critical milestone was IBM's selection in 1980 of the 8088 as the exclusive microprocessor architecture for its first personal computer. The success of the IBM PC placed Intel at the center of the personal computer revolution and established Intel's x86 microprocessor architecture as the de facto industry standard.

Intel continued to produce chips with improved performance over the next decade. In June 1988, Intel introduced the Intel 386 SX microprocessors, which became the backbone of IBM's and other manufacturers' growing PC lines and positioned Intel for its explosive growth over the next five years. In April 1989, the company introduced the next generation microprocessor, the Intel 486 processor. In 1990, Intel sold approximately 7.5 million 386 and 486 microprocessors.[2] Intel's 1990 revenue from 386 microprocessor sales alone was estimated to be $850 million.[3] As of 1990, Intel had $3.9 billion in sales, representing a 360 percent growth in 10 years, and $650 million in earnings, representing a 570 percent growth in 10 years. Intel microprocessors were found in almost 80 percent of all IBM and IBM compatible machines. The company, one of the largest semiconductor manufacturers in the world, was recognized as the undisputed industry leader.

THE MICROPROCESSOR INDUSTRY IN THE EARLY 1990S

Since 1986, Intel had been the only supplier of 386 and 486 technology. A number of competitors, however, had announced intentions to market their own versions of Intel's 386 and 486 microprocessors in the latter half of 1990. The most serious threat came from Advanced Micro Devices (AMD), who in October 1990 announced its own version of Intel's then hottest product, the i386 SX, called the AM386. In January 1991, two small semiconductors firms, Chips and Technologies and NexGen Microsystems, announced their intentions to introduce 386-compatible chips within the year. Many competitors claimed that their 386 microprocessors would rival certain configurations of Intel's i486 chip. Whatever their true technological capabilities, Intel knew these chips could be named "386" or "486" and that it could do nothing to prevent such naming.

Intel's Branding Issues

In the late 1980s, there was a significant shift in the general focus of the personal computer industry toward the mass-market, non-technical business, and home PC users. Recognizing this shift, Intel moved from a "push" strategy to more of a "pull" strategy and began to redirect a portion of its advertising efforts away from computer manufacturers to actual computer buyers. Until this time, the consumer's choice of a personal computer was based almost exclusively on the manufacturer's brand image, such as Compaq, Dell, or IBM. Consumers did not think about the components inside the computer. By shifting its advertising focus to the consumer, Intel hoped to create brand awareness for Intel and its microprocessors, as well as build brand preference for the microprocessor inside the PC. Intel still considered the Management Information Services (MIS) community to be its primary buyer, but also recognized the growing importance of the retail or "Circuit City"[4] buyer, as a significant market segment and wanted a message that spoke directly to them.

As the market and technology leader, Intel was always first to introduce a new generation of products and establish the name and value of the new technology to consumers. With competing products carrying the same or similar names, however, it became increasingly difficult for Intel to differentiate its products from those of its competitors. As a result, consumers were confused about who made a particular generation of microprocessor and what level of performance to expect. Consumers were confronted with a product "alphabet soup" that made establishing a point of differentiation and a distinct brand identity for Intel products increasingly difficult.

In June 1989, the company experimented with its first print campaign targeted to the consumer. The $5 million campaign promoted Intel microprocessors through its numbers—the 286 and 386. The initial ad was an oblique but attention-getting print ad and outdoor billboard that mimicked graffiti by spray painting over "286" and inserting "386 SX." The tag line read, "Now, get 386 system performance at a 286 system performance price." Within months, buyers began asking for personal computers with the Intel 386 SX chip. In 1991, the 80386 SX became Intel's best-selling chip ever, shipping approximately 8 million units.[5] Intel's graffiti ad campaign successfully had introduced the microprocessor to consumers, and market research indicated that an increasing number of consumers identified with 386 and 486 microprocessor technology.

EVOLUTION OF INTEL'S BRANDING STRATEGY

During the fall of 1990 and winter of 1991, Intel was involved in a trademark case with AMD to prevent their use of the "386" name in a new AMD microprocessor. A negative verdict would mean that in the future *any* competitor could market its products under the same marks used by Intel. It would also mean that any computer maker could call a machine "386" without regard to the manufacturer who supplied the chip. Concerned about the possible negative verdict and feeling a general need to clarify strategy, Dennis Carter, vice president of Intel's Corporate Marketing Group, began developing an alternative branding strategy, although he planned to wait until the court's ruling to decide whether or not to implement it.

In March 1991, Intel did lose the "386" trademark case. It was now clear to Carter that Intel needed to change its branding strategy and knowing that AMD would begin selling its own version of the 386 microprocessor within the month, created a sense of urgency. Within a few days Carter proposed a new processor branding strategy to Intel's executive office. The strategy recognized Intel's status as an ingredient supplier to PC Original Equipment Manufacturers (OEMs) and consisted of three elements, combining both push and pull communication strategies: 1) the use of a logo based around the words "Intel Inside" to represent Intel processors used in PCs; 2) the use of coop marketing funds to share PC OEM advertising expenses; and 3) an Intel advertising program to build equity. The strategy was accepted and Carter immediately established a task force whose sole mission was to implement this new branding strategy.

The task force's first action was to raise awareness of the Intel brand name. They launched a new ad using the "Intel: The Computer Inside" slogan. This ad asked the reader, "Quick, do you know the first name in microprocessors?" showing a blank line in front of the numbers 486, 386 and 386 SX. Turning the page, the blanks were filled in with the word "Intel." At the bottom of the ad was the Intel corporate logo with the slogan, "The Computer Inside" below it. The ad copy sought to assure the reader that purchasing a personal computer with an Intel microprocessor inside was a safe and technologically sound investment, providing "the power and compatibility to take you into the future."

The task force established a new branding strategy within a month of the court decision. The primary focus of the new strategy was the establishment of Intel as a brand, transferring the equity of "386" and "486" microprocessors to Intel, the company. Establishing a unique identity for Intel was considered the best way not only to distinguish Intel products, but also to communicate the depth of Intel as a corporation with respect to its competitors. While the majority of the company's revenues were derived from sales of microprocessors, the company offered a broad range of products for the computer industry, including microprocessor peripherals, multimedia products and PC enhancement products. Dennis Carter explained:

> We wanted to brand the whole company, but in a way that was clearly focused on processors. An initial proposal that I rejected early on that Intel Japan was proposing to do within Japan was to brand all components. That would not, however, solve our current problem. The branding program had to carry the Intel name and image but focus on selling processors.

It was critical to reverse the perceptions that Intel was an impersonal, unfriendly technology company. Intel wanted to establish itself as a brand that offered "safety" and "technology" to consumers. Then, the company could position itself as a premium product with a premium price. Consumers did not necessarily need to know exactly who Intel was or what it made as long as they could be convinced that a personal computer powered by the "creator of microprocessors" was preferable. Intel also believed that if it could gain consumer confidence in Intel as a brand, it would be able to transfer the equity of the Intel brand to launch new products and technologies.

Intel Inside
Because Intel's products were always inside the computer, unseen by the average purchaser of a personal computer, the company wanted to make the consumer believe that what was inside the computer was as important, if not more important, than the PC manufacturer. Intel's "The Computer Inside" campaign had not been explicit enough in linking Intel's name to the microprocessor inside the computer. The company needed a slogan, logo, or some other means that more explicitly identified an Intel microprocessor as the essential ingredient when purchasing a computer.

Carter had previously wanted to use "The Computer Inside" campaign in Japan. Intel's agency in Japan, Dentsu, believed the slogan too complex and recommended modifying it to "Intel In It" instead and presenting it in a logo form. Japan adopted this logo and began using it for all Intel products, not just processors. Needing a logo for processors fast, Carter, as part of his recommendation to the executive office, suggested using this logo form as the basis for the new microprocessor logo. In order to keep continuity with "The Computer Inside" tag line being used elsewhere in the world, Carter changed the phrase to "Intel Inside" that clearly conveyed to the consumer that is was an Intel microprocessor in the computer. The new logo—a swirl with "Intel Inside"— placed the company and its name directly in front of the consumer.

Enlisting OEM Support

In order to execute the new brand strategy, it was essential that Intel get support from the OEMs who used Intel microprocessors. PC manufacturers purchased the majority of Intel's microprocessors and were the most important group of OEMs. Intel's first priority was to get these manufacturers to include the Intel logo in their print ads. In addition to this "push" strategy, the team planned Intel-sponsored advertising and promotions to build equity in the logo and create a "pull" preference among consumers for Intel processors.

To enlist the support of OEMs for their Intel Inside program, Intel developed a cooperative (co-op) advertising program available to all computer manufacturers who used Intel microprocessors. Intel offered computer manufacturers rebates between 30 and 50 percent of the cost of a print ad when they included the Intel Inside logo, up to a maximum of 3 percent of the cooperating company's Intel processor purchases. Intel received mixed reactions during negotiations with OEMs in 1991. The smaller, third tier manufacturers in particular loved the idea. They had no brand name of their own and promoted their products primarily on the basis of price. Print was their main medium of communications, so any advertising subsidy was considered very beneficial. In addition, adding the Intel logo to their machines gave an assurance of quality to their product, and they proved eager to sign on.

On the other hand, the first and second tier OEMs were afraid that the Intel campaign would dilute their own brand equity and weaken their points of differentiation from one another. According to Kevin Bohren, a Compaq vice president, Intel's campaign "was leveling the playing field," thereby making Compaq's efforts to differentiate its PCs from clones harder.[6] It was this group, however, that Intel needed most to ensure the success of its strategy.

Launching the "Intel Inside" Program

Intel officially announced the launch of its "Intel Inside" program in November 1991. The company announced its intention to spend approximately $125 million during the next 18 months on a combination of print, billboard, and spot television advertising. Intel also announced that 240 OEM customers had agreed to participate in the co-op advertising program and to carry the new Intel Inside logo on their packaging. Dennis Carter described the program as "trying to create a brand image for products that fall under the Intel Inside umbrella".[7] As one reporter described the campaign, "The 'Intel Inside' campaign. . .is aimed at changing Intel's image from a microchip-maker to a quality standard-bearer."[8]

Relationship with OEMs

IBM was the first major OEM to use the Intel Inside logo, in April 1991. After running this ad, however, IBM did not use the Intel Inside logo again for nearly a year. By December 1991, over 300 OEMs had signed co-op advertising agreements with Intel, including first, second, and third tier manufacturers. Over 100 of these companies featured the Intel logo in their ads, including Zenith Data Systems, Everex Systems, NCR Corp., Dell Computer, and AST Research.[9] Nevertheless, at this time the largest first tier computer manufacturers—including Compaq and IBM—still were not using the Intel Inside logo in their ads.

Intel's Ad Campaign

Simultaneous with the development of its OEM co-op advertising program, Intel developed its own Intel Inside ad campaign. The first Intel Inside ad was a print ad called the "measles" ad and showed the Intel Inside logo splashed across a page. The headline read: "How to spot the very best computers." At the bottom of the page, was the tag line: "Intel: The Computer Inside." The primary objective of this ad was to get the new Intel Inside logo in front of consumers and get them familiar with the Intel name. The ad text promoted Intel as "the world's leader in microprocessor design and development," and reassured the reader that "with Intel Inside, you know you've got unquestioned compatibility and unparalleled quality. Or simply put, the very best computer technology." The ad ran in both computer trade publications and magazines such as *National Geographic* and *Time*.

In November 1991, Intel launched its first television ad, dubbed "Room for the Future." The spot, developed by Intel's ad agency, Dahlin Smith White, used special effects designed by Lucas Arts' Industrial Light and Magic Co. to take the viewer inside the computer, giving them a whirlwind tour of the inside of a microcomputer that showed how the Intel486 SX chip streamlined computer upgrading. At the end of the ride, a flashing "Vacancy" sign indicated where the faster chip of the future might go. Careful not to use any "technospeak," a friendly voice-over said, "Something's waiting inside the powerful Intel486 SX computer. We call it. . . room for the future. Check into it. From Intel. The Computer Inside."

Complementing the television campaign was a print campaign launched one week later. The print ad headline read: "The affordable power source for today's software." A version of this Intel486 SX processor ad was placed on billboards in Los Angeles, San Francisco, Chicago, Toronto, and seven other metropolitan markets.[10] Finally, the company prepared a small booklet describing in detail capabilities of the Intel486 SX microprocessor. Two pages of text were devoted to describing each of the following product attributes: upgradability, power, affordability, compatibility, and the experience of Intel.

The "Room for the Future" ad was Intel's first experiment with television as an advertising medium. Dennis Carter explained, "We thought it might be an interesting cost-effective way of reaching a broader audience more effectively—a more impactful way to augment the print advertising campaigns that we do."[11] Consumer research indicated that most viewers of the commercial remembered the Intel name, rather than the product being advertised. Intel's print ads, on the other hand, proved much more successful in educating the consumer on specific product attributes associated with the Intel486 SX.

"Intel Inside" Campaign Matures

By December 1992, over 700 customers were participating in the program, primarily consisting of second and third tier OEMs.[12] According to Carter, by July 1992, at least half the computer ads in personal computer magazines included the Intel Inside logo.[13] Participating OEMs were pleased with the results of the co-op program, and many claimed that the Intel Inside logo had boosted their advertising effectiveness. Bill Saylor, manger of U.S. advertising for NCR commented, "The Intel Inside program has been a good program for us. It has helped add some credibility and enhancements to our messages. You know our product is a quality product because it has an Intel chip in it."[14]

BRANDING INTEL'S "P5"

Intel expected to introduce its next generation processor, code-named "P5," sometime after the fall of 1992. Unlike previous processors, it was not obvious what Intel should name the "P5" or how it should be branded in light of the developing Intel Inside program.

The Intel Inside program had generated significant awareness for Intel and meant that any branding strategy developed for the "P5" would have to work in conjunction with the existing program. The heightened competition during the prior year within the industry had also generated unusually keen interest in the "P5," and both the technical and business markets were looking for information on the product—its capabilities, its expected introduction date, *and* its name.

Naming "P5"

Carter appointed Karen Alter to manage the P5 naming process. She formed a team whose first concern was choosing a name for this new processor. The team wanted a name that would stand on its own as well as indicate the generation of the new chip. The court's decision that numbers were not trademarkable made the choice of "586" a risky one. In a June 1992 interview with an AP reporter, Andy Grove was quoted as saying, "Over my dead body will this new product be named 586."

With the "586" option eliminated, the team decided to use the "P5" naming process as an opportunity to redefine the industry language for microprocessors. Intel could create a new brand that would acquire its own equity over time and make it difficult for other CPU suppliers to get a "free ride" from Intel's equity. The team decided that it was necessary that the name: 1) be difficult for competition to copy; 2) be trademarkable; 3) indicate a new generation of technology that could effectively transition from generation to generation; 4) have positive associations and work on a global basis; 5) support Intel's brand equity; and 6) sound like an ingredient so that it worked *with* Intel's partners' brand names. The team's primary target audience was the retail consumer.

Intel's sales force surveyed a broad range of customers during a two-month period to get their reaction to the planned naming concept (i.e., to not use a numerical name). Some customers told Intel that changing the industry language by not using "586" was not possible. They argued that the industry moved too fast, that the market was already on a level playing field, and that the product was too complicated to "re-educate" the consumer. Others, particularly the technologically sophisticated OEMs, liked the idea as a way to differentiate Intel technology. A distinctive name would allow the company to distinguish its products from lower tier manufacturers in the PC market, as well as from the competition in the workstation and server markets.

Name Selection

Intel undertook the most extensive search in its history to find a name for the "P5." In addition to hundreds of names generated from the task forces own brainstorming sessions, Intel hired the naming firm Lexicon and ran a company-wide naming contest in which over 1,200 employees worldwide participated. Some of the more humorous entries submitted included, "iCUCyrix, iAmFastest, GenuIn5 and 586NOT! *Computer Reseller News*, an industry trade publication, even held its own contest. In all, the selection process generated 3,300 names. Karen Alter described the process:

> We divided the names into three concept categories: 1) closely linked to Intel; 2) technologically "cool"—e.g., naming an architecture; and 3) completely new with some generational concept embedded. We then discussed the pros and cons of each concept category and selected ten alternatives for extensive review and testing.

The company conducted a detailed global trademark search to ensure that each name on the list could not be copied, as well as a worldwide linguistic review to ensure the name would be effective in all languages. The final three name options for the respective concept categories were: InteLigence, RADAR1, and Pentium.[15] Ten days before the planned announcement of the official name, the company's top executives and the members of the task force met to make the final name selection. Grove led the meeting, asking each participant to choose from the three alternatives and describe what they liked about that name and why. Grove and Carter did not give their opinions, saying that they would make the final decision after the meeting was over.

Not surprisingly, the members of the task force were almost evenly split across the three names. The public relations members of the task force liked the InteLigence name because it was the easiest name for them to explain to the public. The technically oriented members liked the "techie cool" name RADAR1. The sales/marketing-oriented members were partial to the Pentium name because it was new *and* represented the cleanest break—they felt that it would be easier to sell to OEMs and other customers. After everyone had given their opinion, Grove and Carter thanked the group and went into Grove's office to make a final decision.

Communicating the New Name

When the naming options had been narrowed to three choices, the task force considered the impact of each name on the multiple audiences—press, OEMs/dealers, competitors, and employees—to whom they would have to communicate the decision. Without question, many people would react negatively to any name that was not "586" and Intel wanted to counter this reaction as quickly as possible. Intel hoped the computer companies would market the name to users as a key product ingredient, much like NutraSweet, Teflon, and Gore-Tex. As one Intel spokesperson explained, "The market is changing and with other people (competing chip makers) introducing a key ingredient, you don't know what part you're getting inside." Intel also hoped computer companies would market the name to users as a way to convey the power and efficacy of its fifth generation processor family.

Launching the Pentium Processor

Intel officially announced the name of the new chip on October 20, 1992. Andy Grove made the announcement during an exclusive interview on CNN, who provided Intel the ability to make a live official announcement on a worldwide basis. Grove announced that the name of Intel's fifth generation microprocessor was Pentium and said the company would begin shipping production versions of the chip in early 1993. In describing the choice of Pentium for the name, Grove explained, "the name should suggest an ingredient. The 'Pent' of Pentium, from the Greek meaning five, alludes to the fact that the new chip is the fifth generation of the family. The 'ium' was added to make the chip sound like a fundamental element." The company coined the name because it conveyed the positive attributes such as quality, state-of-the-art technology, software compatibility, and performance. Grove explained the rationale for not using a number as a name, "We can't count on another number. It's so much cleaner to designate a name that's protectable."[16]

Immediately following Grove's announcement, the Pentium processor marketing team launched a full-scale effort to ensure the Pentium name was quickly adopted into the everyday industry vernacular. Intel's PR department phoned all leading individuals who wrote about the industry to let them know the new name. A not uncommon response was: "I can't believe this name. This is the most ridiculous name I've ever heard." Intel's PR department carefully monitored all press for references to the Pentium processor, and if they found anyone using "586" or "P5," they immediately sent the author a letter correcting the error. Within one month after the naming launch, over 90 percent of press mentions used Pentium instead of "586."

The Pentium Processor Product Announcement

One week before the Pentium processor-based PCs were available for sale, Intel introduced its first Pentium ad. The four-page magazine insert, the first in a year long "technology briefing" campaign, positioned the Pentium processor at the elitist end of the market, saying "all but the most demanding users" should use personal computers with Intel486 chips. Because of this target market, the insert, which described in some detail how the Pentium processor made PCs run faster, was a shift away from the simpler, consumer-style advertising Intel had done since 1989. As one Intel spokesperson explained, "In the olden days, we would do very "techy," spec-driven ads in engineering books, and then we got very end-user (focused) without much meat on the bones. Now we're going a little bit back to our roots."[17]

Indications of Success

Between 1990 and 1993, Intel had invested over $500 million in advertising and promotional programs designed to build Intel's brand equity. The Intel Inside campaign had constituted the bulk of this investment and plans were to continue with the campaign. Within the industry, there was considerable debate about the effectiveness of Intel's "branded ingredient" strategy. AMD, for example, had publicly rejected adoption of a similar branding strategy. As one AMD spokesman explained, "You wouldn't find an 'AMD Inside' campaign even if we had the kind of deep pockets that Intel has. We don't think it's particularly effective to try to build brand awareness."[18]

The Intel Inside program had won a number of advertising awards, including the Marcom Award for best television campaign in 1992 at the computer industry's premier trade show, Comdex.[19] Also at Comdex, Dahlin Smith White, Intel's ad agency, won the "Grand Marquis" excellence award for its "Power Source" commercial. In presenting the award, Donna Tapellini, editor of *Marketing Computers* magazine, explained:

> This is not just for the best marketing program or campaign, it is for a work that has raised the standard irrevocably and made a difference…Not only have they moved the goal posts in terms of advertising values, but this campaign is a culmination of a brilliant 'Intel Inside' branding strategy. They have done for (computer) chips what Frank Perdue has done for chickens. They have set the standard and become the ones to beat in the industry.[20]

Intel's own market research, both in the United States and in Europe, indicated that end user awareness of the Intel brand name had increased significantly since the introduction of the Intel Inside program. The independent research, performed in June 1992, indicated that users worldwide viewed Intel as the technology leader versus such competitors as AMD and Cyrix and the overwhelming microprocessor of choice. Research in the United States also showed that Intel had the strongest image on quality and compatibility attributes. Over 80 percent of those surveyed had seen the Intel Inside logo in personal computer ads and nearly half had seen the logo in store displays, product literature, or on a personal computer. Over 75 percent of those who had seen the logo said that it conveyed positive attributes, and 50 percent said they looked for the symbol in making their personal computer selection. In Europe, two-thirds of business computer purchasers surveyed had seen the Intel Inside logo and understood that the logo indicated a CPU brand. However, among the non-sophisticated non-technical users, the "Intel" name and Intel Inside logo were often confused. The problem was particularly acute in certain foreign languages, like character-based Chinese, that did not link the Intel Inside brand with the Intel company name.

In 1993, *Financial World* rated Intel as the third most valuable brand, behind Marlboro and Coca-Cola, with an estimated worth of $17.8 billion.

Pentium Becomes a Hit

The price of the original Pentiums targeted high-end consumers—at the time of their launch, Pentium PCs cost around $5,000, compared with 486 systems that cost as little as half as much. The prohibitive cost of the chip and limited availability prevented the Pentium from making an instant sales splash, and a year after the chip's introduction it accounted for only 10 percent of Intel's revenues. When the company increased production and began cutting Pentium prices, sales rose dramatically. In 1994, Pentium sales grew eight times faster than 486 sales did when that chip was new. That same year, the company shipped over 6 million Pentiums. Within two years after the company's decision to use the "Pentium" name for its P5-generation chips in 1992, Intel possessed roughly 90 percent of the world's PC microprocessor market and enjoyed exclusive relationships with several of the biggest computer manufacturers.

EVOLUTION OF THE PENTIUM

The company saw the Pentium sub-brand as an important part of its success, and extended the name in branding its next four processors (by 2000, Intel had unveiled the Pentium Pro, Pentium II, Pentium III, and Pentium 4 chips, see Exhibit 1 for timeline). In 1994, Intel's revenues rose 24 percent from the previous year to $11.5 billion on the strength of over 6 million Pentium processor shipments. Following the success of the Pentium chip, Intel decided to call its next generation P6 processors the "Pentium Pro." The first Pentium Pro chips were released in December 1994.

In 1997, Intel launched its next chip, the Pentium II processor. That year, the company spent a record $100 million on an integrated marketing campaign to promote the Pentium II. The campaign included several high profile advertisements, such as a Super Bowl spot featuring the popular "bunny people" series. The "bunny people," which first introduced the Pentium MMX, were commercial versions of Intel technicians dressed in brightly colored contamination suits. In the ads, the colorful characters danced to a disco soundtrack while they worked inside a processor fabrication facility. The company felt that by taking the audience inside the fabrication plant where the chips were manufactured, the new television spots remained consistent with the original Intel Inside television ads, which had given the viewer a virtual tour of the interior of the computer. Even though the bunny people were popular, some felt that the lively spots strayed too far from Intel's core product placement, the inside of the computer.

Renewed Processor Competition

In 1998, Hewlett-Packard and Compaq chose to buy cheaper chips from Cyrix and AMD instead of buying certain Intel Pentium models. Intel executives initially ignored the discount PC market, noting that PCs priced at less than $1,200 comprised only 27 percent of the total market in 1997 and did not sell well overseas. But as the cheaper PCs attracted American consumers who only needed a simple machine that would allow them to access the Internet, Intel re-thought its strategy. By the middle of summer in 1997, AMD and Cyrix had gained 20 percent of the overall U.S. retail PC market and Intel's share of the low-end market dropped below 30 percent.

By not properly anticipating the surge in popularity of sub-$1,000 PCs, Intel wound up fighting to keep from losing overall market share. To combat the increasing competition from AMD and Cyrix, Intel released the low-end Celeron chip in April 1998. The first Celerons, slower than comparably priced chips, drew unfavorable reviews and sold poorly. As a result of these sluggish sales, Intel's share of the sub-$1,000 PC market dropped from 68 to 56 percent in the third quarter of 1998, while AMD's share rose to from 19 to 24 percent.

In 1999, Intel released the Pentium III. The company positioned the chip as a tool to enhance home PC users' Internet experience. Intel nearly doubled its 1998 advertising budget, spending $300 million on a global campaign that promoted the processor in nearly every available medium. Sensing that the "bunny people" strategy had run its course, Intel shifted back to a more PC-centered campaign for the Pentium III. The new marketing campaign used a theme reminiscent of the original "Intel Inside" slogan: a blue door bearing the Intel Inside insignia accompanied by the line, "This way in."

In October 2000, the company introduced a trio of spokespeople— performance artists Blue Man Group—that appeared in television ads for the Pentium III. The ads featured the Blue Man Group performing acrobatic and musical stunts that reinforced the number "III."

AMD Battles for "Fastest Chip"

In the fall of 1999, AMD unveiled a 700 MHz version of its Athlon chip, which surpassed the latest Pentium in terms of performance. The release of the 700 MHz Athlon put Intel in the unfamiliar position of trailing a competitor's technology advancements. Major PC manufacturers had been reluctant to buy AMD processors, however, and as of late 1999 none of the top PC makers used an AMD processor in its machines. "It's the same reason that people bought IBM for years and nothing else," said an executive with a computer reseller. "There's a sense that there is less risk in Intel."[21]

For much of 2000, AMD and Intel battled for the title of "fastest chip," which usually changed hands with each successive product release. The important issue for AMD was to keep pace with Intel's highest performing chips, a valuable point of comparison that helped AMD's stock rise 353 percent from 1999 to 2000. By June 2000, AMD was selling microprocessors to every major PC manufacturer. Many industry analysts considered AMD's revitalized business to be a "serious challenge" to Intel. [22] Intel experienced a number of product flaws, shortages, and delays in 1999 and 2000, which critics partly blamed Intel's push to beat rival AMD to market with faster processors. Intel's product delays enabled AMD to gain significant inroads in the PC microprocessor business. In 2000, AMD had increased 4 percent to a 17 percent share of the chip market. In addition, nine out of the top 10 PC makers were using AMD chips in their computers in 2000.

INTEL'S SEGMENTATION STRATEGY

The increased competition prompted then-CEO Andy Grove to initiate an aggressive promotion of Intel's low-end chip, the Celeron, while admonishing his co-workers "if we lose the low end today, we could lose the high end tomorrow."[23] Intel quickly increased the processor speed on its Celerons and cut prices 30 percent. These counter measures precipitated an overall microprocessor market share drop for AMD from 16 percent to 13 percent from the third to fourth quarter of 1998. Intel's market share rose to over 80 percent from 75 percent over the same period.

The fear of "losing the high end" drove Intel to restructure its processor business by segmenting it into three price and performance categories. The top processor, the Xeon, was designed for servers and powerful networks and retailed for as much as $3,000. The Pentium class targeted the performance-PC market and sold for roughly half the Xeon's cost. The Celeron retailed for as low as $63. The aggressive promotion of the Celeron eventually had the desired effect: Intel gained a 62 percent market share in the sub-$1000 PC category by the year 2000. Still, Intel made most of its profits from sales of the two upper-level processors, and designed its marketing strategy accordingly. The Pentium II processor received heavy marketing support across nearly every medium, from expensive TV spots to web advertising to print campaigns. The Celeron processor, on the other hand, got no TV time and was marketed using comparatively sparse print and radio.

Pentium 4

In 2000, Intel announced that their next Pentium-generation chip would be called the Pentium 4, and would be the company's first completely new desktop processor design since the 1995 Pentium Pro. The Pentium 4 was a major new weapon in Intel's processor speed battle with AMD. Pentium 4 debuted in November 2000 in PCs starting at $2,000 and soon became the fastest desktop processors on the market, outpacing AMD's 1.5 GHz Athlon.

Intel supported Pentium 4 with a $300 million advertising campaign, Intel's largest outlay for a single chip, which also featured the Blue Man Group. The company decided to keep the Blue Man Group, in order to provide "continuity between the two chips as it phases out the older product."[24] Research found that the Blue Man Group ads scored high among Pentium 4's target audience of well-educated, middle- to upper-income PC consumers. The ads positioned Pentium 4 as a chip that enhanced media and Internet applications with the tagline "The center of your digital world."

At the time of the Pentium 4 launch, the domestic PC market was in less than ideal condition. The percentage of U.S. homes with PCs had stayed at 58 percent since 1999. Faced with a declining PC market, Intel cut prices on Pentium 4 chips by as much as 23 percent in January 2001, only two months following the chip's release. The Pentium 4 got off to a slow start, and less than 4 percent of PCs in the U.S. retail market contained Pentium 4 chips by April.

Itanium Targets High End

Intel continued to increase its research and development budget to fund new technologies (see Exhibit 2). Intel's next big processor development in 2001 was, the Itanium, a 64-bit chip capable of performing advanced operations on complex data much more rapidly than the 32-bit Pentium family of chips (a 64-bit chip can process data twice as fast as a 32-bit chip). Delivered two years late and at cost of $2 billion, detractors quickly labeled it "the Itanic." The Itanium performed poorly, processing data even slower than Intel's current 32-bit chips. The company released a newer version, Itanium 2, in 2002, but this chip was soon overshadowed by AMDs Opteron chip.

Intel's Vision for New Growth

After enjoying ten years of better than 30 percent compound annual growth, Intel executives looked toward the future and saw the PC market declining in the years to come. Consumers in America bought cheaper computers than they had in previous years. These discount computers contained cheaper processors manufactured by Intel's competitors, which meant that expensive Pentium processors often sat in the top-of-the-line computers on store shelves. With sales of Pentium-based computers—which provided Intel with 70 percent margins—dwindling, Intel was forced to lower the prices of its chips during 1997 and 1998 to retain market share. As price drops cut into margins, Intel profits fell and its stock shed about 30 percent from its peak. Intel recognized that the period of high growth and large margins in its PC processor business was ending, and determined that diversification within its processor lines and growth into other technologies would help the company weather the PC market decline.

In 1998, Andy Grove stepped down and Intel appointed company president Craig Barrett as its new CEO. Barrett's vision for Intel's future included broad product offerings and technological developments for the Internet. He understood the limitations of a processor-dominated business strategy, declaring "If Intel wants to continue to occupy a central position [in high tech], it's not just enough to build the hearts and brains of computers."[25] Broadening the company's focus seemed like a bold risk at first glance, since 90 percent of revenues and 100 percent of profits came from Intel's microprocessor business. But with the Internet technology sector growing 30 percent faster than the PC industry and new technology like wireless communication increasing in popularity, Barrett knew that an expanded role on the Internet would be crucial in helping the company grow in the next decade.

From the start of his tenure as CEO, Barrett steered the company into a host of new businesses, such as consumer electronics, e-commerce, and Internet hosting. He also revamped Intel's microprocessor offerings, expanding into chips for network utilities, information appliances, and lower-priced PCs. The company supplemented its expansion by rapidly acquiring competitors and specialists in new growth areas. In 1999, Intel spent $6 billion acquiring 12 different companies. In Barrett's first two years as CEO, the company invested in 25 communications-technology startups. Over half of the more than 250 companies Intel invested in from 1996 to 2000 were Internet-focused startups, including such ventures as online retailer e-Toys and web searching technology developer Inktomi. In part due to Barrett's vision, and in part due to market conditions at the time, Intel's stock price soared (see Exhibit 3 for Intel's stock price, and Exhibit 4 comparison of Intel's stock price versus index benchmarks).

New Product Introductions

Intel also recognized the importance of extending its business beyond processors by developing other electronic products. The company introduced modems and videoconferencing equipment in the mid-1990s, but these brand extensions went virtually nowhere. The company refocused its efforts to establish itself in consumer electronics in 1998 by creating the Home Products Group. This new group developed Internet appliances such as web-ready televisions, set-top boxes, PC cameras, a children's microscope, and wireless keyboards. In 2000, Intel introduced two new digital cameras, the Me2Cam and the Pocket PC Camera. The company also unveiled a digital music player, the Intel Personal Audio Player. For children, Intel's Smart Toy Lab designed a Computer Sound Morpher that enabled users to record sounds and mix and alter them on a computer. Said John Middleton, marketing manager for Intel's consumer products, "These products extend the business and the brand and they make the Internet more fun."

In 1998, Barrett established the New Business Group, a division aimed at growing Intel's business opportunities outside processors. The group worked on small projects, each one of which was treated like a start-up, with "venture capital" coming from Intel's cash reserves. By 2000 the company had spent $50 million on over 20 new projects, including an effort to install 3,000 terminals on seats at Madison Square Garden that sports fans could use to access information about teams and players and a start-up called Vivonic that built handheld computers designed to enable users to monitor their diet and fitness.

CHALLENGES IN THE NEW CENTURY

Craig Barrett remained highly optimistic about the benefits of the company's brand extensions. In 2000, he announced that within five years he expected that every new business Intel ventured into would generate revenues exceeding $1 billion. Barrett also anticipated that Intel's new ventures would be fueling 15 to 20 percent annual growth, compared with 8 percent growth between 1998 and 1999. Not everyone believed that Intel's expansion strategy would yield success, however. While the Internet remained the hottest place for new business growth, Intel was not a proven player in the Internet economy and faced stiff competition from established Internet powerhouses and earnest startups. Additionally, some investors and analysts worried that Intel's rush to develop, in the words of the company's New Business Group head Gerry Parker, "as many ideas as possible"[26] outside its core business demonstrated a loss of focus. Amidst the plaudits and the criticisms, Intel financial performance suffered.

The 2001 fiscal year was Intel's worst in its 34-year history. Revenues that year plummeted 21 percent to $26.5 billion, while net income dropped 70 percent to $3.6 billion as the PC market slowed (see Exhibit 5). Intel's new businesses rang up zero profits, while losses doubled each year since 1998. A former Intel executive said, "They're dabbling in everything and overwhelming nothing."[27]

In order to stem its losses, Intel exited non-processor businesses such as digital cameras, streaming media software for online audio and video transmissions, toys, and networking hardware. The company shut down its Connected Products unit that made many of Intel's consumer products. Intel stopped manufacturing network servers and routers after several of its big chip customers, including Dell and Cisco and Hewlett-Packard, complained that Intel was competing against them. The company spun off its interactive media-services division and scaled back its information-appliance business.

In response to these moves Barrett said, "I think we have cleaned up our product line. In this difficult time [these peripheral businesses] were distracting us from our core strengths."[28] Intel renewed its focus on microprocessors, servers, mobile devices, and networking equipment.

Intel Focuses on a Platform Strategy

Realizing that many computer users were taking their laptops on the road, but not getting the optimal performance they expected, Intel designed and launched a new platform called Centrino in early 2003. Centrino was Intel's first brand to stand for a combination of products. The bundle was based on a new processor (the Pentium M) that was designed to consume little electricity and extend battery life. The package also included other Intel chips that were specifically designed for wireless communication. Intel said the Centrino platform of chips allowed notebook computers to be lighter, smaller, and have better battery life. Centrino was also designed to work together and would provide users with seamless access to Wi-Fi "hot spots."

Intel launched a $300 million effort to promote the Centrino wireless platform. The first phase of the campaign, which ran in 11 countries, was targeted at business users and tech-savvy consumers. Intel created eight-page inserts for major newspapers that urged the wired world to not only "unwire," but also "Untangle. Unburden. Uncompromise. Unstress." Later that year, Intel launched a series of television spots aimed at a broader audience. The ads were designed to appeal to moms and students, and showed everyday people enjoying the benefit of using their laptops without wired Internet connections. To further market its new technology, Intel joined with The *New Yorker* magazine and developed a mini-guide to Wi-Fi hot spots that was published in the magazine. Intel also sponsored "One Unwired Day," where mobile PC users received free access to thousands of hot spots in major cities. Intel even brought back the Blue Man Group for a new round of advertisements.

The most controversial part of the Centrino launch was the co-op advertising subsidies that Intel offered to OEMs. In order to qualify for the subsidies, and be able to show the Centrino logo on their products, computer makers had to purchase the *entire* bundle. OEMs were excited about the new Pentium M chip, but less excited about the wireless networking chip that was the other part of the platform. One computer manufacturer executive remarked, "We can quickly get much better components available unbundled. Intel is trying to get more into systems design, and force us to have less freedom as far as engineering and trying to deliver value to customers." Although this sentiment was echoed by others, OEMs were reluctant to not use the Centrino platform. They feared a cost disadvantage by not getting the advertising subsidies. Also, Intel's heavy promotion of the new brand would indirectly benefit any computer maker that adopted the new technology. Dell, Toshiba, HP, and IBM offered Centrino branded notebooks as one choice, but also gave consumers the option of "upgrading" to other wireless chips, allowing them to get the Centrino marketing subsidies.

AMD Surges in the Marketplace

Competition heated up in April 2003 when AMD launched its Opteron chip, a direct rival of Intel's Xeon. This powerful chip soon found customers with Hewlett-Packard, Sun Microsystems, and IBM. Opteron used much less electricity and generated much less heat than Intel's Xeon server chips, an important difference in corporate data centers. In addition, software makers such as Linux and Microsoft began to write software specifically designed to run on 64-bit chips; this promised to give the chips even better performance.

AMD competed with Intel in other areas as well. In response to the success of the Centrino, AMD launched the Turion chip. Turion was designed to provide optimum performance for mobile computers. It used 32- and 64-bit technology in a chip that allowed OEMs to make thinner and lighter notebook computers with longer battery life, enhanced security, and compatibility with the latest wireless technology. The company also launched the Athlon 64, a powerful 64-bit chip designed for desktop computers.

AMD managed to beat Intel in certain areas. In the commodity-like memory business, AMD had become the global leader in a critical type of flash memory. This memory was the most expensive component in what was the world's hottest technology product—the cell phone. AMD also became the first company to launch a major product aimed at bridging the "digital divide" between rich and poor. In October 2004, it introduced the Personal Internet Communicator (known inside the company as "Emma"). A rugged, shoebox-sized computer, Emma was designed so people in remote villages all over the world could get help with education, agricultural, and health-care information, as well as entertainment. The cost, including monitor, was $230. Emma was being offered along with Internet access for a sub-$10 monthly subscription. This was the first of a variety of products planned by AMD, all aimed at a goal they call 50X15, meaning 50 percent of the world's population should be online by 2015.

AMD only spent $2.6 million on measured media in 2003, and $2.2 million in the first nine months of 2004. AMD realized that it must make branding its new chips and processors a priority. At the end of 2004, the company spent $30 million to advertise its Athlon 64 and Opteron brands. Tracey Brown, AMD's director of worldwide consumer marketing commented, "We are not trying to educate people on the technical specifications of the processor, but letting them know that with AMD processors you get a better experience or a better lifestyle." She continued, "Intel is more than twice our size and so our marketing approaches are very different. You'll probably never see us do a mass-marketing carpet-bombing approach."[29]

Leadership Changes

In May 2005, Craig Barrett stepped down as CEO and was replaced by COO Paul Otellini. Otellini was a 30-year veteran of Intel but many looked at him as an outsider since he was the first Intel CEO without a degree in engineering. His four predecessors each had a Ph.D.—Otellini had a BA in economics and an MBA. Otellini did bring technical experience to the job, however. He fought successfully with engineers over the need to create Centrino. He won, and Centrino paid off. There were significant challenges facing the company, including technical chip design, a maturing PC market, and strengthened competition from AMD. To address these issues, Otellini pushed for what he called a "right turn." No longer would Intel focus on processor speed for speed's sake alone. Instead, it would listen to what customers wanted. "People still want performance, but they want other things, and we need to deliver and discuss performance in a different way."[30]

Otellini's reorganized the company from two operating segments – Intel Architecture Business and Intel Communications Group—six business units—the Mobility Group, the Digital Enterprise Group, the Digital Home Group, the Digital Health Group, and the Channel Platforms Group. The goal was to bring all major product groups in line with the company's strategy to drive development of complete technology platforms.

In addition, Intel also hired a new chief marketing officer, Eric Kim. Kim had been the head of marketing at Samsung Electronics for the previous five years, where he was credited with helping to push the giant consumer-electronics company to be competitive with rivals like Sony, Panasonic, and Sharp.

NEW OPPORTUNITIES

Although Otellini was eager to pursue a marketing strategy of embracing technology "platforms"—which are different than individual microprocessors because they include other chips and software that work together—there were other areas where he wanted the company to explore. One of the largest opportunities for Intel was expansion in China (see Exhibit 6 for a breakdown of Intel's revenue by geographic region). By 2005, China was the world's third largest market for chips. With many analysts predicting that the U.S. market for PCs would grow by only about 5 percent a year, Intel was eager to reap gains from growth in China. Intel controlled 84 percent of the microprocessor market in China, with AMD taking up the remaining 16 percent. AMD gained momentum, however, when they signed an agreement with Lenovo, China's biggest PC manufacturer, to be the exclusive supplier of chips for Lenovo's low-end PCs. Intel further invested in China in 2005 when they established a venture capital fund to invest in Chinese technology companies. Intel hoped that by investing in emerging companies, these companies would create products that would use Intel microprocessors, driving future growth.

In June 2005, Intel announced that Apple Computer would begin using Intel microprocessors in its Macintosh computers in 2006. Apple planned to transition all of its Macs to using Intel products by the end of 2007. Steve Jobs, Apple's CEO commented, "Our goal is to provide our customers with the best personal computers in the world, and looking ahead Intel has the strongest processor roadmap by far."[31]

Intel also looked to what it called the "digital household" for growth. One of the biggest-selling products in the digital household was the flat-panel TV, which a represented a $10 billion market. Intel worked on developing processors that could cut the cost of some flat-panel TV screens in half. A smaller, but growing, market was for entertainment PCs. These computers were specially designed to play movies, music, and be the source for other living room-centered media. Intel had 90 percent of this $120 million market in 2004.

Even with these developments in the microprocessor business, Intel realized PC growth was slow and that in order to keep the $34 billion company growing, Intel would have to expand. As a result, Intel unveiled a new brand strategy in 2006 that acted as a milestone in the evolution of its brand.

Intel Tries to "Leap Ahead"

In January 2006, Intel officially launched a new brand identity campaign. Not only did it include a $2 billion global marketing campaign but also a revised brand architecture strategy that positioned Intel as a "market-driving platform solutions company" instead of a microprocessor company.

There were three significant changes to Intel's new brand strategy. First, the company reorganized its business divisions into four strategic key markets: Mobile, Digital Home, Enterprise and Health. Second, Intel launched a new platform called Intel Viiv (rhymes with five) technology that targeted home entertainment buffs. A PC with a Viiv platform allowed consumers to download and send movies to televisions around the house. Intel also launched two new PC chips code-named Merom and Conroe. Finally, Intel revamped its brand image with a new logo and slogan, to help create the impression of a "warm and fuzzy consumer company."[32] Intel executives also hoped it would better link Intel into areas like consumer electronics and cell phones instead of just PCs.

The company modified the familiar 37-year-old blue encircled Intel logo with a dropped "e" in the name. The marketing group launched a version of the logo with a new font and tweaked the swish that appeared around the company's name. In addition, marketing executives developed a new slogan called "Leap Ahead." Eric Kim explained, " 'Intel. Leap ahead.' is a simple expression that declares who we are and what we do. This is a part of our heritage. Our mission at Intel has always been to find and drive the next leap ahead—in technology, in education, social responsibility, manufacturing, and more—to continuously challenge the status quo. It's about using Intel technology to make life better, richer, and more convenient for everyone."[33]

The new campaign was met with mixed reviews. Samuel Jones, CIO of Trillium Asset Management and a leading Intel shareholder complained, "I understand why Intel would want people to understand that their focus is not just on PCs, but why abandon the existing branding? They have huge recognition globally and I'm not sure they need to go this far."[34] Robin Wight, chairman of advertising agency WCRS, agreed, "It takes a while for a name or slogan to reach the hippocampus (the portion that helps names get into memory). Losing a well-known logo or slogan often means throwing away that investment."[35]

Despite the initial criticism, Intel stood by its new brand image and Viiv platform. CEO Paul Otellini commented at the International Consumer Electronics show, "With our new platforms, we're not only boosting wireless computing, but also advancing digital entertainment a few steps closer to effortless."[36]

Coinciding with the campaign was a shift in Intel's microprocessor strategy. For more than a decade, Intel's main metric was operating speed, expressed in MHz. However, that metric was only one measure of how computing work was accomplished. Other factors included having the circuitry to execute multiple tasks at the same time, how energy-efficient the chips were, and how much built-in memory and communication capacity the chips had. In 2006, Intel announced plans to phase out its Pentium chip architecture in favor of a suite of dual-core processors called Core 2 Duo that use 35 percent less power and improve performance by 80 percent.

CONCLUSION

From its early place as a Silicon Valley pioneer, Intel had become the dominant chipmaker of the PC era. But like other tech stocks after the tech boom, Intel's stock price had swung wildly, from a high of over $71 a share in March of 2000 to a near low of $18 a share in April of 2006. In 2004, Intel was the second worst performer on the Dow Jones Industrial Average. Things began looking up in the first half of 2005. The company was sitting on over $14 billion in cash and had seen its stock rise 22 percent, the Dow's second-best performer. In addition, Interbrand, a brand consultancy firm, ranked Intel the world's fifth most valuable brand that year. However, the first half of 2006 brought more disappointing financial results, even with the launch of a new brand identity. Due to increased competition from AMD in key markets and excess inventory, first-quarter revenues were $500 million under projections, and the stock price fell to its lowest earnings multiple in a decade. Second-quarter revenues decreased 13 percent and net income for the quarter fell 57 percent.

Amid this competitive environment, Intel faced questions of whether the company had the optimal product portfolio and whether the platform strategy would prove successful. Intel executives hoped that changing its 37-year-old logo and introducing a new slogan would be instrumental in helping the brand achieve renewed success. Despite its challenges, Intel had much in its favor, including a strong track record for innovation, lower manufacturing costs, and one of the most powerful brands in business.

DISCUSSION QUESTIONS

1. What were the strengths and weaknesses of the Intel Inside campaign?
2. Evaluate Intel's continued use of the Pentium family of processors. Did Intel make the right decision by extending the name through the Pentium 4 processor?
3. Suppose you were the Chief Marketing Officer for AMD. How would you propose the company position itself to better compete with Intel? Would you propose that AMD institute an Inside-like ad campaign?
4. Evaluate Intel's segmentation strategy. Is having a good/better/best product line (Celeron, Pentium, Xeon) the best positioning for Intel? Should it discontinue a line(s) and focus on the other(s)?
5. In light of Intel's move into the "digital home," did the company's executives make the right decision in launching an entirely new brand identity? Did it make the right decision in changing a 37-year-old Intel logo and dropping the *Intel Inside* campaign for *Leap Ahead?* What other marketing strategies might the company employ?
6. Intel moved into consumer-electronics products, such as digital cameras in 2000, only to withdraw after receiving complaints from OEMs such as Dell. Does Intel face a similar issue with its move into the "digital home?" Does this move too far outside Intel's core competency of producing microprocessors?

Exhibit 1: Intel Processor Introductions

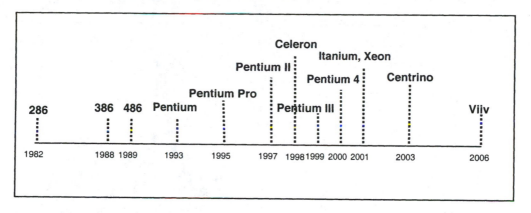

Exhibit 2: Research and Development Spending

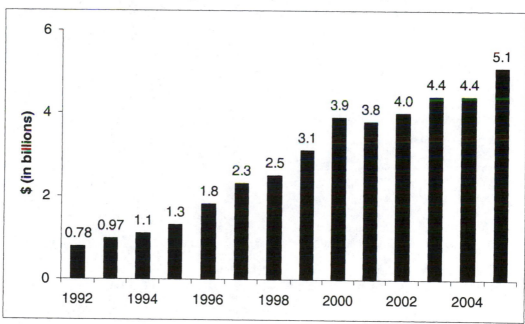

Source: Company Reports

Exhibit 3: Intel's Weekly Closing Stock Price as of April 2006

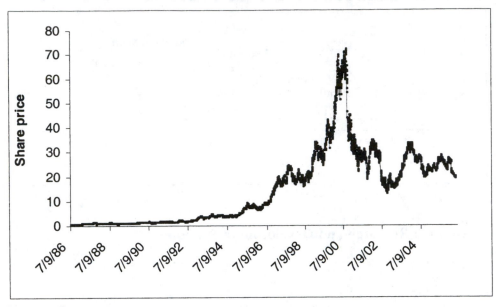

Source: Company reports

Exhibit 4: Intel's Weekly Closing Stock Price versus Selected Indices

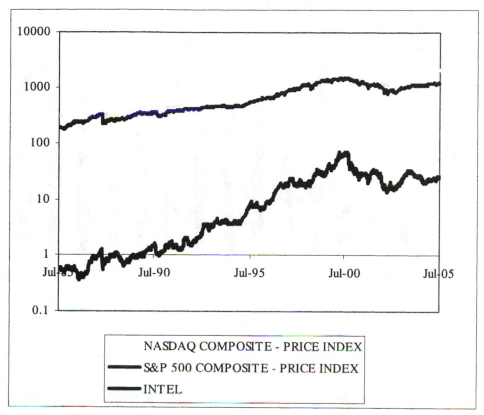

Source: Company reports

Exhibit 5: Net Revenues

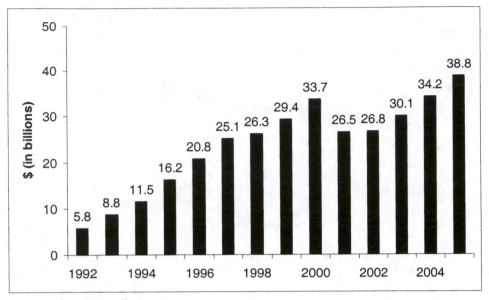

Source: Company Reports

Exhibit 6: Geographic Breakdown of Revenue

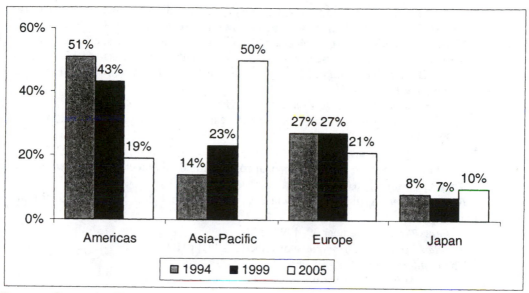

Source: Company Reports

REFERENCES

[1] This case was written with the cooperation of Intel and the assistance of Dennis Carter, Vice President of Marketing, Sally Fundakowski, Director of Processor Brand Marketing, and Karen Alter, Manager, Press Relations, at Intel. Leslie Kimerling prepared this case, with research assistance from Keith Richey. Jonathan Michaels and Lowey Bundy Sichol updated and revised the case under the supervision of Professor Kevin Lane Keller.

[2] The *Wall Street Journal*, April 8, 1991, p. A1.

[3] The 386 revenues are estimates found in Morgan Stanley Analyst reports dated April 1, 1990 and April 11, 1991.

[4] Circuit City is a retail chain selling audio and video equipment, major household appliances, and more recently, personal computer and other technology-based products. They sell primarily to the mass market.

[5] *Business Week*, April 29, 1991. In its best year with the 80286, Intel sold 4.5 million units.

[6] *Business Week*, September 30, 1992, p. 32.

[7] The *San Francisco Chronicle*, November 2, 1991, p. B1.

[8] The *London Sunday Times*, September 13, 1992.

[9] *Business Marketing*, February 1992, p.16.

[10] *Business Marketing*, February 1992, p. 19.

[11] *Business Marketing*, October 1991, p. 48.

[12] *Business Wire*, January 13, 1993.

[13] *Advertising Age*, July 6, 1992, p. S-16.

[14] *Business Marketing*, February 1992.

[15] These are pseudonyms for the actual names chosen but are representative of the names chosen in each of the three concept categories.

[16] The *Wall Street Journal*, October 20, 1992, p. B3.

[17] *Advertising Age*, May 10, 1993, p. 3.

[18] *Advertising Age*, May 10, 1993.

[19] *Marketing Computers*, January 1993.

[20] *Business Wire*, November 18, 1992.

[21] Molly Williams. "Newly Competitive AMD Challenges Intel in Corporate Chip Market." The *Wall Street Journal*, December 27, 2000, p. B1.

[22] "AMD Shows It's Ready for Prime Time." *Forbes*, April 13, 2000.

[23] As quoted in *Business Week*, March 13, 2000.

[24] Molly Williams. "Intel Is Banking on Pentium 4 Ads to Revive Sales." The *Wall Street Journal*, February 15, 2001, p. B1.

[25] As quoted in *Forbes*, May 3, 1999.

[26] As quoted in *Business Week*, March 13, 2000.

[27] Cliff Edwards. "Intel: Can Craig Barrett Reverse the Slide?" *Business Week*, October 15, 2001, pp. 80–90.

[28] Mark Boslet. "Intel's Barrett: Internet Focus of Co's Growth Strategy." Dow Jones Newswires, October 31, 2001.

[29] Beth Snyder Bulik. "AMD chips away at image of rival Intel." *Advertising Age*, January 24, 2005.

[30] Adam Lashinsky. *Fortune*, April 18, 2005, p. 118.

[31] "Apple to Use Intel Microprocessors Beginning in 2006." Intel press release, June 6, 2005.

[32] Don Clark. "Intel to Overhaul Marketing in Bid to Go Beyond PCs." The *Wall Street Journal*, December 30, 2005.

[33] Company press release. "Intel Unveils New Brand Identity." *Intel.com,* January 3, 2006.

[34] Amanda Andrews. "Intel cashes in its chips… and raises the stakes." The *Australian*, January 3, 2006.

[35] Amanda Andrews. "Intel cashes in its chips… and raises the stakes." The *Australian*, January 3, 2006.

[36] *Associated Press.* "Intel Launches Viiv Entertainment PC." *MSNBC.com*, January 5, 2006.

got milk?:
BRANDING A COMMODITY[1]

INTRODUCTION

"got milk?"—one of the most popular ad campaigns of the 1990s—was borne of necessity. In February, 1993, Jeff Manning, newly appointed Executive Director of the California Milk Processor Board (CMPB), was reviewing reports on per capita U.S. consumption of milk over the last fifteen years. To anyone involved in the production and sales of milk, the numbers painted a disturbing picture. There had been a steady decline in milk consumption over the previous two decades and recently the decline was accelerating. Manning only had a $23 million budget to make milk's message heard among the noise.

To revitalize sales of a product in seemingly perpetual decline, Manning and the ad agency Goodby, Silverstein & Partners developed the "got milk?" campaign. The campaign was based on a "milk deprivation" strategy that reminded consumers how terrible it was to be without milk with certain foods like cereal, brownies, or chocolate chip cookies. Consumers in California responded positively to the campaign, embracing the quirky ads and also consuming more milk than if the rate of decline had continued. The campaign was licensed nationally and "got milk?" soon became a catchphrase all over America. "got milk?" was successful in California and reversed the sales and consumption slide, while consumption levels continued to decline nationally. Critics applauded the campaign's success in California, but as "got milk?" entered its twelfth year, some questioned how long the "got milk?" campaign could be effectively sustained.

THE DAIRY INDUSTRY

Three major groups make up the dairy industry: 1) Farmers—who produce the milk, 2) Processors—who convert raw milk into whole and lower-fat milk, and 3) Retailers who sell the final product. There are many groups representing farmers and processors in the United States, including several national milk boards and many regional, state, and local groups. As of 2003, the U.S. milk industry had reached a value of $23.1 billion and milk remained the most frequently purchased item in grocery stores.[2]

Farmers

There are over 2,100 dairy farms in California that are represented nationally by the National Dairy Public Relations Board (NDPRB) and the United Dairy Industry Association (UDIA), and locally by the California Milk Advisory Board (CMAB). Funding to support these groups and their advertising programs comes directly from each of the farmer's profits. As a result, farmers are traditionally tight-fisted and scrutinize all program budgets carefully.

Processors

The processors' primary function is to transform raw milk into the products that ultimately hit the grocer's shelves, e.g., whole, 2%, 1%, and skim milk. There are 40 processors of fluid milk in California, each employing hundreds of people. Concerned about declining sales and consumption, the processors joined forces to create the CMPB.

Retailers

In the early 1990s, Safeway and Lucky food stores were the two leading retailers in California. Fluid milk was one of approximately 50,000 products sold at these retailers but extremely profitable. According to the *Progressive Grocer*'s 1992 Supermarket Sales Manual, milk was the top-selling supermarket product per shelf foot. The dairy department racked up a total of $61.23 per square foot compared to the average of $22.47 per square foot. In addition, direct profit return on inventory dollars, an important statistic for store managers, averaged $84.83 compared to the department average of $5.

Other Distribution Channels

The majority of fluid milk was sold in grocery stores, due in large part to the perishable nature of fluid milk. Convenience stores, schools, and food service establishments such as McDonald's accounted for the majority of remaining milk sales. In California, the latest threat to milk consumption came from the school districts. Prior to 1982, all school lunches in California included milk. Since then, school children chose from five items, including milk, for lunch. The change in school district policy contributed to the 3.8 percent decline in non-commercial food service milk volume from 1986 to 1991. The trend was equally troublesome in commercial food service establishments such as McDonald's. Although the percentage of food dollars spent out of home increased to 33 percent in 1991 from 25 percent in 1971, milk did not enjoy an increase in sales in these types of establishments. In fact, commercial food service milk volume actually dropped 23 percent from 1986 to 1991.

California Milk Processor Board (CMPB).

Consumer research revealed that per capita consumption of milk had been on a steady decline for a number of years. So, in 1993, the processors joined together and established the CMPB to fund advertising and public relations programs with the ultimate goal of increasing milk sales and consumption. The processors agreed to sponsor legislation requiring them to contribute $0.03 per gallon of milk sold in the state in the first year, with slightly smaller contributions in the remaining years of an initial three-year charter for the CMPB. In the first year, the CMPB raised about $23 million, all to promote fluid milk in California. The CMPB hired Jeff Manning, previously a senior vice president with Ketchum, as executive director. Manning had worked with beef, potatoes, bananas, and eggs in commodity marketing and also brought a wealth of branded product marketing experience.

MARKETING BRANDS VERSUS COMMODITIES

The strategies behind marketing a commodity and a branded product are very different. Marketing a commodity is similar to marketing the product category as a whole rather than marketing a single brand within the category. To start, a commodity doesn't have a brand name. This results in many complexities, both on the supply side—how the product is marketed—and on the demand side—how consumers perceive and value the product.

Supply Side Differences

There are four major supply side differences in commodity marketing.

Too many decision makers. Each member of the industry has an input into every marketing program associated with the commodity. Not only does this result in little flexibility, but also all programs require extra paperwork and effort from each group in the industry. As a result, it is difficult to adopt new programs and the industry members typically opt for the status quo, assuming that "everyone needs the commodity." For example, something as "new" as couponing is extremely difficult to execute in commodity markets because the redemption value has to be paid by a broad range of processors, producers, and other intermediaries.

Small budgets. Commodity marketers typically have significantly lower budgets available for advertising, promotion, and marketing research than brand marketers. A national brand can draw on investment funds into the millions but commodity promotional budgets like milk are raised either from the processors or directly from the farmers. The average $200 million brand spends at least $5 million on advertising and another $5 million on promotions to the trade. In contrast, a multi-billion dollar commodity category usually spends about $5 million total, including advertising, promotion, marketing research, and public relations.

Slow budget process. The commodity budgeting process is a slow moving, arduous system of approvals. Funding for budgets are accomplished through assessments—contributions from each producer or processor collected on a unit basis. These assessments are usually in the form of mandatory collections put into law and administered by a government entity. These budgets are fixed and decided upon in advance. In contrast to packaged goods companies, commodity marketers cannot raise short-term capital by selling off assets or dipping into emergency common funds.

Push versus Pull. Commodity marketing differs in the division of promotional funds allocated between push and pull strategies. Commodities generally spend almost all the funds raised to generate some sort of pull with consumers. The most common tools used to increase sales include television advertising, radio, print, billboards, and PR. Most major commodities like milk do not maintain a direct sales force to push product through channels of distribution or build relationships with retailers.

With 100 percent distribution penetration levels and extremely high consumer penetration levels, there was not a pressing need to motivate retailers to carry fluid milk.

Demand Side Differences

The demand side of commodity marketing also differs in two ways from marketing a traditional brand.

Changing a category versus market share. The paramount challenge for commodity marketers is to change consumer attitudes and behaviors toward an entire category as opposed to trying to increase market share of a brand. Although difficult to change, category attitudes do evolve over time, and when they do change, the results can be quite dramatic. For example, a 1 percent increase in the consumption of milk can result in literally hundreds of millions of dollars of extra revenue to the dairy industry. Commodity marketers learned about the potentially deleterious impact of changing consumer attitudes from experiences in the beef industry. In 1950, cattlemen and meat market retailers across the country laughed at the notion of poultry ever coming remotely close to beef in popularity. Yet in 1990, poultry consumption passed beef in terms of per capita consumption. As the level of milk consumption steadily declined for fifteen years, Manning feared a repeat of the beef industry.

Influenced by other industries. Demand for commodities can be dramatically influenced by other food industries. A new product in the food service industry or the consumer packaged goods industry can increase sales exponentially. For example, when Wendy's fast food restaurants introduced hot stuffed potatoes they cleared the entire 8–12 ounce potato market almost overnight. The same is true of the packaged goods industry. A new ready-to-eat raisin cereal from Kellogg's can mean millions of dollars to the raisin industry. Sometimes these new products are introduced as a result of technological advancements that make them possible. Some commodity boards are capitalizing on such opportunities by investing more funds in research and development.

BACKGROUND

The Beverage Category

The beverage industry includes all beverages from beer and liquor to bottled water and soft drinks. In 1993, when the CMPB formed, the beverage category was experiencing intense competition and an ongoing proliferation of new products, especially from soft drinks, bottle water, and fruit drinks. According to a Beverage Industry survey, 1,805 new beverages were introduced in 1991, many experimenting with diet, clear, and non-caffeinated versions. Media spending in the beverage category approached $2 billion, with over half of the total accounted for by beer and soft drinks. Milk spent less than 10 percent what beer spent on media.

The beverage category enjoyed tremendous growth in the two decades prior to the formation of the CMPB. Between 1975 and 1993, total consumption of beverages increased by 18 percent. Although the category has increased substantially, milk was one of the few beverages to actually experience a decline in consumption over the same period. While soft drink per capita consumption increased by 80 percent from 1975 to 1991, milk consumption dropped by 10 percent. In addition, milk's market share dropped from 17 percent to 13 percent.

Previous Milk Promotion Campaigns

The national or regional dairy boards had sponsored a number of advertising campaigns throughout the fifteen years of declining milk consumption prior to 1993. Milk advertising traditionally communicated a three-tiered message to consumers:

> Adults: Milk is good for you and should be a regular part of the diet.
> Teens: Milk makes you beautiful and strong.
> Kids: Milk is cool and fun.

Traditional milk advertising campaigns showed a member of the target group drinking a glass of milk, followed by a brief mention of the nutrients in each glass. A 1992 UDIA national consumer survey revealed the following:

- 80 percent agreed, "I like the taste of cold milk."
- 89 percent agreed, "Milk is a healthful drink."
- 91 percent agreed, "Milk is a good source of calcium."
- 83 percent agreed, "Milk is needed for growth."
- 74 percent agreed, "Adults should drink milk."
- 52 percent agreed, "I should drink more milk than I do."

In the early 1990s there were two dominant campaigns. The "Milk does a body good" campaign focused on the benefits of milk as part of a well balanced diet. In addition, the "Good fast food" campaign promoted milk, cheese, and other dairy products. Both campaigns ran nationally.

CALIFORNIA'S MILK ENVIRONMENT

Trends in 1993

Exhibit 1 reveals the accelerated decline of milk sales from 1990 to 1993. As a result of this decline, the CMPB's goal was clear: increase the sales and consumption of milk in California. In 1992, California's population was 31.3 million people but only 21 million were current or potential milk drinkers. If milk consumption could increase by one glass per week, profits would increase over $100 million per year.

Previous advertising campaigns had been extremely effective in communicating the health benefits of milk to consumers. However, the gains in sales of low fat and skim milk had come at the expense of sales in whole milk. Milk sales had not kept up with population growth either. Total fluid milk sales in California increased by 10.9 percent in the decade of the 1980s but California's population had increased by 26 percent over the same period.

To compound the problem, the U.S. Census Bureau also revealed that the modern family size was shrinking. In 1970, the average family included 2.5 kids. By 1990, the average was 2.1 kids per family. In addition, there were more mothers in the workplace. In 1970, 49 percent of mothers with school age children worked but by 1990, that number had increased to 74 percent. The increase of working mothers meant more meals were eaten outside of the home. These trends did not bode well for milk consumption, a beverage consumed primarily by families in their homes.

The CMPB did see some growth opportunity in the changing ethnic composition of California. Latinos were one of the fastest growing ethnic groups in the state—good news for the CMPB because Latinos also represented an important segment of heavy users. As a group, Latinos drank almost one-third more milk than the average individual. Latinos also drank significantly more whole milk than the rest of the population and usually bought larger sizes of milk.

The UDIA Consumer Study

In 1992, the United Dairy Industry Association (UDIA) commissioned a marketing research study to investigate the reasons behind the perpetual decline of per capita milk consumption. The study attempted to gauge consumer preferences by taking a qualitative approach, conducting 1,252 personal interviews with consumers of all age groups to talk about milk and other beverages. The UDIA study revealed several factors that may have been playing a role in the decline of milk consumption, including:

Proliferation of other beverages—The average American family now had fifteen different beverages in the refrigerator at any given moment in time.

Lack of portability—Eighty-nine percent of all milk was consumed at home. Most consumers drank milk on a regular basis—at breakfast in cereal, at lunch with a sandwich, and at dinner with the family meal—but over half of all of the meal occasions were outside of the home.

Lack of flavor variety —To many, milk essentially came in one flavor. The lack of variety of milk flavors was especially relevant in 1993 because other beverages were flooding the market with a myriad of flavored drinks.

Not thirst quenching—A significant number of consumers noted milk's lack of overall refreshment. The inability to "gulp" when thirsty and the lack of a clean, crisp taste were significant barriers to milk as a thirst-quenching beverage.

Lack of consumer mind share—Milk had always been a fairly "forgettable" beverage. At specific times during the day or with specific foods, milk was irreplaceable.

However, beyond these particular consumption occasions, foods, or outside of the house, milk was usually forgotten.

Shared nature of consumption—With such high penetration levels, virtually all people drank milk at some time during the day. This shared feature of milk often led members of a family to pace themselves and "ration" milk. This restrained behavior could have restricted the overall consumption of milk per household.

Relationship of Milk with Other Foods

The research included a host of transcripts from consumer's experiences with milk. Below are some of the typical quotes from consumers, listed by age and sex:

> "With things like Oreos or any other kind of cookies or cake, none of these would be good without a big glass of milk."
>
> > - female, mid-30s

> "At night with cereal, or for dunking Oreos."
>
> > - female, mid-20s

> "It's a pain in the a— because you usually find out (that you're out of milk) just after you pour the cereal."
>
> > - male, late-30s

> "What are Cheerios? They're nothing. But you add milk and it's everything."
>
> > - male, late teens

These responses highlighted the close-knit relationship between milk and other types of food including cereal, cookies, and sandwiches. Consumer's experiences with fluid milk also emphasized its versatility. For example, milk is used as an accompaniment to sweets, as a necessity with cereal, and as an ingredient in coffee, milkshakes, and soup.

Surprisingly, nutritional requirements were not as important in beverages. As a result, the end user health benefits of milk only moderately motivated consumers to drink milk at any point in time. Some consumers felt that if a beverage must be cold to taste good or if the drink has a strong taste, these were de-motivators to drinking it. For teenagers "done something good for myself," "goes well with sweets," "satisfyingly rich," and "complements a hearty meal" were the most effective motivators.

CMPB'S BRANDING STRATEGY

Developing a Strategy

To meet CMPB's objectives of reversing the declining trend in milk sales and consumption, Manning was considering several strategic options:

1. Invest in R&D to expand the number of flavors available.
2. Expand the potential usage occasions.
3. Cooperate with consumer packaged goods companies for joint promotions.
4. Develop an advertising campaign to clarify the health benefits of milk.
5. Generate a new image for milk through advertising.
6. Target Hispanics and aging Californians.

After carefully considering all the options, Manning and representatives from the CMPB's advertising agency, Goodby, Silverstein & Partners in San Francisco, decided that the best strategy to reverse the declining trends was to embark on a new, innovative advertising campaign. Nobody doubted that previous milk campaigns successfully achieved positive shifts in consumer attitudes toward milk. What was missing, however, was a corresponding change in consumer behavior. Consumers knew milk was good and thought they should drink more of it, but they never thought enough about milk to be motivated to change their consumption habits. The typical milk campaign—emphasizing calcium and other vitamins—caused consumers to tune out. The recommended campaign had to break the mold for milk advertising, grab attention, and shake consumers out of their "milk malaise." Manning knew that other beverages had successfully built up strong brand images over the last decade and he believed that milk could do the same by taking a more light-hearted approach, which talked directly to consumers. Manning reflected back on the decision:

> The dairy industry has taken itself too seriously. Eating is a form of entertainment...the most popular form of entertainment in California, the USA, and the world. Get people smiling at your advertising and they will look, listen, and, we believe, consume more milk.

Campaign objectives
The new advertising campaign had to satisfy three objectives:

1. **Change consumer behavior.** The CMPB's foremost priority was to increase milk consumption by one occasion per week. Because positive attitudes toward milk had failed to reverse the decline in consumption, the new campaign should change *the way* consumers think about milk.

2. **Increase mind share.** Although many people drink milk everyday, milk suffered from a complete lack of consumer mind share. People did not think about milk enough at home and almost never outside of the home. One way to implement this change was to take consumers by surprise by creating a new and different image for milk.

3. **Halt sales decline.** Obviously, sales represented the bottom line for the CMPB. The advertising campaign needed to motivate people to buy more milk and subsequently drink more milk. A high awareness campaign that did not result in subsequent changes in milk consumption would not be acceptable.

Target Market

In order to generate quick results, Manning decided to target "regular" users of milk—70 percent of the California market—who already had favorable attitudes toward drinking milk. Presumably, they could be influenced in the short-term. In contrast, non-users or light users typically restrained from milk for actual or perceived health reasons, which probably could not be changed very quickly. Manning explained:

> If the 21 million people in the state that we regard as our "marketing universe"—those people who regularly consume milk in any form, be it a glass of milk, a bowl of cereal, instant pudding, or whatever—increased consumption by just one serving a week in any form, consumption of milk would increase in California by 9–13 percent.

Because a wide range of demographic and psychographic groups drink milk, regular users were segmented according to behavior. The behavior segmentation strategy focused on *when* and *where* consumers drink milk. First, almost all milk is consumed at home. The UDIA study had shown that consumers rarely drink milk outside of the home, and even when they drink milk at home it is generally during the same usage occasions. Second, milk is considered an essential complement to certain types of foods. The focus groups revealed that consumers talked about milk with other foods, not as a drink by itself. Third, consumers tended to discuss milk and these foods as though they were the same food, i.e. Oreos and milk, peanut butter and jelly sandwiches and milk, etc. It became evident that not only were these foods highly associated with milk, but also that these foods were the driving force behind milk consumption and the potential key to any future increase.

"got milk?" Creative Development

Based on the market research, Manning and the Goodby, Silverstein & Partners advertising agency decided to reach out to the regular users with a "deprivation strategy." Each ad in the campaign paired one of milk's perfect complements: cereal, chocolate chip cookies, peanut butter and jelly sandwiches, etc. The clever creative twist, however, was to deprive the main character of milk, resulting in delicious food *without milk*—the deprivation strategy. In each of the ads, a meal or snack is essentially ruined because of the absence of milk. Manning explained his thought process:

> Sell milk with food. The idea is almost frighteningly simple and obvious. And yet, as we reviewed milk advertising from around the country (and

from around the world), we found that food was almost totally absent. We don't know why. Perhaps in an attempt to compete against soft drinks, the dairy industry lost contact with its roots. Consumers haven't. They will tell you time and time again that food—certain foods—drive their milk decision.

Television Ads

The television ads gradually built the tension that was so critical to the deprivation strategy. Each television ad began with a close-up of one of the food complements such as the peanut butter and jelly sandwich. Once the desire for the food is established, the protagonist takes a big bite. While joyfully chewing the food, the protagonist casually reaches for a glass of milk. Unfortunately, there is no more milk left in the container. A desperate search for even a single drop ensues, but all efforts are in vain. At the height of anguish, the voice-over pronounces: "got milk?"

One memorable ad showed an obnoxious businessperson on a busy city sidewalk talking on a cell phone. After loudly informing the person on the other end of the conversation that he or she is fired, the businessperson gets run over by a truck. The next scene takes place in "heaven"—an all-white room where soothing music is playing. On a table sits a plate of Frisbee-sized chocolate chip cookies that the businessperson greedily devours. Searching for milk to wash down the cookies, he opens the refrigerator and sees row upon row of milk cartons. He reaches for one, but finds it to be empty. Grabbing another, he discovers that it too is empty. Finally it dawns on him: "Wait a minute, where am I?" The "got milk?" logo appears with a flame effect as the man screams.

The "got milk?" tagline urged consumers to run to the refrigerator and make sure the answer was "yes." It was felt that this deprivation strategy would bring back the consumer mind share for milk and begin to recreate a positive image for milk as a necessity. The ads were humorous and well received by focus groups.

The campaign broke away from previous milk advertisements in two important ways. First, there was never any mention of how milk could benefit a healthy diet. Consumers presumably already knew about the benefits, so the new campaign instead urged them to change their behavior. Second, milk was never actually shown in the ads. Whereas in the past, milk was shown without food, in the new campaign, food was shown without milk. The CMPB felt that the deprivation strategy would increase mind share for milk precisely because the ads hit consumers where milk (or lack thereof) hurt them the most.

Additional Communications Programs

The creative strategy lent itself to using complementary foods as promotional tools for milk. If consumers purchased more of the foods that naturally went with milk, they should also buy more milk. The CMPB ran joint promotions with major brands such as Wheaties and Oreos to focus on their relationship instead of trying to pull consumers over to the dairy case. These promotions included coupons, 'got milk?' logos on cereal boxes, point-of-purchase displays, shelf talkers at the complementary food locations, and "got milk?" check-out dividers. Billboards were used extensively to reinforce the television campaign. The billboards featured the same foods as the television ads with one bite taken out and prominently displayed the key question: "got milk?" The complementary television, radio, print, and billboard campaigns all leveraged the food-milk relationship and capitalized on the advertising budgets of several major brands of cereals and cookies.

Media Strategy

According to Manning there were three ideal times to communicate the milk message—at home where milk could be immediately consumed, on the way to the store, and in the store. The media strategy complemented the overall communications message because it reached consumers during these three times. The primary focus was television and concentrated on targeting consumers when they drank the most milk—mornings during breakfast, afternoon snack time, and late evening snacks. Timing ads in this manner and given the "call to action" nature of the campaign, the spots led to more impulse uses of milk. Each usage occasion was further broken down into the type of user and specific ads were used during those times. The spots targeted children in the early morning hours and late afternoons and targeted adults at prime time during their late night snack time.

The CMPB launched a heavy outdoor campaign to target consumers on the way to and inside grocery stores. "got milk?" signs and billboards were located at nearby bus stations and next to supermarkets as a reminder to purchase milk before consumers entered the store.

Finally, the CMPB's annual budget of $23 million doubled the previous year's spending. This placed milk among the top ten advertising spenders in all of California, on a par with Coca Cola and Budweiser. As a result, the campaign possessed the muscle to compete with other beverages for the first time in milk advertising history. Only one question remained: Would the deprivation strategy work?

"GOT MILK?" SUCCESS

Immediate Results

The "got milk?" campaign was launched in November, 1993. Although focus groups indicated that consumers liked the ads, the actual launch exceeded all expectations. The campaign zoomed to a 60 percent aided recall level in only three months, enjoyed 70 percent awareness within six months, and surpassed the long-running "It Does a Body Good" campaign in top-of-mind awareness in less than a year. The "got milk?" campaign quickly became a consumer favorite, prompting a L.A. Times reporter to comment, "Since the ad campaign began, it has reached a near-cult following."

Not only did the campaign get consumers talking, it also exceeded initial sales expectations. In California, milk consumption increased for the first time in years as shown in Exhibit 2. California household consumption of milk increased every month in the first year of the "got milk?" campaign except for the first two months. This performance was in sharp contrast to the rest of the country where consumption declined over the same period. The number of Californian consumers who reported consuming milk at least "several times a week" jumped from 72 percent at the start of the campaign to 78 percent a year later. In addition, sales jumped 6.8 percent that first year of the campaign. Prior to the campaign's launch, California milk processors experienced a decline in sales volume of 1.67 percent or $18 million. A year after the launch, sales volume increased 1.07 percent or $13 million, for a total turnaround of $31 million. On a month-to-month comparison, sales volume increased every month and rose 6.8 percent by the end of the first year. Nationally, sales decreased 0.1 percent that year.

"got milk?" Goes National and International

The "got milk?" advertising campaign was also met with critical acclaim. In 1995, the ads won an Effie Award and top honors from several other major advertising award committees. In September of that same year, "got milk?" was licensed to the national dairy farmers' group Dairy Management Inc. (DMI) who ran the campaign nationally. Thus "got milk?" was receiving national advertising exposure along with the existing "milk mustache" campaign. Even though these two campaigns commonly promoted milk, they were run separately. The CMPB and Goodby Silverstein created and ran the California "got milk?" campaign. The DMI and Leo Burnett USA licensed "got milk?" for the national campaign. In addition, the National Milk Processors' Education Program (MilkPEP) controlled the famous "milk mustache" campaign with Bozell Worldwide managing the creative.

MilkPEP's "milk mustache" campaign launched in 1995 with the slogan "Milk. What a Surprise." The program focused primarily on the healthy "good for you" aspect of milk and leveraged the celebrities in the ads, not milk itself. The following year, MilkPEP changed the tagline to "Where's your mustache?" as a call to action. Then, perhaps in an effort to consolidate the equity achieved by the separate campaigns, MilkPEP obtained licensing rights to the "got milk?" slogan in 1998 and replaced the milk mustache taglines with "got milk?" In 1998, MilkPEP and the DMI forged a partnership that combined their advertising budgets, pooling Dairy Management's $70 million budget and MilkPEP's $110 million budget. However, this joint budget did not compare relative to the CMPB's approximately $30 million budget for California alone.

After seeing the sales results in California, the UK's Milk Development Council (MDC) approached the CMPB to license "got milk?" In 2004, "got milk?" went international and the ads began running throughout England, Wales, and Scotland.

Products and Partnerships

The "got milk?" campaign also fueled a cult status of buying "got milk?" licensed products. Such products included t-shirts, baby bottles, mugs bearing the "got milk?" logo, and even a "got milk?" themed Barbie doll. Manning wrote a book about the "got milk?" campaign. Companies such as General Mills, Nestle, Quaker,

Keebler, and even the Girl Scouts of America agreed to work with the CMPB. These partnerships led to numerous creative advertisements and promotions.

The national campaign also consisted of print and outdoor advertising. Billboards featured the characters Snap, Crackle, and Pop, Cookie Monster, the California Raisins, and the Girl Scouts. The Girl Scouts initially balked at the possibility of a partnership in 1996, because they felt a "got milk?" tie-in would be too commercial. The following year the CMPB pointed out that "got milk?" did not represent a corporate dairy interest and the Girl Scouts agreed to participate. Goodby Silverstein designed a billboard that showed a group of Girl Scouts looking directly at the viewer, with scores of boxes tucked under their arms and lying about behind them. As usual, the words "got milk?" were placed prominently at the center of the ad. The Girl Scouts also agreed to endorse milk by supplying local troops with "got milk?" pins for girls to wear during door-to-door sales of their cookies. Other promotions included a partnership with Dole that placed "got milk?" stickers on 100 million clusters of bananas throughout the country and a venture with Mattel that developed a "got milk?" Hot Wheels milk truck.

In October 1998, the CMPB established the www.gotmilk.com to provide consumers with more information about milk, the "got milk?" campaign, and purchase a full line of "got milk?" products direct. In 2005, the CMPB expanded its distribution channels and licensed apparel maker MJC Corp. to produce men's clothing that would be sold through Wal-Mart. "got milk?" baby products were expanded into Babies "R" Us, Buy Buy Baby, Baby Depot and Macys.com later that same year.

"GOT MILK?" RECONSIDERED

Revising the Deprivation Strategy

The "got milk?" campaign took a step away from its deprivation formula in October 1997. Earlier in the year, focus groups indicated that the deprivation ads had become somewhat familiar or predictable. Concerned that consumers might soon tire of the ads altogether, the CPMB sought alternatives to the deprivation strategy. Goodby Silverstein created the ad that took the deprivation principle and expanded it throughout an entire town, Drysville.

During the ad, the camera passes by daily scenes that one would expect to occur in any town, the difference being that in Drysville the absence of milk made these scenes depressing. The viewer sees a police officer forlornly eyeing a box of donuts, a mother pouring tap water on her child's bowl of cereal, and a teenager paying cash to steal a glance at a photograph of a glass of milk. The "got milk?" tagline appeared at the end of each Drysville spot. The Drysville campaign worked as far as re-engaging the consumer with the "got milk?" campaign, but research revealed that the deprived town did not affect consumers' immediate consumption or purchase decisions to the same degree that the traditional ads did. In his book, Jeff Manning explained the difference:

Drysville's advertising was working more on people's heads than their mouths and stomachs. People felt the deprivation only intellectually, almost abstractly. Deprivation was only happening to "them," the people of Drysville, not to me, [the consumer].[3]

Following a year in Drysville, the CMPB returned to isolated cases of deprivation for its "got milk?" scripts. Several subsequent spots cast the dangers of deprivation in a different light. The "Paws" ad featured a grandmotherly type who attempts to feed her dozens of pet cat's non-dairy creamer when she runs out of milk. An ad called "Y2Kud" spoofed millennium paranoia by showcasing a "Y2K-compatible" cow that continues to graze after a power outage occurs the first minute of 2000.

Milk Branches Out

While milk sales had increased in California, national **per capita** consumption numbers were still declining. In the interest of appealing to young milk drinkers, some dairies began manufacturing portable and flavored milk products. Many of these dairies developed extensive marketing programs in support of their new product launches. One of the biggest dairies in the nation, Midwest-based Dean Foods, invested $40 million to upgrade its plants for the production of Chugs, a portable and flavored milk product packaged in plastic containers made to look like old-fashioned glass bottles. The company spent an additional $12 million on an integrated national marketing campaign to support the new products with television, print, and outdoor advertising. Ads with the theme, "Milk where you want it," showed kids and teenagers with Chugs bottles in their pockets. Jim Page, Dean's Vice President of Marketing, offered the following explanation for his company's independent marketing efforts throughout the Midwest:

> I feel very good about what 'milk mustache' and (national) 'got milk?' has done. It increased awareness but not consumption. Our job is to take it to the next level.[4]

The results of Dean's new initiative were favorable. By 1999, Chugs generated more than $100 million in sales to the company and contributed to 40 percent of the total growth in milk sales that year, despite only comprising 6 percent of total milk sales. Believing flavored milk could stimulate further growth in the following year, the CMPB approved an ad with the extended tagline "got chocolate milk?" The ad showed a teenaged boy looking in the fridge for chocolate milk to drink. Finding none, the boy takes a box of chocolate flavored cereal from the cabinet and pours regular milk into the box. When he finishes drinking the concoction, he puts the milk-sodden cereal box back on the shelf.

While kids and teens took to flavored milk, demands for healthier types of milk like soy and organic continued to grow, too. In response, companies like General Mills and Dean Foods began investing in these areas. General Mills purchased 8th Continent, a soymilk producer in 2002. With $55 million in sales in

2003, 8th Continent was the faster growing business for General Mills. Dean Foods acquired Horizon Organic in 2004 and the company's organic and soy product lines saw record sales that same year.

Growth Slows

The "got milk?" and "milk mustache" campaigns helped fuel a 1 percent growth in national milk sales during 1997. The dual campaigns did not enjoy similar success, however, the following year. MilkPEP spent $84.5 million in 1998 and Dairy Management spent $70 million, but national fluid milk sales dropped 0.4 percent for that year. In the three years since both campaigns began targeting national audiences, milk sales had risen by 1.1 percent, but the growth failed to offset the cost in the minds many in the milk industry. The stalled growth in national milk sales sent many industry executives searching for alternatives to the expensive milk marketing campaigns. MilkPEP executives contended that national price increases between 10 and 15 percent in 1998 accounted for the dragging sales. Milk consumption continued to decline for the rest of the decade and remained flat or down each year during the early 2000s (see Exhibit 1).

Results in California were mixed (see Exhibit 2). After three straight annual consumption increases from 1995 to 1997, sales declined again in 1998. This was partly due to price increases that exceeded the national increases of the same time. A gallon of 1% low fat milk cost as much as $3.48 in San Diego during 1998, compared with a national average of $2.69 per gallon of low fat milk for the same year. By 1999, the cost of a gallon of milk in California had risen to over $4. in some cities. Perhaps fearing that the rising cost of milk would once again yield a disheartening sales decline, the CMPB allocated $23 million to the "got milk?" campaign in 1999. Milk sales rose slightly in 1999, then dropped again in 2001, to the same level they were in 1993 when the campaign began. "We basically stopped the hemorrhaging," said Jeff Manning. In 2002 and 2003, sales hit a 10-year high of 740 million gallons, but then unexpectedly dropped 1 percent in 2004.

NEW DIRECTIONS IN GOT MILK MARKETING

Back to Health

In 1998 the CMPB voted to maintain the "got milk?" campaign through 2002, but also incorporated a "milk is healthy" message into some of the advertisements. Research revealed that a vast majority of women aged 25 to 49 only drank milk to prevent bone disease. In addition, research showed a link between mother's and children's milk consumption. These insights prompted the CMPB to develop two ads with Goodby Silverstein highlighting a health benefit of milk.

The first ad debuted in the spring of 1999 opened with a shot of a mother urging her two children to drink milk at a meal. The children protest that their neighbor, a Mr. Miller, told them he doesn't need milk to stay healthy. At which point the children look out the window to wave at Mr. Miller, who is gardening next door. Mr. Miller waves back, and then stoops to pick up a wheelbarrow. When he lifts, his arms break off at the shoulders. The ad closes with a shot of the two children rapidly gulping down their glasses of milk.

The second ad ran in 2000 and emphasized milk's role in preventing osteoporosis. In the spot, a group of elderly men sauntered into a roadhouse and each ordered milk. Several tough-looking characters teased them so the older men gulp their glasses of milk and invite the bullies to "step outside." The ad closed with shots of the older generation pummeling the younger crowd. A voice-over discusses the preventative health benefits of the beverage as "got milk?" flashed onto the screen.

The CMPB also began a grassroots campaign targeting young teens in 1998 with the launch of the Gravity Tour. The "got milk?" Gravity Tour traveled to high schools throughout the state and featured the world's top professional skateboarders, bikers, and inline skaters. The tour's purpose was to promote the "coolness" of action sports and emphasize how important milk is to young athletes and their bone density. The CMPB also joined forces with MilkPEP and Dairy Management to make milk an official sponsor of Major League Soccer.

In 2003, the CMPB took milk's health message to another level and developed the theme, "Strength comes from within." Half of the CMPB's $30 million budget was spent on a television spot developed to promote milk's importance to healthy bones featuring real x-rays set to haunting music. CMPB also launched a series of print ads, which creatively made bones look like butterflies, exclamation points, and question marks. Each ad included copy that explained the importance of milk and was targeted towards a specific user group—men, women, or children. By 2005, visitors at gotmilk.com saw "got milk?" spelled out in bones when they landed on the home page. The website highlighted significant amounts of research on milk's benefits, including how it increases bone mass in teens and adults, prevents PMS and osteoporosis, and improves sleep.

Another non-deprivation spot was introduced in 2005, making light of the steroid scandals sweeping professional sports. The spots depicted a media frenzy surrounding athletes abusing a new "substance," which happened to be milk. The spots showed surveillance footage of athletes caught "pouring," crying on camera, and offering public denials that they are using milk. The ads positioned milk as a " 'super food'—in all of its health promoting benefits."[5]

Independent Farmers Speak Out
Things seemed to going well for the CMPB as "got milk?" was entering its ninth year and California milk sales rose 2 percent to hit 746 million gallons, the highest level in a decade. However, on April 2, 2002, Joseph and Brenda Cochran, independent dairy farmers from Westfield, Pennsylvania, filed a lawsuit against the Dairy Program. The Cochrans did not want to be forced by law to pay for national advertising, specifically the national "got milk?" and "milk mustache" campaigns. As previously mentioned, dairy farmers must pay a portion of their operating profits to help fund these national and local campaigns. This case was not specific to the CMPB but its outcome would have had major implications on the CMPB's mission.

Specifically, if the Cochrans won their case, the CMPB would not be able to raise funds from California farmers for the "got milk?" campaign.

The Cochran case stayed in the courts for three years however, in May 2005, the Supreme Court made a ruling for commodity marketing campaigns and the Cochran's case was ruled in favor of the milk processors. As a result, the dairy industry remained functioning as it had been and the CMPB continued receiving funds from farmers.

Hispanic Consumers

In 2001, the Hispanic population represented 32.5 percent of California's total population and was growing every year (Exhibit 3). The CMPB understood how important targeting this demographic was to milk's growth. Not only was it a growing demographic population but also Hispanics and Latino were heavy milk drinkers, spending more money on milk than any other demographic (Exhibit 4).

Initial consumer testing of the original "got milk?" ads, though, found that Spanish-speaking households did not find the commercials funny when translated directly to Spanish. As Manning explained, "We found out that not having milk or rice in Hispanic households is not funny: running out of milk means you failed your family."[6] In addition, "got milk?" translated roughly means "are you lactating?" As a result, the CMPB and Hispanic ad agency Anita Santiago Advertising created a series of ads focused on milk being a sacred ingredient and often used the tagline "Familia, Amor y Leche" (Family, Love and Milk). When the campaign did use the "got milk?" tagline, it was left untranslated. Awareness rose among the Hispanic population and in 2002, the CMPB tested its first Spanish-language television spot, La Llorona (pronounced "Yoh-ROH-nah) or "The Crying One." La Llorona is a mythical Hispanic character who, angry with her adulterous husband, drowned her children and then commits suicide. La Llorona wanders the world as a ghost, crying and searching for them.

> In the spot, the tragic La Llorona wafts through a family home late at night searching, of course, for the elusive milk. Finding the refrigerator, La Llorona utters "Leche," stops crying (for the first time in centuries) and joyously grabs the milk. The carton turns up dry and, in a fit of dramatic despair; she slams the door and returns to her wailing. The commercial ends with the now famous question...GOT MILK?[7]

Hispanic consumers were thrilled that the commercial understood their culture and targeted them specifically. In addition, La Llorona won the "TV Silver" award in the *Ad Age* Hispanic Creative Advertising Awards.

That same year, the CMPB created a campaign around the Mexican drink Licuados (pronounced Lee-Kwa-Dohs). Licuados are authentic Mexican smoothies made with milk, fruit, and ice. The print ads emphasized the importance of milk by showing a blender filled with fruit and ice but no milk. A recipe for the drink appeared in the copy and the 'got milk?' logo was spelled out on the blender buttons. The campaign specifically targeted Hispanic Californians, popularized

Licuados throughout California, and introduced non-Hispanics to the next Latin craze. California milk sales continued to rise into 2003 and Manning credited some of that upswing to the new Licuado initiative.

Got Cheese?

The growing Hispanic demographic directly correlated to the steady increase in cheese sales and consumption. Over the past 20 years, U.S. per capita cheese consumption grew every year, reaching an all time high of 34 pounds in 2004 (Exhibit 5). In California, 46 percent of all milk was used for cheese production in 2004, making California the largest producer of Hispanic-style cheese. The CMPB kept a watchful eye on this trend because California was also second largest overall cheese producer in the nation with almost 2 billion pounds in production.[8]

Expanding distribution

Another area of growth developed as the obesity crisis began to make headlines at the turn of the century. The percentage of the population that could be considered obese was above 15 percent in all 50 states by 2003, compared with just 5 states with the same demographics in 1991.[9] Milk producers took advantage of the situation to promote its healthy message and expand distribution into vending machines, schools, and fast food restaurants.

Improved portable packaging and a variety of milk flavors naturally led to the expansion of milk into vending machines. Vending machine sales of milk increased 45 percent in 2003 compared to other cold beverages that declined 1 percent. Beverage Marketing Corporation estimated that vending sales of milk could generate up to $1.2 billion over the next five years as vending machines continue to take on a healthier variety of foods and beverages.[10]

Some of the $1.2 billion vending machine sales increase was expected to come from schools like the Los Angeles Unified School District that banned the sales of all soft drinks during school hours in 2004. In addition, milk got another boost when President George Bush signed into law the Child Nutrition Act in 2004. This law gave schools more flexibility as to how they serve milk and required at least two different types of milk be served. Varieties of milk could include different flavors, low or non fat, and lactose-free.

In 2003, McDonald's, under pressure to promote healthier eating, teamed up with the CMPB. Research revealed that 53 percent of parents preferred milk in their Happy Meals and 70 percent of parents want their children to drink milk when they eat out. Using the "got milk?" logo under the golden arches, McDonald's franchises in California pushed sales of milk with its Happy Meals instead of soft drinks. Milk sales soared 20 percent during the pilot test and the program rolled out to 1,000 franchises in Southern California.[11] In addition, more fast food establishments and restaurants started to promote milk instead of soft drinks, including Wendy's who took actions to promote milk in their locations with point-of-sale.

What's next?

The "got milk?" campaign obviously resonated with consumers in California. Not only did it increase sales and slow down a two-decade decline in milk consumption, but it launched a market for licensed merchandise and "got milk?" knockoffs. By 2005, other advertisers had co-opted the slogan for such marketing projects as "Got Wine?" "Got Jesus?" "Got Porn?" "Got Stickers?" and "Got Books?" Jeff Manning contended that the success of the "got milk?" campaign demonstrated both the value and power of advertising. In his opinion, "got milk?" accomplished more than stopping the disastrous slide of milk sales:

> "got milk?" changed the world of advertising. It proved, perhaps more convincingly than any other campaign…that products, even ancient products like milk, can be resurrected with smart, creative advertising.[12]

The "got milk?" campaign initially revitalized solely with effective marketing, since the product itself and consumer attitudes about its health benefits remained constant throughout. When the attempt by the CMPB to break with the deprivation formula with Drysville failed to entice consumers in the same manner as the original ads, the CMPB returned to its original strategy. In 2005, even with exciting initiatives toward health, expanded distribution, and Hispanic-marketing, the CMPB always came back to its roots—the deprivation strategy. The spot, "Russian Family" ran in 2005.

> The commercial opens in St. Petersburg on a dreary winter's night. The snow is falling as a Russian family soberly slurps their watery soup. From nowhere we hear the unmistakable voice of the *Pillsbury Doughboy*. Dad looks up, grandma drops her pot, and the music begins to play as the Doughboy pushes in a huge plate of his freshly baked, chocolate chip cookies. Everyone takes a bite of the warm, irresistible cookies, hugs and begins to dance around the kitchen. Life is good. However, the celebration comes to an abrupt halt when the horrified mother emerges from the kitchen, screaming "Moloko" (milk in Russian) and shakes an empty milk carton. The music ends, faces drop, mouths clog with warm cookies and once again milk deprivation reins terror on the world. The commercial closes on the shocked face of the *Pillsbury Doughboy* and, of course, GOT MILK?

As the "got milk?" campaign celebrated its 12-year anniversary in 2005, the CMPB pondered the contemporary impact of its strategy. Milk sales in California had fallen again in 2004, after a decade of mixed results. Per capital milk consumption had been flat or down in the United States each year since 1997. Still, if milk consumption had continued to decline at its early-1990s rate, the situation would be much worse. The question remained, how long will the "got milk?" catchphrase last? What will fuel the next cycle of milk growth? Specifically, should the CMPB focus on new demographics, fresh creative, new innovative products and packaging, expanded distribution, or something else? Or should the CMPB just keep doing what it had been doing successfully since 1993?

DISCUSSION QUESTIONS

1. What associations do consumers have for milk? What are the implications of these associations in terms of building brand equity for and increasing the consumption of milk?
2. Evaluate the CMPB marketing program now and back in the early 90s. What do you see as its strengths and weaknesses? What changes would you make?
3. Evaluate their Hispanic marketing initiatives. Does the CMPB risk alienating its current consumer base?
4. There are several areas of growth that lay ahead of the CMPB—health, cheese, Hispanic, and new channels of distribution. Given the trends, what should they do and how should they do it?
5. How long can the CMPB keep running the "got milk?" campaign? What can they do to keep the message and strategy fresh in the consumer's minds? Are there other examples of other successful campaigns that ran this long?

Exhibit 1: Fluid Milk Consumption per Capita (gallons)

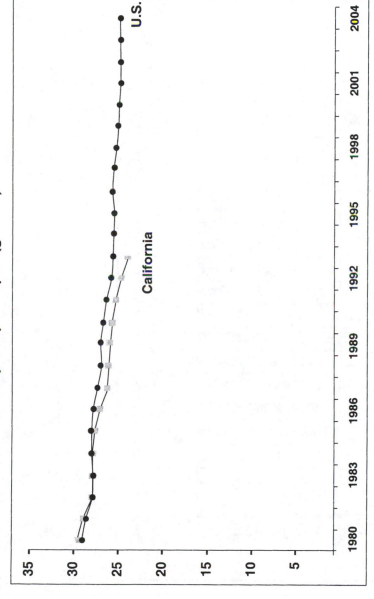

Source: USDA Economic Research Service

49

Exhibit 2: California Class 1 Milk Sales in Millions of Gallons

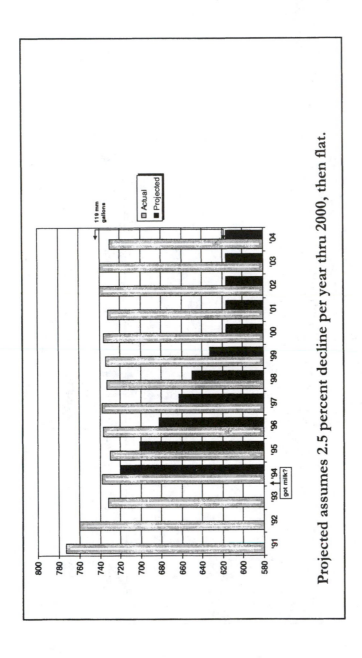

Projected assumes 2.5 percent decline per year thru 2000, then flat.

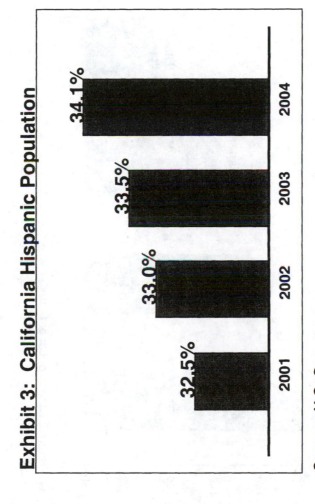

Exhibit 3: California Hispanic Population

	2001	2002	2003	2004
	32.5%	33.0%	33.5%	34.1%

Source: U.S. Census

Exhibit 4: Annual Expenditures on Milk per Household, 2002

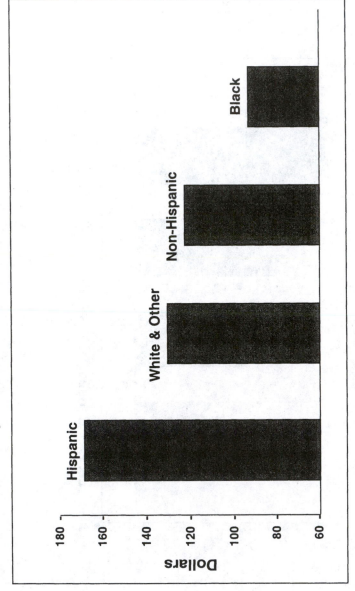

Source: Bureau of Labor Statistics

52

Exhibit 5: U.S. Cheese Consumption per Capita (pounds)

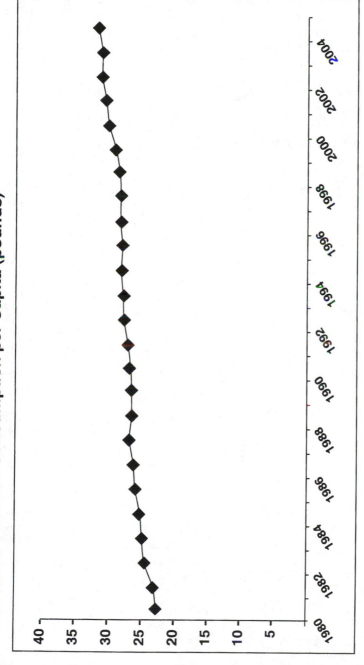

Source: USDA Economic Research Service

REFERENCES

[1] This case was made possible through the cooperation of the California Milk Processor Board and the assistance of Executive Director Jeff Manning. Sanjay Sood prepared this case with additional assistance from Keith Richey and Lowey Sichol under the supervision of Professor Kevin Lane Keller, Tuck School of Business, Dartmouth College as the basis for class discussion.

[2] Datamonitor: Milk in the United States, Industry Profile, February 2004.

[3] Jeff Manning, *got milk?: the book.* p. 182.

[4] As quoted in *Advertising Age*, January 1998.

[5] "New got milk? Messages spoof steroid scandals." *Dairy Foods*, November 2005, p. 16.

[6] The *Wall Street Journal*, March 6, 1996.

[7] www.gotmilk.com

[8] California Department of Food & Agriculture.

[9] www.obesityinamerica.org

[10] http://milkdelivers.org/vending

[11] Dairy foods, October 2003, Vol. 104, Issue 10.

[12] Jeff Manning, *got milk?: the book.* p. 185.

GENERAL ELECTRIC:
BRANDING IN BUSINESS-TO-BUSINESS[1]

INTRODUCTION

When General Electric's ninth chairman, Jeff Immelt, took office as Chairman of the Board and Chief Executive Officer on September 7, 2001, few could imagine what would happen in those following days. The events on September 11th changed the world politically and economically. Not only did these changes create some of the most difficult challenges any CEO would ever face in the company's 125 year history, but additionally Immelt was stepping into a role that some of America's most famous businessmen had undertaken. His predecessors included Thomas Edison, Reginald H. Jones, and Jack Welch, who over time had shaped one of America's most enduring companies into a diverse portfolio of businesses ranging from light bulbs to jet engines to financial services. This unique combination of businesses had enabled the General Electric Company to grow into one of the world's biggest businesses, with $157 billion in revenues and over $350 billion in market value in 2005.

As Immelt entered office, a struggling economy, rising fuel costs, and global warming were the major concerns of the day. Immelt believed that the future of the company lay in innovation and emerging technologies such as fossil fuels and wind power. He began to implement this vision, first dropping the well-known slogan "We Bring Good Things to Life" for "Imagination at Work" in 2003. Then, as stricter global regulations and environmental concerns became more prominent, he launched a company-wide initiative called "Ecomagination" in 2005, which set aggressive goals for GE to produce cleaner technologies. This major shift in marketing and business strategies did not immediately boost GE's stock, however, which hovered around $30 per share after Immelt took over as CEO. Nevertheless, Immelt continued to believe that focusing on innovation and eco-friendly technology was the best, most profitable direction for the company.

GE HISTORY

The Early Years (1878–1954)

Thomas Edison once stated in the late nineteenth century, "I find out what the world needs, and then I proceed to invent"—a motto that has served as the foundation for innovation at General Electric. The history of the company started when Thomas Edison founded the Edison Electric Light Company in 1878. A year later he developed his most famous invention, the incandescent lamp (now called the light bulb) from his laboratory in Menlo Park, NJ. The first ads for Edison Electric invention were simple, informative signs that read: "This room is equipped with *Edison Electric Light*. Do not attempt to light with match. Simply turn key on wall by door."

In 1892, Edison General Electric merged with Thomson-Houston Company to create the General Electric Company. Thomson-Houston's leader, Charles Coffin, was named GE's first president and Edison was appointed director. Inventions continued to flourish in those early years and the first business divisions included lighting, transportation, medical equipment, and appliances. By the turn of the century, print ads explained one of

General Electric's products in lengthy detail and provided information about its benefits. A poster from the 1900s exclaimed, "Everyone wants Electric Light, its luxury—comfort—cleanliness—convenience. Everybody can now afford it." Another ad read, "Electric Light is Now Cheaper. Ask your Electric Light Company about this new lamp tomorrow morning. Find out why it is so economical. Learn how you can have Electricity Light at one half of the old cost."[2]

In the 1900s and 1910s, most of GE's revenue came from GE Transportation, which manufactured large electrical equipment for railroads and public utilities and began working on jet engines as early as the late-1910s. GE Appliances, which produced percolators, toasters, grills, irons, refrigerators, and ranges under various brand names like Hotpoint Stoves, Thor Washing Machines, and Premier Vacuum Cleaners, made up most of the company's remaining revenue. Other early divisions included GE Plastics, GE Financial Services, GE Medical Supplies, and a joint venture with AT&T and Westinghouse that formed the Radio Corporation of America (RCA). Despite the fact that GE produced so many products, few consumers recognized the GE brand.

General Electric's marketing and sales made improvements following World War I thanks to the expansion of electricity. In 1919, electric lines only reached 25 percent of Americans. Five years later, that number had increased to approximately 65 percent of Americans. In 1922, GE hired ad agency, BDO, whose executives firmly believed that the company needed to do two things. First, BDO recommended that GE unify its diverse portfolio of products under one corporate brand. Second, they recommended that GE create a more personal brand identity. Bruce Barton, one of BDO's founders, suggested that GE drop the name "Company" from the end of the General Electric Company. In addition, he helped GE launch a full corporate campaign called "The Initials of a Friend…GE." Many employees did not approve of this corporate advertising, insisting that executives were spending their money to educate the public. Consequently, GE executives recognized the importance of selling GE's corporate campaigns to the employees first—a strategy that has become one of the keys to GE's marketing success over the years.

BDO also helped create the now famous GE script logo. The signature logo, which has gone unchanged for decades, had two basic parts. First, the letters, G and E, were written in script black and white font. Second, the letters were surrounded by counter-clockwise waves, symbolizing the company's wide range of products. By the mid-1920s, the logo appeared on all of the company's products and in its print ads.

In addition to its early marketing campaigns, GE became renowned for developing innovative products. The inventiveness and entrepreneurial talents of founder Thomas Edison lived on in GE's main research lab in Schenectady, New York. The lab, which became known as "The House of Magic," was responsible for a number of innovations, including the X-ray tube and the high-frequency alternator, the latter of which made radio and television broadcasting possible. Importantly, GE was able to develop commercial applications for many its inventions, as evidenced by translating its invention of the high-frequency alternator into a founding role in the Radio Corporation of America (RCA) and the National Broadcasting Corporation (NBC), two early pioneers in television and radio. The House of Magic was responsible for many other commercially successful products that former GE chairman Owen Young remarked in 1930 that the research lab "is the balance sheet itself."[3]

The next round of company slogans came about in the 1930s. "More Goods for More People at Less Cost" reflected customer's concerns during the depression years. By the late 1940s, GE adopted, "You can put your Confidence in General Electric" which fit the postwar sentiment appropriately. The baby boom and housing explosion that followed the end of the war helped fuel tremendous growth for the company. Consumers stocked their homes with GE products like televisions, portable mixers, hair dryers, dishwashers, radios, and light bulbs. In addition, GE was one of the first companies to take advantage of television advertising, which helped humanize the corporation.

The Growing Years (1954–1980)

In 1955, after decades of successful expansion into a diversified technology powerhouse, GE underwent a major restructuring based on the decentralized management approach of its president at the time, Ralph Cordiner. Cordiner's approach created a bureaucratic corps of professional managers who were frequently rotated across businesses, even if it meant they entered a sector where they had no scientific knowledge. This decentralized approach, while it occasionally led to employee frustration with the many layers of management, was credited with enabling GE to continue its growth despite its immense size.

GE continued its marketing strategy of using high-profile corporate branding campaigns. One of the company's most successful corporate advertising campaigns - "Progress is Our Most Important Product"—launched in the mid-1950s. "Progress is Our Most Important Product" became a household slogan within a few years thanks to the *General Electric Theatre*, a half-hour television broadcast featuring top Hollywood stars in a variety of movies and shows. Future President of the United States Ronald Reagan joined *General Electric Theatre* as its host in September 1954, before he gave up acting to venture into politics. Reagan introduced the program and closed it with personal comments. Most of GE's commercials featured Nancy and Ronald Reagan in a complete electrical kitchen talking to the viewers about the benefits of GE and its products. A typical plug for GE sounded like this:

> "In the meantime, remember: From electricity comes progress; progress in our daily living; progress in our daily work; progress in the defense of our nation; and at General Electric, progress is . . . When you live better electrically, you lead a richer, fuller, more satisfying life. Progress in products goes hand in hand with providing progress in the human values that enrich the lives of us all."[4]

Reagan's mannerism and *General Electric Theatre* were so effective at reaching consumers across the country that experts from the polling firm, Gallup-Robinson, stated it was "the leading institutional campaign on television for selling ideas to the public."[5]

In 1972, when Reginald Jones became Chairman and CEO, GE revised "Progress is Our Most Important Product" to "Progress for People." The advertisements in the 1970s focused more on innovation and the product's benefits rather than their features. "Progress for People" ran for nine years. In that time, GE pushed to expand internationally and made significant investments in R&D. As a result, the company generated 40 percent of its earnings abroad in 1980 compared with 30 percent in 1970. The company also focused on nuclear technology as an alternative source of power, a consequence of the energy crisis that gripped the globe in the late 1970s. Furthermore, it placed a renewed focus on consumer products, which accounted for 22 percent of the company's net income by 1976.

Sales more than doubled from $10 billion to $22 billion during Jones nine-year tenure, primarily coming from GE's medical, transportation and appliance divisions. As GE expanded, it became more difficult to manage. Jones admitted that "moving General Electric is like trying to change the direction of a supertanker. It takes five miles to get one degree of change."[6] Exploiting new growth opportunities and anticipating market moves would be key challenges to the company's continued growth in the upcoming years.

A NEW ERA OF GROWTH AND EXPANSION

The Jack Welch Years (1981–2001)
Jack Welch joined General Electric in 1960 as a junior engineer and quickly became frustrated with the company's strict bureaucracy. He came close to leaving GE a year later but was persuaded to stay by his former boss who saw Welch's leadership potential. Welch was promoted to general manager of GE Plastics in 1969, vice president in 1972, senior vice president in 1977, and vice chairman in 1979. In 1981, Jack Welch succeeded Reginald Jones as General Electric's eighth CEO. Over the course of his two decade leadership as CEO, Welch helped grow GE from an "American manufacturer into a global services giant," and increased the company's market value from $12 billion in 1981 to $280 in 2001, making it the world's most valuable corporation.

Welch's success came much in part to his leadership skills. He was a great communicator and created an open, informal learning environment at GE. But he was also very demanding and once stated, "Reward those who meet expectations and discard those who don't."[7] Welch kept to his word and fired the bottom 10 percent of performers at the company every year. In his first five years as CEO, Welch eliminated 130,000 jobs, or a 25 percent of total number of GE employees, and earned the nickname, Neutron Jack.

Welch also set very aggressive goals for each division of the company. He explained, "When I became CEO of GE in 1981, we launched a highly publicized initiative: 'Be No. 1 or No. 2 in every market, and fix, sell, or close to get there.' . . . GE was going to move away from businesses that were being commoditized and toward businesses that manufactured high-value technology products or sold services instead of things."[8] As a result, GE sold 118 businesses in 1982 alone, including most of its consumer products brands except for light bulbs and large appliances. Welch always focused on the bottom line and supported the company's high growth businesses such as aircraft engines, power turbines, commercial finance, plastics, and medical equipment, often augmenting them through acquisitions. Roughly 40 percent of GE's revenue growth during Welch's tenure came from acquired businesses.

Welch's Marketing Strategy
Welch's management style (see Exhibit 1) was not the only thing that made him such a successful leader. He also understood the importance of marketing and building a strong corporate brand. Welch explained, "Brands take time, patience, and understanding that only senior management can provide inside the firm."

Early on, Welch also showed that he believed in taking risks and using marketing techniques from consumer products to market B2B products. As general manager of GE

Plastics, Welch helped develop a "marketing and promotion campaign…that was being promoted more like Tide detergent."[9] The spot featured St. Louis Cardinal pitcher, Bob Gibson, throwing pitches at Welch who held up a Lexan plastic sheet. GE Plastics had a record year in sales and the spot received extensive media attention for being different, risky, and effective.

In 1979, GE launched "We Bring Good Things to Life," perhaps one of the best known and most successful advertising campaigns of all time. Welch embraced this campaign from the start and the company spent over $1 billion nurturing it throughout his tenure.

We Bring Good Things to Life

"We Bring Good Things to Life" ran for 24 years and in that time, humanized the conglomerate by demonstrating the benefits that GE's products brought to people. The tagline, "We Bring Good Things to Life," was created by Phil Dusenberry—the former creative director and chairman of BBDO North America. Dusenberry came up with the famous slogan in a cab, 12 hours before presenting it to Jack Welch. The tagline was set to a jingle, which stuck in consumer's heads because it was a simple musical scale. The campaign also included a print element, which targeted consumers by explaining the benefits of its consumer products. A print ad in the 1980s for a GE microwave stated, "GE didn't design a microwave that works over a grill just to impress home builders. We did it to impress home buyers."

Back when the slogan was developed, GE's revenues came from a diverse array of products, including light bulbs, plastics, consumer appliances, jet engines, and nuclear reactor divisions. The new campaign, however, focused primarily on light bulbs and appliances because GE believed those products touched an emotional side of consumers. GE board member Walter Wriston explained that "millions of people across the country open their refrigerator door, and the light goes on, and they see GE. That monogram stares them in the face every time they turn on the light."[10]

A classic GE spot from the 1980s called "Patricia" did an effective job of communicating the wide range of GE products, but cleverly started and ended with the classic GE light bulb:

> A Man's hand reached and turned on a GE light bulb. A narrators' voice explained, "This is the hand . . . that turned on the light . . . that lit up the desk . . . where the idea was born for a quieter jet engine . . . that flew the technician . . . who works at the power plant . . . which produces its energy far more efficiently. . . as it lights up the city . . . powers the hospital with its life saving images . . . where Sam is found healthy . . . "
> As a young boy is shown skipping off to a football game, the voiceover continued, "in time for the game . . . held under the lights . . . broadcast to millions by a satellite system . . . designed with precision . . . sent by powerful locomotives . . . that ride past a factory that helped build a car with advanced thermo-plastics . . . that sits in the drive at the home of Patricia who went to the fridge and got a drink for her dad . . . who works in a room where he turned out the light as he puts his young daughter to bed. GE—Everyday GE technology touches the lives of just about everybody."

Over the following two decades, GE faced several public relations disasters, including PCB dumping in the Hudson and Houstonic Rivers[11] and a tax scandal in the early 1980s.[12] However, board member Wriston remembered that GE's slogan helped deflect these issues by reinforcing only the good things GE did. He explained, "The result is that the public perceives GE as bringing good things to life. The lights work, the refrigerator keeps the beer cold, the washing machine gets the spots out of your pants. And the concept of some guy ripping off the government on work parts is sort of an esoteric thing that doesn't affect me and GE because my relationship with GE is the light bulb."[13]

Welch's Strategy Led to Results

Throughout the 1980s and 1990s Jack Welch kept the media and marketing strategy focused and simple. Welch even eliminated the Chief Marketing Officer position during this time. He embraced "We Bring Good Things to Life" and did not change it much throughout his tenure. The television spots ran primarily during early Sunday morning business and political talk shows, which targeted a small group of business and political "influentials."

Welch's primary focus was to be number one or two in each of its 11 business divisions (Exhibit 2). Welch explained, "When you're number four or five in a market, when number one sneezes, you get pneumonia. When you're number one, you control your destiny."[14] GE achieved these market positions primarily by focusing on existing business and growing through acquisitions. In contrast, GE under Welch did not invest as much in technology, innovation, or building new businesses. George Wise, a retired historian for GE noted, "Since its founding in 1892, General Electric has mastered the art of acquiring technologies invented elsewhere, then throwing in enough capital, research and salesmanship to dominate the market."[15] In 1986, GE re-acquired NBC, which kept its own separate brand name, and at the time was considered one of the riskiest moves Welch made. It also proved to be one of his most profitable decisions.

In 1991, *Forbes* magazine ranked GE the number one company in America for the first time ever. By 1997, many of GE's businesses were number one in terms of global market share, including industrial motors, medical systems, plastics, transport, power generation, and aircraft engines. Lighting and household appliances held the number two share in the world. The company had also made a successful push into financial services, eventually generating more then $50 billion in revenue from commercial and consumer finance operations such as credit cards, real estate, leasing, insurance, and loans. Exhibit 3 shows GE's growth in revenue and earnings during the latter half of Welch's reign.

In 2000, GE announced the $41 billion buyout of Honeywell. The GE-Honeywell deal would have been the largest merger in the history between two industrial companies and Welch delayed his retirement to see the deal through. But the FTC blocked the GE-Honeywell deal on antitrust grounds. Hence Welch retired on September 6, 2001, known as one of the greatest corporate leaders of all time. He had successfully led GE to phenomenal global achievements, delivered high returns for shareholders, and built up GE's brand equity through the world.

GE IN THE NEW CENTURY

The Jeff Immelt Years (Post-2001)

On Friday, September 7, 2001, Jeff Immelt succeeded Jack Welch as the ninth chairman and Chief Executive Officer of General Electric at the age of 44. The Dartmouth College and Harvard Business School alum started his career at GE in 1982. Over the course of the next two decades, he held senior roles in GE Appliances, GE Plastics, and most recently was President and CEO of GE Medical Systems, an $8 billion division of GE. Len Vickers, a former GE executive who helped create the "We Bring Good Things to Life" campaign commented, "I think Jeff early on was spotted as 'A' material and a real leader. What I liked about him was that he had a marketing head, a marketing mind-set. He always thought and talked in terms of opportunity, not challenges."

Immelt's initial strategy during the challenging post-9/11 business climate was to continue to shed GE's consumer businesses as his predecessor had.[16] Despite this similarity, the differences between Immelt and Welch were evident from the beginning. While Welch had focused on financial services and expanding through acquisitions, Immelt believed the future lay in technology and innovation, including emerging technologies such as solar energy, hydrogen storage, nanotechnology, and fuel cells. Immelt explained, "In the late 1990s, we became business traders and not business growers. Today organic growth is absolutely the biggest task of every one of our companies....The crisis in [corporate America] today is a little bit about governance and a lot about a rampant lack of innovation."[17]

To realize his vision, Immelt added 5,000 engineers in three years, including several to senior management. He built three more Global Research Centers—as the "House of Magic" was renamed—in Shanghai, Munich, and Bangalore. He reduced the acquisitions team, though GE still made some large acquisitions, buying Vivendi Universal for $14 billion and $10 billion for medical imaging company Amersham. He appointed Beth Comstock as Chief Marketing Officer—a position that Welch had eliminated. In addition, Immelt appointed a marketing leader to each of GE's major business lines to help develop new ideas and visions for each division.

A New Campaign

Immelt, Comstock, and GE's longtime agency BBDO Worldwide, believed that the best way to communicate this new vision and direction for the company was to create an innovative marketing campaign. A source at GE explained, "Welch wanted advertising that was touchy-feely. Something you could put your arms around. [Immelt] doesn't want to walk away from the [We Bring Good Things to Life] line, but he wants to come up with his own style of advertising. Something that would be an extension of himself. He wants advertising that's more high-tech, more innovative and contemporary. Something that will make GE look more advanced, out in front."[18] So, after 24 years and $1 billon of supporting "We Bring Good Things to Life," GE dropped its signature slogan for the new tagline "Imagination at Work."

The company did not launch "Imagination at Work" without engaging its employees first. Beth Comstock explained the initial internal branding strategy, "The company talked to employees around the globe to find out what they held as the core attributes of GE, what they held in high esteem, and what they valued about their company.

The employees validated the research we did. But we didn't start off by saying we were going to change 'We Bring Good Things to Life.' "[19] She further explained that GE developed an internal campaign, which would ensure that employees understood the importance of a re-branding effort, felt part of the campaign's creative process, and were supportive of the new slogan. Once Comstock and her team felt good about the internal branding process and the support of GE's employees, they launched "Imagination at Work" to the public.

Imagination at Work

The initial "Imagination at Work" campaign began in January 2003 with a $100 million launch. The creative emphasized the company's revived focus of innovation and targeted three distinct audiences. First, the campaign reinforced to GE employees that the company's new primary focus would be innovation and technological advances. Immelt backed up this promise by increasing the R&D budget to $2.7 billion in 2003. Second, the campaign communicated to analysts and investors on Wall Street that innovation would be central to GE's future growth and profitability. Finally, "Imagination at Work" communicated to consumers how GE products made their lives better. Comstock noted the importance of this corporate campaign encompassing the company's entire portfolio, "When you're a company like ours, with 11 different businesses, brand is really important in pulling the identity of the company together. Integration was important in communicating the brand across the organization and to all of our constituents."[20]

The television ads highlighted three of GE's divisions—GE Transportation, GE Plastics and GE Medical Systems—because they told the best story of recent innovation. Judy Hu, general manager of advertising and brand, stated, "One of the reasons that we picked these operating units is that we wanted to get the message out about the diversity of the units, the diversity of the products and services that we have at GE. We did a lot of consumer research, and most people today - investors and customers—only think of GE in terms of lighting and appliances. It was really important to tell them this is a new GE."[21]

The television spots took on a humorous tone and the first featured the Wright Brothers' rickety Kitty Hawk plane from 1903:

> A GE aircraft engine strapped to the plane helped transform it into a jet. The Kitty Hawk-turned-jet soared high into the sky as Johnny Cash's "We'll Visit the Man in the Moon" played in the background. The message to viewers was that GE's products could take things to places people never imagined.

Another spot for GE Healthcare featured a brain surgeon and his team performing an operation:

> The scene switched from an operating room to an outer space sci-fi look and feel. The surgeon and his crew members zapped troubled spots with laser guns - depicting how GE technology helped doctors perform difficult medical procedures with precision. The spot cut back to the operating room where another doctor said incredulously, "You just told us to go back to the ship." The surgeon snapped out of his fantasy as the GE voice explained, "GE Healthcare's medical imaging allows doctors to navigate a patient's brain in ways that seem like science fiction."

GE's black and white logo underwent a "facelift" for the first time ever. The logo, which appeared at the end of the TV spots, changed to one that quickly flashed colorful symbols of the company's different products (for example, the NBC peacock, a jet engine, a wind mill, an x-ray, a locomotive, and a leaf) before ending with its signature black and white logo. This fresh new logo not only communicated the diverse areas of GE but also symbolized a contemporary company, focused on innovation and technology.

The campaign also included print ads like one that featured GE's founder, Thomas Edison, with his head opening up. Out of his head spilled visions of aircraft engines, high-tech windmills, refrigerators, and other GE products. GE spent over $200 million on the campaign in print, TV, and online advertising during the first two years.

Reaction to the Campaign

The "Imagination at Work" tagline met with mixed reviews. Some criticized GE for abandoning decades of equity built up in the "Good Things to Life" slogan and of not being able to "breathe new life into the current theme."[22] Critics called the new slogan 'unimaginative' and pointed out that the "_____ at Work" theme had already been used. Black & Decker had used "Ideas at Work," Ford, ABB, and Bank of America had all used "Ingenuity at Work," and Sony had once used on "Innovation at Work."[23] In addition, many felt the $200 million campaign budget was wasted, especially since few of GE's products advertised were sold to consumers. One research study conducted in 2004 found that 39 percent of consumers recognized "We Bring Good Things to Life," whereas only 5 percent recognized "Imagination at Work."[24]

On the other hand, GE executives and BBDO defended its campaign. Comstock stated, "We're a 120-year old company, and you don't get to your third century without changing with the times. We certainly were not looking to change for change's sake, but you also can't stay still."[25] Some marketing experts agreed with Comstock, noting that the campaign helped return GE to its roots as an innovative company, focused on shareholder value.[26] One brand strategist commented, "These ads have nothing to do with getting consumers to buy GE light bulbs—and everything to do with getting investors to buy GE stock. They realize the investor community will not regard them as highly for consumer goods that it is looking for innovation and new technology. These ads imply a product and innovation mindset at GE that will put them at the heart of the economy in the future."[27]

Early surveys indicated that the campaign was resonating with consumers. *USA Today's* Ad Track, a weekly consumer survey, found that 19 percent of the consumers surveyed liked the new GE commercials "a lot"—just 2 percent shy of the weekly average of 21 percent.[28] In addition, only 1 percent of those surveyed "disliked" the ads—much less than the Ad Track average of 13 percent. The low percent of 'disliked' responses surprised many critics because GE had dropped such a popular campaign. But, Hu responded, "We haven't seen a single negative response, given the changes we've made." [29] Other studies showed that the ads were changing consumer's attitudes toward GE. Perceptions of GE being seen as 'innovative' increased by 35 percent; offering high tech solutions increased by 40 percent; being dynamic increased by 50 percent.[30] In addition, there was a 14 percent increase in traffic on GE.com, and 1.7 million individuals received GE's interactive ads virally.

GE Goes "Green"

GE spent the 18 months after "Imagination at Work" was launched conducting extensive consumer research. Executives wanted to understand the effectiveness of the new campaign, their customer's major concerns, and current global economic trends. Several themes emerged from the research, including concerns about rising fuel costs, tighter global environmental regulations, and increased expectations of the value of a company's products and services. One reporter summarized the times by saying, "In an era of corporate scandals....consumers trust companies that are responsible citizens they mistrust companies that appear selfish or wasteful."[31]

One major finding from "dreaming sessions" with managers of energy and heavy-industry companies who were GE customers was a "wish list" of eco-friendly products they wanted to use in their businesses, such as hydrogen fuel cells, which reflected the changing global environmental regulations. GE recognized that finding optimal means of serving these changing demands would give it a competitive advantage. As one reporter for *Forbes* pointed out, "GE's new philosophy... is this: If you can't beat the environmentalists, join them. Immelt's GE is going to make a business out of being green."[32] What materialized was a new company-wide initiative called "Ecomagination."

"Ecomagination" launched in May 2005 and represented a commitment from GE to develop cleaner products and technologies like solar energy, lower-emission engines, and water purification technologies.[33] The campaign involved several major initiatives. First, GE would double its investment in R&D. By 2010, GE would invest $1.5 billion or 35 percent of its total research budget a year in R&D for cleaner technologies. Second, GE would double its revenue from "Ecomagination" products to $20 billion by 2010. The Ecomagination initiative promised to reduce greenhouse gas emissions by 1 percent by 2012. That number was impressive considering that emissions were predicted to have increased 40 percent by 2012 if no action had been taken. Finally, Immelt promised to keep the public informed of GE's Ecomagination results.[34] In an interview, Immelt elaborated on his Ecomagination strategy:

> We're not doing it just to be do-gooders. We're not doing it because it's trendy or because it's, quote, unquote, 'moral.' We're doing it because we think it can help lower our internal costs and help us grow our revenue at the same time.[35]

"Ecomagination" Launches

To communicate the "Ecomagination" initiative, GE and agency BBDO launched a integrated campaign targeting a broad audience. The campaign included a series of television spots, print ads, online ads, an informative website, and billboards. The first television spot, entitled "Signin' in the Rain," introduced the "Ecomagination" concept with an ad that stated "At GE, we're using what we call Ecomagination to create technology that's right in step with nature. GE—Imagination at Work."

A subsequent spot for GE Energy was called "Model Miners:"

> Set to the thumping tune of Tennessee Ernie Ford's "Sixteen Tons," the commercial took place in a dark, steamy coal mine. However, instead of traditional-looking miners, the spot looked more like a music video and featured attractive, half-naked, sweaty men and women models shoveling coal. A voice clarified, "Imagine if a 250 year supply of energy were right here at home. Now, thanks to emission-reducing technology from GE Energy, harnessing the power of coal is looking more beautiful every day. Another product of Ecomagination. GE—Imagination at Work."

One reporter from the *New York Times* questioned GE's use of combining sex with a pro-labor miner's song. "No one expects GE to preach a Marxist sermon, but the use of "Sixteen Tons" ("You load sixteen tons, and what do you get?/ Another day older and deeper in debt/ Saint Peter doncha call me 'cause I can't go / I owe my soul to the company store.") as a jokey soundtrack is an odd public relations move."[36] A reporter for *Adweek* agreed, "… the slickness has a trivializing effect that could actually make light of environmental issues. Isn't it kind of shallow to think that the only metaphor for natural beauty is a supermodel?"[37]

Critics agreed that the "Ecomagination" spots did a good job of explaining to its audiences *what* GE was doing—producing cleaner, better technologies for the environment. It was Immelt's job to tell Wall Street *why* GE was doing it. As one reporter for the *Washington Post* explained, "Mr. Immelt is so convinced that clean technologies will be the future of GE that, invoking the color of American money, he has made his new mantra: 'Green is Green.' "[38]

CHANGES FOR GE

Company Reorganization

In July 2005, two months after "Ecomagination" launched, GE reorganized its businesses from 11 business units into six industry-focused businesses units: GE Infrastructure, GE Commercial Financial Services, GE Consumer Financial Services, GE Industrial, GE Healthcare, and NBC Universal (Exhibit 4). Immelt believed that the restructuring would do two things. First, it would save costs. Immelt explained in a company statement, "These changes will accelerate GE's growth in key industries. We have been moving toward a more customer-focused organization for several years. In addition, we believe we can reduce $200 to $300 million of cost in savings and structural redundancies."

Second, the restructuring would help GE achieve loftier global expansion goals, an important initiative for GE. Immelt explained the rapid rate of international growth, "Revenue in developing markets is increasing 20 percent a year compared with 5 percent to 10 percent in developed countries outside the U.S." It was expected that by the end of 2006, 45 percent of GE's total revenue would come from outside the United States. By the beginning of 2006, GE held the number one or two global or U.S. market share in many of its divisions, including light bulbs, store credit cards, plastic, jet engines, motors, generators, TV broadcasting, and appliances.

Immelt also hoped that the restructuring in tandem with "Ecomagination" would help boost GE's stock price, which had lingered in the low 30s since 2002 and had dipped down to as low as 22 in October of that year. Unfortunately for GE, this was not the case (Exhibit 5). Despite the fact that GE was earning more income and generating more cash than when the stock was at its peak, the stock remained in the 30s during 2005 and underperformed the market. To boost the stock, it seemed, GE would have to generate even more growth, a fact that spurred Immelt to spend 30 percent of his time on growth initiatives in 2005.

Healthcare Re-Imagined

In January, 2006, GE announced more changes to the marketing department. Beth Comstock, who had helped launch and manage "Imagination at Work" and "Ecomagination," was named president of NBC Universal Digital Media. GE appointed Dan Henson as the new chief marketing officer. Henson's responsibilities included driving GE's marketing and branding strategies, leading the "Ecomagination" initiative, and expanding "Imagination at Work." Two weeks after Henson became CMO, GE launched a campaign called "Healthcare Re-Imagined" in February 2006. The latest marketing campaign focused on GE Healthcare and the products that detected, cured, and prevented diseases.

"Healthcare Re-Imagined" launched in the United States during the opening ceremonies of 2006 Winter Olympics and ran for 10 weeks. The campaign included print ads, an online interactive campaign, and four new commercials that ran on NBC, MSNBC, CNBC and USA. All four commercials took on a more serious tone than earlier "Imagination at Work" spots. Research had showed that consumers felt the topic of health was too significant to joke about.

One commercial called "Welcome to the Earth" sent the message that the world was filled with opportunities. Another commercial entitled "Beats" highlighted how everyone is connected through the commonality of a beating heart—from athletes competing in a match to children playing on the playground to an elderly man walking down a lone road. The spot explained that the breakthrough technology of GE's Lightspeed CT scanner enabled physicians to scan the human heart "in a truly remarkable way."

"Healthcare Re-Imagined" included print ads, most notably, an eight-page pullout section that ran in the *USA TODAY*, the *Wall Street Journal*, and the *New York Times* during the first week of the campaign launch. The print copy directed consumers to visit a specific website and submit pictures of how they keep healthy:

> "At GE we picture a world without disease or illness... And we're working on it.... It's an approach we call Early Health... A completely new way of looking at healthcare that we can all share... How do you stay healthy?"

GE launched a similar campaign overseas in March 2006 where consumers in each country saw print, outdoor, online and television ads in their native language.

CONCLUSION

By 2006, GE had accomplished many magnificent feats as a corporation. It was a $157 billion dollar global company with 310,000 employees worldwide and the most widely held stock in the world. With over $1 billion in ad expenditures, GE's brand health was strong and often ranked at the top of many lists. In 2004, *BusinessWeek* ranked GE as the fourth most valuable brand in the world, after Coca-Cola, Microsoft and IBM. *Fortune Magazine* ranked GE as the number one "Global Most Admired Company" in 1999, 2000, 2001, 2002, and 2006. The *Financial Times* ranked GE as the World's Most Respected Company in 1999, 2000, 2001, 2002, 2003, and 2004. As one *Fortune* reporter noted, "No other U.S. company has been as dominant for as long as GE. Of the 12 firms that Charles Dow put into his original Dow Jones industrial average in 1896, GE is the only one still in the index, and most of the others are dead. Survival is another achievement to admire."[39]

In his first five years as CEO, Jeff Immelt had successfully introduced his vision for GE. The company had launched a new campaign called "Imagination at Work," and adopted an aggressive company-wide environmental initiative called "Ecomagination." With the marketing campaigns in full gear but GE's stock continuing to hover around $30, Immelt needed to ensure that the innovations developed at his company would yield competitive advantages. GE would have to find opportunities that were innovative enough to drive growth but stable enough to sustain it. A brand that had been flexible enough to incorporate a diverse portfolio of businesses during its 127-year history would likely stretch to accommodate whatever new directions Immelt charted for it.

DISCUSSION QUESTIONS

1. Discuss the importance of B2B marketing and a strong B2B brand. How does it differ from consumer marketing?
2. Did Jeff Immelt and Beth Comstock do the right thing by dropping "We Bring Good Things to Life" for "Imagination at Work"? Why or why not?
3. Has "Imagination at Work," "Ecomagination," and "Healthcare Re-Imagined" changed GE's brand? If so, how? Is it a good change or not?
4. Can Immelt transform GE's approach of innovation (risky, unknown areas like fuel cells, solar energy, hydrogen storage, and nanotechnology) versus past strategies of improvement of current technologies?
5. What should Henson do next for GE's brand strategy?

Exhibit 1: Jack Welch's 25 Lessons

Lead More, Manage Less
1. Lead
2. Manage Less
3. Articulate Your Vision
4. Simplify
5. Get Less Formal
6. Energize Others
7. Face Reality
8. See Change as an Opportunity
9. Get Good Ideas from Everywhere
10. Follow up

Build a Winning Organization
11. Get Rid of Bureaucracy
12. Eliminate Boundaries
13. Put Values First
14. Cultivate Leaders
15. Create a Learning Culture

Harness Your People for Competitive Advantage
16. Involve Everyone
17. Make Everybody a Team Player
18. Stretch
19. Instill Confidence
20. Have Fun

Build the Market-Leading Company
21. Be Number 1 or Number 2
22. Live Quality
23. Constantly Focus on Innovation
24. Live Speed
25. Behave Like a Small Company

Source: Jack Welch. *Jack: Straight from the Gut.*

Exhibit 2: GE's 11 Business Divisions

Advanced Materials (Plastics, Silicones/Quartz)
Commercial Finance
Consumer Finance
Consumer & Industrial (Appliances, light bulbs)
Energy (Power plant products and services)
Equipment and Other
Transportation (Jet engines, rail systems, replacement parts and services)
Insurance
Infrastructure (Chemical water treatment)
Healthcare
NBC Universal

Exhibit 3: GE Revenue and Earnings 1991–2005

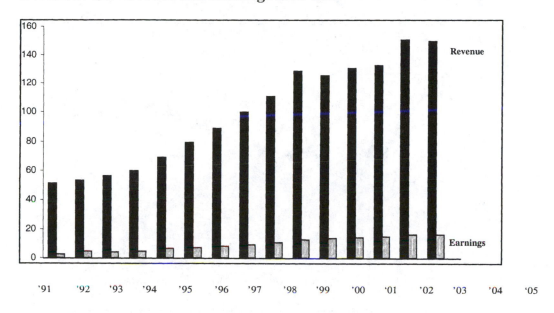

Source: GE.com

Exhibit 4: 2005 Restructure into Six Divisions

Infrastructure (Aircraft Engines, Rail, Energy, Oil & Gas, Water, related financial businesses)
Commercial Financial Services
Consumer Financial Services
Industrial (Plastics, Silicones/Quartz, Consumer & Industrial, Security & Sensors, Automation and Equipment Services)
Healthcare
NBC Universal

Exhibit 5: GE's Stock with Immelt as CEO (as of 3/29/06)

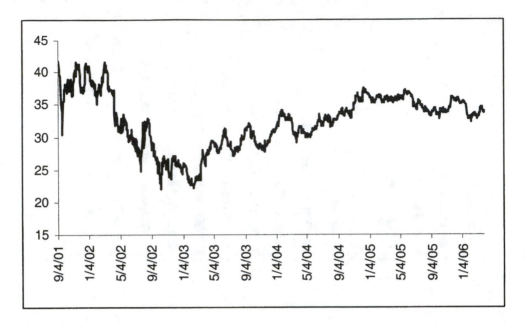

Source: GE.com

REFERENCES

[1] Lowey Bundy Sichol prepared this case under the supervision of Professor Kevin Lane Keller as the basis for class discussion. The case was later updated and revised by Keith Richey.

[2] Robert Slater. *The New GE—How Jack Welch Revived an American Institution.* Business One Irwin, p. 7.

[3] Jerry Useem, "Another Boss, Another Revolution." Fortune, April 5, 2004, p. 112.

[4] William L. Baird, Jr. The Museum of Broadcast Communication.

[5] William L. Baird, Jr. The Museum of Broadcast Communication.

[6] "General Electric: The Financial Wizards Switch Back to Technology." *BusinessWeek*, March 16, 1981, p. 110.

[7] Bill Rothschild. Strategyleader.com. Based on Jack Welch's *Jack: Straight from the Gut.*

[8] Robert Slater. *Jack Welch and the GE Way.* McGraw-Hill. 1999. p. 61.

[9] Bizrum.com, Business Summaries—*Jack: Straight from the Gut.*

[10] Robert Slater. *The New GE—How Jack Welch Revived an American Institution.* Business One Irwin, Pg. 108.

[11] In August of 1975, Richard Severo, a Pulitzer Prize reporter for the *New York Times*, released a story that revealed GE had been dumping polychlorinated biphenyls (PCBs) into New York's Hudson River and Massachusetts' Houstonic Rivers from its Hudson Falls and Fort Edward plants. PCBs were commonly used by manufacturing companies as a fire-prevention material and GE used them to make electric products. However, because PCBs did not burn, they were difficult to dispose of, and GE chose to dump them (legally at the time) into the rivers for approximately 30 years. The U.S. government banned PCBs in 1977 after studies showed that PCBs were linked to cancer, skin rashes, liver damage, and other health risks. But, by then, GE had dumped over 1.3 million pounds of PCBs into the two rivers. In the early 1980s, GE acknowledged that the rivers contained PCBs from their plants, however the legal battle on how to clean up the toxins went on for decades. EPA officials and local environmentalists argued that GE should be responsible for the clean up, which could cost "hundreds of millions of dollars." GE argued, and some scientists agreed, that cleaning up or dredging the rivers would actually do more harm than good – releasing the PCBs that were deeply embedded into the bottom of the two rivers.

[12] In 1981, Congress adopted the 1981 Tax Act, which allowed profitable companies like GE to write off large tax concessions. Although legal, GE avoided paying federal taxes between 1981 and 1983 and only paid $185 million in 1984.

[13] Robert Slater. *The New GE—How Jack Welch Revived an American Institution.* Business One Irwin, Pg. 108.

[14] Robert Slater. *Jack Welch and the GE Way.* McGraw-Hill, 1999. p. 61.

[15] Daniel Fisher. "GE Turns Green." *Forbes,* August 15, 2005.

[16] As of 2003, light bulbs and appliances only made up 7 percent of the company's revenue.

[17] Commencement speech—Harvard Business School. June 5, 2005.

[18] "A new life. General Elective to change corporate image." *Delaney Report*, Volume 13, Issue 22, June 10, 2002.

[19] Andrew Gordon. "Profile—Workers for change." *PR Week US,* October 13, 2003.

[20] Kate Maddox, Beth Snyder Bulik. "Integrated Marketing Success Stories." *B to B*, Vol. 89, Issue 6, June 7, 2004.

[21] Judy Hu, GE's general manager-corporate advertising and marketing communications. "GE campaign brings 'good things' to an end: Emphasis on b-to-b divisions an attempt

to move image of industrial giant beyond light bulbs and appliances." *B to B*. February 10, 2003

[22] "GE to spend $100 million promoting itself as Innovative." The *New York Times*. January 16, 2003.

[23] Timothy Foster. "Creative Eye—The best a brand can get. A memorable advertising slogan can ensure the future's bright..." *Financial Times*, September 9, 2003.

[24] "Second Annual Slogan Survey." Emergence Creative Labs, Atlanta, GA. 2004.

[25] Beth Comstock. "General Electric Drops Longtime Slogan." Associated Press, January 16, 2003.

[26] "GE campaign brings 'good things' to an end: Emphasis on b-to-b divisions an attempt to move image of industrial giant beyond light bulbs and appliances. *B to B*, February 2, 2003

[27] Michael McCarthy. "Imagination at Work for GE." *USA TODAY*, May 4, 2003.

[28] Michael McCarthy. "Imagination at Work for GE." *USA TODAY*, May 4, 2003.

[29] Michael McCarthy. "Imagination at Work for GE." *USA TODAY*, May 4, 2003.

[30] Kate Maddox, Beth Snyder Bulik. "Integrated Marketing Success Stories." *B to B,* June 7, 2004.

[31] David Ignatius. "Corporate Green." The *Washington Post*, May 11, 2005.

[32] Daniel Fisher. "GE Turns Green." *Forbes,* August 15, 2005.

[33] GE.ecomagination.com

[34] Topping off the "Ecomagination" initiative, Immelt and GE accepted responsibility in the Hudson River PCB cleanup process. As of 2006, the dredging process was scheduled to begin in the spring of 2007. In addition, the company planned to pay up to $78 million to the EPA, in addition to the $37 million already spent.

[35] "General Electric's plans to increase spending on cutting-edge environmental technologies." NPR: Morning Edition, May 10, 2005.

[36] Josh Ozersky. "Working in a Coal Mine: Lord I Am So Tired, but Good-Looking." The *New York Times,* April 3, 2005.

[37] Barbara Lippert. "Barbara Lippert's Critique: When Nature Calls." *Adweek*, May 16, 2005.

[38] "The greening of General Electric: A lean, clean electric machine." *Economist Intelligence Unit*, December 16, 2005.

[39] Geoffrey Colvin. "What makes GE Great?" *Fortune,* March 6, 2006.

RED BULL:
BUILDING BRAND EQUITY IN NON-TRADITIONAL WAYS[1]

INTRODUCTION

Red Bull GmbH was founded in 1985 by Dietrich Mateschitz, an Austrian who was a former marketing manager for Procter & Gamble's Blendax (where he managed products like toothpaste and shampoo). Mateschitz hit upon the idea of Red Bull during one of his many business trips to Asia, where an energy drink called "Krating Daeng" ("red water buffalo" in Thai) was very popular. After working for two years to create a carbonated version in a colorful can, Mateschitz launched Red Bull Energy Drink in Austria in 1987 using the slogan "Red Bull verleiht Flüüügel" ("Red Bull gives you wiiings"). Red Bull was available exclusively in Austria for five years, then gradually rolled out in other European nations. Part of the growth strategy was to enter new markets slowly and methodically in order to maximize buzz and build anticipation.

Red Bull achieved remarkable growth considering the product was available in only one stock-keeping unit (SKU)—the now-famous silver 250 ml (8.3 oz.) can—and received little traditional advertising support. Red Bull's above-the-line marketing activities were limited to television commercials that adhered to the same format: using animated shorts to reinforce the "Red Bull gives you wiiings" message. By 1997, a decade after it was launched in Austria, Red Bull was available in 25 markets globally, including Western and Eastern Europe, New Zealand, and South Africa. During that same period, Red Bull sales volume grew from 1.1 million units to over 200 million units. By 2004, the company had worldwide annual sales of nearly 2 billion cans in 120 countries. For all this growth, Red Bull still remained a relatively small company; it had only 1,800 employees worldwide and a mere 200 on the headquarters staff.

Several major beverage companies, including Coca-Cola, Anheuser-Busch, and PepsiCo, began introducing similar products in the year 2000. Despite the additional competition, Red Bull maintained its energy drink market share lead in every mature market. Its meteoric rise and continued dominance of its category made Red Bull one of the most successful new beverages in history. The challenge for the brand would be to continue its stellar growth as current competitors became more aggressive and additional competitors entered the market.

DESIGNING THE PRODUCT

After witnessing firsthand the potential of energy drinks in the Asian market, Dietrich Mateschitz negotiated with a Thai beverage manufacturer called TC Pharmaceuticals for the rights to license its energy drink recipe. In exchange for a 51 percent stake in Red Bull, TC Pharmaceuticals sold the foreign licensing rights in 1984. Mateschitz adapted the product to Western tastes by diluting it, lowering the caffeine content, and adding carbonation. Red Bull essentially invented the "functional energy" beverage category in Western markets, named thus because the beverages were meant to be consumed for energy, not enjoyment, purposes.

Both the Thai version and Mateschitz's version of Red Bull contained the following energy-enhancing ingredients: caffeine, taurine, and glucuronolactone. One 250 ml can of Red Bull had 80 mg of caffeine, about as much as a weak cup of coffee; a small coffee at Starbucks may contain more than 200 mg of caffeine (see Exhibit 1 for caffeine amounts in common drinks). Both taurine and glucuronolactone are chemicals that occur naturally in the human body. Taurine is a conditionally-essential amino acid, a detoxifying agent, and a metabolism transmitter. Glucuronolactone is a metabolism transmitter and a detoxifying agent. These three ingredients, along with a variety of sugars and vitamins, contributed to the following properties claimed by Red Bull:

- Improves physical endurance
- Stimulates metabolism and helps eliminates waste substances
- Improves overall feeling of well-being
- Improves reaction speed and concentration
- Increases mental alertness

Between 1984 and 1986, Dietrich Mateschitz led a team of professional marketers developing the product and packaging concept for Red Bull. The process was extensive: the team conducted large amounts of market research and tested more than 200 packaging proposals.

Flavor

Red Bull's flavor was intended to communicate the product's value as a functional energy drink. It was sweet and carbonated like a cola, but also had what some consumers described as a "medicinal" taste. The strong taste indicated to consumers that the product was more than mere refreshment. "We never cared about the taste a lot because we are more concerned about the function of the product,"[2] said Norbert Kraihamer, Red Bull's Group Marketing and Sales Director. Still, directions printed on Red Bull's can recommended that the drink be served "well-chilled," since most consumers found the taste more pleasant when they drank it cold.

Package

Red Bull came in a single package, a slender silver-and-blue 250 ml can. The small can, which originated in Japan, signaled to consumers that the contents were different from and stronger than traditional soft drinks. The Red Bull logo—an Oriental-themed depiction of two (red) bulls about to collide head-on in front of yellow sun—appeared prominently on the front of the can. Under the logo, the words "Energy Drink" succinctly communicated the product's benefits. Consumers could only buy the cans singly; they were not offered in six-packs or cases. Some retailers sold Red Bull in these larger denominations for convenience purposes, but still charged the same amount per can (i.e., a case of Red Bull cans would cost the same as 24 cans bought separately).

Red Bull also developed a brown glass bottle for use in locations where it could not list the can, but the bottle design was less preferable to consumers than the can. When Red Bull launched in Germany, demand quickly outpaced supply and the company was forced to sell bottles when it ran out of cans. Sales of the product fell off the torrid pace as soon as the bottles were introduced. Red Bull used this example to show retailers the revenue they could lose if they only allowed the glass bottles.

Positioning

Mateschitz also devised the brand positioning: "Revitalizes body and mind." This phrase conveyed the tangible benefit of the product in an easy-to-grasp manner. It also covered a broad set of appropriate consumption occasions. Mateschitz intended Red Bull to be drunk whenever consumers needed a lift, whether it was morning, noon, or night. This way, Red Bull consumption would not be limited to certain occasions or activities, the way other energy-related beverages had been positioned. This broad positioning was designed to enable growth into a variety of market segments. Red Bull's advertising did not specify any consumption occasions, which further facilitated an elastic positioning.

The early adopters of Red Bull in Austria and surrounding markets were dancers, clubbers, and ravers who used the drink to stay fresh at late-night parties. This party association was crucial for Red Bull as it expanded into other markets because hip nightspots generated significant buzz. In these venues, Red Bull was used primarily as a mixer. Red Bull appreciated the business that mixing brought, but the company emphasized a variety of usages in its marketing. "We are not against mixing," said Norbert Kraihamer. "We even appreciate it to a degree. But over time we must make sure that the product is regarded as much more than a mixer. This is not a drink for a restaurant, this is a nutritional item."[3] Other early adopters of Red Bull included truck drivers who used the drink to stay awake on long drives and students who drank it to help them concentrate during their studies. Though most of the original Red Bull customers were young, the company intended the brand to appeal to consumers of all ages.

Price

From the start, Red Bull pursued a premium pricing strategy. Mateschitz reasoned that consumers would be less likely to believe in Red Bull's energy-enhancing properties if it was priced the same as a traditional cola beverage. By charging a premium price, Red Bull could reinforce the energy positioning and also stake out a unique territory in the beverage market. In every market, Red Bull set a price at least 10 percent greater than the most-expensive competitor in order to maintain a "best of class" positioning. Kraihamer explained the rationale:

> We are much more expensive than [cola]. This is OK because ours is an efficiency product, so we can charge this price premium, which is the secret of its success. . . . Due to the respect for a price premium brand . . . we can charge what is fair for the benefit.[4]

Priced between $1.99 and $3.00 in convenience stores, the 250 ml can of Red Bull cost up to 300 percent more per ounce than traditional soft drinks.

LAUNCH IN AUSTRIA

Red Bull encountered difficulty getting approved for sale in Austria. The Austrian government at the time had three categories for food and drug: 1) traditional food, 2) dietary food, and 3) pharmaceutical. Red Bull sought categorization as a traditional food, but this category restricted its ability to make claims about performance benefits. Therefore, Red Bull lobbied to create an entirely new category: functional food. Functional foods, which also came to be known as nutraceuticals, had some medicinal benefits beyond a dietary product, but also contained food properties that made them different from a pharmaceutical. The functional food category combined regulations from the three other categories and required almost as much documentation as a pharmaceutical product. For example, any health benefit claims had to be supported by scientific evidence.

In order to support its claims about performance benefits, the company commissioned various studies from scientists. Red Bull's product documentation totaled more than 3,000 pages, almost as much evidentiary support as required for a pharmaceutical product. The heavily regulated functional foods category in Austria created a barrier for entry that competitors were initially unwilling to overcome. The cost of commissioning the required scientific studies was simply too high. This economic barrier, combined with the fact that the energy drink category was still unproven, led to a lack of competitors in Austria for over five years after its 1987 introduction.

While Red Bull needed reams of scientific evidence to enter a market, it did not oversell consumers on the science behind the product. Kraihamer explained, "We do not force volumes of scientific evidence down the consumer's throat. Out principle is to make the product available in the right places at the right time with the right message. Consumers then try it and make up their own mind if it works."[5] Encouraging product trial was the keystone of Red Bull's marketing strategy. Red Bull's above-the-line marketing was minimal, and for the first five years in Austria (1987–1991) the company's marketing expenditure ranged between only $700,000 and $1.4 million annually. During that time, net sales grew from $700,000 to $10 million.

MARKETING RED BULL

Dietrich Mateschitz reasoned that the best method to get consumers to try the product was testimonials from peers who bought into Red Bull. Therefore, word-of-mouth—which Norbert Kraihamer called "the oldest and best media in the world"[6]—was the central component of all Red Bull marketing activities. Word-of-mouth drove awareness of the brand in the early stages of entering a market. As knowledge of the product spread, a buzz would build around the brand. Red Bull supplemented its word-of-mouth strategy with event sponsorships, athlete endorsers, sampling programs, point-of-purchase marketing, and select electronic media buys. Eventually, the company hoped, consumers everywhere would be talking about (and purchasing) Red Bull.

Developing the Red Bull Mystique

From the start, Red Bull was a source of intrigue for consumers. The functional energy category was brand new for Austrians, so curious and adventurous customers tried the brand and spread the word. Not content to let the word-of-mouth evolve naturally, the company aided this effort. Shortly after the product launched in Austria, the company would place empty Red Bull cans in clubs and bars to create the illusion of popularity. Between 1987 and 1992, when Red Bull was available only in Austria, consumers in adjacent countries like Germany and Hungary who had not been to Austria heard about the product from word-of-mouth testimonials. In this way, consumers outside Austria were made aware of product benefits, the unusual ingredients like "taurine," and the state regulations. Because the product could not be exported, it was bootlegged across the Austrian border by enterprising individuals. These factors contributed to the buzz surrounding the product, and led to what Kraihamer referred to as the "over-mystification" of Red Bull.

Most consumers outside Austria had not seen any official Red Bull marketing, and if they had not tried the product themselves they would not know what to make of it. Some thought it was a beer, others believed it was a liquor product. Rumors about the product's special ingredients (one inaccurate rumor was that Red Bull contained bull testicles) and energy benefits fueled gray markets in several countries, most notably Germany.

The mystification of Red Bull, however, fueled negative rumors as well. Because Red Bull was popular in the European rave scene, rumors linked it with drug overdoses and even deaths. Though the beverage was never directly responsible for the overdoses or deaths, this fact did not prevent rumors from persisting. As a result, Red Bull garnered press coverage, which added to the buzz surrounding the product.

Market Entry Strategy

When it entered a new market, Red Bull strove to build buzz about the product through its "seeding program," where the company micro-targeted "in" shops, clubs, bars, and stores. This enabled the cultural elite to access the product first and hopefully influence consumers further down the pyramid of influence through word-of-mouth. Red Bull also targeted "opinion leaders" who were likely to influence consumer purchases. These included action sports athletes and entertainment celebrities. The company attempted to reach these individuals by making Red Bull available at sports competitions, in limos before award shows, and at exclusive after-parties.

Red Bull's limited availability in the early stages of development contributed to the brand's cachet, as evidenced by the presence of gray markets in countries bordering Austria. After six-months of selectively seeding a new market, the company gradually expanded its presence to locations surrounding these "in" spots.

These locations were typically less price-sensitive than the seeding locations and served to widen access to the brand. Availability was still limited and word-of-mouth continued to be a main driver of awareness. However, any consumer who wanted to purchase the product could do so if they sought it out. Finally, Red Bull reached the mass-market via supermarkets. As Norbert Kraihamer explained, "We are very focused on consumer base building and not just heading for maximum weighted distribution."[7]

Additionally, Red Bull engaged in "pre-marketing" to establish awareness in markets where its product was not yet sold. Pre-marketing involved sponsoring events that took place in a country where Red Bull was not available, such as the Red Bull Snowthrill of Chamonix ski contest in France. The international ski contest exposed French consumers to the product and the athletes it sponsored. Red Bull also exported its television productions to countries it had yet to enter. The television programs, which featured Red Bull sponsored events and athlete endorsers, acted as ambassadors for the brand in the absence of any market presence. For example, if a Colombian athlete sponsored by Red Bull was competing in a televised Red Bull event, Colombian television stations would have interest in broadcasting the event. Colombian television viewers would then gain knowledge of the brand's involvement with their countryman or countrywoman and would associate Red Bull with that person and his or her event. Of the pre-marketing strategy, Kraihamer said, "We want to be recognized as the pre-eminent brand, even if we are not there."

Red Bull Target Market

Red Bull did not define a specific demographic or psychographic segment as its target market. Rather, the company sought to reach a broad range of consumers based on their need for a stimulating drink. Kraihamer said, "We only have two dimensions: people who are mentally fatigued and people who are physically fatigued or both."[8] These consumers fell into five broadly-defined categories: "students, drivers, clubbers, business people and sports people."[9] By not defining a narrow consumer target, Red Bull ensured that it could grow into numerous market segments. In mature markets, Red Bull achieved its highest penetration in the 14–19 age range, followed by the 20–29 range (see Exhibit 2). As its consumers aged, Red Bull hoped they would continue to use the product, increasing the older end of the age distribution. As Kraihamer explained:

> The kids that are 18 or 19 years old and drink Red Bull in a nightclub have years of use ahead of them. These same people will use it in the future as a sporting drink, or for driving, or as a conference drink because business meetings are always tiring.[10]

MARKETING ACTIVITY

Red Bull engaged in a variety of marketing programs, including traditional television, print and radio advertising, event marketing in sports and entertainment, sampling, and point-of-purchase promotion. The bulk of Red Bull's marketing activity was directed toward encouraging product trials. This was accomplished primarily through sampling, word-of-mouth, and point-of-purchase efforts. According to Kraihamer, "We do not market the product to the consumer, we let the consumer discover the product first and then the brand with all its image components."[11] The company rapidly increased its marketing expenditures during the 1990s (see Exhibit 3).

Advertising

Dietrich Mateschitz created the familiar Red Bull "adult cartoon" advertising with the aid of Johannes Kastner, a colleague who owned an advertising agency. All ads featured an intelligent dialogue about product benefits using one character with an energy deficiency and others who proposed the solution: Red Bull. Unlike most beverage marketers, Red Bull did not reinforce the taste of the drink, the direct benefit of the drink, or the image associations of the drink.

In one ad, a dentist informs Dracula that his teeth will have to be removed. Dracula complains that without his teeth, he will not be able to drink blood. Dracula laments, "But without fresh blood my body will wither and my mind will fade." The dentist tells Dracula "one revitalizing Red Bull and you'll be prince of the night again." A shot of the product appears on the screen, with the copy "Red Bull energy drink. Vitalizes Body & Mind." The dentist samples a Red Bull himself and tells Dracula, "You know, Red Bull gives you wings," before sprouting wings and flying away. Other classic characters to appear in Red Bull ads include Leonardo da Vinci, Adam and Eve, Frankenstein, William Tell, Rapunzel, Sisyphus, and the Devil. The tagline "Red Bull gives you wiiings" grew directly out of the positioning statement "Red Bull vitalizes body and mind."

The ads were effective because they clearly communicated product benefits without promising specific physiological results. The literal message of "Red Bull gives you wiiings" was obviously an exaggeration, but taken figuratively it was clever and believable. The animated television spots also refrained from defining a specific target group; anyone with a sense of humor, no matter how old, would be able to appreciate the ads. This enabled the company to establish as wide a consumer base as possible.

The Red Bull animated ads were adopted uniformly across the company's global markets. Not only did the colorful images travel well, but also the simple execution and universal concepts of the ads ensured that they would cross cultural boundaries easily. Said Kraihamer, "Even in a country where they speak a different language, we send the same message using the cartoon...We more or less translate it word for word—the power of our marketing mix works."[12]

Sampling

Product trial was an essential part of the Red Bull marketing program. Whereas traditional beverage marketers attempt to reach the maximum number of consumers with a sampling, Red Bull sought to reach consumers only in ideal usage occasions, namely when the consumer needed or wanted a boost. For this reason, Red Bull sampling campaigns took place at concerts, parties, festivals, sporting events, at the beach, at highway rest areas (for tired drivers), and at campus libraries. Kraihamer explained the importance of getting the consumer to try the product at the proper time:

> We have to make sure that people experience the product the right way at the right moment and in the right situation when they have met with particular fatigue or are in need of food.[13]

Red Bull sent sampling teams to the ideal locations equipped with Red Bull branded vehicles and plenty of cans of cold Red Bull. The sampling team's job was to explain the product benefits and encourage the consumer to drink a full can for maximum benefit. For its sampling teams, Red Bull employed individuals who could energetically and believably endorse the brand. The sampling teams were typically comprised of college students called Red Bull Student Brand Managers. Aside from sampling, student managers researched drinking trends, designed on-campus marketing initiatives, and wrote stories for student newspapers. According to Henry Drnec, Red Bull's managing director in the United Kingdom, "Sampling [is a] key element of our marketing strategy. The customer feedback we get is invaluable and the conversion rates are huge."[14] Kraihamer elaborated:

> It is our people that give us real power in the field. This is one of the reasons we are not at all afraid of the big companies, the Coca-Colas and the PepsiCos and the Cadbury Schweppes of this world. They'll find it difficult to put the same kind of focus and dedication into one product, one item, because they are spreading their marketing across a whole range.[15]

Event Marketing

Red Bull had an extensive network of events that it was involved with. Red Bull either invented the event from the ground up, or brought the product to an existing event. When Red Bull created the event, it controlled all aspects of the event, including the name, logo, promotion, and media production. Classic Red Bull-owned events included the Red Bull Soapbox Race and the Red Bull Flügtag ("Flying Day"). The Red Bull Flügtag was a comical event in which participants constructed a flying object and attempted to launch it off a ramp into a lake or ocean. The event was a perfect fit for Red Bull because it required use of both the mind (in the design of the flying object) and body (in the power to get it off the ground). The winner of the event received free lessons for a pilot's license.

Sporting events developed by Red Bull include the Red Bull Snowthrill extreme skiing competitions in France and Alaska, and Red Bull Cliff Diving World

Tour Finals event in Hawaii. These events enhanced Red Bull visibility and also reinforced the brand's positioning as an independent, stimulating beverage. "People who attend one of our events have the indelible awareness that it was sponsored by Red Bull because of the unusual amount of control we can exert over our own events,"[16] said Red Bull corporate communication manager Emmy Cortes. The more unique an event, the more likely television stations would want to broadcast it, or newspapers would want to cover it. Kraihamer explained, "We want to have the most creative ideas and do the best things so that they get automatically into the media."[17]

Sports Marketing

In addition to sponsoring sporting events, Red Bull also sponsored individual athletes. Red Bull engaged in sports marketing first and foremost to establish credibility among opinion leaders who participated in action sports such as surfing, snowboarding, skydiving, skateboarding, rock climbing, mountain biking, and many other non-mainstream athletic endeavors. The athletes who played these sports exhibited many of the qualities Red Bull wanted to project in its brand personality: innovative, individual, non-conformist, unpredictable, and humorous. The company started its sports marketing by simply making the product available to athletes at competitions, allowing interested athletes to seek out Red Bull and become authentic users. Following these low-key introductions, Red Bull would then work out sponsorship deals that put its logo on the athletes' equipment. Red Bull sponsored a number of athletes, but was very selective about which athletes it chose. First, the sport had to fit with the Red Bull image. According to Norbert Kraihamer, "Generally, these are extreme sports, but if there is an energetic golfer, no problem."[18] As athletes began to use Red Bull for its stimulating effect, they subsequently drove awareness among their audiences.

Once Red Bull became an international brand, it was able to sign influential and leading athletes such as Robby Naish (windsurfing), Eddie Irvine (Formula 1), and Shane McConkey (skiing). Red Bull also inked a blockbuster sponsorship deal with the Sauber-Petronas Formula 1 team, which gave Red Bull a globally recognizable symbol—the racing car—competing at the highest level. Already having a sponsorship presence in the sport for some time, Red Bull acquired its own Formula 1 team in November 2004 when it purchased the Jaguar team from Ford Motor Company, creating Red Bull Racing. It was estimated that the racing team would cost $100 million a year to keep on the track, while generating revenue of $70 million. Red Bull later expanded its participation in racing by sponsoring the "Red Bull Junior Team" and the "Red Bull Driver Search."

In 2006, Red Bull announced its plans to move into American motor sports by starting a two-car NASCAR team in the 2007 season. One of the cars would bear the number 83 that represents the 8.3 ounces in each can or Red Bull. The company also earned headlines in 2006 by buying the New York Metro Stars of Major League Soccer for more than $100 million and renaming the team the New York Red Bulls. The choice of name was controversial, since contemporary American sports teams were not named after their corporate sponsors. In international soccer, however, clubs typically bore the name of their sponsors in a prominent place on the jerseys, and the Red Bulls followed this well-established precedent.

At the other end of the competitive spectrum, Red Bull sponsored athletes who engaged in sports that have no official competitions. One example was kite-surfing, an aquatic sport where participants strapped their feet to a sort of wakeboard and used a kite sail to then skim across the water. Red Bull sponsored two dedicated kiteboarders from Florida by giving them gas money and a cooler full of Red Bull. The two kiteboarders drove around to different beaches and wherever they went, they attracted a crowd with their cutting-edge kiteboarding. After their sessions, the assembled crowds would witness the pair refueling with Red Bull. If the sport were to become official, Red Bull would already be sponsoring the best competitors. Norbert Kraihamer described the kiteboarding case as a "great example of synthetic involvement in sport."

Point-of-Purchase Marketing

Red Bull's primary point-of-purchase tool was the branded refrigerated sales units. Red Bull placed these miniature glass refrigerators, which prominently displayed the Red Bull logo, in convenience stores, bars, clubs, sports shops, office buildings, cafeterias, and commissaries. These refrigerators set the brand apart from other beverages and ensured Red Bull a prominent location in the retail environment. If a location would not accept the Red Bull mini-fridge, the company would rent space in existing store refrigerators. To ensure consistency and quality in its point-of-purchase displays, Red Bull hired teams of delivery van drivers whose sole responsibility was stocking Red Bull. Red Bull also used a highly visible aluminum window sticker to indicate availability, rather than the traditional clear plastic. Believing the can itself to be the best promotional tool, Red Bull limited the use of posters, shelf talkers, and ceiling hangers in the store.

EUROPEAN EXPANSION

In the mid-1990s, Austria was not yet part of the European Community (now called the European Union, or EU), and the company was concerned that a competitor would enter the energy drink category ahead of Red Bull. The EU's policy for approved food products dictated that if a food was approved in one EU country, it could be sold in all EU countries. The problem for Red Bull, however, was that most EU countries had a list of allowable food ingredients, and taurine was not on any of the lists. Lobbying to get taurine added to the list would be too costly and time-consuming. Fortunately, Scotland—an EU country—had a "negative list" of food ingredients, in other words all ingredients not on the list were allowed. Red Bull ingredients were not on the list, so the company had an entry point. Red Bull set up its first EU test market in the United Kingdom, and rapidly entered the rest of the EU markets. Red Bull was unable to enter the French market, however, because the product was banned until it could be proven "100 percent safe." The French government was especially conservative about new food products because of recent health scares involving foot-and-mouth disease and mad cow disease (bovine spongiform encephalopathy, or BSE). The ban in France did have the benefit of adding to the mystification effect for French consumers.

Marketing Steps in the United Kingdom

Red Bull varied its market entry strategy only in the United Kingdom, which it entered in 1995. Believing the British market to be too different from Austria, the management team in the United Kingdom altered the Red Bull marketing formula in three significant ways: 1) the company marketed Red Bull as a sports drink, not a stimulation drink; 2) it did not pursue a word-of-mouth strategy, choosing instead to sell via the largest beverage channels; and 3) it created new advertising and focused on billboards rather than electronic media. As a result, Red Bull was considered a failure in the United Kingdom after losing more than $10 million during the first 18 months in that market. This was in part because the United Kingdom had an established sports drink brand, Lucozade, which had been on the market for decades. Consumers were very familiar with the sports drink category, but Red Bull did not meet their expectations of what a sports drink should be. Usually, Red Bull sought to create its own new category when it entered new markets, so when U.K. managing director Harry Drnec took over in 1996, he repositioned Red Bull as a stimulation drink, by changing the word "energy" on the can to "stimulation," and thus established a new category.

The second strategic mistake in the United Kingdom was a departure from the word-of-mouth strategy that had fuelled Red Bull's popularity in other markets. The original U.K. management skipped all the preliminary steps and started by selling Red Bull in the largest supermarkets and convenience outlets. This move essentially precluded any buzz from building, because it did not allow a discovery phase or an opinion leader program to establish the brand as cutting edge. Said Norbert Kraihamer, "The U.K. team started from the wrong end, in the big chains, hoping the consumer would pick it off the shelf. But they were wrong, they totally misunderstood how to create a consumer base."[19] In response, Drnec and his new management team pursued the traditional word-of-mouth strategy.

Finally, the original U.K. managers overhauled the Red Bull advertising concept to suit the needs of the market as they saw them. They used the slogan "Never underestimate what Red Bull can do for you," which did not clarify Red Bull's positioning at all and was too long to be catchy. By contrast, the "gives you wiiings" slogan communicated Red Bull's positioning as a stimulation drink and translated effectively into any market. The original U.K. team also focused the ad spending on billboards that were not as effective in communicating Red Bull's benefits as electronic media. "We go for electronic media, because energy needs movement and dialogue," said Kraihamer. "You can hardly get smart drinks across on a billboard—it doesn't talk."[20]

After new management made the necessary changes, Red Bull took off in the United Kingdom Between 1997 and 2001, Red Bull's share of the sports and energy drink market rose from under 2 percent to 48 percent. This share exceeded that of Lucozade, the entrenched leader for the previous 74 years. Red Bull went from selling 3.2 million cans per year in 1995 to more than 290 million in 2000. The brand claimed an 86 percent share of the "functional energy" drinks market in 2001. That same year, Red Bull was the third biggest product by value in the soft drinks market, behind Coca-Cola and Pepsi. The United Kingdom was Red Bull's second-largest market by volume and sales in 2001, behind the United States.

Competition

As Red Bull began to exhibit exponential sales growth internationally, beverage companies that had previously dismissed the drink as a fad or fashion started moving into the energy drink segment. In the United Kingdom, Red Bull faced competition from Virgin, which developed Virgin dt; Anheuser-Busch, which entered the market with 180; Coca-Cola, which debuted a drink called Burn; Pepsi-Cola with SoBe Adrenaline Rush and Mountain Dew Amp; and a host of other brands with names like Indigo, Hype, Bawls, XTC, and Magic. Speaking about the emergence of major brands in the market, Red Bull U.K. managing director Harry Drnec said, "It's a lucrative market, and the many players who have been jumping in are finding it's not a game. You can't market a functional drink like you do a soft drink. But we're excited about Coke's entry—it could push the category even further forward."[21] Between 1995 and 2000 in the United Kingdom, the beverage consultancy Zenith International reported that more than 40 product launches occurred in the functional energy category. Many of these competitors used packaging that resembled Red Bull: small, thin metal cans, metallic hues, and animal imagery. Red Bull dominated all other competitors in the United Kingdom functional energy drinks market with a 72 percent share in 1999. None of its competitors had more than a 6 percent share of the market.

The competitors often employed marketing tactics similar to Red Bull's. Coca-Cola used a word-of-mouth strategy that targeted influencers and opinion leaders first. PepsiCo's Mountain Dew Amp used a sponsorship and sampling strategy that resembled the Red Bull approach. To reach its target 18- to 24-year-old demographic, Pepsi hired young sales representatives to promote Amp on college campuses by giving away samples of the drink. Pepsi also sponsored emerging music acts with the Amp name. PepsiCo's SoBe Adrenaline Rush also pursued a grass-roots strategy involving sampling teams, point-of-purchase materials, sponsored SoBe Team Lizard athletes, and distribution concentrated on bars, convenience stores, and restaurants. In Britain, Red Devil sponsored the Asprilla motorbike team and Virgin dt sponsored the Radio One Love Parade dance festival.

Other brands used sex appeal to try and take market share from Red Bull. The Red Devil brand claimed that its product would "ma[ke] you horny," while the Go-Go Passion brand marketed itself as "Viagra for girls." The tagline for SoBe Adrenaline Rush was "Get it up. Keep it up. Any Questions?" While most competitors used below-the-line marketing activities in attempts to develop a viral marketing effect, some brands, like Virgin dt and Red Devil in the United Kingdom created radio and television advertisements. Red Devil used celebrity spokesperson Vinnie Jones, a former soccer tough and actor, to star in ads with the tagline "You can always repent."

Lots of smaller competitors attempted to capitalize on the energy drink trend as well. In 2001, Red Bull had more than 140 competitors in Germany. These competitors combined for less than 5 percent market share, and typically had lifecycles around six months. The number of competitors diluted the category because few were seriously committed to the market and most pitched consumers with a limited usage message that focused on one dimension of stimulation. In 2001, Red Bull got an injunction imposed on a Swiss mineral water company that was marketing a knockoff product called "Red Bat." In the ruling, the judge noted that since Red Bull was a very recognizable brand, it had a greater need for copyright protection. The judge also stated that competitors were able to choose brand names that were sufficiently different from Red Bull. Still, knockoff products such as Red Devil and Red Rooster continued to saturate the market.

Red Bull had the advantage of originating the energy drink category in most markets it entered, and could therefore establish the brand's prominence on its own terms (i.e., by gradually building awareness through seeding and relying on word-of-mouth to build buzz around the brand). In markets where it was not the first mover, Red Bull often had to overcome image perceptions for the energy drinks category that competitors had engendered with their marketing. For example, Red Bull was not the first energy drink to be sold in Brazil; other European competitors had moved in first. For the most part, the competition set prohibitively high price points and marketed their beverages strictly for nightlife usage occasions. In Brazil, Red Bull set its standard 10 percent price premium and worked to reinforce its message using its proven marketing formula, eventually overtaking the competition in terms of volume. Once it established volume leadership, Red Bull pressured the competitors to lower prices while maintaining the premium.

In spite of this competition, Red Bull maintained its dominant position in international markets. In 2004, Zenith International, a U.K.-based consultancy, reported that Red Bull owned two-thirds of overall energy drink volume across Western Europe. The brand was present in 13 Western European countries and held the lead in 12 of those. The remaining top 20 brands took a combined 17 percent share.

RED BULL IN THE UNITES STATES

For Red Bull's 1997 entry into the United States, the company used a "cell" approach to divide key markets in the country into targeted geographic segments, rather than attempt a nationwide launch. "Our intention was never to go to the States and say 'We are launching Red Bull,' " said Kraihamer. "We chose small market cells."[22] The brand's first test market was Santa Cruz, California, a beachside town known for its active lifestyle built around surfing and skateboarding and for the University of California Santa Cruz. The population of Santa Cruz represented a good target audience for the brand because it contained a large number of sports enthusiasts and university students. From Santa Cruz, Red Bull moved into the nearby urban market of San Francisco, and then to Venice Beach, a trendy beachside city near in Los Angeles. Following success in these locations, Red Bull established a presence in adjacent Santa Monica and then Hollywood. Norbert explained the development of the cell approach:

> When one small cell became a success story, we moved onto the next cell. Of course, after three years, these cells are becoming bigger and bigger. But initially it was towns or part of towns.[23]

To manage the cells, Red Bull established eight separate business units in the United States. The regional office in New York, for example, was responsible for the brand in Maryland, New Jersey, New York, Pennsylvania, and Virginia.

When Red Bull entered a cell, it initially targeted high-end nightclubs, bars, plus exclusive health clubs and gyms in order to reach the trendy and active consumers. Like it had done in Europe, Red Bull gradually increased distribution to include downmarket bars and clubs, restaurants, convenience stores, and grocery chains. On college campuses, Red Bull recruited student brand managers to organize on-campus promotions such as renting out study rooms during finals week and stocking them with free cans of Red Bull and school supplies. Because the drinking age in the United States was much higher than in most other European countries, the college marketing events in the states never had an alcohol link. Red Bull also implemented its sampling program, using Red Bull branded trucks and cars and teams of "consumer educators" that worked on a street level to promote the brand.

Red Bull gradually expanded its distribution eastward in 1999, moving first into Texas and then to mountain resorts in the Rocky Mountains. After establishing seeding programs in the Midwest and Chicago area, Red Bull moved into the East coast and Florida in 2000.

Red Bull's growth in the American market outpaced the company's expectations. In 2000, the company achieved sales of 108 million cans, well above the 80 million can target. That year, the company's U.S. market share stood at 65 percent.

Effective Use of Media

Only when a cell was considered mature did Red Bull begin a media program in that area. "Media is not a tool we use to establish the market," said vice president of marketing David Rohdy. "It's a critical part. It's just later in the development."[24] Of the $100 million marketing budget for the United States in 2000, Red Bull spent less than $20 million on measured media. The company's most visible media efforts were the two new animated cartoon commercials it developed each year.

Red Bull also kept up its aggressive event marketing efforts in the United States. In addition to the Red Bull Cliff Diving World Finals in Hawaii and the Snowthrill of Alaska winter sports event, Red Bull held the Red Bull Wings Over Aspen hang-gliding event and a street luge competition in San Francisco. In 2000, Red Bull introduced the Red Bull Rock 'n' Air festival, a day of extreme sports demonstrations and progressive live music. Another unique Red Bull event was the Red Bull Music Academy. Started in 1998, this annual event that was held in a different city each year, brought DJs and music producers together for two weeks of collaboration, learning, and performance.

Red Bull's initial results in the United States mirrored the brand's success in Europe. In 2001, Red Bull was the number one seller in Store24 convenience stores, bigger than any single beer, milk, water, or soda brand. "It's the number one beverage and the gap is widening," said Andy Steele, a beverage buyer for Store24. "I've never seen anything like it." One new age beverage executive said, "Red Bull seems to have a cooler in every bar in every city."[25] By mid-2001, Ohio, Tennessee, and the Dakotas were among the few states that did not have Red Bull. The company's U.S. case volume more than quadrupled that of its nearest competitor and its market share hovered near 70 percent.

OBSTACLES TO GROWTH

Proliferation of Energy Drinks in the United States

In the years since Red Bull's introduction, more than 1,000 smaller players had entered the energy drink market, according to *The Beverage Network*. More importantly, the rate of new product introductions skyrocketed (see Exhibit 4 for new beverage introductions). Some of these competitors were from established brands like Coca-Cola and Pepsi, while others came from upstarts like Monster Energy drinks.

Hansen Natural Corp. introduced the Monster brand in April 2002 as a direct competitor to Red Bull. Monster's ingredients were similar to those of Red Bull, but Monster came in 16-ounce cans, giving consumers twice the amount of beverage for roughly the same price. Monster followed the lead of Red Bull in many areas of its marketing. Teams of Monster "ambassadors" gave out samples of the drink at concerts, beach parties, and other events. The company also sponsored motocross, surfing, and skateboarding competitions. Monster launched a new program in 2004 dubbed the "Monster Army." This program was an online way for Monster to coordinate with amateur action sports athletes in the United States. Aside from skateboarding and surfing, amateur athletes could apply to be sponsored by Monster in diverse sports such as wheelchair racing, paintball, or rodeo. Those selected received products and exposure from Monster Energy.

Monster was extremely successful in its first few years. In 2004, the company posted sales of $180 million, up 63 percent from the year before. More importantly, it commanded an 18 percent share of the U.S. energy drink category.

Competition came from more traditional companies as well. Coca-Cola's KMX had been on the market for years, but lagged far behind Red Bull. Looking to gain a foothold in the market, Coke launched a new product, Full Throttle, in early 2005. This drink came in black, 16-ounce cans that closely resembled Monster's cans. Coke made another move in the category a few months later when it announced it would distribute Rockstar Energy Drink in the United States and Canada. Rockstar, founded in 2001, originated the 16-ounce energy drink. Rockstar experienced triple-digit growth every year since its inception, and by 2004 was the 10th largest carbonated soft drink (CSD) company in the United States.

With the energy drink segment growing rapidly, companies not usually associated with this segment soon entered the fray. In early 2001, Anheuser-Busch introduced its 180 Energy Drink. Lightly carbonated, this orange citrus-flavored energy drink with vitamins   B-6, B-12 and C, was enhanced with guarana. The company soon followed with 180 Sport; water enhanced with vitamins and minerals. Anheuser-Busch made another move into the energy drink category in 2004 with Bud Extra, labeled on the can as B^E (pronounced "B-to-the-E"). This was traditional Budweiser beer with caffeine, ginseng, and guarana. This 10-ounce drink contained 4.5 percent alcohol by volume and 54 mg of caffeine (about the same as a 12-ounce Mountain Dew). The product was aimed at consumers in their 20s, with the website touting, "You can sleep when you're 30" and "You can go home when you are married." Suggestions for consuming the drink were titled B^E Cool (B^E over ice), B^{E}Kini (B^E with vanilla rum and coconut rum), and Royal B^{E}atch (B^E with raspberry liquor and pineapple juice).

One of the biggest developments of 2005 was the extension of the energy drink segment into organics and spirits. BevSpec, of Austin, Texas, introduced the first certified organic energy drink, Syzmo. The $2.5 million marketing campaign played off the fact that Syzmo is one way to say "earthquake" in Spanish. The company that made Hpnotiq, a popular tropical vodka liqueur in the early 2000s, launched Everglo, a lime-green blend of vodka and tequila infused with caffeine and ginseng that came in a glow-in-the-dark bottle. Two other energy vodkas soon entered, Zygo and Pink. In a sign that some Red Bull employees might not have been happy at the company, two Red Bull executives left the company and paired with Nestle to launch Returnity, a functional milk drink that was promoted in Europe as a "brain shake." Other entrants in the energy drink category included musician Lil Jon's Crunk brand, Bong Water, Pimp Juice, Shark, and Gay Fuel.

Other competition came from a new beverage segment, hybrid drinks. Realizing that energy drinks were not designed for hydrating purposes, Coca-Cola's Powerade division created a hybrid drink that offered the hydrating benefits of sports drinks and the stimulating boost of an energy drink. As part of a $60 million brand relaunch in July of 2003, Powerade offered two new hybrid drinks, Psych and Raize.

This competition proved challenging for Red Bull. Red Bull's market share in the United States was over 80 percent in 2000; two years later, it had fallen to 51 percent. By early 2005, it had dropped to 47 percent. Still, the company remained strong. Sales in the United States continue to grow at 40 percent (see Exhibit 5 for U.S. sales data). Over 700 million cans were sold in the United States in 2004, with sales rising to 1 billion cans in 2005. Red Bull also benefited from the growth in the energy drink category it founded, as total sales rose 75 percent in 2004 to $3.5 billion.

Health Concerns Over Red Bull

Although Red Bull was a strong global brand with millions of loyal consumers, there were some countries that did not allow sale of the drink. Stories like that of Ross Cooney, though rare, concerned many. Ross Cooney was a healthy, 18-year-old basketball player from Limerick, Ireland who collapsed and died on the court in 2000. Cooney reportedly drank four cans of Red Bull before playing that day. The connection between Cooney's death and Red Bull remains inconclusive; a coroner's inquest found that he died as a result of Sudden Arrhythmia Death Syndrome (sudden death due to cardiac arrest brought on by an arrhythmic episode). This is just one of many reported stories of people experiencing health problems after drinking Red Bull and then exercising vigorously. Because of health concerns, France, Norway, and Denmark prohibited the sale of Red Bull. In Norway, for example, Red Bull was classified as a medicine and had its sale banned in retail outlets due to what was judged to be an excessive amount of caffeine.

In 2004, the European Court of Justice (Europe's highest court) upheld the French ban on Red Bull. The judges said that studies by the French Scientific Committee on Human Nutrition and the European Commission Scientific Committee on Food raised enough concerns to continue the ban. These two groups did not agree that caffeine levels in Red Bull were excessive, but they did agree that more studies were needed to assess the dangers of taurine and glucuronolactone.

Other countries came up with new regulations to allow the sale of Red Bull. Once banned in Canada, Red Bull was approved for sale in 2004 after Health Canada (equivalent to the Food and Drug Administration in the United States) created new laws that covered "natural health products." As part of the approval, cans of Red Bull sold in Canada had to carry the warning:

> Not recommended for children, pregnant or breast-feeding women, caffeine sensitive persons or to be mixed with alcohol. Do not consume more than 500 ml per day.

Controversy over energy drink ingredients continued into 2005. Caffeine has been generally regarded as safe since 1958, but debate persisted regarding the acceptable level of caffeine in energy drinks. As of 2005, the FDA had no regulation in place pertaining to the use of many of the ingredients found in energy drinks; it did not issue a specific approved list, rules on levels of legal use or guidelines on what mixtures are safe. The result, according to one analysis, was that "the average consumer does know whether 200 mg or 80 mg of caffeine is safe, and may be unaware of the effects of 100 mg, 10,000 mg, or even 1 mg of taurine."[26]

RED BULL MARCHES ON

Continued Event Marketing Innovation

Since the early 1990s, Red Bull had supported a local flying club in Innsbruck, Austria. This relationship became official in 1999 with the creation of "The Flying Bulls," a group that flew both new and restored aircraft at airshows around Europe. Red Bull expanded this idea and created the "Flying Bulls Aerobatics Team" in 2001. This team flew a combination of jets, helicopters, and World War II-era aircraft at airshows across Europe. The company further increased its presence in aviation with the building of "Hangar-7" in Salzburg, Austria in 2003 to house its squadron of aircraft. This architecturally unique hangar not only included maintenance space for the planes, but a restaurant, several lounges, a café, and two bars.

Moving into new markets and sports, Red Bull began the "Red Bull Big Wave Africa" competition in 2000. This event brought big-wave surfers from around the world to Cape Town, South Africa. Desirable, big waves were not present every year, causing cancellation of the 2002, 2004, and 2005 competitions due to lack to waves. This lack of consistent big waves has not hurt the event, as it continued to draw some of the best surfers in the world.

In 2003, Red Bull sponsored the first "Divide and Conquer" competition in Colorado. This rigorous, four-part event included running seven miles (with a 4,125 foot elevation gain), kayaking 27 miles down class IV and V rapids, and biking 27 miles (with a 6,280 foot elevation gain). Winners of the event received prize money and transportation to the Dolomitemann competition in Austria—a Red Bull sponsored, male only, race that was billed as "the worlds toughest team relay race".

In 2005, the company sponsored its first ever "Red Bull Dragsterday" in Michigan. Teams of five built and raced human-powered dragsters, while being judged not only on speed, but also on the creative designs of their "dragsters."

Product Innovation

Red Bull spent considerable time and money sponsoring sports-related events like those above. In 2003, however, noting that 21 percent of all soft drinks consumed in the United Kingdom were of the sugar free diet variety, as were over 30 percent in the United States, the company focused its innovation on adding a new product, Red Bull Sugarfree. This new drink contained the exact same amounts of taurine, glucuronolactone, and caffeine as the original, but Red Bull Sugarfree contained artificial sweeteners and only 10 calories, compared to 110 calories in the original. The drink was sweetened with NutraSweet and claimed to be the first global energy drink to address growing consumer demand for diet beverages. Red Bull Sugarfree was sold in the readily identifiable Red Bull can, with two differences. The dark blue color of the original can was replaced with a lighter blue, and the word "Sugarfree" replaced "Energy Drink."

First launched in the United Kingdom, Red Bull Sugarfree was quickly expanded globally. The product proved to be successful; by mid-2005 it accounted for nearly 20 percent of brand volume. Mateschitz continued to invest heavily in marketing the Red Bull brand; in 2004 he spent $600 million, or 30 percent of revenue, on marketing (for comparison, Coca-Cola spent 9 percent).

Evolution of Red Bull Usage

Red Bull marketed its product to appeal to a broad range of consumers and to be appropriate in a variety of usage occasions. Still, the vast majority of Red Bull's business came from the youth market. In many markets Red Bull was used predominantly as a mixer. During 2001, half of all Red Bull consumption in the United Kingdom was in nightclubs and bars. Other European markets had similar figures. In mature markets like Austria, however, the product remained relevant even as consumers aged. Because usage was not limited to one or even a few occasions, Red Bull users could continue to use the product even as their priorities shifted. For example, a Red Bull consumer first attracted to the product as a nightlife enhancer in his or her early twenties might later use the drink as a morning pick-me-up or a revitalizer during a long day of meetings. In a 2001 interview, Norbert Kraihamer explained, "The reasons for consumption change, but the basics are always there: the real benefit." The benefit "keeps the consumer loyal through the years."[27] Evidence in Red Bull's debut market, Austria, where it has been sold since 1987, suggested the product was not a fad. Kraihamer continued, "We are continuing to expand our consumer base in the initial Austrian market and are growing there at a rate of 20 percent."[28]

Mateschitz had plans to grow the Red Bull brand with new products. The company had sold an herbal tea drink in Europe called Carpe Diem that supposedly boosted the immune system and improved metabolism. As of 2005, the product was being tested in Los Angeles, but did not seem to have the success of Red Bull. In February 2005, he also announced plans to open a fast-food chain call Carpe Diem in Austria and Switzerland, with plans to expand into Germany. Finally, Mateschitz had plans to launch a quarterly magazine in Europe devoted to the Red Bull lifestyle of music, extreme sports, night life, and social trends.

CONCLUSION

Red Bull experienced tremendous growth during the 1990s and early 2000s. In many markets, it commanded an 80 percent share. Even in the United States, where competition was especially tough, the company maintained a market share near 50 percent and an annual growth rate that exceeded 40 percent. This growth culminated in the company becoming the 7th largest CSD company in the United States in 2004 (see Exhibit 6). Even with the rapid growth of Red Bull and its competitors, there was still room for expansion; with $3.5 billion in U.S. sales in 2004, energy drinks barely represented a rounding error in the $66 billion carbonated soft drinks business.

As the functional energy category became increasingly competitive, and as major beverage industry players like Coca-Cola and PepsiCo grew more serious in their efforts to establish a foothold in the category, Red Bull's dual challenge would be to maintain growth in established markets and succeed in growing into new markets. Including the United States, Red Bull was sold in 100 markets, most of which had room to grow in terms of increasing per capita consumption. In existing markets, Red Bull needed to remain relevant to consumers in existing markets or risk experiencing slowed growth. The highly competitive beverage industry would require Red Bull to work hard to replicate its success in Europe and North America as it expanded.

DISCUSSION QUESTIONS

1. Describe Red Bull's sources of brand equity. Do these sources change depending on the market or country?
2. Analyze Red Bull's marketing program in terms of how it contributes to the brand's equity. Discuss strengths and weaknesses.

3. How can Red Bull maintain its marketing momentum? Would you recommend that Red Bull develop any brand extensions? If so, what would they be? Would you use the same marketing strategy?

4. Evaluate Red Bull's move into herbal teas, fast-food chains, and magazines. Does it make sense for the company to expand into these areas? What are the potential benefits and dangers?

5. Because product usage was not marketed as being limited to one or even a few occasions, Red Bull users could continue to use the product even as their priorities shifted. The case states that, "a Red Bull consumer first attracted to the product as a nightlife enhancer in his or her early twenties might later use the drink as a morning pick-me-up or a revitalizer during a long day of meetings." How effective is Red Bull at advertising to these varied groups?

Exhibit 1: Caffeine Content of Popular Drinks

Soft Drinks 12-ounce beverage	milligrams	Other Beverages 8-ounce beverage	milligrams
Red Bull (8.3 oz)	80.0	Coffee, drip	115–175
Jolt	71.2	Coffee, brewed	80–135
Mountain Dew	55.0	Coffee, espresso (2 oz)	100
Tab	46.8	Coffee, instant	65–100
Diet Coke	45.6	Tea, iced	47
Dr. Pepper	41.0	Tea, brewed, imported brand	60 (average)
Diet Dr. Pepper 41.0		Tea, brewed, U.S. brands	40 (average)
Sunkist Orange	40.0	Tea, green	15
Pepsi-Cola	37.5	Hot cocoa	14
Diet Pepsi	36.0	Coffee, decaf	2–4
Coca-Cola Classic	34.0		
Snapple Sweet Tea	12.0		
Sprite, 7UP	0		

Source: Netrition.com

Exhibit 2: Red Bull Market Penetration in 2000, Austria and United Kingdom

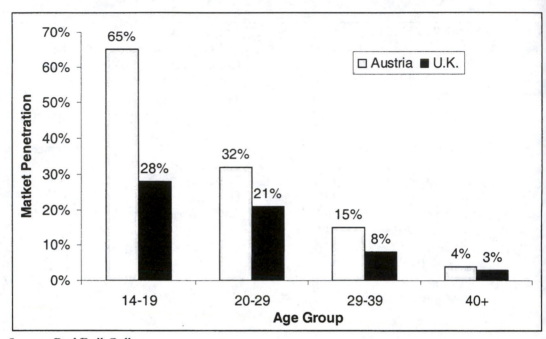

Source: Red Bull College

Exhibit 3: Red Bull Worldwide Marketing Expenditures

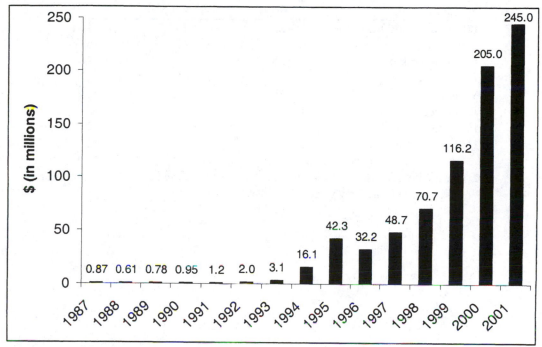

Source: Red Bull College

Exhibit 4: New Beverage Introductions in the United States

Segment	2004	2003	2002
RTD juices and juice drinks	293	197	144
Energy and sports drinks	101	65	68
Carbonated soft drinks	85	52	48
Beer and cider	77	48	52
Water	77	57	45
RTD iced tea and coffee	53	41	36
Flavored alcoholic beverages	41	19	21
Hot beverages	30	37	25

Source: Mintel's Global New Product Database, defined as "new formulation," "new product," or "new variety."

Exhibit 5: Red Bull U.S. Revenues

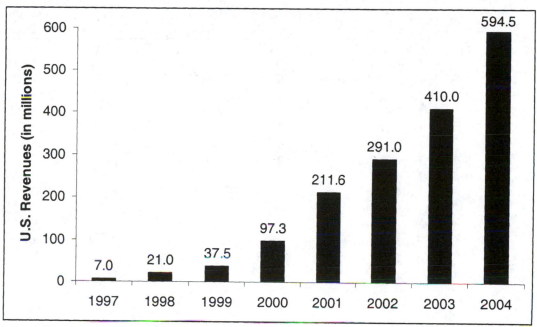

Source: Beverage Marketing Corp.

Exhibit 6: Top 10 CSD Companies—2004

Rank	Company	Market share	Share change	Cases (millions)	Volume % Change
1	Coca-Cola Co.	43.1	-0.9	4,414.8	-1.0%
2	Pepsi-Cola Co.	31.7	-0.1	3,241.7	+0.4%
3	Cadbury Schweppes	14.5	+0.2	1,485.9	+2.3%
4	Cott Corp.	5.5	+0.8	564.9	+18.2%
5	National Beverage	2.4	flat	249.4	+2.2%
6	Big Red	0.4	flat	41.5	-0.5%
7	Red Bull	0.3	+0.1	30.0	+45.0%
8	Hansen Natural	0.2	+0.1	20.2	+56.6%
9	Monarch Co.	0.1	flat	9.8	+7.6%
10	Rockstar	0.1	+0.1	9.7	+154.5%
	Private label/other	1.7	-0.3	171.5	-11.2%
	Total Industry	100.0		10,239.4	+1.0%

Source: Beverage Digest

REFERENCES

[1] This case was made possible through the cooperation of Red Bull and the assistance of Norbert Kraihamer, Group Marketing and Sales Director. Keith Richey prepared this case, which was revised and updated by Jonathan Michaels, under the supervision of Professor Kevin Lane Keller as the basis for class discussion.

[2] Claire Phoenix. "Red Bull: Fact and Function." Interview with Norbert Kraihamer. *Softdrinksworld*, February 2001, pp. 26–35.

[3] Ibid.

[4] Ibid.

[5] Ibid..

[6] Norbert Kraihamer. Personal Interview, August 2001.

[7] Claire Phoenix. "Red Bull: Fact and Function." Interview with Norbert Kraihamer. *Softdrinksworld*, February 2001, pp. 26–35.

[8] Ibid.

[9] Ibid.

[10] Ibid.

[11] Norbert Kraihamer. Personal Interview, August 2001.

[12] Claire Phoenix. "Red Bull: Fact and Function." Interview with Norbert Kraihamer. *Softdrinksworld*, February 2001, pp. 26–35.

[13] Ibid.

[14] John Cassy. "Enragingly Ubiquitous: Aged Only 22 but Already Branded." *The Guardian*, June 26, 2001.

[15] Claire Phoenix. "Red Bull: Fact and Function." Interview with Norbert Kraihamer. *Softdrinksworld*, February 2001, pp. 26–35.

[16] Kate Fitzgerald. "Red Bull Charged Up." *Advertising Age*, August 21, 2000, p. 26.

[17] Norbert Kraihamer. Personal Interview, August 2001.

[18] Claire Phoenix. "Red Bull: Fact and Function." Interview with Norbert Kraihamer. *Softdrinksworld*, February 2001, pp. 26–35.

[19] Ibid.

[20] Ibid.

[21] Cordelia Brabbs. "Can Coke Break Into Clubland?" *Marketing*, October 26, 2000, p. 25.

[22] Ibid.

[23] Ibid.

[24] Kenneth Hein. "Brand Builders: A Bull's Market." *Brandweek*, May 28, 2001, p. 21.

[25] Ibid.

[26] OneSource, "United States energy drink sales in dollars and percent change for 1998 to 2003." June 1, 2004, p.2.

[27] Norbert Kraihamer. Personal Interview, August 2001.

[28] Claire Phoenix. "Red Bull: Fact and Function." Interview with Norbert Kraihamer. *Softdrinksworld*, February 2001, pp. 26–35.

MTV:
BUILDING BRAND RESONANCE[1]

Introduction

Over the course of 25 years, MTV has built a powerful youth-oriented brand that has spanned the globe. When the all-music channel debuted in 1981, few dreamed that it would attain such a prominent place in popular culture. Few also imagined that MTV would attract as many international viewers as it did—over 421 million households in 167 countries by 2005. Domestically and abroad, MTV developed its programming and content that consistently resonated with viewers over the years. MTV attracted loyal followers starting in America in the early 1980s and in each of its international broadcast regions in the 1990s and early 2000s. The channel built more than just its own brand equity. Throughout the years, MTV served as a star-making vehicle for pop-artists and on-air talent. Experts credited the channel with changing the course of music and television and in some cases even having an impact upon socio-political events, including the collapse of the Eastern Bloc communist regime, participation in the 2004 Presidential election, and the aftermath of September 11th and Hurricane Katrina.

MTV's rise to cultural prominence was not achieved without difficulty. MTV endured a lengthy stretch of flat U.S. ratings in the mid-1990s as music tastes shifted and the channel lost touch with its core audience. However, MTV managed successfully to reinvent itself and establish a following from a new core audience by embracing "long-form" programming. MTV reduced the number of music videos shown by 36.5 percent from 1995-2001 while ratings increased 50 percent. By 2005, music videos made up only 25 percent of MTV's programming.

The 2000s brought on a new era of growth for MTV. In 1999, Viacom formed MTV Networks to offer its advertisers a full spectrum of demographic groups. MTV Networks included sister channels such as VH1, Nickelodeon, Nick at Nite, Comedy Central, and Spike TV. MTV also expanded globally—launching its 100th channel, MTV Base Africa, in 2004—and becoming the largest global media brand in the world. Additionally, MTV saw record household penetration even as it replaced several hit long-form programs, including *The Osbournes*, *The Ashlee Simpson Show*, and *Newlyweds: Nick & Jessica* with newer, unproven shows. Through its strong core brand values, MTV continued to stay focused on its central challenge: remain current within the fickle world of popular culture.

MTV'S HISTORY

The Channel's Origins

MTV originated as an unlikely offshoot of a cable broadcasting joint venture between Warner Communications and American Express called Warner Amex Satellite Entertainment Company (WASEC). A number of future MTV executives worked at WASEC and germinated the idea for a music video cable channel. Jack

Schneider, president of WASEC, recognized the opportunity inherent in a music channel. He reasoned, "If you have a disc jockey with a microphone, a transmitter, and 40 records, you've got yourself a radio station. So why don't we put a disc jockey on TV?"[2] Steve Casey, original director of music programming, came up with the name for the channel:

> We were under pressure to do something, so we were writing out different possibilities. Finally, I came up with "MTV." I didn't like the way it sounded so much as the way it looked. It really seemed cool. No one said "Great," but no one had a better idea, and that ended the meeting.[3]

An independent designer named Patti Rogoff came up with the MTV logo, a blocky three-dimensional "M" with a graffiti-scrawled "TV" on top. The channel's creative team came up with the idea of using a picture from the first moon landing—of Neil Armstrong in his spacesuit holding the American flag—as its television signature. Tom Freston, current CEO and chairman of MTV Networks and one of the channel's first employees, explained the development of the design:

> We knew we needed a real signature piece that would look different from everything else on TV. We also knew that we had no money. So we went to NASA and got the man-on-the-moon footage, which is public domain. We put our logo on the flag and some music under it. We thought it was sort of a rock 'n' roll attitude: "Let's take man's greatest moment technologically, and rip it off."[4]

Instead of disc jockeys (DJs), MTV employed video jockeys, called VJs. MTV producers explained that VJs would be joining the audience throughout its MTV viewing experience instead of just hosting the program.[5] The original VJs were a diverse group including Alan Hunter, an actor; Mark Goodman, a DJ; and Martha Quinn, a radio station intern. The VJ segments were filmed in a studio that resembled a cross between "a SoHo loft . . . and a rec room"[6] and was designed to seem welcoming, interesting, and avant-garde to the viewers. The VJ personalities added value to the channel beyond the videos and the viewership conferred celebrity status on them alongside the pop stars whose videos they introduced and those they interviewed. MTV's approach to showing videos included packaging them with VJ introductions and station promos, which helped MTV establish a unique brand identity. Co-founder and original programming chief Bob Pittman had an eye on brand building from an early stage:

> The concept I had was to have a clear image, to build an attitude. In other words, to build a brand, a channel that happened to use video clips as a building block, as opposed to being a delivery system for videos. The star wouldn't be the videos, the star would be the channel.[7]

Music Videos Hit the Air

MTV's business plan mirrored that of a radio station. The channel got its content—in this case videos or "clips" instead of audio tracks—from record companies for free and earned revenues by selling advertising. Warner Amex approved the plan and gave the channel $25 million in financial backing. Record companies were reluctant at first to give away videos, which they had to pay to produce in addition to the original recording. When MTV first launched, its video library contained a scant 250 videos.

MTV's success was contingent on receiving free videos, and the record companies eventually relented. The record companies primarily gave MTV clips from their second- and third-tier artists, however. MTV's first-ever aired video was a minor record titled, appropriately enough, "Video Killed the Radio Star" by an English band called The Buggles. The video aired at midnight August 2, 1981, when MTV hit the airwaves for the first time. The opening broadcast was simple, with a voice-over intoning "Ladies and gentlemen, rock 'n' roll" over footage of a space launch, followed by the Buggles video. The success of the channel, which was practically overnight, was evidenced by the fact that the channel created stars from the lower-tier acts. Artists such as Adam Ant and Billy Idol, who received little radio play, emerged as genuine talents after their videos aired on MTV. Billy Idol recounted how MTV's influence as a burgeoning cultural phenomenon helped propel him to stardom:

> Radio guys would take one look at my picture with the spiky hair and say, "Punk-rocker. Not playing him." Then MTV airs my videos, and kids start calling up radio stations saying, "I want to hear Billy Idol!" It really broke the thing wide open. We'd never touched the charts, and the next minute we had a Top 10 album. It was amazing. Nobody'd ever noticed me before. Now I'm walking down the streets, and people are yelling: "Billy!"[8]

In addition to creating fame, MTV broadcasts also created record sales. The executive vice president of Warner Bros. Records, Stan Cornyn, said at the time, "It was reported back to us that records were selling in certain cities without radio airplay. We asked, 'Why?' and it turned out that there were music videos playing on MTV. An act like Devo is dancing around in their funny masks and stuff like that—and they take off in a market where nothing else is happening."[9] John Sykes, MTV's original director of promotions noted a similar phenomenon:

> We finally hit pay dirt when we went into a record store and asked if there was any reaction to the songs we were playing that weren't being played on the local radio stations. The manager said, 'Yeah, we sold a box of Buggles albums.' . . . Within two weeks we had trade ads in Billboard, with quotes from all the store managers in Tulsa, claiming that MTV was having this profound impact on record sales.[10]

Soon record companies began producing more videos from bigger artists, in part because of the sales figures and also because artists were demanding to have their own videos played on MTV.

MTV Raises Awareness

Financially, the first year was difficult for MTV, because advertisers were reluctant to embrace an unproven cable upstart. Adding to MTV's trouble was the fact that many cable operators refused to carry the channel, keeping its audience well below the targeted 2.5 million for the inaugural year. In 1982, MTV devised an advertising campaign designed to spike demand in unserviced markets. The concept was simple: have famous rock stars endorse the brand by uttering the phrase "I want my MTV," then air these commercials in areas where cable providers were not showing MTV. The first star to sign on was Mick Jagger, at the time the biggest rock star in the world. Other stars to cut promos included Pete Townshend, David Bowie, John Cougar, and Pat Benatar. The results of the $2 million ad campaign were dramatic.

Prior to launching the campaign, MTV conducted an awareness study and found that the percentage of respondents in the U.S. who had heard of MTV or seen the channel was just below 20 percent. Four weeks after the campaign, awareness had risen to 89 percent. Still, the financial picture for MTV remained bleak. In two years, the channel had recorded $33.9 million in losses and advertisers did not respond to the channel with the same enthusiasm young viewers had. MTV sold only $6 million in advertising in 1982.

MTV developed a number of contests and promotions in order to build viewership. These were starkly different from traditional promotional campaigns. For one contest, the prize was a "lost weekend" with Van Halen. In another early contest, MTV bought a somewhat dilapidated house and gave it away to a lucky viewer. One of the most coveted items was a T-shirt with an MTV logo on it, because MTV neither sold nor gave its T-shirts away. MTV would eventually develop a lucrative licensing operation.

Music Videos Take Off

The era of modern music videos started with the Michael Jackson video for his song "Billie Jean" from the landmark album *Thriller*. The video featured Jackson's energetic dance moves and applied advanced production values to achieve a sleek look. The video helped propel sales of *Thriller* to more than 800,000 a week. The follow-up to "Billie Jean"—"Beat It"—added a street fight narrative that involved complex choreography. The title video from *Thriller* took the music video to an entirely different level. Running an unprecedented 14 minutes, "Thriller" cost $1.1 million to make, a figure more than 20 times the cost of the most expensive video on record to that point. The video, which was modeled on the horror classic *Night of the Living Dead*, featured Jackson as the star of a miniaturized feature film in which zombies him and his date. MTV paid $250,000 for the right to air the video first and played the video three times every day. The channel also pre-promoted the video before each playing and noticed a rating spike each time. *Thriller* went on to be the biggest-selling album up to that point, and Michael Jackson vaulted to mega-stardom.

Hot on the heels of Jackson's breakout success, MTV broke in another new star with Madonna. Madonna's videos, though not as elaborate as Jackson's, were still more expensive than the average video. Other artists began demanding more money for videos. Budgets rose from around $10,000 to over $100,000, which raised the music video aesthetic further. Accordingly, artists became more concerned about their image and appearance. They were not competing primarily on the basis of sound anymore, and the look of an artist took on a newfound importance.

Early Competition

Several networks attempted to replicate MTV's success with weekly video programs. NBC developed "Friday Night Videos" and USA launched "Night Flight." The syndicated "FM-TV" also contained two hours of videos and interviews. MTV created VH1 to counter Ted Turner's 1984 launch of Cable Music Channel, itself an answer to MTV's popularity. VH1 stood for "video hits" and was positioned to be distinctly different from MTV by airing adult-oriented videos. Kevin Metheny, director of programming, described the VH1 format:

> We picked three musical genres that wouldn't cannibalize MTV: R&B, country, and adult contemporary. We'd have Tony Bennett, followed by Kool and the Gang, followed by Willie Nelson; the Judds, followed by Latoya Jackson, followed by Air Supply. It was very odd . . . but the point with VH1 was to monopolize shelf space, rather than create a successful entity.[11]

A month after VH1 went on the air, Turner shut down the Cable Music Channel and sold its assets to MTV for $1 million.

Success Leads to New Ownership

In 1984, MTV had the highest Nielsen ratings over the average 24-hour period of any advertiser-supported cable network. At that time, the channel reached more than 21 million households. As ad revenues in the first quarter of 1984 rose 223 percent from the previous year, MTV turned its first quarterly profit of $3.4 million. Not only was MTV making strides financially, it was being recognized for its impact on American music culture. In 1984, the National Association of Record Manufacturers honored MTV with its Presidential Award in recognition of the channel's role in reviving the record industry. This recognition of the channel's success was also expressed in financial terms, as in 1985 media giant Viacom bought MTV for $525 million, folding the channel into its vast media empire.

MTV PROGRAMMING EVOLVES

Changing Formats

After four years of growth, MTV suffered a ratings decline in 1985 and 1986. From a high of a 1.2 share in 1983, MTV ratings dropped from 0.9 in the third quarter of 1985 to 0.6 in the fourth quarter. MTV addressed the ratings slide by developing "long-form programming" that would keep viewers tuned in for longer periods of time, hopefully over the course of a season. Analysts applauded the format change, noting that MTV "can't get by showing clips for 24 hours a day, seven days a week."[12]

Between 1986 and 1989, MTV introduced a number of long-form programs. *120 Minutes* was a weekly two-hour showcase of progressive and underground music. *Headbanger's Ball* launched in 1987 and was dedicated to hard rock and heavy metal. *Unplugged* featured artists playing songs acoustically in an intimate small theatre setting. *Unplugged* premiered in 1989 and over the years featured legendary artists like Paul McCartney, R.E.M., Eric Clapton, and Neil Young. Many of these new programs were successful but remained focused on music videos or live performances.

MTV eventually tapped into programs that did not revolve around music. In 1989 MTV introduced a fashion program called *House of Style* where host model Cindy Crawford took a weekly look at the world of fashion. Two of MTV's most popular long-form programs ever were introduced in 1992 and 1993, *Beavis and Butthead* and *The Real World*. *Beavis and Butthead* was a half-hour animated cartoon series about two low-IQ teenaged title characters with an MTV obsession. When they were not watching videos, Beavis and Butthead caused trouble in their neighborhood or at school. The show resonated with different types of viewers and even *Time* magazine's pop-culture critic called the show "the bravest show ever run on national television."[13] The show's popularity led to lucrative licensing agreements with clothing and toy manufacturers, and even a feature-length film called *Beavis and Butthead Do America*.

The Real World, introduced in 1992, was credited as first modern "Reality TV" program. Conceived by a news producer and a soap-opera producer, the show recorded the lives of seven people between the ages of 19 and 25 sharing a loft in New York City's SoHo district. The producers selected the seven occupants to precipitate some racial, gender, and sexual tension. The seven individuals then gave MTV unlimited access to videotape their personal lives and story rights for a three-month period. The first 13-week season was an instant hit and captured a large viewing audience of approximately 700,000 people. By 2002, *The Real World Chicago* was the most watched episode of the series with 5.5 million viewers and a 6.1 rating among 12–34 year olds. In 2005, *The Real World Key West* became the program's 17th season—making it MTV's longest running series ever. The popularity of these new non-music-video shows indicated a new direction of growth for MTV. Tom Freston acknowledged MTV's expansion beyond music in 1993 when he said, "We're not just about music. We're about all issues associated with pop culture."[14]

MTV EXPANDS GLOBALLY

During the time MTV was reconnecting with its core audience via long-form programming, it also was achieving unprecedented growth in its international markets. MTV first went global with its MTV Europe launch in 1987. At the time, MTV had a single satellite feed that broadcasted primarily American programming and used English-speaking VJs. The music and entertainment tastes of the people varied widely among European nations, and soon competitors took advantage of

MTV's undifferentiated broadcast by establishing locally-produced music channels. MTV watched much of its audience, and consequently, its advertiser base, abandon the channel in favor of local competition. As a result, MTV learned early on that the key to successful international growth was to "think and act locally." That is, MTV needed to offer local content that catered to the region's tastes and culture. Bill Roedy, president of MTV Networks International explained, "We've had very little resistance once we explain that we're not in the business of exporting American culture."[15] By 2005, MTV provided unique programming for most European countries, including the newest channel, MTV Ireland, which broke off from MTV UK that same year.

MTV Latin America went through a similar initial launch in 1993. The channel was criticized early on for the prominence of English-language videos, which outnumbered Spanish-language videos by a 4-to-1 margin. MTV Latin America increased the Spanish-language content and customized its programming in accordance with regional tastes and by 2003, the channel aired its own MTV Video Music Awards Latin America. The number of subscribers rose from 3.2 million in 16 countries in 1993 to 13 million in 24 countries households in 2005. With similar success, MTV Brazil reached 18 million households by 2005.

MTV India also had success once it aired local programs and videos. MTV India produced local shows, including *MTV Cricket in Control* about the game of cricket, *MTV Houseful* featuring Hindi film stars, and *MTV Bakra* modeled after *Candid Camera*. MTV India's VJs spoke "Hinglish," a hip mix of Hindi and English popular in the countries urban areas. Between 1996 and 2000, ratings for MTV India increased 700 percent. In addition, MTV India increased household penetration by 11 million from 2000 to 2005 and produced more than half of its shows in Hindi.

MTV Networks also focused attention on fast growing countries, like Asia. MTV first targeted the region in 1995 with the launch of MTV Mandarin, MTV Southeast Asia, and MTV China. MTV Korea debuted in 2001 and each of these Asian channels played native-language music videos as well as international videos. In 2003, MTV China and Nickelodeon China became the first global brand to launch a 24-hour TV channel in the country. Two years later, MTV Network launched Nickelodeon Korea, the country's first 24-hour format targeting children 2 to 14 years old. By the 2005, MTV's distribution hit more than 150 million households in Asia and Nickelodeon reached more than 105 million households in Asia.

MTV Network International grew at such record pace around the world that by 2005, it was the first media company to achieve the 100-channel milestone with the launch of MTV Africa. MTV Networks had launched into 167 countries in 22 languages (see Exhibit 1). As Judy McGrath, CEO and Chairman of MTV Networks, stated, "We are a truly global operation that is fuelled by the exchange of creative ideas and cultures."[16]

DOMESTIC CHANNEL DIFFICULTIES

MTV Addresses Ratings Slump

Despite the success of its long-form programming and its success connecting with local audiences during its global expansion, MTV's ratings continued to hover near 0.5 in the United States between 1992 and 1996. In 1994, Tom Freston spoke of the difficulty of staying relevant to young viewers:

> MTV is in rather a vulnerable position because it's sort of out there on the leading edge of what's going on in the popular culture. It has, for 13 years, managed to reinvent itself, stay interesting, keep its audience levels up, and I think that's quite an accomplishment.[17]

By 1996, this difficulty had manifested itself as MTV's ratings stayed low through that year. Despite the success of its long-form programming, the channel's ratings continued to hover near 0.5. The grunge genre that MTV and its viewers had embraced in the early 1990s—typified by Nirvana, Pearl Jam, and Soundgarden—was falling out of favor. So too was the gansta rap genre popular with young viewers especially. The channel had yet to find any suitable musical replacement that resonated with its core audience. Though MTV did have competitors in the music channel space (see Exhibit 2), these channels' smaller audiences meant they did not contribute significantly to MTV's ratings decline.

Viewers and analysts alike criticized MTV for the level of non-music video content of its programming mix. In December 1996, MTV addressed these concerns by adding six additional hours of music video programming each week but continued to develop long-form programming that kept viewers tuned in on a regularly basis. In comparison, the video-only mix encouraged viewers to watch only the videos they liked and tune out during others. In 1996, MTV's two highest-rated programs were *Road Rules*, a reality-TV road trip, and *Singled Out*, a dating show. Tom Freston explained how long-form programming was evolving MTV from a channel about music to a channel about culture.

> [Long-form programming] works. The consumers like it. We think it's a way to sort of stretch ourselves out and make MTV a bigger, more interesting, more vital place for its audience. . . . Long-form programming serves sort of as a punctuation mark, if you will, and as a way to bring attention to the network. . . . I think the diversification of MTV from a pure music network to a network that's not only about the music but about the things the music is about has worked well for us.[18]

While long-form programming took off, MTV launched an all-music channel called MTV2. MTV2 catered to an older audience, 18 to 49 year olds, for whom music video viewing was important and enabled MTV to continue to build its ratings with long-form programming. The company also changed the genres of music it played on MTV, briefly programming an eclectic mix of styles, ranging from electronic dance music to traditional pop tunes. This mix was soon all usurped by the teen pop phenomenon epitomized by the success of acts such as the Backstreet Boys, *NSYNC, and Britney Spears.

MTV responded to this phenomenon by repackaging its music video offerings into discrete shows, such as *Total Request Live*, or *TRL*. *TRL* was a call-in video request program that sought to establish stronger connections with its viewers. Host Carson Daly would count down the top 10 videos of the day, as chosen by viewers voting on the net and via telephone. The show also featured live interviews in the studio with famous artists and movie stars, as well as celebrity guest-hosts and videotaped interviews. The Times Square studio where *TRL* was taped became something of a touchstone for viewers, who lined up outside daily in the hopes of getting on camera. The crowd outside eventually became so large that police were required to provide crowd control to keep the throng from spilling out onto the street. Fans lucky enough to make it into the studio audience would get to see and hear the action up close. The truly lucky fans got the opportunity to plug their favorite video on camera, usually spoken fast and breathlessly, signing off with the exuberant "WHOOOOOO!" that became standard on the show.

In response to this surge of support, *TRL* expanded from one hour to a 90-minute show in the summer of 1999. At that time, the show attracted more than one million viewers every afternoon. Many of the bands featured on the *TRL* countdown became big stars, including Britney Spears, Backstreet Boys, and *NSYNC. Carson Daly also became a celebrity of the same magnitude as many of the artists and actors featured on the program.

TRL was an unqualified success, particularly among viewers aged 12–17. In 1999, MTV news chief, Dave Sirulnick, referred to the show as "the franchise of the channel."[19] The success of *TRL* thrived into the 2000s and prompted other MTV programs to hold contests, promotions, and original types of live interaction.

Bringing Back Male Viewers

While the focus on the teenage girl demographic helped MTV ratings to climb from 1997 to 2000 (see Exhibit 3), the emphasis of teen pop programming was alienating some of its viewers. Males and older individuals were experiencing a disconnect with the channel. MTV executives recognized that teen pop was just the latest in a series of trends and the channel could not afford to exclude large numbers of its audience. In response, MTV altered its programming and created a number of shows aimed at an older audience.

The *Tom Green Show* premiered in 1999 and featured oddball Canadian host, Tom Green, performing madcap sketches and stunts. A racy nighttime soap-opera called *Undressed* centered on the sex lives of high school and college students. And, *Jackass*, a show in which a pseudo-stuntman and his friends performed absurd and sometimes dangerous stunts like lighting himself on fire, riding a bull, and allowing himself to be shot at close range with a paintball gun, debuted in October 2000. *Jackass* was MTV's highest rated show in 2000 attracting 1.6 million viewers. Other popular shows reached a broad range of viewers, including *MTV's Cribs*, which debuted in 2000, and gave viewers an insider's look at stars homes such as Nelly, Tommy Lee and Destiny's Child. *The Andy Dick Show* featured comedian Andy Dick, in sketches, short films, and music video parodies during the half-hour comedy show.

The result of MTV's new programming approach was a more balanced audience across the 12–17 year-old and 18–24 year-old demographic. Between 1996 and 2001, the 18–24 demographic grew 33 percent compared with 17 percent for ages 12–17. Advertisers took note of this trend and ad sales rose 20 percent in 2000.

Big Hits Help Ratings

In early 2002, the biggest MTV hit to date aired—*The Osbournes*. The show chronicled the domestic life of heavy metal legend Ozzy Osbourne, his wife, Sharon, and his teenaged children, Jack and Kelly, as they went through daily routines in their Beverly Hills mansion. Viewers watched plotlines such as Ozzy, Sharon, and Kelly attempting to use a vacuum cleaner, the family feuding with noisy neighbors, and everyone trying to housebreak their pets. The show built a buzz almost immediately, attracting almost eight million U.S. households—the highest rating in cable history—and averaged a 4.4 rating for the show. MTV capitalized on the success of the show by airing various episodes 15 times a week and charging $135,000 for each 30-second commercial, up from $10,000 when the show debuted and a record for the channel. MTV also paid the Osbournes $20 million to renew the show for two more seasons. The success of the show proved somewhat unsustainable, however. In 2003, ratings dropped 50 percent overall and 15 percent within its core 12–34 year old audience.[20] Analysts noted that, "Once something becomes too popular, it goes out of vogue with teens. MTV always has to reinvent a new programming genre."[21] MTV cancelled *The Osbournes* after three seasons but the program helped lift MTV's overall ratings from 2002–2004 (Exhibit 4).

During the Osbourne years, MTV released a number of other hit shows, including *Laguna Beach: The Real Orange County, Pimp My Ride, Punk'd, Newlyweds: Nick and Jessica,* and *The Ashlee Simpson Show. Laguna Beach,* most notably, became a huge hit among 12–24 year olds. A reality counterpart to the popular Fox primetime soap *The OC, Laguna Beach* gained complete access to eight rich and beautiful teenagers who lived in Laguna Beach, CA. The show revealed the friends' true-life experiences, parties, and relationships. In its second season, *Laguna Beach* reached over 73 million viewers and became the most watched program for 12–24 year olds during its time slot.

In addition to long-form programming, MTV also focused on its Video Music Awards or VMAs, an awards show honoring top music performers in all genres. The VMAs had become a critical event for MTV and artists alike. Over the years, the VMAs have had scandal—e.g. Britney and Madonna's 2003 kiss—as well as hosts and performers who have continually tried to outdo the previous years "shock" factor. In 2004, the 20th annual VMAs aired for an audience of 10.3 million, ranking in the top five cable shows of the year. The VMAs also started adding "reality TV" contests with text messaging and online voting understanding that viewers preferred to watch MTV in an interactive way.[22]

MTV's numerous programming shifts in the late 1990s and the early 2000s demonstrated one of the channel's key properties: dynamic programming. MTV was able to represent itself as a leading source of entertainment for each of the major music trends that have swept the nation since the early 1980s: new wave, hair metal, grunge, gangsta rap, teen pop, and hip-hop. MTV Entertainment President Brian Graden explained how important it was to stay dynamic:

> Music television is a term that has to be redefined for each generation. You have to find new ways to package it, celebrate it, reinvent it, or somebody else would create tomorrow's music television.[23]

A NEW ERA FOR MTV

Throughout the early 2000s, MTV led cable TV with original and hip programs and music videos as it had in decades past. MTV ended 2004 with its highest household penetration ever and its highest ratings for 12–34 year olds ever. The channel was focused in its music selection, primarily playing hip-hop artists such as Nelly, 50 Cent, and Kanye West as well as pop artists like Madonna, Britney Spears, and Kelly Clarkson. While the music strategy remained consistent, MTV emerged as a source of information and education for its viewers as significant disasters struck throughout the world starting in 2001. Understanding that it was a true global media brand, MTV evolved into more than a channel about music and culture. During these crises, it became an educational destination, connecting young viewers around the world.

MTV Educates Its Viewers

On September 11, 2001 MTV and VH1 broadcast CBS News all day following the terrorist attacks on New York City and Washington, D.C. In the week after the attacks, MTV pulled all its long-form programming and broadcast only videos and news updates. The *New York Times* reported that during that period, 31 million 12–34 year-olds watched MTV in order to get information. MTV quadrupled its daily news coverage in the weeks following in order to air special programs ranging from the life of Afghani teens, domestic anti-Arab sentiment, Islam, to military activity. Similar coverage was offered on the MTV.com website. "MTV has provided more in-depth coverage and explanation as to why the Taliban is the way it is than I have seen on any other channel," said Aasma Khan, spokeswoman for Muslims Against Terrorism, a youth group organized by young Muslim professionals since Sept. 11. "They're reaching out to people of Muslim and Arab descent and bridging that gap."[24] MTV received positive feedback from many corners of the world for its coverage of the war on terror.

The channel had a similar impact on young adults prior to the 2004 presidential election. MTV and MTV.com helped educate young viewers on domestic and international issues such as the war in Iraq, education, and global warming to help motivate them to vote. The *Choose or Lose* campaign, which MTV had implemented in every presidential election year since 1992, exceeded it goal of getting 20 million 18-30 year olds to vote by 17 percent from the previous presidential campaign. Executives at MTV believed that the channel had even changed the way the candidates ran for office, noting that candidates paid more attention to the issues important to young Americans.[25]

MTV responded similarly to 9-11 in the wake of several devastating natural disasters, including the 2004 tsunami in South East Asia and 2005 Hurricane Katrina that devastated much of New Orleans and surrounding areas. MTV China won awards for its coverage and efforts following the tsunami. After Katrina, MTV showed special news broadcasts as well as joined forces with VH1 and CMT to launch a relief campaign that included live performances and volunteer and donation opportunities.

Around the world, teenagers and young adults turned to their local MTV channel and website to learn more about world events and connect with others. And, in 2005, MTV launched *think*MTV, an initiative to help viewers learn more and respond to domestic and international crises. The separate on-air and online sections of MTV and MTV.com were developed to "inform and empower young minds to take action on issues, including education, discrimination, the environment, sexual health, and global concerns." *think*MTV helped connect MTV viewers with common concerns around the world and build its credibility as a trusting resource. The Internet and MTV.com continued to play a critical role within this connectivity.

MTV.com Broadens the Experience

The MTV brand made an unauthorized debut online in 1991 with an unofficial newsgroup hosted by former VJ Adam Curry called MTV.com. Independently, Curry had built a website on which he posted music reviews, industry gossip, and concert dates. In 1993, MTV sued Curry, who then relinquished the site. In 1994 MTV launched MTV.com. In 1994, MTV partnered with America Online to produce MTV Online, its first official Internet site. By 1999, MTV.com attracted more than two million visitors each month. That year, MTV formed a separate business unit called MTVi (for MTV Interactive) that oversaw the brand's music sites.

MTV also established websites for MTV2 and for each of its international channels. These sites resembled the MTV.com site, but with content designed specifically for the local market. For example, MTV France's website (www.mtv.fr) offered live footage from the annual Printemps de Bourges music festival. Both MTV Japan's website (www.mtvjapan.com) and MTV Brazil's (www.mtv.com.br) website contained content relating to each country's Video Music Awards. The international sites featured local artists and information on local concert events. Some local content was just for fun, such as a game featured on MTV's Russian website (www.mtv.ru) called "Kill 'Em With a Pillow" in which players walked through a virtual MTV studio and hit Russian and international celebrities with a pillow to earn points. By 2005, there were 14 individual international MTV websites, each unique to its target country.

MTV.com received a boost when the music industry came to recognize the Internet as an excellent medium for music after first pursuing aggressive litigation to prevent illegal file-sharing. Several record companies and other Internet firms started services that enabled consumers to download mp3s legally. In 2001, MTV contracted RioPort, a music-download service, and offered downloadable music on MTV.com for a fee. By 2005, this service was free to MTV.com members and was one of the most popular sections of the website. That year, the company also launched a pay-for-download service called URGE, in partnership with Microsoft.

URGE offered more than 2 million songs to download and featured exclusives from MTV.

In 2001, MTV launched a campaign called "MTV 360" designed to lure MTV viewers to MTV.com and MTV2. The campaign, which involved spending of $100 million over twelve months, involved integrated programming on all three channels. For example, during a live performance by the Dave Matthews Band on MTV's TRL, MTV2 played a block of older videos by the band, and MTV.com offered visitors the opportunity to download a live performance of a song from the band's upcoming album. In April 2002, traffic to MTV.com approached 2.5 million visitors for the month. By 2005, traffic had grown to more than 18 million visitors each month and was the number one music content site.

In 2005, MTV.com launched MTV Overdrive, a web channel dedicated to streaming MTV programs, live performances and music videos. MTV Overdrive pioneered online broadcasting—giving non-cable subscribers a chance to get involved with the brand, listen to the music, meet the personalities, watch the programs, and get involved with the communities without paying for the station. In addition, it gave current viewers more reasons to interact with the brand. For example, fans could click on the latest Madonna video, watch a preview of the next *Laguna Beach* episode, or catch news clips of current global events. MTV had become an important part of teens' and young adults' lives around the world. MTV Networks aimed to do the same with its other channels.

MTV Networks Span the Globe

Six years after MTV Networks launched as a global brand in 1999, it was the leading music entertainment company in the world. MTV International had become a part of most cultures around the world through its TV channel, online presence, and grass roots involvement. In addition, other MTV Networks channels touched viewers where MTV did not (see Exhibit 5). As of 2005, the MTV Networks offered the following music video channels to digital cable and satellite subscribers:

- **MTV**—The largest global television network where young adults turn to find out what's happening and what's next in music and popular culture.
- **MTV2**—An innovative, free-form mix of music videos, series, and special programs spanning musical genres. MTV2 targets older viewers who discover, control, and connect to the music they love.
- **mtvU**—A television channel just for colleges that takes a look into dorm life, cafeteria eating, and student centers on 730 college campuses.
- **MTV Desi**—A music video channel dedicated to the culture and style of South-Asian Americans.
- **VH1**—The music network for 18- to 49-year-olds. VH1 takes audiences behind the music and beyond with original series, concerts, live events, music movies and new music videos.
- **VH1 Classic**—Features 24 hours of the greatest music from the 1960s, 1970s and 1980s.

- **CMT**—The number one country music channel and recognized worldwide authority. CMT brings you original programs, live concert series, exclusive world premiere videos, and a diverse playlist.

Viacom Split

In early 2005, Viacom announced that it would divide the company into two separate, publicly traded companies by the end of the year. The new Viacom, headed by long-time MTV employee and then co-President and co-COO of Viacom Tom Freston, would include all of the high-growth properties such as MTV Networks, BET, and Paramount Pictures. Separately, CBS Corporation would include CBS Television with slower-growth businesses such as Infinity Broadcasting, Viacom Outdoor, and Simon & Schuster. Executives noted that the separation would achieve better growth results due to more similar strategic focus within the Viacom and CBS groups, respectively. When the two companies were officially split in January 2006, analysts expected the new Viacom to perform better initially than CBS, given its stable of successful cable channels that had generated a 16 percent annual revenue growth since 1994.

Yet, paradoxically, CBS performed better than the new Viacom in terms of share price. In the nine months following the split, CBS stock rose 9 percent, while Viacom stock fell by 16 percent. Viacom's sagging performance was due, in part, to its revenue growth rate falling to 10 percent in the first nine months of 2006 as advertisers shifted spending away from cable television to the Internet, where Viacom's presence was not as established (see Exhibit 6). MTV.com had enhanced its offerings with the addition of broadband content on MTV Overdrive, but it still attracted far fewer visitors than MySpace.com, the leading teen Internet content site (MTV.com had 7.5 million unique visitors in January 2006, compared with 30 million for MySpace).

In a move to renew growth at Viacom that surprised many in the industry, chairman Sumner Redstone elected to install a new management team at Viacom, replacing the CEO Freston, who had been with MTV since 1981. Analysts speculated that Redstone was unhappy that Freston, who had been credited with building MTV networks into its present state as a cable giant, had not aggressively pursued growth opportunities in new media. For example, Viacom lost a bidding war for MySpace when rival News Corporation purchased the site's parent company for $580 million in 2005. "It was there for the taking," Redstone later lamented.[26] MTV Networks had spent some $600 million on a number of Internet acquisitions, including video hosting site iFilm, children's online community Neopets, and content site Atom Entertainment, none of which had approached the audience levels of MySpace.

Freston's replacements, Philippe Dauman as CEO and President and Thomas Dooley in the newly-created role of Chief Administrative Officer, were members of Viacom's board that had previously worked at Viacom, helping guide it through its largest growth period, when its stock price tripled between 1996 and 2000. They had left Viacom after its 2000 merger with CBS to form a private equity concern, and asserted that this experience enabled them to bring "a very entrepreneurial culture" to Viacom in order to "be ahead of the curve."[27] This new management team was expected to look outside the company for growth opportunities, but with MTV still playing a critical role in the new Viacom, the brand was expected to remain Viacom's strongest asset.

CONCLUSION

From its roots as a start-up cable network, MTV grew into a dominant youth brand in the music and television industry. Within a decade of its first broadcast, MTV established itself as one of the premier media properties in American cable television. Over the next decade, MTV expanded and strengthened its brand both domestically and abroad. In 2005, MTV was the number one television network in the world, reaching more people across the globe than any other network. In addition, *Interbrand* ranked MTV the second-most valuable media brand (after Disney) in 2005, as the 50th most valuable brand in the world.[28] With over 421 million household subscribers in 167 countries around the world, MTV was a true media force.

As the channel continued to grow, MTV contended with a number of issues. First, the cable advertising market was slowing, with more advertising dollars shifting to the Internet, where MTV was not as strong. With the company's tentative steps regarding new Internet properties playing a role in the firing of veteran Tom Freston, MTV's new management had to determine an Internet strategy that would help the company meet its growth objectives. It would be necessary to understand how technology was changing the way viewers watched television and figure out how best to interweave technology with the brand. Furthermore, within MTV Networks, executives needed to evaluate MTV's position relative to its sister channels, in order to maximize viewership and minimize overlap with other channels and websites. As always, the biggest challenge would be to remain relevant to the core audience of young consumers through dynamic programming and compelling content. In order to ensure growth, MTV needed to stay on top of musical and cultural trends as it had in the past. Because the network had managed to do so for more than two decades, MTV executives were confident that the channel would continue to succeed.

DISCUSSION QUESTIONS

1. What is the MTV brand image? How valuable are the MTV brand associations? What should its core values be?
2. Describe the current sources of MTV's brand equity. How have they changed over time? How have they remained constant?
3. What is the role of music within MTV?
4. Technology is changing the way viewers watch television and interact with programs. Discuss the role of the Internet and technology within MTV. What has MTV done well to date to integrate technology with the brand and what else should MTV do?
5. MTV Networks includes many sister channels such as Nickelodeon and Spike TV. How has MTV been positioned within this network versus the

other channels? Is this the right strategy? What else would you do to optimize the MTV Network brand portfolio?

6. Over the years, MTV has evolved from a channel about music to a channel about the culture of music to a channel about culture. What does the future holds for MTV—globally and domestically?

Exhibit 1: MTV Channels Across the Globe

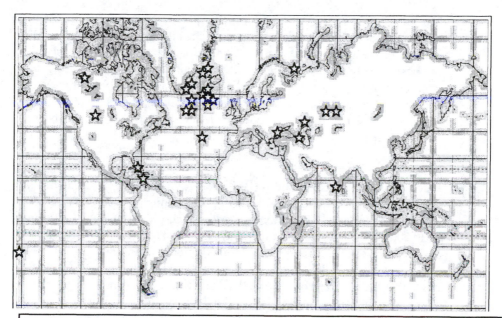

United States (MTV, MTV2, mtvU, MTV Desi, MTV Overdrive, *think*MTV), MTV Canada, MTV Latin America, MTV Brazil, MTV Base Africa, MTV European, MTV France, MTV Spain Germany, MTV UK, MTV Ireland, MTV Holland, MTV Italy, MTV Nordic, MTV, MTV Portugal, MTV Poland, MTV Romania, MTV2 Europe and MTV2 Germany, MTV Adria, MTV Australia, MTV China, MTV Japan, MTV South East Asia, MTV Thailand, MTV Korea, MTV India

Exhibit 2: MTV's Television Competition

Throughout its history, MTV did not encounter a powerful competitor that challenged its category leadership in a significant way. The first-mover advantage was a powerful brand-building tool in the case of MTV, since it established early on a connection with the youth audience and worked to maintain this connection. The fact that MTV remained the leader after two decades of broadcasting did not guarantee its future leadership, however. What follows is a historical overview of MTV's major competitors, both domestically and abroad:

BET

Black Entertainment Television (BET) was founded in 1980 to address the underserved African-American audience. Programming included music videos, college sports, movies, news, and talk shows. In the late 1990s and early 2000s, BET developed a niche by showcasing cutting edge hip-hop and R&B videos. Audience reach doubled to 60 million households between 1991 and 2000, and BET was seen as a legitimate competitor to MTV as a source for urban music. Viacom bought BET in late 2000 for $2.3 billion and added it to the MTV Networks unit.

The Box

The Box was an innovative music video channel where viewers could tune in for free to watch videos voted on by other viewers using call-in system. The Box also functioned like a jukebox, where viewers could pay a small fee to watch a selection of their choice. MTV purchased The Box in 2000 and combined it with MTV2.

MuchMusic

MTV's acquisitions of The Box and BET left MuchMusic as the closest competitor. MuchMusic, a Canadian music channel, launched in the United States in 1994. The channel received limited distribution primarily on satellite and digital cable networks, and was available in only 14 million U.S. homes at the beginning of 2001. The channel initially broadcast the Canadian feed to the United States, which by Canadian law had to include 30 percent of its videos from Canadian bands. In Canada, MuchMusic was the dominant channel, with more than 6 million households to its name. The company created a separate entity—MuchMusic USA—in 2001 in order to cater to the American pop music tastes. In 2003, MuchMusic sold its U.S. entity to Fuse Networks, which became Fuse TV (fuse.tv).

Fuse TV

Fuse TV launched in 2003 after it acquired MuchMusic USA. "Fuse is the nation's only all-music, viewer-influenced television network featuring music videos, exclusive artist interviews, live concerts and specials—all rooted in the music experience." As of 2005, it had a subscriber base of 38 million. Fuse was in the process of offering its subscribers content via VOD (Video on Demand), mobile phones, and PSP (Play Station Portable).

International Competition

MTV's success abroad inspired competitors such as News Corp.'s Rupert Murdoch and AOL Time Warner. Channel V—a 24-hour music channel based in Hong Kong and owned by Murdoch's Star TV satellite network. With channels in Hong Kong, India, Indonesia, China, Malaysia, Middle East, Philippines, Taiwan, Thailand, and Asia, Channel V reflected the tastes and culture in each local market. MTV's largest European rival, VIVA, was part-owned by AOL Time Warner, EMI, and Vivendi Universal.

Exhibit 3: MTV Ratings by Demographic Group

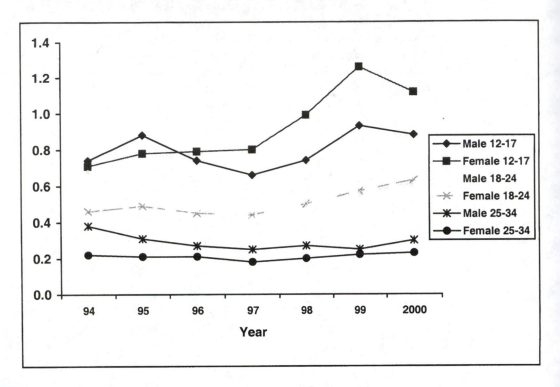

(Source: Average of Nielsen Quarterly Data)

Exhibit 4: MTV Overall Ratings

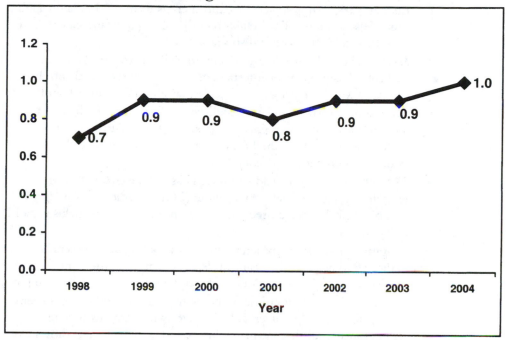

(Source: Nielsen)

Exhibit 5: MTV Networks (Non-Music Channels, 2005)

- **Nickelodeon**—Animation, adventure, comedy and live action shows for kids. Nickelodeon was the number one channel targeting children 2–11 in 2005, reached more than 180 million households worldwide and complemented MTV in terms of its younger target audience and programming.
- **Comedy Central**—The only 24-hour, all-comedy network. Spotlights popular animated series for adults like "South Park" and Emmy Award-winner "Dr. Katz: Professional Therapist," plus sitcoms, sketches, stand-up, talk shows and movies.
- **SpikeTV**—The first network developed for men. Spike TV inspires and defines the modern man through programming that appeals to his lifestyle interests. This is the one place men can find all the comedy, movies, sports entertainment, and innovative originals they want, from a male point of view.
- **Nick at Nite**—Classic TV for an ever-expanding audience. Nick at Nite presents America's best-loved, family-friendly, classic TV sitcoms like "I Love Lucy."

- **TV Land**—Cable's 24-hour classic TV network. Home to the best dramas, variety shows, westerns and sitcoms from the 1950s through the 1990s—with hits like "Hill Street Blues," "Sonny and Cher," and "Gunsmoke"—plus original specials.
- **BET**—The 24-hour television network for the African-American audience. Keeps viewers entertained, educated, and excited with hard-hitting news, electrifying music videos, family entertainment, and more.
- **Showtime**—Movies and more: where you'll see great Hollywood hits and ground-breaking original pictures and series that you can't see anywhere else—PLUS the best in championship boxing, only on America's number one Boxing Network.
- **LOGO**—MTVN's new ad-supported basic cable channel for the lesbian, gay, bisexual, and transgender (LGBT) audience providing a mix of original and acquired entertainment that is smart, inclusive, and authentic.
- **Noggin**—The first commercial-free network for preschoolers dedicated to helping 2–5 year olds learn and grow to meet the challenges of their world. Airs seven days a week from 6 a.m. to 6 p.m.
- **The N**—The N is nighttime on Noggin, dedicated to helping tweens (9–14) figure out their lives. It is the place where tweens tune in to shows tuned in to them, with exclusive and award-winning shows like *A Walk in Your Shoes, DeGrassi: The Next Generation, Radio Free Roscoe,* and *Daria.* N can be seen every day from 6 p.m. to 6 a.m. ET.

Exhibit 6: MTV Networks—Total Revenue ($ millions)

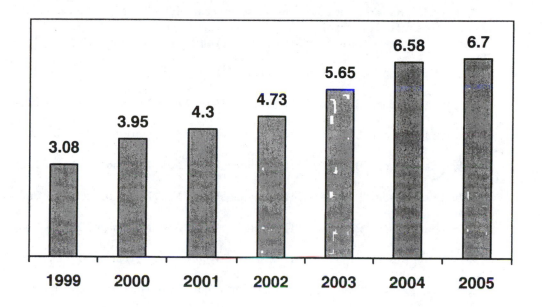

(Source: Viacom Annual Report)

REFERENCES

[1] Keith Richey prepared this case under the supervision of Professor Kevin Lane Keller as the basis for class discussion.

[2] Robert Sam Anson. "Birth of an MTV Nation." *Vanity Fair*, November 2000, pp. 206–248.

[3] Robert Sam Anson. "Birth of an MTV Nation." *Vanity Fair*, November 2000, pp. 206–248.

[4] Robert Sam Anson. "Birth of an MTV Nation." *Vanity Fair*, November 2000, pp. 206–248.

[5] Robert Sam Anson. "Birth of an MTV Nation." *Vanity Fair*, November 2000, pp. 206–248.

[6] Robert Sam Anson. "Birth of an MTV Nation." *Vanity Fair*, November 2000, pp. 206–248.

[7] Robert Sam Anson. "Birth of an MTV Nation." *Vanity Fair*, November 2000, pp. 206–248.

[8] Robert Sam Anson. "Birth of an MTV Nation." *Vanity Fair*, November 2000, pp. 206–248.

[9] Robert Sam Anson. "Birth of an MTV Nation." *Vanity Fair*, November 2000, pp. 206–248.

[10] Robert Sam Anson. "Birth of an MTV Nation." *Vanity Fair*, November 2000, pp. 206–248.

[11] Robert Sam Anson. "Birth of an MTV Nation." *Vanity Fair*, November 2000, pp. 206–248.

[12] Steven Rea. "Who Wants Their MTV?" Knight-Ridder News Service, June 22, 1986.

[13] Rick Marin. "Beavis and Butt-head: You Have to Ask?" The *New York Times*, July 16, 1993, p. 41.

[14] Brenda Hermann. "How Do You Like Your MTV?" *Orange County Register*, April 2, 1993, p. 58.

[15] Kerry Capell, et al. "MTV's World." *Business Week*, February 18, 2002, p. 81.

[16] Viacom.com, press release. November 15, 2004.

[17] Rich Brown. "Tom Freston: The Pied Piper of Television." Interview. *Broadcasting & Cable*, September 19, 1994, p. 36.

[18] Rich Brown. "Tom Freston: The Pied Piper of Television." Interview. *Broadcasting & Cable*, September 19, 1994, p. 36.

[19] Dave Karger. "'Total' Eclipse: MTV's Total Request Live Is Interactive Hitmaking at a Fever Pitch." *Entertainment Weekly*, October 22, 1999, p. 25.

[20] *Electronic Media*, February 3, 2003, pg. 4.

[21] *Reality TV world*, UPI News Service, May 2, 2005.

[22] *Advertising Age*, August 19, 2003, pg. 3.

[23] Lorraine Ali and Devin Gordon. "We Still Want Our MTV." *Newsweek*, July 23, 2001, p. 50.

[24] Jim Rutenberg. "MTV, Turning Serious, Helps Its Generation Cope." The *New York Times*, October 2, 2001, p. E1.

[25] Stuart Miller. "MTV Choose or Lose." *Broadcasting & Cable*, June 28, 2004.

[26] Thomas S. Mulligan and Sallie Hofmeister, "Once Again, Redstone Shakes Up Viacom." *Los Angeles Times*, September 6, 2006, p. A1.

[27] Thomas S. Mulligan and Sallie Hofmeister, "Once Again, Redstone Shakes Up Viacom." *Los Angeles Times*, September 6, 2006, p. A1.

[28] "Best Global Brands 2006." Interbrand.

NIKE:
BUILDING A GLOBAL BRAND[1]

INTRODUCTION

Nike, which began as a two-person enterprise in Oregon, leveraged its technological prowess and marketing savvy to become the largest footwear and apparel company in the world. Along the way it surpassed the incumbent Adidas and withstood challenges from upstart Reebok in the 1980s. The company successfully expanded to Europe and other international markets in the 1990s by tailoring its marketing to blend locally-relevant products and advertising with broadly appealing global campaigns. Additionally, Nike weathered an image crisis involving its labor practices in developing countries by creating a corporate responsibility division, among other moves to address the problems.

Despite its successes in the 1990s, challenges for Nike remained. The company had not fully embraced some major sporting trends, including the "action-sports" trend, typified by ESPN's X-Games, which generated billions in footwear and apparel sales to teens across the globe. Additionally, global revenue growth was stagnant in 1999, with only the European division rising slightly. Nike needed to connect with new consumer segments at home, spur revenue growth in existing markets, and tap emerging markets such as China. The company's ability to achieve these objectives would determine whether it success in the global footwear and apparel market.

NIKE'S DOMESTIC HISTORY—The Early Years

The Nike story begins with its founder, sports enthusiast Phil Knight. Knight grew up in Oregon, a haven for the running micro-culture, with a deep passion for athletics and running, in particular. In 1962, Knight started Blue Ribbon Sports, the precursor company to Nike. At the time, the athletic shoe industry was dominated by two German companies, Adidas and Puma. Knight recognized a neglected segment of serious athletes that had specialized needs that were not being addressed by the major players. The concept was simple: Provide high quality running shoes designed especially for athletes *by* athletes. Knight believed that "high-tech" shoes for runners could be manufactured at competitive prices if imported from abroad. After completing his degree in 1962, Knight embarked on a world tour that included a visit to Japan. During his visit, Knight contacted Onitsuka Tiger, an athletic shoe manufacturer with a reputation for high-quality products, to convince them of his vision for the athletic shoe market. When asked who he represented, Knight made up a name—and Blue Ribbon Sports was born.

In December 1963, Knight received his first shipment of 200 Tiger shoes, which he promptly stored in the Blue Ribbon warehouse—his family's basement. In the 1960s, Oregon was filled with impassioned runners who possessed a hard-wired dedication to their sport. Without much cash for advertising, Knight crafted his "grass roots" philosophy of selling athletic shoes. He spoke to athletes on their level, shared their true passion for running, and listened to their feedback about his products and the sport. Each weekend, Knight traveled from track meet to track meet talking with and selling Tiger shoes from the trunk of his green Plymouth Valiant.

In 1964, Knight asked Bill Bowerman, his track coach at the University of Oregon, to join him at Blue Ribbon Sports. Bowerman had a knack for designing running shoes for the track team and constantly experimented with new products. Knight approached Bowerman with the concept for his business plan, and that year the Blue Ribbon Sports partnership was formed, with Knight and Bowerman each contributing $500. In the first year of their partnership, Blue Ribbon Sports sold 1,300 Tiger running shoes totaling $8,000 in revenues.

In 1965, sales rose to $20,000 and profits rose to $3,240. Needless to say, Knight kept his job as an accountant and Bowerman kept his job as a track coach. In 1967, Bowerman developed the Marathon, the first running shoe made with a lightweight, durable, nylon upper. Sales for Blue Ribbon began to rise as word about the innovation spread in the running community. The next year Bowerman developed two new products: the Cortez—Blue Ribbon's best seller—and the Boston—the first running shoe with a full-length cushioned midsole, a radical innovation in running shoe design. By 1969, sales reached $300,000, and Knight, then an Assistant Professor of Business Administration at Portland State University, resigned to dedicate himself full time to Blue Ribbon Sports, which then employed 20 workers.

The Formative Years

By 1971, the company had reached $1 million in sales and Knight decided to venture out on his own. Manufacturing his own line of shoes required choosing a new, marketable brand name as the Blue Ribbon name seemed too cumbersome for consumers. Knight wanted to use the name "Dimension Six" to reflect the six dimensions of sports—the fan, the event, the arena, the equipment, the media, and the shoes or apparel. Other Blue Ribbon executives felt the name was too long and lobbied for something else.

Just days before the product was to go out to distributors, Jeff Johnson, the company's third employee, suggested the name Nike, which had come to him in a dream the night before. Nike was the winged Greek Goddess of victory. Although nobody else liked the name or knew what it stood for it seemed better than Dimension Six. Around the same time, Knight had asked a designer friend to propose some ideas for a logo for the new product. She submitted twelve proposals, none of which were liked by anybody at Blue Ribbon. Due to time constraints—the product was set to hit the shelves in days—the management team finally decided to go with the least objectionable logo, "a fat check mark." Thus, the famous Nike "swoosh" was born for a total cost of $35.

In 1973, University of Oregon running star Steve Prefontaine became the first athlete to be paid to wear Nike shoes. Prefontaine epitomized "the athlete against the establishment" attitude that was at the foundation of the company's irreverence and challenge to the status quo. Knight explained, "Pre(fontaine) was a

126

rebel from a working-class background, a guy full of cockiness and pride and guts. Pre's spirit is the cornerstone of this company's soul." Knight had founded the company with the attitude to do whatever it would take to defeat established running shoe companies and "the system." Just as Prefontaine did not care what other people thought, Knight was nurturing a corporate culture along the same lines. Knight explained,

> We were able to get a lot of great ones under contract—people like Steve Prefontaine and Alberto Salazar—because we spent a lot of time at track events and had relationships with the runners, but mostly because we were doing interesting things with our shoes. Naturally, we thought the world stopped and started in the lab and everything revolved around the product.[2]

Nike's first sponsorship of athletes was relatively inexpensive but, more importantly, very productive. Prefontaine never lost a race in four years at the University of Oregon and went on to set a number of U.S. running records. Jon Anderson, another long distance runner, won the Boston Marathon in a pair of Nike shoes. The early success of these Nike-sponsored runners led Knight to sign up athletes in other sports. The abundantly talented, mercurial Ilie Nastase became Nike's first tennis athletic endorser shortly before becoming the world's top-ranked tennis player. The budget was still tight so only the most cost-effective athletes could be signed.

In 1974, Nike introduced to the general public a Bowerman prototype called the Waffle Trainer. The diffusion of the Waffle Trainer benefited from the so-called "pyramid of influence." That is, Nike believed that consumers chose products and brands in the mass market based upon by the preferences and behavior of a small percentage of top athletes. The reality was that the vast majority of athletic shoes were never actually used "on the court" but rather were used in other settings, or just for "walking around." Nevertheless, Nike was convinced that the choices of these more casual users were affected by the choices of more serious athletes. Fueled by this "trickle-down" marketing, it quickly became the best-selling training shoe in the country.

By the end of 1974, Nike revenues had reached $4.8 million and the company employed over 250 people. In 1978, the company officially changed its name from Blue Ribbon Sports to Nike, Inc., reflecting the growing recognition of the Nike brand name and the popularity of the Bowerman innovations. By 1980, the company had 2,700 employees and sales of $270 million, surpassing Adidas as the number one athletic shoe company in the United States with almost 50 percent market share.

The Troubled Years

The popularity of running, however, was beginning to give way in the early 1980s to new categories such as fitness and aerobics. The new trends were dominated by women, a market segment that had thus far remained largely unaddressed by Nike. As a result, growth for Nike started to trail off as competitors such as Reebok were better positioned to ride the aerobics wave. Reebok made a batch of aerobic shoes with soft, garment leather instead of the traditional "tough" athletic shoe leather and introduced "style," "fashion," "comfort," and "for women." Their soft leather shoes were supple, comfortable to wear, and made women's feet look smaller. Suddenly, Reebok became the industry darling.

Nike's reputation for performance and innovation, its dedication to serious athletes, and its focus on the male consumer segment did not help them much in the more fashion-conscious aerobics market. Market share began to drop, and warehouses became overstocked with running shoes. Nike's first layoffs occurred in 1984, followed by two money losing quarters in 1985. Finally, although Nike reached $1 billion in sales in 1986, they lost the market share lead to Reebok. By 1987, Reebok dominated the U.S. athletic shoe market, owning 30 percent of the market as compared to Nike's 18 percent. Phil Knight elaborated:

> Reebok came out of nowhere to dominate the aerobics market, which we completely miscalculated. We made an aerobics shoe that was functionally superior to Reebok's, but we missed the styling. Reebok's shoe was sleek and attractive, while ours was sturdy and clunky. By the time we developed a leather shoe that was both strong and soft, Reebok had established a brand, won a huge chunk of sales, and gained momentum to go right by us.[3]

The Transition Years

Reebok's meteoric rise forced Nike to chart a new direction with a fresh approach to the market. Nike had learned some valuable lessons. Subsequently, the company would put the spotlight on the consumer—not just the product—and become more marketing-oriented as a result. Nike would broaden their marketing effort to embrace consumers and the brand as well as the design and manufacture of products. Rather than copy Reebok's emphasis on style, however, Nike decided to keep their focus on performance but devote more attention to basketball that had continued its recent rise in popularity. Perhaps more importantly, Nike set out to change how they marketed new products, creating a new marketing formula which linked concepts related to shoes, colors, clothes, athletes, logos, and their first-ever wide-spread, mass market television advertising.

Nike had never advertised much because they felt advertising came between the intimate relationship that a runner had with his or her shoes. Advertising and commercialism were felt to be nothing short of heresy for the purist athlete. Nike had only advertised in peer-group running journals, which they tolerated only because they were published by runners themselves. Even then, all advertising remained performance-oriented, with no models, no gimmicks, and no hype. As part of "reinventing" Nike the company, however, decided to take to the airwaves for a new basketball campaign. For the task of developing the campaign, Nike turned to Dan Wieden, president of Wieden and Kennedy, a little-known advertising agency just a short drive from Nike headquarters. Wieden fondly recalls Phil Knight's first word, "Hi. I'm Phil Knight, and I don't believe in advertising." Wieden and Kennedy would soon change his mind.

Nike developed an innovative new cushioning technology that was used first with the Air Max running shoes. The ad that showcased this new shoe debuted in March 1987 and was in its own way a bold innovation, albeit a daring and risky one. The "Revolution in Motion" spot used the there-to-fore untouched Beatles song as an anthem (at the cost of hundreds of thousands of dollars in licensing fees) in a television ad that used novel black and white, 16mm, hand-held cinematography to depict professional athletes and "regular people" of all ages involved in sports. Close-up shots in the ads clearly depicted the heel of the shoe compressing and springing back after contact with the ground. Complimentary print ads were run in horizontal and vertical publications. The campaign debuted in March 1987. Scott Bedbury, Nike's Director of Advertising at the time, recalled:

> The Revolution ad was a powerful brand statement and a massive handshake from Nike to the consumers. The ads successfully got across, both implicitly and explicitly, the product technology. It was able to communicate to a wide range of people but still was true to the Nike brand. It reflected Nike's "soul" and a deep, almost genetic understanding of what it meant to be "Nike" and how that could and should be expressed in advertising.

Air Max was a huge success, selling $75 million at retail in its first year.

In 1985, Nike managed to sign then-rookie guard Michael Jordan to endorse Nike basketball shoes after Adidas, Jordan's first choice, refused to match Nike's offer. Although Jordan was still an "up-and-coming" basketball superstar, most basketball followers agreed that he was going to be something special. Nike bet on Jordan, and it paid off in a big way. His very first commercial began by showing a basketball rolling along an outdoor court toward the future superstar. As Jordan picked up the ball and drove toward the basket, the sound of jet engines roared in the background. As Jordan took flight, the engines screamed louder. The slow motion camera followed Jordan's body as he gracefully glided toward the basket for a full ten seconds. At the end of the thirty seconds, Michael Jordan was a household name and later became the premier superstar in basketball.

The Air Jordan line of basketball shoes literally flew off the shelves. Nike sold over $100 million of Air Jordans in the first year alone. Knight reflected on the success of Air Jordans:

> Basketball, unlike casual shoes, was all about performance, so it fit under the Nike umbrella. And the shoe itself was terrific. It was so colorful that the NBA banned it—which was great....Michael Jordan wore the shoes despite being threatened with a fine, and of course, played like no one has ever played before. It was everything you could ask for, and sales just took off....(Air Jordan's) success showed us that slicing things up into digestible chunks was the wave of the future.[4]

The Dominant Years

The Air Jordan line sparked a new wave of momentum for Nike. As Michael Jordan flew through the air on his way to six championships, the image-consciousness of the market gave way to a re-emphasis on performance. This time it was Reebok who got lost in the midst of a transition. Just as Nike had paid too little attention to the rise of the aerobics trend of the mid-1980s, Reebok paid too little attention to a consumer desire for performance-related products in the late 1980s. Also during this time, new competitors entered the market chasing Reebok, not Nike. Nike stayed on the forefront of performance, while competitors such as L.A. Gear vied with Reebok for control of the fashion market.

While Reebok tried to breathe life into the fashion segment, Nike continued pushing the performance of its shoes. In 1988, Nike aired its first ads in their new "Just Do It" campaign. The $20 million month-long blitz, urging Americans to participate more actively in sports, featured 12 television spots in all. The campaign marked the launch of a category—cross-training shoes designed for athletes who played more than one sport—which was new to Nike and the athletic shoe industry as a whole. One non-celebrity ad featured Walt Stack, an 80 year-old long distance runner, running across the Golden Gate Bridge as part of his daily morning running routine. The "Just Do It" trailer appeared on the screen as the shirtless Stack made his way past the center of the bridge on a chilly San Francisco morning. Talking to the camera as it zoomed in and while still running, Stack remarked, "People ask me how I keep my teeth from chattering when it's cold." Pausing, Stack matter-of-factly replied, "I leave them in my locker."

By 1990, sales had surpassed $2 billion, and Nike had reclaimed the market share lead from Reebok in the United States. Nike successfully applied their new marketing formula of blending performance and attitude through strategic product development, endorsements, and advertising to other categories including tennis and baseball. Nike ads, reflecting the company's character, addressed controversial issues head-on. The ads ranged from Charles Barkley pronouncing that he was "Not a Role Model" to a 1995 ad showcasing a long distance runner afflicted with the AIDS virus. Sports marketing at Nike was now of huge importance. Knight recalled:

> The whole thing happens on TV now. A few years back we were extremely proud of a novel, three-quarter-high shoe we'd developed. But we only sold 10,000 of them the first year. Then John McEnroe had ankle trouble and switched to the shoe. We sold 1 1/2 million pairs the following year. The final game of the NCAA basketball tournament is better than any runway in Paris for launching a shoe. Kids climb up next to the screen to see what the players are wearing.

Nike kept their "finger on the pulse" of the shoe-buying public, in part, through their use of "EKINs" (Nike spelled backwards)—sports-loving employees whose job was to hit the streets to disseminate information about Nike and find out what was on the minds of retailers and consumers. Nike's "Brand Strength Monitor" more formally tracked consumer perceptions three times a year to identify marketplace trends. Nike's inventory control system, called "Futures" also helped Nike to better gauge consumer response and plan production accordingly. Nike required retailers to order up to 80 percent of their purchases six to eight months in advance in return for guaranteed delivery times and a discount of up to 10 percent. Nike sweetened their relationships with retailers such as Foot Locker by also giving them early looks at new models as well as the rights to exclusively sell certain models.

Sales soared past $3 billion in 1991 as Michael Jordan took the Chicago Bulls to their first of six championships. By 1993, Nike athletes included 265 NBA basketball players, 275 NFL football players, and 290 baseball players. Half the teams that won the NCAA college basketball championships over the past ten years had worn Nike shoes. In total, Nike had arrangements with college coaches and athletic departments that resulted in over 60 top tier "Nike schools."

In 1993, Nike decided to put more emphasis on top-of-line performance wear—uniforms and apparel worn in actual competition—through their Organized Team Sports group and F.I.T. lines. Although representing only a small percentage of apparel revenues, these new initiatives were thought to provide halo to other apparel lines and be consistent with broadening the Nike brand meaning to encompass "performance in sports" and not just shoes.

NIKE'S GLOBAL BRAND BUILDING

In 1980, when Nike overtook Adidas as the number one athletic shoe company in the United States, Phil Knight dispatched five employees to Europe to establish a European presence. Though Nike had succeeded in breaking Adidas's dominance in the United States, taking over from the leader in its home arena would be a greater challenge.

Initial Growth

In the early 1980s, the most popular sports in Europe were soccer, track and field, and tennis. If Nike wanted to have a significant presence in Europe, the company would have to establish its name in each of these sports in each of Europe's five primary markets—Germany, France, England, Italy, and Spain—which accounted for the bulk of the European sports shoe and apparel sales.

Nike faced formidable competition in Europe. Adidas, the German shoe company, dominated the European sports market. Together with Puma, a spin-off of Adidas, the two companies controlled over 75 percent of Europe's athletic shoe and apparel market. For decades, the two companies developed a grassroots allegiance of local sports teams, particularly soccer, track and field, tennis, and rugby. They both had endorsement contracts with top European athletes in each of these sports and sponsored many local teams in cities and towns across Europe. Adidas, in particular, was respected for the quality of its shoes and had earned the reputation as the European performance brand. Establishing a presence in Germany, Europe's largest country market, in the face of these two companies was considered nearly impossible.

Nike's European marketing team attacked one sport at a time. Given the company's track and field heritage, Nike initially focused on developing links in track and field, whose sizable popularity in Europe was reflected by the fact that it was the second most televised sport (after soccer). The company sought ex-runners with the same devotion and intensity to the sport as Nike to help develop the brand. Finding such athletes to work with, however, proved to be an elusive task. Nike was typically forced to partner with the largest local athletic shoe and apparel distributor.

In 1981, Nike highlighted American tennis star, John McEnroe, in a set of print ads that were run around the time of Wimbledon. These ads played on McEnroe's "nasty boy" image, showing a Nike tennis shoe and a headline underneath that read, "McEnroe Swears by Them." In another version, the headline read "McEnroe's Favorite Four Letter Word." McEnroe's triumph at Wimbledon that year helped Nike gain badly needed exposure and credibility among European consumers.

Regaining control

By the end of 1987, Nike's European revenues had grown to $150 million, representing 5 percent of the European athletic shoe market and a growing percentage of Nike's total revenues. Compared to its U.S. position, however, Nike's penetration of the European market was insignificant. Perhaps even more disturbing to Nike was its inability to control the growth of its brand. In most countries, the Nike distributor who controlled marketing and advertising rights was not necessarily highly motivated about selling Nike. To overcome this limitation, but still maintain its quality image, Nike restricted its product line to primarily high-end, higher priced shoes. In doing so, the company forfeited volume and market share. Though the company also sold some low-end, relatively inexpensive shoes, it had no product offerings for the expansive "middle market." As a result of this pricing policy, many European consumers saw Nike as an aggressive, expensive American brand.

Because Nike distributors controlled advertising in their local markets, each continued to develop their own interpretation of the Nike brand and identity programs. While Nike embarked on the "Just Do It" umbrella campaign in the U.S., Grey Advertising, the agency that managed the Nike account in five countries, developed separate, and not necessarily reinforcing, ad campaigns in each European country. Nike also did not have the same means of displaying their shoes and retailing them to customers as in the United States—athletic shoe specialty stores did not really exist in Europe.

In late 1987, Nike sent David Kottkamp to head its European operations with a focus on brand building. Kottkamp decided that the only way to take control of the brand was to take greater control of advertising and product strategies. He then focused on repurchasing licensing rights to Nike products from their licensed distributors in Europe.

While Kottkamp was initiating these negotiations with Nike distributors, a task that would take several years, he launched Nike's first centralized print campaign in 1988 as a means to introduce "Air" technology in that market. Despite objections from Nike's European distributors, the campaign achieved some success. In 1989, Nike introduced its "Gospel" campaign. This powerful, uplifting campaign was unquestionably American in its look and Nike in its attitude. Using the tag line,

"True to its [Nike] soul," the campaign ran primarily on MTV Europe and Star TV in Asia, as well as various national television networks.

Regaining Control

Over the next three years, while Kottkamp worked on repurchasing licensing rights, Nike relied heavily on advertising to promote its brand. The direction to take with that advertising, however, was not obvious. Research revealed that a 2-minute TV spot designed to portray Nike products and attitude—featuring Jimi Hendrix's adventurous rendition of the National Anthem at the Woodstock rock festival and the tag line, "Play Hard. Die Old."—was seen as too aggressive and was not well received. Nike attempted to blend centralized and localized work. Nike imported some of its American heroes to promote the brand in Europe; European marketing managers could look at Wieden & Kennedy's latest creations and chose ads they felt were relevant. For example, the "Tennis Lessons" spot that spoofed Andre Agassi's and McEnroe's rebellious image was shown in Italy, Germany, and elsewhere.

By the end of 1991, Kottkamp had successfully regained control of 90 percent of Nike's European distribution. In comparison, Adidas only controlled 65 percent and Reebok only controlled 40 percent of their European distribution. Getting European retailers, who were used to ordering whatever they wanted, whenever they wanted from the Adidas warehouse, to adopt Nike's Futures program—which was very successful in the United States—was a harder sell. Nevertheless, now that Nike had greater control over their marketing, they could concentrate on developing their brand in the manner that they desired.

Nike in 1992

In 1992, Europe represented a tremendous growth opportunity for Nike. At that time, 400 million pairs of athletic footwear were sold in the U.S. Europe, with 130 million *more* people than the States, bought 280 million *fewer* pairs of shoes. The largest buying group there, those in their teens and 20s, owned an average of just two pairs each (compared to an average of at least four pairs in the United States).

There were several explanations for the discrepancy. First, Europeans had a different view of the role of sports and top athletes and were not as idolizing of their sports heroes as were Americans. The American workout ethic, epitomized by health and fitness clubs and a firm belief of the essential importance of exercise, was not as widely embraced in Europe. Moreover, as a general rule, Europeans were slower to embrace sneakers as off-court shoes and were more likely to wear fine leather shoes even in casual settings. Either on or off the court, Europeans just needed fewer athletic shoes.

The image of athletic shoes was changing, however, and sneakers were no longer a dead giveaway that a person was, more likely than not, an American tourist. European teens seemed captivated by the "American" image of Nike and Reebok. By 1992, Nike's European sneaker revenues were approximately $1.1 billion—nearly six times the 1987 figure. Adidas, with over $1.5 billion in revenues, still had more than double the market share of Nike in Europe. Though Adidas still dominated the European market, Nike had made significant inroads in the last five years, and the German giant and its counterpart, Puma, had lost market share to Nike and Reebok.

Nike's two main competitors, Adidas and Reebok, posed very different challenges. Adidas was the established brand with a loyal consumer base, especially among the 35-and-older generation. Its strong grass-roots presence and entrenchment in amateur sports sponsorships, particularly soccer, had bolstered Adidas' number one market position in Europe. Reebok was a relatively new company in Europe, but its success in the U.S. women's fitness market had carried over to Europe. Reebok was the third-place brand in most European countries, behind Adidas and Nike. Determined to overtake Adidas and prevent Reebok from continuing to gain ground, Nike focused its attention on the 1992 Barcelona Olympics, raising their overall global advertising and promotion budget to $240 million, up from $150 million the previous year, committing $50 million to Europe.

With the rise in popularity of basketball as an international sport, Nike planned to lead its marketing charge with its strong stable of basketball superstars. Leading up to the Olympics, U.S. Olympic "Dream Team" members such as Charles Barkley, Michael Jordan and others were featured in European exhibition tours and in a series of ad campaigns. Nike also sought to play up its endorsements of other top flight world-class athletes who would spotlight Nike products in the Olympic Games.

Many European consumers, however, still found the brand intimidating and aggressive. Moreover, retailers bristled at the Nike's Futures program and product mix, viewing the company as arrogant. To reach its growth goals in Europe, Nike needed to find a way to change consumers' perceptions there of Nike as an expensive, aggressive American brand.

Hitting its Stride

Despite some successes, Nike was clearly struggling to extend its U.S. reputation for performance and innovation into the European market. A more grassroots approach was needed to build credibility and relevance with the Nike brand in European sports—especially soccer. As an important first step, Nike became more actively involved as a sponsor of soccer youth leagues, local clubs, and national teams. Unlike their approach to other categories, apparel—not footwear—would provide the entry point to build the consumer franchise for the Nike brand in soccer.

As luck would have it, Brazil, the only national soccer team for which Nike had any real sponsorship during the 1994 World Cup—a number of the Brazilian stars had individual contracts to wear Nike shoes—won the premiere event. Their victory provided two very different benefits for Nike. Internally, it inspired confidence and motivation; externally, it lent credibility to a soccer-crazed world. Other soccer endorsements (in the form of national team and individual sponsorships) soon followed. A Nike ad created for the 1994 World Cup, dubbed "The Wall," showed many of these prominent players springing to life from billboards as they literally kicked a soccer ball around the world. Nike also out-bid Adidas and Reebok for the sponsorship rights to the men's and women's U.S.

national team. Beyond soccer, Nike tried to sign up the best athletes in other countries to push Nike products locally, such as baseball player Hideo Nomo in Japan and Formula I race car champion Michael Schumacher in Germany.

Nike's new focus was to be seen as culturally, geographically, and personally relevant to local consumers abroad. Building on the success of its "Just Do It" campaign in the United States, Nike attempted to introduce the tag line into its European advertising in the spring of 1993. Nike hoped the campaign would successfully communicate Nike's core values of authenticity, performance, and athletics, and help establish an emotional connection with European consumers through sports. The new campaign was a good counterpart to the flashy, Barcelona-inspired Olympic spots featuring celebrity athletes. The "Just Do It" ads featured inspirational visuals of common folk displaying a passion for sport. The four spots featured kids and adults running and playing soccer in the streets, wheelchair athletes climbing mountainous hills as part of a race, and two runners winding their way beside a picturesque lake. Four commercials showing professional athletes engaged in competitive sports were translated and shown in 52 local markets. Overall, Nike allocated $80 million to $100 million to European advertising and promotion in 1993.

NIKE MARKETING EVOLVES

By 1993, Nike's marketing strategy had evolved to a two-tiered approach. Individual markets featured ads with local heroes and local settings while all of Europe saw ads that featured popular sports such as soccer, tennis, and track. This approach enabled Nike to earn credibility at the local level and reach a broad consumer base at the same time. The company increased its marketing intensity, allocating as much as $100 million to European advertising in 1993 alone. As a result of its reworked advertising strategy, Nike's European revenues climbed from $920 million in 1994 to $1.3 billion in 1996, and its lofty goal of European market leadership seemed attainable.

Soon after Nike's ambitious market expansion into Europe the company experienced several setbacks domestically. First, as fashions inevitably changed, Nike found itself behind the curve, much like their experience with the aerobic fitness wave in the 1980s. Many consumers viewed trainers or running shoes as out-of-style, useful only for exercise. Second, Nike's corporate image suffered, due in part to controversial marketing projects (such as contributing $25,000 to the legal defense fund for Tonya Harding—the figure skater accused of conspiring to injure a competitor before the 1994 Winter Olympic Trials) and accusations of unethical labor practices in its Asian factories. Perhaps worst of all, Nike was losing its appeal in the eyes of its core consumers—youths between 12 and 18 years of age. According to one research firm,[5] 40 percent of kids surveyed considered Nike to be one of the "coolest" brands in 1998, a 12 percent drop from the previous year. As Nike pursued global business, the company faced the dual challenges of increasing its international market share while ensuring that its image did not tarnish in the process.

Growth Through Soccer

Nike's first truly global advertising campaign consisted of sponsorships and advertisements during the 1994 World Cup. Recognizing that soccer represented one of the best entry points into new markets, Nike embarked on a mission to become the world's leading soccer equipment provider by 2002. Domestically, Nike began sponsoring the U.S. national teams in 1994, and shortly thereafter signed on with Major League Soccer to sponsor five of the ten teams in the league. In 1997, Nike spent an unprecedented $200 million to sponsor Brazil's national team for ten years, and added several other countries to its list, including Italy and Nigeria. Nike also supported their high-profile campaigns by sponsoring youth soccer leagues in Europe and formed a tournament called the Nike International Premier Cup that featured the best youth teams from throughout the continent. Nike's goal in sponsoring both world champion teams and local clubs was to become a household name in all levels of soccer competition, as market leader Adidas had been for decades.

A Kinder, Gentler Marketing Approach

Throughout its campaigns in the years between 1994 and 1997, much of Nike's advertising kept in the tradition of its irreverent, rebellious spirit. For example, in 1996, Nike targeted audiences worldwide during the Summer Olympics with 32 separate print and television ads. Among the most notable advertisement from the $35 million campaign was a controversial series featuring athletes pushing themselves to physically and visually agonizing limits. The television version of this ad used a boisterous Iggy Pop song called "Search and Destroy" as its soundtrack and showed graphic footage of a boxer losing his mouthpiece after a punch as well as a clip of American marathoner Bob Kempainen vomiting on his shoes after winning the U.S. marathon trials in 1996. The latter image appeared in a print campaign with the caption "If you can't stand the heat, get out of Atlanta."

This irreverence did not sit well with many European consumers, however. An ad that ran during the 1996 European Soccer Championships pitted a team of international soccer stars against a satanic figure and assorted demons on the pitch of a rather hellish stadium. Called "Nike vs. Evil," the controversial ad received a strongly ambivalent response, meeting with success in some markets but drawing considerable ire from the media in others. Some television stations even refused to run the ad during prime time, for fear of upsetting child viewers.

Compounding this image problem was the company's extravagant spending as it burst onto the soccer scene. Nike's deep pockets enabled it to have an impact immediately, in terms of marketing and sponsorships, but some consumers resented what they saw as a powerful corporation muscling in on smaller heritage brands like Umbro, Diadora, and Puma. Even market leader Adidas, which was several times larger than Nike in European soccer sales for most of the 1990s, met with success when it marketed itself as an underdog to Nike. Phil Knight, responding to these image problems, said, "Now that we've reached a certain size, there's a fine line between being a rebel and being a bully."[6] For Nike, casting itself as anti-establishment fit poorly with consumers who perceived the company as *the* establishment.

As a result, Nike adjusted its global advertising strategy in 1997. In soccer, the local and national team sponsorships were kept because they were seen to provide links to soccer's heritage. The violence in the advertising was toned down considerably, and new ads featured famous American Nike pitchmen like Michael Jordan and Charles Barkley playing soccer with Euro stars. Nike spent considerable R&D funds sending a research team on a global expedition to study foot morphology for application to better soccer shoe. Nike applied the results of this research to the design of their flagship soccer shoe, the Mercurial, which debuted in 1998. To fine tune their general global advertising so it resonated with regional tastes, the company sought cultural input from experts residing in major national markets like Japan, Germany, and Brazil. Nike used two of its best-recognized athletes, Tiger Woods and Brazilian soccer star Ronaldo, in global ads to project a more international image.

Growth in Asia

After Nike had safely established itself as a contender in the European market, with sales exceeding $1 billion in 1996 and growing another 38 percent in 1997, the company sought global growth in Asia, Latin America, South America, Africa, and the Middle East. Of these other regions, Asia harbored the most potential in terms of customers since over half of the world's population resided there. Nike had long operated manufacturing plants in Asian countries such as Japan, Taiwan, and South Korea, but before the 1990s the company had not focused on Asia as a target market. Japan was the first country to embrace Nike products. As early as 1992, Japan imported $100 million worth of Nike products, and by 1997, Nike had surpassed Japanese brands Asics and Mizuno to occupy the market leader position.

In the last few years of the decade, Nike began marketing projects in an effort to capitalize on the large number of potential customers in other Asian countries. China received much of the advertising attention, primarily since its population of over one billion spent over $2 billion annually on sneakers. Nike abandoned its brash advertising attitude in China, learning from the mixed reactions it received in Europe. Nike's Asian ads celebrated local athletes as heroes, with hopes to improve the local perception of its brand.

Asian sales soared into late 1997. Rapid international growth drove Nike's stock price above $70 a share for the first time in the company's history. Japan, where sales had grown fivefold over the previous seven years, now constituted Nike's second-largest market. Then the bottom fell out of the Asian economy, and suddenly Nike's booming business there stalled. The collapsed economy withered sales figures and left Nike facing canceled orders from retailers everywhere. In Japan, where shoes had sold for as much as $200 dollars a pair in recent years, sales dropped precipitously and distributors were left with excess Nike products exceeding 2 million units.

The results were disastrous for Nike's overall business. In 1998, its stock price fell sharply and the company reported its first earnings decrease in thirteen years. Nike's employee base had expanded from 9,500 in 1994 to almost 22,000 in 1998 but in early 1998 the company announced plans to trim this figure by 7 percent. Nike also cut $100 million from its advertising budget, dropping many lower profile endorsers and sponsorships. In spite of the prolonged Asian recession, Nike executives remained optimistic about growth in the region. By mid-1999, despite a continuing sales decline, orders were up 19 percent in the region while canceled orders dropped from 40 to 15 percent. Growth in Asia had returned, though not to pre-recession levels.

NIKE'S IMAGE CRISIS

The Asian economic collapse was not the only factor contributing to Nike's global sales woes during fiscal 1998. Domestically, and to some extent abroad, Nike's corporate image suffered from negative public perceptions and increasing public outcry over the company's labor practices in Asia and the ubiquity of its corporate logo, the swoosh.

In 1997 a labor watchdog agency published the results of Ernst & Young's 1996 audit of a Nike factory in Vietnam that found unsafe working conditions there. The audit included findings that workers were forced to work 65-hour weeks and improperly compensated for overtime labor, worked in areas with poor ventilation, exposed to dangerous levels of the carcinogens, and earned little more than ten dollars a week. As the media reported further findings of low wages, teenage laborers, and poor treatment of employees, human rights and workers' rights groups lined up to attack Nike. Organized opposition to Nike's global practices ranged from boycotts of the company's products to letters-of-protest from congresspersons to a lawsuit against the company charging that "lies" about the company's labor practices constituted false advertising.

Nike's Counter-Measures

In response to the allegations and condemnations pouring in, Nike implemented comprehensive changes in its corporate labor policy. With respect to the audit, the company first stated that the unsafe conditions reported in the 1996 had already been improved, via the installation of new ventilation systems, and the enforcement of its pre-existing limit of 60-hour weeks. Furthermore, Nike asserted that though wages for its Vietnam factory workers were extremely low by Western standards, Nike workers enjoyed an average salary well above the national average. In 1998, the company formally announced the implementation of new global labor standards. These new standards included age requirements for footwear workers of 18 years, the use of water-based solvents and adhesives in manufacture, compliance with OSHA indoor air quality levels, and monitoring of labor practices by independent agencies.

The same year, Nike created a Corporate Responsibility Division that consolidated the labor, environmental, and community action groups already part of the company. The stated mission of this new division was "to lead in corporate citizenship through programs that reflect caring for the world family of Nike, our teammates, our consumers, and those who provide services to Nike." Additionally,

Nike became a charter member of the Fair Labor Association, a White House initiative that establishes a code of conduct for global manufacturers and accredits monitoring processes in the industry. Nike enlisted FLA-approved PriceWaterhouseCoopers to conduct annual audits of each of their 500 global factories.

Nike's measures to improve and monitor its global manufacturing conditions met with decidedly mixed responses. Although some commended Nike for its community involvement, its environmental consciousness, and its comparatively high wages and clean factories, others continued to condemn the company. Some activists claimed that annual audits paint an inaccurate portrait of actual conditions, since in some cases the factory management knew the date of the audit in advance and modified conditions so they appeared more favorable. Others complained that Nike employees' yearly pay did not constitute a "living wage" and continued to accuse Nike of using "sweatshop labor." To respond to the continued accusations, Nike initiated measures to provide the public with access to information about its labor practices and the results of audits.

In 2001, Nike released its first Corporate Responsibility Report in an attempt to assess and communicate the impact of how the company ran its business. The report included a series of detailed reports of Nike's efforts at developing environmental sustainability, its efforts toward understanding and managing global labor compliance, its commitment to diversity, and the company's involvement in local communities. Nike continued these efforts in the ensuing years, with Phil Knight acknowledging past troubles. In response to continuing criticism of working conditions in underdeveloped countries, Knight wrote in the 2004 Corporate Responsibility Report, "After a bumpy original response, an error for which yours truly was responsible, we focused on making working conditions better and showing that to the world." He continued, "Just producing this report goes far beyond transparency. It becomes a tool for improving both our management of business and in giving us clues about what we need to do next."

Swoosh Ubiquity

As Nike's labor crisis in Asia seeped into the American public's consciousness, so did an increasing awareness of the company's corporate ubiquity. Nike's shorthand symbol—the swoosh—appeared on shoes, jerseys, hats, billboards, and soccer balls across the globe with remarkable and, to some consumers, alarming frequency. One shoe model in particular boasted swooshes in nine different locations. Writers sometimes referred to newspaper sports sections as the "Nike Pages" because of the abundance of swooshes on pictured athletes. One author wrote a piece for *Sports Illustrated* entitled "The Swooshification of the World" that imagined a future in which the swoosh transcended sports to become a letter of the alphabet and the new presidential seal, among other things. As of 2000, 97 percent of American citizens recognized the brand logo, which perhaps explained why the average American spent $20 a year on Nike products. But many consumers felt that the overabundance of swooshes was symptomatic of Nike's aggressive corporate philosophy, which had fallen out of favor with consumers in recent years. In the eyes of many members of the American public, the swoosh represented one or both of two modern societal ills—the commercialization of sports and the globalization of capitalism.

Because the swoosh was rapidly accumulating negative connotations, Nike executives began searching for ways to downplay the logo's visibility. Nike spokesman Lee Weinstein explained that "having the swoosh be the ID for everything we do is probably too much pressure on that symbol."[7] Phil Knight later joined in the criticism of the swoosh's ubiquity by saying, "If you blast [the swoosh] on every T shirt, every sign in the soccer match, you dilute it."[8] Mark Parker, Nike's vice president for global footwear, put it more succinctly when he stated "clearly, we had the swoosh on everything and it was just ridiculous."[9]

Beginning in 1998, Nike often removed the swoosh from its corporate advertising and letterhead and replaced it with the script lowercase word "nike." The company developed separate business units for its proprietary Jordan, All Conditions Gear (ACG), and NikeGolf brands. Each brand claimed its own logo, and management was empowered to develop a unique marketing strategy using the advertising firm of their choice.

A sub-brand of shoes and apparel called the Nike Alpha Project emerged as a strategy to diversify the brand's appearance and subdue the swoosh. Though products in the Alpha Project line bore the Nike name, a new logo made up of five small dots arranged in a horizontal line usually replaced the swoosh. Nike positioned the Alpha Project products as the company's most technologically advanced products, and company president Tom Clarke referred to them as "the modern-day version of what Nike's mission has always been, creating breakthrough products for people who compete and recreate." Despite all the efforts to de-emphasize the swoosh, Nike officials recognized that the logo aided the company's rise significantly and stressed that the swoosh would not be abandoned. Subsequently, the Alpha brand was gradually phased out, and two new swoosh-bearing brands replaced it as technological torchbearers for the brand, Nike+ running shoes and apparel and Nike Pro athletic apparel.

NIKE IN THE NEW MILLENNIUM

Positive Indicators

In spite of financial and market setbacks that occurred in the late 1990s, Nike had reason to think positively about its global corporate position in coming years. Despite falling domestic revenues in 1998 and 1999, Nike's total revenues rose on the strength of growth in international markets, especially Europe (Exhibit 1). In 1999, a year in which every other regional market experienced tapered revenues, the company's European revenues rose, albeit slightly. Two significant contributors to continuing annual revenue growth in Europe were Nike's success in soccer and apparel. Their global market share in soccer products increased more than sevenfold between 1994 and 2000, and sales exceeded $375 million in fiscal 1999. Additionally, in 1999 the company's soccer orders from Europe grew over 100 percent from the previous year. Nike's total apparel sales rose against declining footwear sales in 1997 and 1998. Though global apparel sales flattened in 1999, apparel revenue in Europe rose 26 percent, on top of 34 percent the previous year.

Though soccer was Nike's most important global game in 2000, a Nike athlete from a different sport garnered international attention. Tiger Woods provided the new sub-brand NikeGolf with a marketing boost as he dominated the PGA tour in 2000 using Nike's specially designed Tour Accuracy ball. With victories at the U.S. Open, British Open, and PGA championships, Tiger became only the second player in the history of modern golf to win three major tournaments in one year. After his record 15-stroke victory at the U.S. Open in June, Nike estimated that sales of their golf balls rose between 50 and 75 percent within one month. Nike also stood to gain additional advertising power in international markets from Tiger's exceptional play, since Nike had successfully employed the international superstar in worldwide advertising campaigns before. According to Mike Kelly, vice president of marketing for Nike Golf, in 2000 Tiger enjoyed even greater popularity in Asia than he did in the U.S. and compared the golfer to Michael Jordan in terms of "transcend[ing] his sport."[10]

Nike scored big again in 2005 when Tiger won the 2005 Masters. Clinging to a one-stroke lead when starting the par-three 16th hole, Woods hit his tee shot past the green. He chipped from the rough and sent the ball 25 feet toward the hole. The ball slowly rolled toward the cup and settled on the lip for almost two full seconds—with the black Nike swoosh logo visible—before dropping into the hole for a birdie. The live shot and subsequent replays were estimated to be worth over $1 million in free advertising for Nike.

Expansion of Brand Portfolio

Nike had always focused on growing their core brand and had a spotty record of acquisition activity. In 1988, Nike made its first acquisition, purchasing the luxury shoe, handbag, and accessory maker Cole Haan. It was not until 1995 that Nike made their next move and purchased Bauer, the world's leading manufacturer of hockey equipment and skates. Nike made this purchase for $409 million.

Acquisition activity picked up starting in 2002. That year, Nike purchased Hurley, a company that focused on apparel and footwear for teenagers participating in board sports such as surfing and skateboarding. Realizing that the "retro" look was back in vogue and consumers were increasingly looking for brands that had been popular years ago, Nike acquired Converse in 2003 for $310 million. Converse's biggest product was the Chuck Taylor basketball shoe, a model first produced in 1923 but became immensely popular in the 1950s. Nike followed this move in 2004 by paying $43 million for Exeter Brands Group, maker of the Starter brand of athletic apparel.

Nike had multiple goals in mind when making these acquisitions. They were looking for brand diversity and ways to provide additional avenues for growth. More importantly, they were looking to segment their business by customer. Hurley was a teen brand that was mostly fashion focused. Converse was lower priced (relative to Nike) and capitalized on the strong classic and retro trend. It was hoped that Starter would provide an opportunity to address the low end through distribution at retailers like Wal-Mart. These new brands had an immediate impact on Nike's financial performance. In fiscal 2004, "Other Revenues," of which these acquired brands are all a part, rose 51 percent to $1.4 billion, with the Converse acquisition accounting for 24 percent of this increase. This operating segment continued to grow, rising to $1.9 billion in 2006.

Strengthened Competition
Athletic footwear had always been a competitive market, but the competition heated up in the new millennium.

Adidas was the number two sportswear company in the world behind Nike, and fought aggressively to close the gap. In 2004, the company unveiled a new slogan, "Impossible is nothing." Initial ads starred boxing legend Muhammad Ali and international ads featured local stars. They continued to sign world-class athletes to endorse their products, including soccer star David Beckham and NBA players Kevin Garnet and Tim Duncan. Adidas drew strength from the Sport Heritage division of the company; this division put out classic, old-style shoes and apparel that targeted urban youth and accounted for 20 percent of sales in 2003. The company added the "mi adidas" custom-fit shoe technology to many of its performance stores. This technology allowed trained store personnel to not only measure length and width of a customer's foot, but also measure weight distribution to determine the exact size and support needed to create a perfect fit. Adidas had a strong international presence with 1,500 stores in China in 2005 and 40 new stores per month. The biggest opportunity, and perhaps greatest risk, for the company came with the introduction of the Adidas 1 shoe in early 2005. This $250 shoe had an in-sole computer that adjusted heel cushioning in real time according to changes in the running surface. Adidas planned to produce only 10,000 of the shoes in the first year, to both drive exclusivity and hedge their bet on this expensive new technology. Adidas launched television ads in 2005 and 2006 to support the product launch.

Reebok, who briefly dominated the U.S. shoe market in the late 1980s but realized that consumers did not recognize their logo, looked to regain dominance in 2003 with a $50 million global campaign that centered on its "vector" logo. They hoped to make the vector symbolize both performance and authenticity. Reebok continued to use athletes to endorse their products, focusing on NBA stars like Allen Iverson and tennis players such as Andy Roddick. Reebok scored a coup in 2003 when they wrestled Yao Ming, a 7-foot-5-inch Shanghai native from Nike and signed him to a deal worth $100 million.

Aside from athlete endorsements, Reebok looked to get another kind of credibility—street credibility. In 2002 the company launched its Rbk division to address the global youth culture through the connection between sports and music. In 2003, the company created signature shoe lines for rap stars Jay-Z and 50 Cent. 50 Cent (aka Curtis Jackson) said, "Reebok's Rbk collection is the real thing when it comes to connecting with street and hip-hop culture."[11]

New Balance was another major competitor in performance footwear. The company, whose global sales topped $1.5 billion in 2005, took an opposite approach to their advertising. Eschewing professional athletes, a trademark tenet of the company has always been "Endorsed by No One." New Balance launched a new ad campaign in 2005 asking people to consider why they play sports and what values they get out of it. The full tagline reads, "There are two motivations in sports. Which is yours? For Love or Money?"

Product Innovation

Phil Knight continued to focus on innovation. The Nike Sport Research Lab (also called the "Innovation Kitchen") was housed on the ground floor of the Mia Hamm building on Nike's 175-acre headquarters campus in Beaverton, Oregon. There, over 30 personnel studied biomechanics, physiology, and sensory/perception in order to develop cutting edge products for all types of athletic gear. In 2000, Nike introduced its Shox technology. Shox were small columns, made mostly of rubber and usually used four at a time in a square formation in the heel of the shoe. Nike claimed that Shox not only absorbed impact from heel strike, they also "spring back" adding more power to a runner's stride. Nike also introduced the "Total 90" concept, a range of equipment to help players perform over the 90 minutes of a soccer match. These products included the Air Zoom Total 90 shoe, the Total 90 Aerow soccer ball, and the Total 90 apparel featured Nike's Cool Motion technology to keep players cool.

In 2005, the company launched Nike Free. This shoe was designed to strengthen legs and feet by imitating bare foot movement. The principle was that a bare foot landed more evenly than a foot wearing a typical athletic shoe. This even landing distributed pressure over a greater area—which reduced stress on the legs, and encouraged the body to align more correctly. Nike Free provided runners with the benefits of being barefoot, yet still protected their feet.

Nike explored some non-traditional areas as well. In 2005 they announced the introduction of an exclusive brand of urban-themed clothing under the name Blue Ribbon Sports. These products—which included jeans, belts, sweaters, and woven shirts—were sold at high-end retailers like Barney's and Fred Segal. Industry insiders said that Nike had brought in rapper Sean Combs (aka P. Diddy) to help design the line. Nike also teamed up with eye-care-products maker Bausch & Lomb to create special contact lenses that would make baseballs and golf balls easier to see. The company also planned to introduce special high-contrast balls that were designed to be more easily picked up by the lenses' filtering optics.

Marketing Innovation

In order to keep growing the brand and reach new consumers, Nike determined that it needed to place more emphasis on women and their specific needs. The task of heading up Nike apparel division was given to Mindy Grossman, a veteran of companies such as Chaps, Polo, and Tommy Hilfiger. Upon her hiring in 2000, Grossman did not relocate to Nike headquarters in Oregon, but remained in New York City, where she could be close to Seventh Avenue and the latest fashion trends. In 2002, Nike opened six Nike Goddess boutiques, featuring workout gear for running, biking, yoga, and Pilates. At the end of fiscal year 2003, apparel sales had climbed 11.7 percent, compared to just 5.4 percent for footwear sales.

Nike furthered its offerings directed at "real" women and dealt a blow to the wafer-thin body image in 2005 when they introduced a campaign that celebrated women's "big butts, thunder thighs, and tomboy knees." The ads, created by Wieden & Kennedy, portrayed six different parts of the body, including a set of bruised knees with copy that read:

> My knees are tomboys. They get bruised and cut every time I play soccer. I'm proud of them and wear my dresses short. My mother worries I will never marry with knees like that. But I know there is someone out there who will say to me: I love you and I love your knees. I want the four of us to grow old together. Just do it.

There were no television spots in the campaign, which was designed to drive women to Nikewomen.com and, ultimately, to its fitness apparel. Nancy Monsarrat, Nike's U.S. ad director, explained, "Women come in all shapes and sizes, which is no surprise, but when you talk to women in an honest way, they respond."[12]

Additionally, Nike created a way for customers to design their own Nike products through its NIKEiD.com website. A customer could pick a style of Nike shoes, golf balls, watches, or gym bags, and then customize the color scheme and even add their own name. Finished products were delivered in three to four weeks in stylish suede-lined boxes and suede bags for the product.

Nike took the idea of allowing customers to design their own products one step further in 2005 when they purchased a 23-story billboard in Times Square. Passersby with a cell phone could call a toll-free number and use their keypad to choose aspects of a sneaker they prefer and then build it in real time on the giant billboard, for the entire city to see. "The more you allow people to stop what they are doing and interact with a brand, the better it's going to be," said John Mayo-Smith, vice president of technology at R/GA, the agency that handled the campaign. He added, "But just as important, the people who are watching the sign are getting a brand experience, too."[13]

International Push Pays Off

In 2003, Nike took in more revenue from its international divisions than from the United States—$5.1 billion versus $4.6 billion. This trend grew through 2005, as the company posted revenue from international divisions of nearly $6.9 billion, compared to $5.1 billion from the United States (see Exhibits 1 and 2 for a breakdown of Nike revenue. See Exhibit 3 for a comparison of Nike geographic revenues compared to its competitors).

The 2004 Summer Olympics in Athens proved to be a windfall for Nike. Athletes wearing Nike products took home 50 gold medals, and dozens more earned silver and bronze. In the men's 1,500-meter run, all three medallists wore the same Air Zoom shoe. The top four finishers in the men's 100-meter dash all wore Nike apparel as well. More importantly, the company used the Olympics to make a stronger push into China. When hurdler Liu Xiang won gold and became China's first Olympic medallist in a short-distance speed event, Nike swung into action before most Chinese new they even had a new hero. Moments after the race finished, Nike launched a television ad in China showing Xiang destroying the field and then raising his arms in victory with the trademark swoosh on his shoulder.

China was a major battleground for footwear and apparel sales. The market there was valued at $3 billion in 2004, but had been experiencing double-digit growth since 2000, and was expected exceed $6 billion by 2008. Of the companies jockeying for position in China, Nike led the pack, with 10 percent of the market. They had 1,200 stores across the country and added about 10 new shops a week. In 2004, Nike sales rose 66 percent, to $300 million. Adidas doubled its sales in 2004 to $280 million, allowing the German company to creep into the number two spot with 9.3 percent of the market. Adidas had 1,300 stores in 250 cities and planned to have 4,000 stores in 400 cities by 2008. Both companies recently surpassed Li-Ning, the previous market leader. Li-Ning, founded by the gymnast who won three gold medals at the 1984 Los Angeles Olympics, slipped to the number three position, with an 8.7 percent share and sales of about $260 million for the year. The Chinese company had 2,500 stores covering every province in China, and planned to open 1,500 more by 2008.

Some analysts believed that Nike success in China resulted from China's one-child policy. That is, parents were willing to spend more on their one child, which bode well for high priced brands like Nike. Others believed that Nike realized the new middle class in China desired Western culture and brought many aspects of American culture to its marketing efforts in China.

Nike's goal in China was to migrate inland from the richer east-coast towns and be prepared to take advantage of the outpouring of interest of sports that would presumably accompany the 2008 Summer Olympics in Beijing. At those Olympics, 21 of China's 28 squads would compete in Nike shoes. But in a possible situation reminiscent of the 1992 Olympics, where the U.S. Dream Team resisted wearing Reebok warm-ups to the medal ceremony, any Chinese medal-winners in 2008 will pick up their medals wearing the official Adidas-sponsored uniform (Adidas bid to be the Official Sportswear Partner of the 2008 Olympics, at a cost of approximately $80 million).

Competition Heats Up

In August 2005, Adidas announced that it had agreed to purchase Reebok for $3.8 billion. This deal initially gave Adidas a combined 21 percent of the U.S. athletic shoe market, compared to Nike's 36 percent (which equaled half of all athletic shoes sold in the entire world).[14] However, by 2006, Nike's U.S. share had risen to 38 percent and Adidas-Reebok had dropped to 16.5 percent.

Internationally, the deal gave Adidas a combined 28 percent of the athletic shoe market that trailed Nike by only 3 percent and put more pressure on Nike internationally. [15] Adidas's spokesperson, Jan Runau, explained that the company planned to expand Reebok sales in Europe and Asia, "where Reebok is relatively small and Adidas is very strong." [16] Nike executives remained optimistic and remarked that the new combined company was "like and athlete: When you get some good competition, you tend to raise (performance) to the next level." [17]

After the announcement, Adidas's stock tumbled 22 percent in the fourth quarter of 2005, however it recovered soon thereafter based on its strength in the soccer market and upcoming World Cup. One analysts explained, "I think Adidas would have fared much better if it had really concentrated on its own brand." In 2006, Adidas went forward with an aggressive marketing strategy and announced and 11-year deal to provide the NBA and WNBA with its uniforms. Executives hoped this would help the company break into new markets and increase market share.

Executive Shuffle in the Corporate Office

In late 2004, Knight relinquished the title of CEO and passed those duties off to Bill Perez, former President and CEO of privately held S.C. Johnson, maker of Drano, Windex, and Ziploc bags. Though Perez had experience in managing a family of brands, many questioned how this experience in household goods would translate to Nike's footwear and apparel brands. After little more than a year into Perez's tenure, Phil Knight approached the Nike board to address the problems with Perez as CEO. According to Knight, Perez did not fit with the company's culture or industry and, with the board's approval, eventually forced him to resign on January 20. Even though he was an outsider, some were surprised that Perez did not fit in at Nike, since upon giving him the job Knight had cited his belief that Perez would work well with the culture.[18] Yet lack of fit proved too much to overcome, even for an experienced manager like Perez. Said one management consultant who worked with Nike in the past, "People who don't get the culture don't stick around very long. They know they don't fit. That's it."[19]

Following the Perez saga, Nike looked inside the company for its next CEO. In January 2006, Knight approached Mark Parker, a 27 year veteran with the company and President of the Nike brand since 2001 to take the reigns of CEO. Parker accepted the position stating, "I've had a great relationship with Phil through the years. We have the same philosophy, same approach to business, same view on the industry."[20] Knight expected a better working relationship with Parker as well, stating, "There is no question communication between Mark Parker and me will be better than between me and Bill."[21] Knight stayed on as Chairman, and was expected to maintain an active role in the company as he owned 36 percent of Nike's common shares and 80 percent of the voting stock.

CONCLUSION

Entering 2006, Nike's business looked sound. It was the number one athletic footwear and apparel company in the world. In fiscal 2005, Nike had earned over $13 billion in revenue and the company's stock was soaring around $82 per share (Exhibit 4). Nike had over 24,000 employees around the world. The company continued to sign high-profile athletes such as LeBron James and reap the benefits of those associations. In fact, research showed that 64 percent of all teens had a positive view of the Nike brand.

Despite the positives, some challenges lay ahead for the company. Although Nike held a strong lead in footwear and apparel markets in the United States, Parker and Knight faced the difficult task of maintaining the company's international growth, especially given the potential market power of the combined Adidas-Reebok. New CEO Parker also had to preserve Nike's reputation as an innovator and maintain Nike's strong brand equity domestically and perhaps more importantly, abroad.

DISCUSSION QUESTIONS

1. How would you characterize Nike's brand image and sources of brand equity in the United States?
2. How have Nike's efforts to become a global corporation affect its sources of brand equity and brand image in the United States, Europe, and Asia?
3. Are sponsorships and endorsements vital to Nike's business? For instance, what effect would Nike becoming an official sponsor for the Olympics have on the company's relationship with consumers?
4. Why did Nike become a target for critics of globalization? Do you think Nike's response to allegations of unfair global labor practices was appropriate and/or effective? Is Nike truly concerned about these issues?
5. Evaluate Nike's acquisitions and the brands now under its control. Do these acquisitions make sense for Nike? What, if any, brands should Nike try to acquire next?
6. How important is "fashion" to Nike? Are they a performance apparel company, or a fashion company? What is more important for Nike when they enter a new market like China? Fashion or performance?
7. Should Nike do anything different to defend its position now that Adidas and Reebok have joined forces?

Exhibit 1: Breakdown of Nike Revenues (in millions)

U.S. Region	FY2006	FY2005	FY2004	FY2003	FY2002	FY2001	FY2000	FY1999
Footwear	$3,832.2	$3,358.2	$3,070.4	$3,019.5	$3,135.5	$3,208.9	$3,351.2	$3,244.6
Apparel	1,591.6	1,457.7	1,433.5	1,351.0	1,255.7	1,260.3	1,154.4	1,293.4
Equipment	298.7	313.4	289.8	287.9	278.4	349.8	226.5	212.7
Total	5,722.5	5,129.3	4,793.7	4,658.4	4,669.6	4,819.0	4,732.1	4,750.7
EMEA Region								
Footwear	2,454.3	2,500.0	2,232.2	1,896.0	1,543.8	1,422.8	1,309.4	1,207.3
Apparel	1,559.0	1,497.1	1,333.8	1,133.1	977.9	976.3	933.9	917.7
Equipment	313.3	284.5	268.4	212.6	174.8	185.7	163.7	168.8
Total	4,326.6	4,281.6	3,834.4	3,241.7	2,696.5	2,584.8	2,407.0	2,293.8
Asia Pacific Region								
Footwear	1,044.1	962.9	855.3	730.6	638.2	632.4	557.0	455.3
Apparel	815.6	755.5	612.3	497.8	400.6	374.8	321.0	319.8
Equipment	194.1	178.9	145.8	120.8	96.1	102.8	77.1	69.4
Total	2,053.8	1,897.3	1,613.4	1,349.2	1,134.9	1,110.0	955.1	844.5
Americas Region								
Footwear	635.3	478.6	412.0	337.3	359.1	359.6	343.9	311.2
Apparel	201.8	169.1	165.8	148.1	167.1	152.2	137.7	146.2
Equipment	67.8	48.1	47.0	41.6	41.9	27.3	12.5	11.7
Total	904.9	695.8	624.8	527.0	568.1	539.1	494.1	469.1
Other brands	1,947.1	1,735.7	1,428.3	920.7	823.9	435.9	406.8	418.8
Total Revenues	$14,954.9	$13,739.7	$12,253.1	$10,697.0	$9,893.0	$9,488.8	$8,995.1	$8,776.9

Source: Company Reports

148

Exhibit 2: Breakdown of Nike Revenues by Region
(as percentage of total Footwear, Apparel, Equipment revenues, 2006)

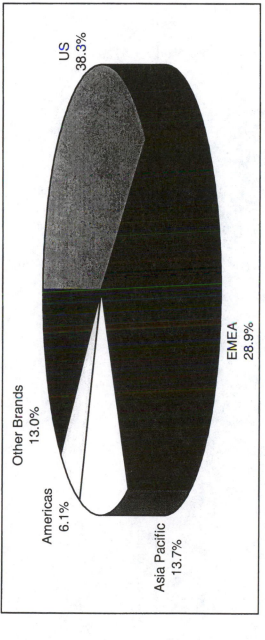

US
38.3%

Other Brands
13.0%

Americas
6.1%

Asia Pacific
13.7%

EMEA
28.9%

Source: Company Reports

Exhibit 2 (cont.)

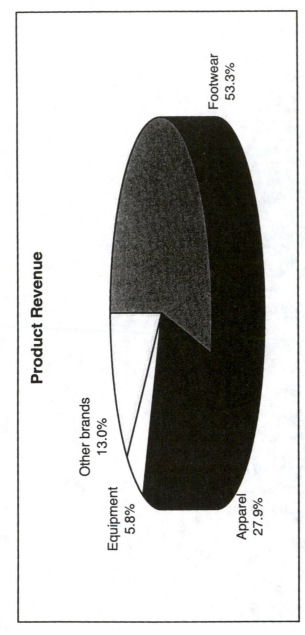

Product Revenue

Other brands
13.0%

Equipment
5.8%

Apparel
27.9%

Footwear
53.3%

Source: Company Reports

150

Exhibit 3: Geographic Distribution of Sales, 2004

Company	U.S.	Americas	EMEA	Asia/Pacific	Other
Nike	39%	5%	31%	13%	11%
Puma	20%	0%	69%	11%	0%
Adidas	25%	3%	54%	18%	1%
Reebok	58%	0%	33%	0%	9%
Timberland	62%	0%	30%	7%	1%
K-Swiss	87%	0%	6%	0%	7%
Others	82%	2%	%	6%	7%
Total	45%	3%	34%	11%	7%

Source: Company Reports

Exhibit 4: Nike's Stock Price Performance (1996 - April 2006)

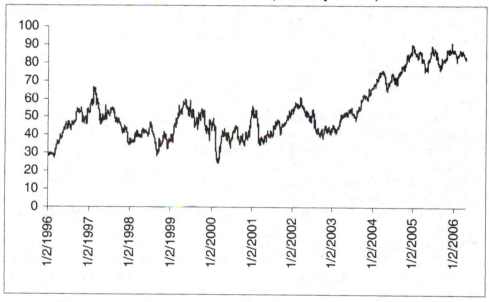

REFERENCES

1 This case was made possible through the cooperation of Nike and the assistance of David Kottkamp, General Manager of Nike International; Liz Dolan, VP of Marketing; Bill Zeitz, Director, International Advertising; Steve Miller, Director, Sports Marketing; and Nelson Farris, Director, Corporate Education. Leslie Kimerling, Sanjay Sood, and Keith Richey assisted in the preparation and writing of the case, which was last updated and revised by Jonathan Michaels and Lowey Bundy Sichol, under the supervision of Professor Kevin Lane Keller.

2 Geraldine E. Willigan, "High Performance Marketing: An Interview with Nike's Phil Knight." *Harvard Business Review*, July-August 1992, pp. 91-101.

3 Ibid.

4 Ibid.

5 Teenage Research Unlimited

6 *Time*, March 30, 1998.

7 CNNSI.com, September 16, 1998.

8 *BusinessWeek*, February 21, 2000.

9 The *New York Times Magazine*, September 13, 1998.

10 The *Chicago Tribune*, July 5, 2000

11 Rich Thomaselli, "Reebok Signs Rappers Jay-Z and 50 Cent to Shoe Deals." AdeAge.com, June 16, 2003.

12 AdAge.com, August 15, 2005.

13 Kris Oser, "Build Your Own Nike Shoe—Above Times Square." AdAge.com, May 9, 2005.

14 Matthew Karnitsching and Stephanie Kang, "Adidas Tries to Broaden Appeal with Acquistion of Reebok." The *Wall Street Journal*, August 4, 2005.

15 William McCall. "Adidas-Reebok merger poses challenge to Nike." *AP Business Writer*. January 26, 2006.

16 William McCall. "Adidas-Reebok merger poses challenge to Nike." *AP Business Writer*. January 26, 2006.

17 Helen Jung, "Nike's CEO Parker looks forward to next steps." The *Oregonian*. January 29, 2006.

18 Daniel Roth, "Can Nike Still Do It Without Phil Knight." *Time*, April 4, 2005, p. 58.

19 Daniel Roth, "Can Nike Still Do It Without Phil Knight." *Time*, April 4, 2005, p. 58.

20 Helen Jung, "Nike's CEO Parker looks forward to next steps." The *Oregonian*. January 29, 2006.

21 Stanley Holmes, "Inside the Coup at Nike." *BusinessWeek*, February 6, 2006, p. 34.

IPOD:
CREATING AN ICONIC BRAND[1]

INTRODUCTION

In the few short years since its introduction, the iPod portable digital music player had become a true cultural and social phenomenon. It was both a ubiquitous design icon and an indispensable piece of personal technology for over 50 million iPod owners. In the first quarter of 2006, which corresponded with the holiday season, Apple sold 14.1 million iPods —that was more than two per second of every waking hour during those three months. In January 2006, the company's family of digital music players owned a 78 percent share of the market for portable digital music players.

Apple reached this state of market domination through a combination of shrewd product innovation and clever marketing. The company continually updated the iPod and released new versions to the public. When the iTunes Music Store was launched, a dynamic duo of legally downloadable music and a cutting edge portable music player caused iPod sales to skyrocket. The product became indispensable to its users and spawned an "iPod economy" of third-party accessories and add-ons. Apple also developed memorable, creative advertising that helped drive the popularity of the iPod. The device had become so popular that numerous competitors lined attempted to dethrone it and be dubbed the "iPod killer."

The question for Cupertino, the California-based company remained— Would they be able to sustain this competitive advantage, and for how long? Apple had a history of developing innovative technology and bringing it to the market first, only to be overtaken by competitors who offered similar products. Given the number of competitors in the digital music player space, and the fickle nature of technology consumers, Apple would have to stay a step ahead of competitors if it wanted the iPod to remain the industry standard.

APPLE'S HISTORY

Apple's origins date back to 1974 when Steve Jobs and Steve Wozniak met while working at a summer job at Hewlett-Packard. That fall, the two began attending meetings of the "Homebrew Computer Club," a group of electronic enthusiasts in Palo Alto, California. They believed that inexpensive home computers would soon be in demand. To raise capital, they sold some of their prized possessions, including Wozniak's HP scientific calculator, and Jobs' Volkswagen van. With the $1,300 they scraped together, the two built their first computer in the Jobs' family garage in 1976 and called it the Apple I. On April 1, 1976 the two formed the Apple Computer Company.

New versions of their computer rapidly followed. The Apple II was introduced in 1977, and the growing company went public in 1980, making both men millionaires. This newfound wealth did not stop Jobs' determination to grow Apple Computer (Wozniak was in a plane crash in 1981 and did not return to the company after his recovery). The company began looking for corporate management talent to help manage its expansion. In 1983, Jobs lured John Sculley, an executive with Pepsi-Cola to serve as Apple's CEO, reportedly challenging him, "Do you want to spend the rest of your life selling sugared water, or do you want to chance to change the world?" Sculley took the job.

The year 1984 saw the introduction of the Macintosh, the first commercially successful computer with a graphical user interface (GUI). The GUI was based on the now-familiar idea of having programs running in "windows" that could be opened, closed, resized, and moved. The success of the Macintosh led Apple to abandon the Apple II in favor of the Mac product line. An internal power struggle developed in 1985, and Jobs was stripped of his duties by Sculley and ousted from the company.

As the 1980s and 1990s went on, Apple struggled to find its place in the market. Apple had a licensing dispute with Microsoft, who agreed not the use Mac GUI technology in its Windows 1.0 operating system. The agreement did not, however, cover future versions of the product, which directly borrowed from the original Mac GUI. By 1990, the market was flooded with cheap PC clones and Microsoft had launched Windows 3.0 to run on them. PCs running Windows became the industry standard, pigeonholing Apple computers in the process as the "alternative" choice. Apple market share of the total retail computer market fell to 10 percent in 1990, down from 28 percent in 1985.

In 1994, Apple announced the PowerMac computer based on the PowerPC chip. The new chips allowed Macs to compete with the speed of Intel PC processors. Apple still had problems, though—in 1995 the company had a $1 billion order backlog. These problems were compounded by the launch and subsequent success of Windows 95. The company suffered its worst financial performance in its history to that point, when in 1996 it lost $68 million for the year.

To effect a turnaround, Apple bought NeXT (a computer company Jobs founded after leaving Apple) in 1996 and Jobs returned to the company he founded as CEO. In the years after Jobs' return, Apple focused on creating personal computers, software, and peripherals. In 1998 the company launched several critically acclaimed computers, including the small, colorful iMac that led Apple to its first profitable year since 1993. The main consumers of Apple's products remained students, educators, and creative professionals. Despite its renewed focus on innovation and new product launches, Apple's market share stalled below 5 percent globally and its financial performance remained inconsistent, driving its stock down. The dawn of the digital music age would enable Apple to return to form as a technology pioneer and market leader.

DIGITAL MUSIC EXPLOSION

The adoption of digital music by consumers was limited until 1999, when 18-year-old college student Shawn Fanning wrote the code for a file-sharing program called Napster that enabled users to swap digital music files from any point on Earth that had an Internet connection. Although Napster's index of music and directory resided on a central server, the transfer of music files occurred directly from user to user. Users were able to share their music libraries with others and increase their own music collections with ease, all without paying a cent for any of the songs they downloaded. Adoption of Napster spread quickly to more than 25 million users in less than one year of operation.[2] The rapid rise of file sharing did not sit well with the Recording Industry Association of America (RIAA), an industry body representing record labels that subsequently filed a copyright infringement lawsuit against Napster in December 1999. The RIAA sought up to $100,000 in damages for each copyright-protected song allegedly exchanged using Napster software. By July 2001, Napster's service was shut down and the company filed for bankruptcy less than one year later.

Though Napster —the most popular file-sharing software at that point— was finished, the consumer appetite for digital downloading of songs continued to grow. The next generation of music sharing services were pure peer-to-peer (P2P) networks that did not require a central server to catalogue the songs—users could search and swap files directly from desktop to desktop. The RIAA filed suit against these services, once again charging that their services enabled the unlawful exchange of copyright-protected music and movies. The RIAA was dealt a major setback in April 2003, when a federal judge dismissed much of the lawsuit. In response, The RIAA shifted its strategy and began filing lawsuits against individual file swappers. Though this legal tactic eventually slowed demand for illegal downloads, users were downloading more than 100 million songs per day in 2001. This file-sharing activity contributed to a 100 million unit drop in annual album sales between 2000 and 2004.

Fearing for their profitability, all the major record companies were aggressively pursuing online music distribution strategies by the end of 2001. Pressplay, a joint venture between Sony and Universal Music Group, and Music Net, developed by AOL Time Warner, Bertelsmann, EMI and Real Networks, were launched in 2001. For users accustomed to the flexibility and freedom of Napster, these high-profile legal services were restrictive and confusing. As an example, the owners of Pressplay initially refused to license their songs to Music Net, and vice versa, so subscribers to one service were unable to purchase songs from artists represented by the labels that were affiliated with the other service. With RIAA ramping up its lawsuits against individuals, the public was eager for an easy-to-use digital music service that would keep them out of trouble with the law and offered the convenience of existing file-sharing software.

Apple: Latecomer to the Digital Music Party

Though Apple was an innovator in many areas of computer design, the company was not ahead of the curve in recognizing the power of music in digital form. Various other portable digital music players were already on the market before the iPod was even an idea. Furthermore, Apple trailed others, such as Winamp and RealPlayer, in creating jukebox software for storing and organizing music collections on computers. In the late 1990s, when Napster and other file-sharing networks were gaining popularity, Apple was focused on the relationship between computers and video. The company had developed a technology called FireWire, which was a means of transferring large files between peripheral digital devices and computers very quickly. Apple added FireWire ports to its iMac computers and created new video editing software. This capability led Apple to develop iMovie and iPhoto to manage users' digital movie and photograph files. These programs fit into the company's strategy of turning a home computer into a "digital hub," allowing users to connect and manage a wide range of digital devices and software. Realizing that music was a natural extension of its iMovie and iPhoto programs, Apple unveiled iTunes in January 2001.[3] This program allowed users to manage their music files and play them on their computers.

LAUNCHING THE IPOD

Development

Apple was unique among computer companies in that it employed both hardware and software engineers; this allowed them to create many products "in house" that would integrate seamlessly. Surprisingly, the iPod concept initially came from an unlikely source, an engineer from outside the company. Computer engineer Tony Fadell had worked for various tech companies after graduating from the University of Michigan in 1991. Through this experience, Fadell designed his own MP3 player as an independent contractor, but had difficulty finding funding to develop it. He demonstrated his design (the predecessor to the iPod) first to RealNetworks, and then to Apple, where soon after he was hired to bring it to market.[4]

Development started in May 2001 under the code name "Dulcimer." Apple wanted to have the product ready for Christmas that year. Other requirements included having a fast connection to the computer (available through Apple's FireWire technology), a close synchronization with iTunes, and an interface that would be simple to use. Jonathan Ive, Apple's vice president of industrial design later commented that there were no "epiphanies" in the development of the iPod. There was, however, constant communication between the design group and the engineers and manufacturers. Ive commented, "[The design team's functions are] not serial. It's not one person passing something on to the next. It's almost easier to talk about it as what it's not."[5] One of the key design aspects of the device was that it not tried to do too much. Consumers were increasingly befuddled with the complexity of their handheld devices—Jobs would not stand for that. Ive continued,

What's interesting is that out of simplicity, and almost that unashamed sense of simplicity, and expressing it, came a very different product. But difference wasn't the goal. It's actually very easy to create a different thing. What was exciting is starting to realize that its difference was really a consequence of this quest to make it a very simple thing.[6]

These ideas about how the unit should work directly influenced its design. There were many other music players on the market at the time, and using flash memory allowed them to be very small. Apple decided instead to use a larger hard disk drive in the iPod, giving users the ability to store up to 1,000 songs. The unit, encased in a white plastic front and silver metal back, had a small screen to display song information. The most striking feature, however, was the mechanical scroll wheel located below the screen. The scroll wheel allowed users to quickly and easily sort through and manage their music library. There were a mere four buttons

(Menu, Play/Pause, Back, and Forward) arranged around the circumference of the wheel and a small internal speaker, which generated the scroll wheel clicking sound.

When the iPod was finally complete and ready to be unveiled to the public, Jobs looked back on the process of how the iPod was designed:

> Most people make the mistake of thinking design is what it looks like. People think it's this veneer—that the designers are handed this box and told, 'Make it look good!' That's not what we think design is. It's not just what it looks like and feels like. Design is how it works.[7]

He later added what may have been the iPod's ultimate accolade, "It's as Apple as anything Apple has ever done."[8]

Product Launch

The iPod was first launched to the public on November 10, 2001 into a challenging market. It was barely six weeks after the terrorist attacks of September 11th, with economy and the tech industry in decline. The 5GB (gigabyte) unit was originally priced at $399, causing many skeptics to refer to it as "Idiots Priced Our Device." This first generation iPod was also not Windows compatible, limiting its market to the small, but loyal, group of Apple users. The iPod also did not use the most common digital audio file format, MP3, but a less widespread format called Advanced Audio Coding (AAC) that happened to be higher quality. In spite of these obstacles, the iPod was a hit. Music fans jumped at the chance to own Apple's first non-computer device since ahead-of-its-time Newton personal digital assistant. Apple used the tagline "1,000 songs, in your pocket" in its advertising. Television ads featured a young man sitting as his desk, downloading compact discs to his Apple computer. He then unplugged his iPod and danced his way out of his apartment.

The first generation iPod was a success, but not yet a sensation. Apple built momentum with a quick upgrade cycle that increased the number of songs that could be stored, while decreasing the unit price. Apple introduced the second generation iPod in July 2002. These iPods had much larger hard drives, with capacities of 10GB and 20GB. The mechanical scroll wheel was replaced with a touch-sensitive, non-mechanical one called a "touch wheel." Due to the larger hard disk drives, these units were slightly thicker and heavier than the original. During the month that Apple also announced it would release a Windows compatible version of the iPod.

The iPod had become a big hit for Apple. The company sold 381,000 units during FY 2002, accounting for $143 million in revenue (2 percent of the company's total revenue). The iPod won a gold medal from *Business Week*'s Industrial Design Excellence Award for 2002 and a gold medal from the Design and Art Direction awards in the United Kingdom. This initial success was just a hint of what was to come.

iTunes Music Store Changes the Game

April 28, 2003 was a watershed moment for Apple and digital music offerings. Steve Jobs not only announced the next generation iPod, but he also unveiled an online music store that was run by Apple and built into the revamped iTunes software. This new service was called the iTunes Music Store (iTMS) and it helped propel the iPod to become an international sensation.

The third generation iPod was slightly smaller than its predecessors, had more distinctively beveled edges, and came with a docking station. It also had increased storage capacity, allowing users to store up to 40GB of music. This device had touch-sensitive buttons located beneath the display that featured red backlighting, allowing easier use in darkness. When purchased through the online Apple store, a purchaser could get two lines of text laser engraved on the back of their iPod. Although these were welcome changes, it was the launch of the iTMS that made big news.

Apple's iTunes music software was originally just a "jukebox," allowing Mac users to manage their music collections and iPods. With the iTMS, Apple successfully identified and fulfilled the key customer needs that no legal service had been able to do since Napster's demise. According to JPMorgan research, the iTMS had three main differentiating factors:[9]

> *First,* Apple allowed users to own the music. Unlike subscription services, with iTMS the customer received permanent ownership of music that did not go away if the customer stopped paying fees. This ownership structure most closely resembled the way customers had become accustomed to purchasing music throughout their lives.

> *Second,* the iPod enabled portability. Music subscription services failed to develop adequate digital rights management (DRM), preventing seamless ties between portable music players and online music catalogs. Apple changed this by allowing iTMS to easily download purchased music to the iPod.

> *Third,* and most importantly, iTMS was the first legal digital music store to offer music from all five major record labels. After closely working with the recording industry to develop a strong DRM framework, iTMS offered a 200,000-song library across all five majors and featured rules for downloads and copying that were uniform across all available songs. Thus, iTMS served as a centralized and user-friendly destination for purchasing a wide variety of digital music.

iTMS users could download an individual song (all songs were in AAC format) for $0.99 or an entire album for $9.99. In its first week, the iTMS software was downloaded one million times, while more than one million songs were sold. After 16 days, the number of downloaded songs topped two million—by early September, it had reached 10 million.[10] Seeing this remarkable growth, Apple released a Windows compatible version of the iTMS in October. Sales of iPods had been small, but steady, up until this point. Introduction of the iTMS —with its low prices, legal downloads, and ease-of-use—caused iPod sales to skyrocket (see

Exhibit 1). Later additions to iTMS increased the music library to over one million songs and 11,000 audiobooks.

THE ECONOMICS OF THE IPOD

The Razor Model Turned Upside Down

The iPod and iTunes Music Store combination proved to be extremely profitable for Apple. What surprised many financial reporters and industry analysts, however, was the breakdown of how revenue was earned by this combination of products. The term "razor model" had been in use for many years to describe how companies such as Gillette would sell hand-held razors for little or no profit, but reap large, sustained profits when consumers purchased multiple replacement razor blades over a period of years. More recently, the razor model was adopted in high-tech industry by printer manufacturers that make small margins on the printers but earn large margins on repeat purchases of printer cartridges. Many analysts wrongly believed this was the model Apple was following with the iPod and iTMS combination: sell the iPod at little or no profit, and earn high revenues when consumers download millions of songs from the online music store. When it was announced that the iTMS earned little profit, the industry first thought that Apple's entire revenue model had collapsed. Upon further investigation, analysts discovered that Apple had turned the razor model on its head.

Analysts noted that the iTMS had significant revenue growth potential, but that profit margins were quite slim. It was estimated that for every $0.99 song that was downloaded, the record labels took between $0.65 and $0.70 in royalties. Credit card fees accounted for approximately $0.22, while other operating expenses ate up $0.08. This meant that for every song sold through the iTMS, Apple might actually lose $0.01, or take in meager profits of only $0.04.[11] As of July 2005, Apple had sold over 500 million songs through its online music store. Assuming Apple earned $0.04 on every song, this would translate into $20 million in profits for the company.

By contrast, profits for the iPod exploded. At the end of 2004, the average selling price of an iPod was $296 (this included all models). The cost of goods sold (COGS) was approximately $233 per unit, while other operating expense totaled $37.[12] This meant there was a profit of $26 on each iPod sold. As of June 2005, Apple had sold 15 million iPods, bringing in over $390 million in profits. Clearly, the iPod was a big money maker for the company, surprising many who thought Apple would make little on its iPods in order to exploit the "razor model" and earn big profits from iTMS. Earnings from the iPod/iTMS combination helped Apple's stock price out of the slump caused by the tech slowdown in the early 2000s (see Exhibit 3).

Based on the history of Napster and the rest of the digital music business, the iTunes Music Store was widely seen as a pivotal moment in the process of creating a legitimate digital music source that consumers were willing to pay to use. However, because Apple made significantly more profit from the sale of iPods, and didn't rely on its digital music store for profits, it appeared that Apple had attempted to reinvent the entire music business in order to sell more iPods (see Exhibit 4).[13]

With its bundled music player and music store model Apple was maintaining a "closed system" that created significant barriers to entry for competitors seeking to exploit the popularity of either iTunes or the iPod. While consumers could run iTunes on Windows and hook it up to an iPod, that iPod could not play songs in the formats used by any other seller of digital music. iPod owners could only listen to songs in AAC format, which were only sold at the iTMS.[14] Moreover, music bought through Apple's store would not play on any rival device. With every song purchased through iTMS, a consumer was more and more likely to purchase an iPod—there was no other device that could play the song.

Continued Product Innovation
With the success of the iPod and iTMS combination firmly established, Apple sought to expand its market presence by developing a portfolio of iPod music players. This was partly due to the fact that the company's success had encouraged dozens of competitors to mimic design elements of the original iPod. Regarding this competition, Jobs remarked, "They're all putting their dumb controls in the shape of a circle, to fool the consumer into thinking it's a wheel like ours. We've sort of set the vernacular. They're trying to copy the vernacular without even understanding it."[15] Jobs continued to push his designers and engineers to make a great device even better.

Apple entered the market for "mini" digital music players in January 2004 with the introduction of the iPod mini. This device had 4GB of storage and was priced at $249. This was only $50 below the 15GB third generation iPod and critics panned it as too expensive. Once again, the critics were mistaken and Apple had trouble keeping the model in stock. The iPod mini introduced the popular "click wheel"—this touch-sensitive wheel allowed users to move their finger around the wheel, while the unit's Menu, Play/Pause, Back, and Forward buttons became part of the wheel itself. Instead of pushing a separate button to activate those functions, the user simply needed to press down on a section of the wheel to operate that function. The iPod mini came in a broader range of colors, namely silver, gold, blue, pink, and green. Silver models sold best, followed by blue ones. The second generation iPod mini came out a little over a year later, offering more storage, longer battery life (up to 18 hours), and richer case colors.

The fourth generation iPod was released in July 2004. The most obvious difference from its predecessors was that it carried over the click wheel design that was introduced with the iPod mini. Some users criticized the click wheel because it did not have the backlight that the third generation iPod's buttons had. Others noted that having the buttons on easily remembered compass points (top, bottom, left, right) largely removed any need for backlighting. This model came in 20GB ($299) and 40GB ($399) versions, both of which boasted battery life of 12 hours.

In October of that year, Apple made two major announcements. The first was the release of the iPod photo, with a 65,536-color, 220 x 176 pixel screen and the ability to store and display JPEG, BMP, GIF, and TIFF images. It could also play music for 15 hours on one battery charge. The iPod photo originally came in 40GB ($499) and 60GB ($599) sizes. That month, Apple also released a black and red edition of the fourth generation iPod called iPod U2 Special Edition. Originally retailing for $349, it was black with a red click wheel (the colors of U2's latest album), and featured the signatures of U2's band members engraved on the back. It also included an iTMS coupon redeemable for $50 off of the price of "The Complete U2," a digital boxed set that featured over 400 tracks of U2 music. In June 2005, Apple merged the iPod and iPod photo lines, removing all grayscale models from the main iPod line. Apple also added a color screen and photo capabilities for the iPod U2 Special Edition.

Apple announced a newer, smaller iPod in January 2005. The iPod shuffle introduced flash memory (rather than a hard drive) to iPods for the first time. The shuffle came in two sizes, 512MB (up to 120 four-minute songs) and 1GB (up to 240 songs). The iPod shuffle, weighing less than an ounce and approximately the size of pack of chewing gum, had no screen and therefore had limited options for navigating between music tracks —users could either play songs in the order set in iTunes or in a random (shuffled) order. Toshiba, the maker of the flash drive Apple used in the Shuffle, reported having trouble with meeting demand for its drives. Demand for the iPod shuffle was "so vast that [Toshiba's] current capacity can in no way meet [Apple's] needs," Toshiba's corporate vice president Masashi Muromachi said at a news conference in February.[16]

In September 2005, Apple released another, slightly bigger flash-memory device called the iPod nano. The nano, which replaced the mini, held 1, 2 or 4GB of music depending on the model and was priced between $149 and $249. Its lack of a hard drive enabled it to be small, about as tall as a stick of gum and only twice as wide. It featured a small color monitor, photo display capabilities, and 12 hours of battery life. The nano was an immediate hit, selling one million units in its first 17 days of availability.

Only a month later, Apple unveiled the fifth generation iPod, the main feature of which was the ability to play high-quality color video on an enlarged 2.5-inch screen. Prices per gigabyte were again lower than previous generations for the video iPod, which was offered in 30GB ($299) and 60GB ($399). To complement its video features, Apple began selling ad-free videos and television programs on the iTMS for $1.99 apiece. Initially these videos were limited to 2,000 music videos and limited programming from Disney and ABC, but the selection was soon expanded to include thousands more music videos, 38 TV channels including all the major networks, Discovery, A&E, MTV, and Comedy Central, plus movie trailers and short films. The iTMS video site attracted 20.7 million visitors in December 2005, more than the traffic to Google, MSN, and Yahoo's video sites combined.

Apple's continual upgrading and innovating of its iPod portfolio was credited with helping the company maintain its leadership in the digital music market. One technology consultant observed, "The thing that's got most of their competitors scared is how fast they can move."[17] Apple lacked the size of some of its larger consumer electronics competitors such as Sony and Toshiba, but this gave them an advantage "because they don't have an 85-person audio consumer marketing department spread over three continents, [thus] decisions can be made over dinner."[18] This enabled Apple to push the pace of new product introductions and prevent its competitors from catching up (see Exhibit 2 for a timeline of iPod introductions).

Silhouettes Everywhere

As the iPod line continued to expand, so too did Apple's marketing plan. A new series of iPod ads appeared in April 2003, in conjunction with the launch of iTMS. They featured plainly dressed people wearing their iPods and giving acapella renditions of popular songs, ostensibly while they listened to the original version on their iPod. The ads featured a wide range of music, including The Who's "My Generation," Sir Mix-a-lot's "Baby Got Back," and Eminem's "Lose Yourself."

Apple changed course in October of that year with a media blitz centered on a new theme that reinforced the iPod's status as a design icon. These television and print ads featured actors as black silhouette against a solid color background, dancing while listening to their bright white iPod and signature white headphones. Print ads were displayed in major magazines such as *MacWorld*, *Newsweek*, and *Wired*. The silhouetted figures also appeared on buildings in Dallas, by bus stops in Paris, and adorned the Apple Store in Tokyo. Apple brought the ads to even more "everyday" locations—the steps leading down to a Toronto subway were painted with a black silhouette against a bright colored background, while newspaper recycling collection bins sported the eye-catching ads. Billboards were eventually placed near colleges in Beijing.

Television ads from the silhouette campaign featured many trendy songs, but the most popular ad featured U2 commemorating the launch of the iPod U2 Special Edition. Members of the band were featured in a 30-second commercial pushing their latest single, "Vertigo," which was available exclusively through iTMS during its first few weeks in release. The spot, a cross between a music video and Apple's catchy silhouette ad campaign, received heavy rotation on prime-time television. "Vertigo" topped the iTunes download charts for weeks after its release.

Aiming to poke fun at its file-sharing predecessors and remind the public that iTMS was a legal service, Apple aired a set of ads during the 2004 Super Bowl that starred a number of teenagers who had been sued by the RIAA for illegally downloading music. These spots featured punk band Green Day doing a cover of the famous Bobby Fuller song "I Fought the Law (And the Law Won)." This song was later sold on iTMS as single.

THE IPOD BECOMES UBIQUITOUS

iPod use spread beyond hardcore Apple fans and music lovers and soon became part of the American mainstream. It wasn't long before Hollywood celebrities embraced the product, and their support made the iPod even more desirable to the public. The product had appeared on "Saturday Night Live," in a video by rapper 50 Cent, and on Oprah Winfrey's list of her "favorite things." As a guest on "The Tonight Show," actor Will Smith told Jay Leno how he was infatuated with the "product of the century." Gwyneth Paltrow confided her love of the iPod in an interview with *Vogue* magazine. Pop artist John Mayer commented, "The layout reminds the musician of music." Stories circulated of celebrities who had collections of over 60 iPods.

Nightclubs began having events like "iPod night," where users could bring their iPod and take a turn at being a DJ and sharing the music from their collection. Where once people might have asked, "What's your favorite record?" or "What's your sign?" the new greeting became, "What's on your iPod?" Internet sites specifically for iPod users appeared by the thousands. Sites such as ipodworld.co.uk and ipodhacks.com touted themselves as "your source for latest hacks, mods, tips, and tricks."

There was no doubt that the iPod had become an icon, but it came as a surprise that the products' distinctive white headphones had become just as popular. After some initial debate, Apple decided to make the earphones white, in order to match color of the original iPod. The white headphones were a prominent element in the Silhouettes campaign, because the long white wires stood out against he black silhouetted figures. The signature earphones turned out to have such high recognition that they became a liability—after crime in the New York City subway system rose dramatically due entirely to iPod theft, the New York Police Department issued a warning advising iPod owners to replace the earphones, so as not to make themselves a target. It was reported that most people did not take the advice.[19]

The "iPod Economy"

When people could not get enough of the iPod, they could buy third-party accessories to add to the product's utility. The iPod created a large and growing aftermarket industry that Jobs referred to as "the iPod economy." This economy included accessories such as voice recording modules and docking stations to turn an individual iPod into a speaker system. TEN Technologies created the naviPod, an infrared remote control that allowed users to select songs, adjust the volume, and perform other tasks from across the room. A popular accessory was an FM tuner called the iTrip that plugged into the iPod and allowed users to listen to their stored music through their car stereo. Somewhat less utilitarian, but no less popular, were iPod cases made from faux fur, feathers, organic hemp fiber, mohair, and corduroy. Tony designers Coach, Burberry, and Gucci all made iPod cases. Some of these accessories were available at the online and brick-and-mortar Apple Store.

Seeing the success of these accessories, especially the FM tuners for cars, Apple decided to extend its product line and create an accessory of its own. In June 2004, Apple and BMW announced the BMW iPod Adapter, the first seamless integration between the iPod and a car audio system. After the iPod was plugged into a port in the glove compartment, drivers could enjoy high fidelity sound through the car's stereo system and control the iPod using the standard button on the steering wheel. This feature was initially offered on BMW 3 Series, Z4 Roadster, X3 and X5 Sports Activity Vehicles, and the Mini Cooper. Apple later announced that Mercedes-Benz, Volvo, Alfa Romeo, and Ferrari would add similar capabilities to certain models of their cars.

Expansion of Distribution Channels

Apple had long been criticized for trying to exert too much control over the retail experience. While Apple computers were once sold in both Best Buy and Circuit City retail locations, those relationships broke apart in 1998. Attempts to get iMacs back into those stores were stalled when the retailers balked at stocking iMacs in all five colors due to space restrictions. Aside from insisting on this point, Apple executives also claimed the "consumer experience" at those stores were not satisfactory. Thus, many analysts concluded Apple's computer sales were diminished because the company offered few retail locations from which consumers could purchase the product. Commented IDC analyst Roger Kay, "The Apple brand has plenty of strength, but it's got limited reach."[20]

In an effort to make the iPod available to a wider audience, Apple pursued a variety of distribution strategies. The most important was getting the product back onto the shelves of major electronic retailers. In September 2002, Apple announced that iPods would be sold in 500 Best Buy stores across the country, in addition to the 225 CompUSA locations already selling the devices. Less than a year later, iPods were available at all Circuit City stores across the country and at circuitcity.com. Apple continued to expand its distribution of the iPod in a 2005 partnership with Radio Shack that had 7,000 outlets. One of the terms of the deal was that Radio Shack agreed to purchase at least 450,000 iPods during the initial three-month sales period.

One aggressive method to make iPods available to consumers was airport vending machines. iPods were offered along with other electronic gadgets like digital cameras and earphones at Zoom Systems' Zoom Shop machines at the San Francisco and Atlanta airports. Analysts were impressed with the way Apple had opened up to outside retailers and distributors. "With the iPod, Apple is much more willing to expand their distribution and make sure the product gets into as many hands as possible," said NPD Group analyst Steve Baker.[21] The company had 4,000 distribution points for Mac computers, but boasted over 21,000 distribution points for the iPod.

Another important distribution channel for Apple was its own Apple Stores. The company began constructing these retail spaces in May 2001; by June 2005 the company had 110 locations at upscale malls around the country. For the quarter ended in June 2005, revenues at these stores were $555 million, representing almost 16 percent of Apple's worldwide sales.[22] An important benefit for the company was what many called the "halo effect." Selling millions of iPods at various locations provided the company with a greater scope of awareness for its other products. A Windows user might enter an Apple Store looking for an iPod, but leave with an iMac computer.

Evidence suggested that this halo effect was indeed present. According to a study from Morgan Stanley in March 2005, 19 percent of PC owners who also owned iPods purchased a Mac within the previous year.[23] Nearly 90 percent of those iPod/PC owners polled purchased a Mac in part because of the positive experiences they had with their iPods. This halo effect drove Apple's retail computer market share in the U.S. up to 4.5 percent in July 2005 from 2.8 a year before.

INNOVATIVE USES FOR THE IPOD

As iPods spread throughout the world, users found new and innovative ways to exploit Apple's technology. The devices started turning up in schools and universities, and even inspired a new form of communication.

Duke University Embraces the iPod

Apple received valuable media attention when Duke University announced they would be giving iPods to every member of the class of 2008. The *Duke iPod First Year Experience* was an initiative the school embarked on to "intensify the use of information technology" through a variety of means including effective use of technology to enhance teaching and learning.[24] iPods were used as teaching aids and to record and distribute lecture audio in a variety of classes during the 2004 school year, including Theory and Practice of Tonal Music I, Intensive Elementary Spanish, and Economic Principles. The program was renewed for the 2005 and 2006 academic years, although the iPods were no longer free, but available at a subsidized price of $99.

The Growth of Podcasting

A new use for the iPod became popular in late 2004. "Podcasting" (a combination of the words "broadcasting" and "iPod") described the process of creating audio content and sharing it on the Internet, or downloading radio content from the Internet, allowing the user to listen to it at a time of their choosing. Former MTV VJ Adam Curry was an early podcaster and is credited with coining the term. This term could be misleading, because neither podcasting nor listening to podcasts required an iPod or any portable music player. But in the minds of American consumers, listening to music meant listening to it on the go, and 78 percent of the time (iPod's market share) that meant using an iPod.

Users could defy radio programming schedules by listening to whatever they wanted, whenever they wanted, wherever they wanted. People could subscribe to free podcasts using iTMS. Once they subscribed, iTunes automatically checked for updates and downloaded new episodes to their computer. When users synced their iPod and computer, all podcasts were automatically downloaded to the iPod.

Apple introduced this feature in a new version of the iTMS available in June of 2005. Two days after the release of the program, Apple reported one million podcast subscriptions.[25] Two months later, there were over 6,000 free podcasts available on iTMS. Apple did not earn revenue from these free podcasts, but once downloaded, the only way to listen to them was on an iPod.

LINING UP TO BE THE NEXT "IPOD KILLER"

Global sales of MP3 players doubled in 2004, to more than 20 million units, and were expected to grow at an average annual rate of almost 45 percent up until the year 2010. At that rate, total sales would rise to slightly more than 194 million units.[26] It was no surprise that many new products had entered the market and bragged that they were the "iPod killer."

From a design standpoint, the iPod could be easily replicated. MP3 players were already in existence prior to the introduction of the iPod, although they were not considered as user-friendly from either a size or user-interface perspective. Newer designs, however, were gaining ground on the iPod. Creative Technology launched the Zen Micro that was roughly the same size as the iPod Mini and offered 1GB more storage space. In addition, the Zen Micro offered users touch-pad navigation similar to the iPod's scroll wheel and included features not available on the iPod, such as FM radio reception. While iPod's design remained the standard, some analysts believed it was quickly losing ground as competitors imitated product features such as the scroll wheel.

In addition to Creative Technology, other makers of MP3 players included Gateway, RCA, Panasonic, Phillips, Dell, Rio Carbon, and SanDisk. These companies originally copied the iPod format and built a small, rectangular-shaped device that was designed to play music. Other companies took a page from Apple's playbook and came up with cutting edge designs. Phillips teamed with Nike to produce a music player that also measures exercise performance and heart rate. Sunglass maker Oakley combined their trademark high performance eyewear and music playing devices to offer a unique design that offered a music player built into the frame.

By the summer of 2005, it appeared that the next "iPod killer" might be something that hundreds of millions of people around the globe already owned—a cell phone. Wireless operators around the world were working with music studios, phone makers, and artists in a sweeping effort to turn the mobile phone into a go-anywhere digital jukebox. Many telecom companies saw the mobile phone as central to the future of music. "The iPod is great," said Frank Nuovo, chief designer for Nokia, the world's largest handset maker. "But no one has a stranglehold. There is nothing that keeps the mobile phone from moving into that area."[27]

This challenge to Apple's dominance appeared real. One quarter of the world's population (1.4 billion people) owned cell phones, and the vast majority of these users already paid a monthly phone bill, making it easy to add an additional charge for music. This would also eliminate the need for credit card charges, a significant cost in Apple's structure. Ringtones—short digital music clips that played whenever there was an incoming call—were already popular, generating $245 million in revenues in 2004. Cell phone providers Verizon, Sprint, and Cingular charged as much as $2.50 for wireless downloads of full songs, or twice the $0.99 per song on iTMS. One knowledgeable source close to Apple said those operators were simply being unrealistic if they expected customers to pay $2 or $3 for a song, especially with restrictions. "If you can get something for a buck, why would you buy it for $3? Do they think people are that dumb?"[28]

Apple opted to embrace this new threat by developing an iTunes-enabled phone with Motorola, called the ROKR (for "Rocker") that was released in September 2005. Many wireless operators were skeptical of this plan, though. Operators prefer to have customers download songs over the air directly to handsets. But with the ROKR phone, customers would download songs to a PC, and then copy them to the phone. "It's hard for people in any industry to support something that cuts them out of potential future revenue streams," said Graeme Ferguson, director for global content development at Vodafone Group, one of the world's largest wireless players.[29] For this reason, Cingular initially did not subsidize the price of the ROKR. Consumers were not thrilled with the ROKR either, particularly since its digital music capacity was limited to a mere 100 songs and transfer of songs from computer to phone was markedly slower than transfer to an iPod. Sales were sluggish, and many analysts theorized that Apple had designed the ROKR in such as manner as to ensure that it did not cannibalize iPod sales.

In May 2006, would-be iPod killer SanDisk began targeting iPod more aggressively with a series of "attack ads" that attempted to de-position iPod—which shared Apple's positioning as an innovative alternative for creative types—by insinuating that its users were mindless trend-chasers, or "iSheep." Poster and billboard ads designed to look like poster and stencil street art showed images of sheep wearing the iconic white iPod headphones and directed users to a site called iDon't.com that contained a manifesto of sorts written by "several of us renegades behind the new [SanDisk] Sansa player" that began "Greetings fellow radical" and continued with a not-too-subtle anti-iPod screed:

> Yeah, we're just fed up with the ever-expanding flock of iSheep swarming through our cities. You've seen them. They're everywhere. Every bus, train and city sidewalk is a mass of white headphones. Blindly they've bought into the hype without ever realizing there are other mp3 players out there.[30]

The iSheep ads helped propel SanDisk into the number two rank for digital music player sales in the U.S., though its 10 percent market share was far less than iPod's 78 percent. The iSheep campaign was replaced by a new campaign designed around the Lil' Monsta character, a cartoon monster made from a Sansa MP3 player that is depicted eating vast volumes of digital media, including music, photos, and video.

Software giant Microsoft initiated its own challenge to iPod's dominance by creating the Zune, a combination portable media player and download store. The Zune, scheduled for release in time for the 2006 holiday season, would also be WiFi-enabled for wireless downloading of media content. Given Microsoft's past history overcoming once-dominant competitors, and the success of the closed system "reverse razor" model that it apparently adopted for the Zune, analysts expected Microsoft's challenge to be a legitimate one.

CONCLUSION

In a few short years, the iPod had truly become a cultural phenomenon. College students carried them around campus, businessmen and women had them in their briefcases, and people who were once intimidated by technology found themselves not wanting to leave the house without one. To the delight of Apple (and the chagrin of competitor Sony), the iPod became known as "the Walkman of the twentieth century." Even though some analysts thought sales might slow, consumers continued to snap up the music players. By August 2006, more than 58 million iPod's had been sold and the iPod's halo effect had brought Apple's market share in retail computers up more than 2 percentage points to 4.8 percent.

Beyond spurring sales, the iPod was central in changing the way people listened to and used music. The shuffle feature of iPods helped people make connections between different genres of music. According to musician John Mayer,

"People feel they're walking through musicology" when they use their iPods, leading them to listen to more music, and with more passion.[31] Podcasting enabled users to replace radio broadcasts and listen to DJ sets without commercial interruption. The new video and photo features had the potential to change how people interacted with those media as well.

The question facing Apple was how to maintain its dominant position in the digital music market. Aside from the competition it faced, Apple also faced lobbying and legislative pressure—particularly in the European Union—aimed at getting Apple to open its closed system and allow songs of any format to be played on the iPod. If forced to open its system, Apple's dominant market share could be significantly eroded. At the same time, it was certainly possible that customer loyalty and the steadily increasing appetite for the products Apple had established could prove sufficient to overcome the obstacles, both competitive and legislative, that await it in its future.

DISCUSSION QUESTIONS

1. What is the most important feature of the iPod? Why?
2. Apple continues to operate a closed system (i.e. music downloaded from iTMS can only be played on iPods). Do you recommend Apple continue this strategy, or should it open its system to users of any type of digital music player?
3. Has Apple done a good job of marketing the iPod, or have they relied too heavily on word of mouth and buzz to grow the brand?
4. Apple has extended its distribution network to include large retailers such as Circuit City and Best Buy. How important are these outlets to Apple? Should they be concerned with not having full control over the customer retail experience—control that they have in the Apple Stores?
5. What should Apple do next to sustain iPod sales? Create a new ad campaign? Introduce a new version of the iPod that plays videogames?

Exhibit 1: Sales of iPods by Quarter

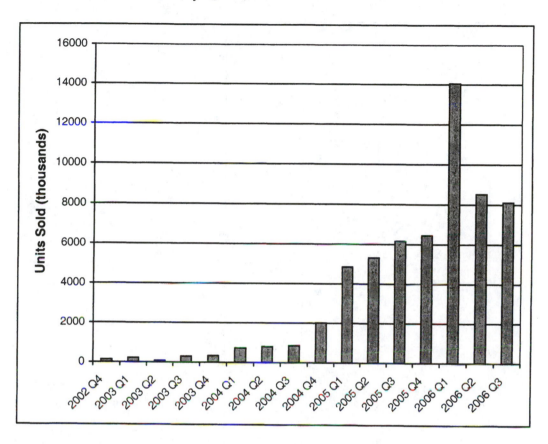

Source: Company reports

Exhibit 2: iPod Introductions Timeline

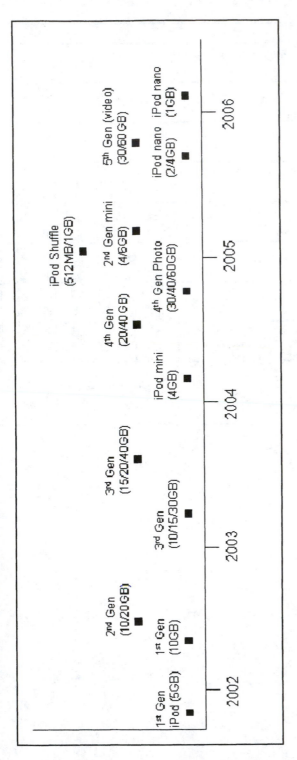

Exhibit 3: Apple Weekly Closing Stock Price

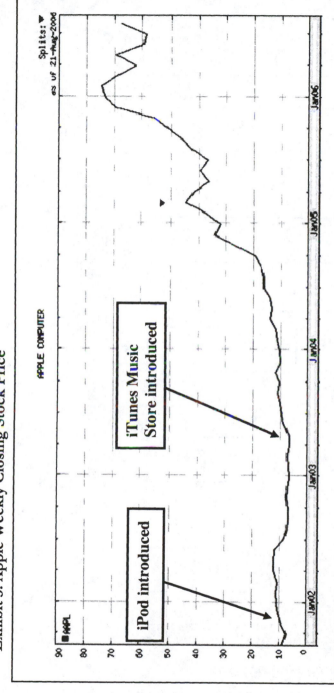

Exhibit 4: Apple and iPod Revenues as Percent of Total

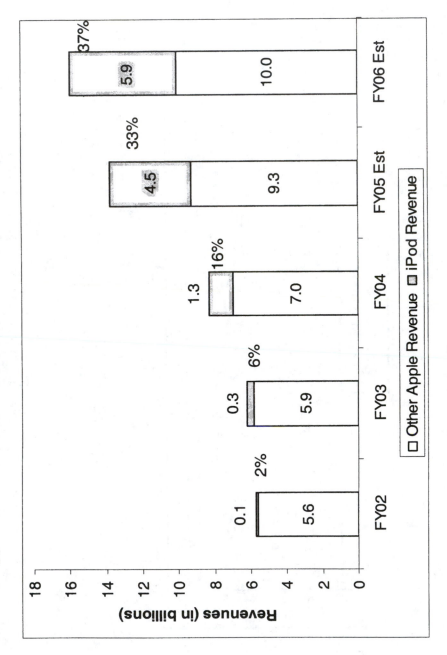

REFERENCES

[1] Jonathan Michaels prepared this case under the supervision of Professor Kevin Lane Keller as the basis for class discussion. The case was later updated and revised by Keith Richey.

[2] JPMorgan Equity Research, "Apple Computer Inc, iPod Economics." November 15, 2004.

[3] Rob Walker, "The Guts of a New Machine." The *New York Times,* November 30, 2003.

[4] Leander Kahney, "Cult of Mac." http://wiredblogs.tripod.com/cultofmac, April 26, 2004.

[5] Rob Walker, "The Guts of a New Machine." The *New York Times*, November 30, 2003.

[6] Ibid.

[7] Rob Walker, "The Guts of a New Machine." The *New York Times*, November 30, 2003.

[8] Steven Levy, "iPod Nation." *Newsweek,* July 25, 2004.

[9] Ibid.

[10] Apple company press releases.

[11] JPMorgan Equity Research, "Apple Computer Inc, iPod Economics." November 15, 2004.

[12] Ibid.

[13] Rob Walker, "The Guts of a New Machine." The *New York Times*, November 30, 2003.

[14] It was possible, however, to convert non-copy-protected MP3s to AAC format.

[15] Rob Walker, "The Guts of a New Machine." The *New York Times*, November 30, 2003.

[16] www.macdailynews.com, February 21,2005.

[17] Terril Yue Jones, "How Long Can the Ipod Stay on Top?," *Los Angeles Times*, March 5, 2006, p. C1.

[18] Terril Yue Jones, "How Long Can the Ipod Stay on Top?," *Los Angeles Times*, March 5, 2006, p. C1.

[19] http://en.wikipedia.org/wiki/podcasting

[20] Beth Snyder Bulik, "Grab an Apple and a Bag of Chips." *Advertising Age*, May 23,2005.

[21] Beth Snyder Bulik, "Grab an Apple and a Bag of Chips." *Advertising Age*, May 23,2005.

[22] Charles Wolf, "The Apple Stores —It's All About Brand Building." Needham & Company Investment Analysis, July 19, 2005.

[23] Kasper Jade, "iPod Halo Effect Estimated at a Staggering 20%." *AppleInsider*, March 18, 2005.

[24] Memo to Duke Faculty from Provost Peter Lange, April 6, 2005.

[25] Apple company press release, June 30,2005.

[26] Normandy Madden, "Spotlight." *Advertising Age*, July 11, 2005.

[27] Roger Crockett, "iPod Killers?" *BusinessWeek* (International Edition), April 25, 2005.

[28] Ibid.

[29] Ibid.

[30] www.idont.com

[31] Steven Levy, "iPod Nation," *Newsweek*, July 25, 2004.

DUPONT:
MANAGING A CORPORATE BRAND[1]

Over the nineteenth and twentieth centuries, E.I. DuPont de Nemours & Co. (DuPont) transformed from a small, Delaware-based gunpowder manufacturer into a Fortune 500 powerhouse with a diverse array of chemical, fiber, polymer, life science, and petroleum products. Since 1802, DuPont used its superior scientific research strengths to make discoveries that have made the lives of millions easier and the operations of businesses around the world safer and more efficient. DuPont, which had risen to become the third-largest chemical company in the United States. and one of the top ten in the world, continued to show impressive growth in the high-performance materials and life sciences sectors. By 2005, the company maintained a portfolio of more than 2,000 trademarks and brands, many of which had attained the highest levels of recognition among consumers for ingredient brands.

DuPont has long been revered for its success with corporate branding. Since the 1930s, the "Better Things for Better Living" slogan helped win brand recognition among DuPont's business customers and consumers alike. In 1999, DuPont launched a new corporate image with the introduction of its "Miracles of Science" campaign. The new strategy raised some important questions. How would DuPont's broader focus on biology affect its traditional chemical science business? Would the corporate brand remain an asset in marketing and supporting DuPont's sub-brands? The company addressed these and other questions as it developed its strategy for the new century.

COMPANY BACKGROUND

Early History

Founded near Wilmington, Delaware in 1802 by E.I. du Pont de Nemours, DuPont's first century of operations was devoted to the production of a variety of gunpowder product lines. DuPont's early research with sodium nitrate led to a replacement for traditionally used explosives in 1857, a revolutionary development in the warfare technology of the time. Three decades later, DuPont established itself as a leader in polymer chemistry research by inventing a process to manufacture smokeless gunpowder. Throughout the rest of the nineteenth century, the growing company continued to dominate the explosives market as the primary manufacturer of dynamite, nitroglycerin, guncotton, and smokeless powder for the U.S. government. While DuPont's production of explosives technologies decreased dramatically in the twentieth century, the company continued to serve as the U.S. Armed Forces' primary supplier of explosives during World War I.

In 1902, DuPont began to pursue new business opportunities as its competitive advantages in the explosives business started to erode. Pivotal to the reorganization of the company from an explosives manufacturer into a diversified chemical company was DuPont's investment in one of the first American industrial research laboratories, the Eastern Laboratory, located in New Jersey. Another research facility, DuPont's Experimental Station in Delaware, was built soon after. In addition, during the 1910s, DuPont began acquiring a diverse group of smaller companies within the nitrocellulose, fabrics, heavy chemicals, dyes, and finishes industries. A major restructuring in 1920 further facilitated DuPont's growth into a multi-billion dollar enterprise. That year, DuPont reorganized its various business units into autonomous operating departments whose production activities were organized by a central corporate headquarters. This modern form of corporate organization allowed the company's business units to pursue growth independently, and thus free from the inefficiencies associated with more centralized organizational structures of other industrial giants of the time. The 1920s also saw DuPont's first expansion of production activities abroad with the establishment of subsidiaries in Mexico and Brazil.

The efforts of DuPont's major research facilities in combination with R&D support from its acquired businesses, led to DuPont's early developments in cellulose-based products including fibers, plastics, finishes, and films. Realizing that the company's future success hinged on continued commitment to scientific research, DuPont created an internal department in 1927 charged with "establishing or discovering new scientific facts." This department advanced DuPont's understanding of various processes in polymer chemistry, leading to an explosion of both consumer and industrial products in the decades that followed.

Early Branding Lessons
It was in the 1930s that DuPont officials gained a curious insight—sometimes, in order to protect the company name it was important not to trademark a product. Early in the decade the company trademarked its new synthetic rubber as DuPrene, but found it could not safeguard the integrity of the product name. DuPrene was an unprocessed material, and unreliable finished goods manufacturers who produced poor goods that used DuPrene as an ingredient threatened to give the product and DuPont a bad reputation. As a result, DuPont abandoned the trademark in 1936 and applied the generic name "neoprene" to distinguish it as an original ingredient, not a finished product. DuPont applied similar logic when it chose not to trademark the revolutionary synthetic fiber, nylon.

DuPont learned another important lesson in the rules of trademark registration during the 1930s. In 1936 the company sued Sylvania for marketing a plastic wrap using the DuPont trade name cellophane. Sylvania argued that no other common name for the material existed. The court agreed, finding that DuPont had not properly protected its trademark by distinguishing the branded product from the generic cellulose film. The company responded to the defeat by strengthening and expanding the legal department's trademark division.[2]

DUPONT'S BRANDING LEGACY
Although DuPont's scientific research strengths engendered top-quality products, many marketing professionals argued that the company's expertise in corporate branding had been the cornerstone of DuPont's success. Marketing experts praised

DuPont for integrating its corporate branding campaigns with ingredient branding efforts geared at promoting the company's various sub-brands. Experts credited DuPont's creation of a strong corporate identity with enhancing the company's bargaining power with other players in the value chain and creating consumer loyalty. In essence, efforts to build a strong corporate brand identity paved the way for the healthy growth of DuPont product sales in a variety of categories—many argue that sales of popular DuPont products such as Teflon, Lycra, and Stainmaster would never have been as impressive without the support of the DuPont name.

DuPont Corporate Marketing Program

DuPont's first advertisement appeared in a newspaper in 1804 and read:

> The subscriber offers for sale, American manufactured Gun-Powder, from the Brandywine Mills, of a quality which is warranted equal and believed to be superior, to any imported from Europe, and at prices much under those of the imported Powder.[3]

Throughout the nineteenth century, DuPont advertising appeared primarily on handbills and lithographs that depicted hunting scenes. The company was largely content to meet existing demand, and therefore the products were not advertised aggressively. By the nineteenth century, DuPont looked to expand into new markets and induce demand for its products. The familiar oval DuPont logo was conceived in 1907, and in 1909 the company officially established the corporate umbrella brand when it dictated that the DuPont name would be attached to each product. That same year, the company established an Advertising Division. One of the first series of advertisements developed by the Advertising Division was titled "DuPont American Industries." One ad indicated that products originally thought of as luxury items were in fact necessities. Another ad connected DuPont with the revolutionary automobile by highlighting the company's Rayntite car tops, Fabrikoid artificial leather upholstery, and Duco exterior finish.

DuPont's experience with corporate branding extended back to the 1930s, when market research revealed that consumers still associated the diversified chemical company with its past involvement in the explosives industry. DuPont's heritage as an explosives manufacturer became a liability during the 1930s, when a Senate committee investigating the munitions industry grouped DuPont with other so-called "Merchants of Death." To promote a new socially-conscious image that conveyed DuPont's emphasis on scientific discovery as a means for the creation of products that made the lives of Americans easier, the company hired Batton, Barton, Durstine & Osborn (BBDO) to lead its direct consumer advertising efforts. BBDO's branding efforts led to a tag line that became associated with the DuPont brand for the next five decades—"Better Things for Better Living Through Chemistry." In addition, the red DuPont "oval" became the company's primary marketing symbol and was used to build brand identity in marketing campaigns geared both toward promoting specific sub-brands as well as those tailored specifically to promoting the corporation as a leader in industrial sciences.

DuPont's largest advertising investment in the 1940s was a weekly radio show called Cavalcade of America. The Cavalcade of America moved to television in 1952, and after a few years the company sponsored the DuPont Show of the Month and Show of the Week. For each episode, DuPont ran a commercial that showcased "the other 99 percent" of the company's products, or its non-munitions offerings. By 1957, consumer polls showed that nearly 80 percent of the public had a favorable impression of DuPont.

DuPont continued to expand its marketing program through the years. By 1980, the company employed six major advertising agencies and worked with more than sixty others globally. In 1980, DuPont dropped the "Through Chemistry" from the slogan to change popular consumer perceptions that DuPont was solely a chemical company. The company wanted to emphasize that it was developing "Better Things for Better Living" that included energy products and well as a growing number of brands related to the biological sciences.

Domestically, DuPont continued to use a product-oriented strategy to convey its "better living" message to consumers. One memorable television ad featured real-life amputee Bill Demby, who was able to play basketball with the help of prosthetic legs made from DuPont plastic. The ad showed Demby on a playground basketball court removing his warm-up pants to reveal the prosthetic limbs. Demby competed one-on-one with another man while a voiceover intoned, "When Bill Demby was in Vietnam, he dreamed of coming home and playing a little basketball—a dream that died when he lost both legs to a Viet Cong rocket." The ad emphasizes DuPont's role in Demby's ability to play with a line about the "remarkable DuPont plastic that could help make artificial limbs more resilient, more flexible, more like life itself." DuPont also used corporate advertising to convey its environmental achievements. One television spot highlighted DuPont's double-hulled oil tanker design. In the spot, assembled sea creatures applaud and cheer DuPont while "Ode to Joy" played in the background.

DuPont augmented its corporate advertising with other marketing activities, including sponsorships and public relations. DuPont sponsored numerous scientific events and programs, which fit naturally with the company's core competency of science research. Science projects funded by DuPont included the world's first human-powered airplane, which flew from England to France, and the first solar-powered airplane. As a company spokesperson explained, DuPont sought events "that involve innovative uses of our products, events that have contests or prizes that have an engineering orientation."[4]

The company also engaged in several high-profile sponsorships. Between 1991 and 1996, DuPont sponsored the American cycle race formerly called the Tour de Trump and renamed it the Tour DuPont. One of DuPont's most visible marketing programs was its lead sponsorship of National Association for Stock Car Auto Racing (NASCAR) driver Jeff Gordon, started in 1993. The sponsorship was logical considering Gordon raced with the help of numerous DuPont products, including a driver's suit made of Nomex heat-resistant fiber, a helmet with Kevlar body protection fibers, and a car painted with DuPont automotive finishes. The brightly painted car that prominently displayed the DuPont logo earned Gordon, who became one of the most successful drivers in Winston Cup racing during the 1990s, the nickname "Rainbow Warrior." In 2002, DuPont included Gordon's car in its 200th anniversary celebration by using the DuPont 100 Years logo, which depicts a flask with confetti streaming from the top, as the primary logo on the car. Corian solid surfaces and Suva refrigerants were some of the DuPont products advertised on the car during the racing season. DuPont signed a contract to sponsor Gordon's team, Hendrick Motorsports Car 24, through 2008. Though specific figures were not available, it was estimated that it cost between $15 million and $20 million to sponsor a car for one season.

In addition to sponsoring Jeff Gordon, DuPont was also a sponsor of NASCAR. DuPont Automotive was recognized as the Official Automotive Finish of NASCAR, while DuPont's Tyvek was a promotional partner of NASCAR. NASCAR was an increasingly popular sport in the United States. and an effective marketing platform for DuPont. Aside from boasting a fan base of 75 million people, NASCAR was the number one sport in fan loyalty, the number one spectator sport (with 17 of the top 20 attended events in the United States.), and number two rated regular season sport on television (trailing only the National Football League).[5] NASCAR also offered DuPont an affluent audience—the average household income for a NASCAR fan was $60,200 in 2004, according to one study. That was higher than the national average of $58,036 in 2003, according to the Census Bureau. NASCAR fans in the 18- to 39-year-old category were even more affluent, averaging $64,500 per household.[6]

INGREDIENT BRANDING

One of DuPont's most successful and long-standing marketing strategies was *ingredient branding*. When DuPont found consumer applications for its scientific discoveries, as was the case with Teflon, Stainmaster, and Lycra, the company licensed its technology to consumer products companies. A variety of manufacturers, therefore, made goods containing trademarked DuPont products. The DuPont technology was an *ingredient* in the finished product, and the company sought to build consumer awareness in the ingredient name, so that, for example, consumers would look for cookware made with Teflon or clothes made with Lycra. DuPont advertised its ingredients as early as the 1950s, when it developed campaigns to raise consumer awareness for brands such as Cordura and Orlon fabrics.

The ingredient brand strategy had several advantages compared with finished product branding. For one, it transformed what consumers considered to be fiber and chemical commodity products into sought-after branded merchandise. As a result, rather than buying a carpet for its color and weave, for example, consumers specifically sought out Stainmaster carpets. Additionally, an ingredient with multiple uses could be marketed as a component in more than one product. Teflon, originally developed for the military, was an example of an ingredient with various industrial and consumer product applications. Difficulty can arise when the ingredient brand appears in products representing diverse markets. As one DuPont executive noted about the Kevlar ingredient brand, "It's always a challenge to make sure that the message that we're using for the overall Kevlar brand is still consistent for a police officer, for a canoe owner, versus [an] aircraft company."[7]

DuPont also leveraged its corporate name with ingredient brands, particularly in business-to-business applications. For example, the company's automotive finishes business, which produced ingredients for the auto industry, did not have a coined ingredient brand name but was called simply DuPont Automotive Finishes. Other ingredient brand products that also carried the DuPont corporate name included DuPont Flooring Systems, DuPont Polyglide, and DuPont XTI Nylon. This strategy enabled the company to establish awareness for its ingredient brands by leveraging the well-known DuPont name.

The benefits of ingredients branding also translated to manufacturers and retailers. Manufacturers who made products containing DuPont ingredients enjoyed the positive associations consumers had with the ingredient name and/or the DuPont name. DuPont also shared some of the production, development, and promotion costs with its manufacturers. Retailers could attain larger operating margins because of the price premiums commanded by products containing DuPont ingredients. Retailers also received additional promotional support from DuPont. Two highly successful ingredient brands for DuPont were Teflon and Stainmaster.

The Teflon Ingredient Brand

Teflon chemical coating was developed by DuPont in the 1930s primarily for military applications and remained outside the consumer product realm for the first twelve years after its introduction. After World War II, DuPont scientists and product development teams thought that consumers would find Teflon as useful as the military because of its non-stick properties and stability at extreme high and low temperatures. Specifically, DuPont pegged Teflon as a perfect candidate for the cookware market since consumers had long expressed a desire for cookware that prevented heated food from sticking to its surface. Adapting Teflon coatings for consumer use was a challenge because of the fact that they were non-stick on both sides, making it difficult to apply Teflon coatings to surfaces of standard pots and pans. But by the early 1960s, DuPont had perfected a method for adhering the non-stick surfaces to cookware and began preparing to market the product to cookware manufacturers and consumers.

As with many other DuPont products, the Teflon brand name was selected from a list of possible product names generated by a computer program that randomly combined words and sounds. Teflon was chosen because it sounded scientific enough to convey the wonders of non-stick surfaces yet it was simple enough for the average consumer to remember. Early Teflon branding efforts centered on television advertisements that stressed the "easy clean" properties of Teflon cookware. DuPont brand managers felt that television was the only advertising medium that could successfully convey the benefits of Teflon because consumers in the 1960s were unfamiliar with the concept of non-stick surfaces and needed to be shown how they worked and could be of use in their daily lives. By pursuing a mostly direct-to-consumer campaign, DuPont depended on a pull strategy in which Teflon sales would be supported by demands for non-stick cookware as consumers realized its advantages.

In the 1990s, DuPont developed improved versions of Teflon as well as a new type of non-stick coating branded by DuPont as Silverstone. At the same time, the company scaled back marketing of Teflon and Silverstone cookware applications—most likely because both brands achieved 95 percent recognition among consumers according to DuPont branding research. While consumer advertising of Teflon has waned during the 1990s, DuPont continued to market its non-stick surfaces for industrial uses. The stable heating and cooling properties of these surfaces facilitated its use in myriad industrial applications from rocket engines to cryogenics. In 2001, DuPont started a consumer campaign for its Teflon brand that highlighted Teflon's use as a stain- and wrinkle-repellant in fabrics. Said Teresa Kleinhans, global textiles manager for Teflon, "We are progressively increasing our presence and refining our strategy in ready-to-wear, which represents a significant opportunity."[8]

Marketing the Stainmaster Brand

Stainmaster was unique to DuPont's portfolio of trademarks because it was designed in response to a specific consumer preference or need—most other DuPont products were discovered through years of scientific research and then had to be marketed to appeal to specific end-users who could potentially find the product useful. It was widely believed that DuPont's launch of the Stainmaster brand—the largest advertising and promotion campaign in the carpet industry's history—was a well thought out and executed, two-part, "push" and "pull" strategy.[9]

Production Program—DuPont used a "push" strategy by giving mills incentives to use the new Stainmaster nylons in their carpets. For example, DuPont supplied mills with Stainmaster chemical agents for free as long as they continued purchasing DuPont's premium nylon fibers. Offering incentives like free use of stain resistant chemical agents was important because competitors began entering the market with similar, low-cost stain resistant agents that employed the same chemical formulas as DuPont's products.

Trade Program—DuPont furthered its "push" strategy by targeting retailers with extensive trade promotions, including supplying merchandisers with marketing tools such as posters, banners, labels, tags, and retail display units, which could be used in stores to attract customers to buy the Stainmaster brand. A key feature was a demonstration unit that allowed customers to dip a toothbrush-like "swizzle stick," with one treated and one untreated group of tufts, into various stains and go through the simple stain-removal process to see for themselves how Stainmaster worked. This encouraged carpet retailers to demand more Stainmaster products because they could rely on DuPont to fund the marketing program while the retailers directly benefited from the dramatic increases in carpet sales that resulted from the branding efforts. Furthermore, DuPont spent more than $35 million on training and support for exclusive Stainmaster distributors. With the launch of

Stainmaster, DuPont sent 50 field representatives to train more than 1,500 retailers to best employ the marketing tools provided by DuPont to boost sales.

Among the cooperative advertising options available to retailers were Stainmaster newspaper ad slicks with room to add the showroom name, Stainmaster TV tapes (which became 30-second television spots when dealers added their names to the 8-second tag), and 30-second radio commercials with time included for the dealer's tag. Any retail carpet dealer purchasing a total of more than 5,000 square yards of Stainmaster carpet in a six-month period accrued co-op advertising dollars for DuPont Stainmaster carpet.

Consumer Advertising—Although marketing to mills and retailers was important, DuPont's consumer advertising of Stainmaster—the "pull" aspect of the campaign—was the more critical aspect of the branding program. The Stainmaster promotional campaign was the biggest marketing endeavor ever pursued by DuPont, totaling $65 million alone for the initial branding campaign, an amount unheard of in the floor covering market. The initial advertising program featured two television spots that creatively and humorously captured the stain resistance, comfort, and durability qualities associated with Stainmaster carpets. DuPont's "Landing" commercial, which featured an infant tossing his airplane shaped plate full of messy food onto Stainmaster carpet, won the Clio Award for Best Commercial of 1987.

Warranty—DuPont's "repair or replace" warranty consisted of a full five-year stain-resistance warranty (covering most common household food and beverages), a five-year wear-resistance warranty (no more than 10 percent wear in any area, except stairs), and a lifetime anti-static warranty.

Toll-Free Number—For Stainmaster carpet dealers and buyers, DuPont introduced a toll-free 800 number tended by operators trained in carpet-stain treatments and backed up by a sophisticated computer system for dealer ordering of sales material and recording of warranties. Initially, the vast majority of the calls were from dealers requesting sales aids, point-of-purchase materials, extra warranty cards, swizzle sticks for in-store displays, and product information. Mills called for extra swizzle sticks, training tapes, or information literature. Later, more calls were placed by consumers.

Calls from consumers fit three categories: those wanting product information, those asking where to buy carpets of Stainmaster, and consumers with questions on performance and cleanability. After verifying the latter's purchase and warranty coverage, operators would talk the caller through the cleaning process. The method of stain removal varied as to length and number of steps by the type of stain and length of time it had lain untended. Operator training required them to have tested Stainmaster carpets personally. If an operator could not correct the problem, he or she would take the customer's number and have one of the DuPont scientists call back the next day. If all these approaches failed, DuPont would send a local professional cleaner to the resident. As a last resort, DuPont replaced the carpet.

Results—The marketing program for Stainmaster exceeded DuPont's expectations. Consumer research indicated that recall of Stainmaster advertising far surpassed that of competitors. More importantly, 60 percent of carpet sold at retail in 1988 had enhanced stain resistance and roughly three-fourths of those sales went to Stainmaster, often at a price premium.

Other Ingredient Brands

Although many DuPont brands were well known (Lycra, Kevlar, Teflon), there were hundreds of other less well-known brands. These brands were not direct consumer products, but were the unseen components in an incredibly wide variety of goods. DuPont had brands that were used in:

- Auto Safety. DuPont had over 60 products that were used in modern vehicles. These included the nylon used in airbags, SentryGlass that kept windows from shattering, and the automotive finishes that were used in half of cars produced in Canada, Europe, and the United States.
- Toothbrushes. DuPont filaments had been used in the oral care industry for over 60 years as manual and electric brushes, floss threaders, and tongue brushes.
- Sneakers. The company's Hytrel thermoplastic polyester elastomers provided the flexibility, strength, and processibility needed to produce athletic shoe parts.
- Detergent. The company produced Elvanol, a water-soluble synthetic polymer that was a packaging ingredient that allowed dissolvable package innovation.
- Cheeseburgers. The BAX system from DuPont was a fast, accurate DNA-based method for detecting bacteria in raw ingredients and finished products. DuPont packaging also helped keep food fresh longer and provided longer-lasting protection.
- Space Exploration. The Mars Exploration Rovers contained numerous DuPont products, including Pyralux (for flexible cable circuits) and Kapton (a polyimide film to control vibration).
- Cell Phones. The typical handheld device contained up to 14 DuPont products, helping to make cell phones smaller and more durable, while allowing them to do more, faster and better.
- Music. Guitar manufacturers used DuPont Performance Coatings to get the look of vintage lacquer on their products. The companies that made drumheads for drum sets, concert, and marching drum instruments used DuPont's Teijin Films polyester film.

Brand Extensions

DuPont sought to build awareness for its brands by bolstering its ingredient branding program. To do so, the company used a two-part initiative that 1) developed new uses for core brands, and 2) fostered relationships with partners who use DuPont ingredients. For example, DuPont partnered with Ciba Specialty Chemical to jointly create a new brand called Easy Care that marketed Teflon as wrinkle- and odor-repellant. Carol Gee, global brand director of DuPont Textiles &

Interiors said, "Teflon will come to mean more than non-sticking and stain-resistance."[10]

Another example of DuPont expanding the market for a particular ingredient brand was its high-end kitchen countertop Corian. Originally developed as a more cosmetic alternative to plastic laminated countertops, DuPont created new uses for Corian that included sculpture and furniture. To showcase these products, DuPont sponsored a private exhibition of sculpture made of Corian called "Exercises in Another Material" at Chicago's Museum of Contemporary Art in 2000 and donated a number of armchairs made of the material to Grand Central Terminal in New York. Whereas Corian had previously been available only through DuPont-selected kitchen and bath boutiques, the company also began selling Corian in mass-market retailers such as Home Depot in order to attract more customers. Since the late 1990s, sales of Corian grew 15 percent annually, to more than $500 million in 2000.

The ingredient brand Kevlar, which was five times stronger than steel on an equal weight basis, had long been used to protect members of the military and law enforcement from dangers such as bullets, shrapnel, and knives. DuPont extended this technology to create residential storm shelters that could protect homeowners from deadly flying debris caused by the strong winds of tornadoes and hurricanes. The DuPont StormRoom, engineered to withstand wind speeds of up to 250 miles per hour, met the Federal Emergency Management Agency (FEMA) performance criteria for hurricane and storm shelters. The StormRoom looked like a small room inside a house or garage. The ventilated room could be finished to match the look of the home, and could even be outfitted with plumbing and electricity. All that was needed for installation was a slab concrete floor.

The brands created by DuPont were components in a wide variety of products that were marketed to make everyday life better, safer, and healthier. The innovations represented by these brands came as a result of the company's massive R&D program ($1.33 billion spent in 2004).

DUPONT RESEARCH

Supporting Two Centuries of Growth

The driving force behind DuPont's history of consistent growth had been the company's aggressive investment in scientific research. DuPont's discoveries and technological improvements led to what company executives described as "dramatic leaps forward," making significant differences in the lives of consumers throughout the world (see Exhibit 1 for a timeline of well-known DuPont innovations). Chad Holliday, current DuPont CEO, explained that the company had never been interested "in serving transitory needs. The kinds of products that DuPont manufactures help to feed, cure, clothe, and shelter humanity."[11] DuPont avoided developing products that meet short-term consumer demands resulting from ephemeral trends, but rather, the company invested in research that met the long-term needs of businesses and consumers alike.

DuPont's annual R&D expenditures, which exceeded $1 billion annually in the 1990s, supported research activities aimed at the creation of new or improved product lines across six major areas: chemicals, fibers, polymers, petroleum, biology, and diversified businesses. The company's extensive R&D budget supported more than 3,700 scientists and engineers working at 24 major industrial research laboratories in 11 countries. In addition to the $1 billion spent on pure scientific research, DuPont invested close to another $1 billion on manufacturing, technical, marketing, and engineering technologies, all of which were instrumental in the company's growth.

In the 1990s, an increasing percentage of DuPont's research funds were dedicated to improving the environmental soundness of the company's products. For example, DuPont engineers developed processes in which bio-hazardous waste generated in the production of certain plastics could be broken down to simple molecular forms so they could be reused later in the manufacture of other products. Moreover, researchers initiated studies on how to refine the production processes of its plants so that zero hazardous waste was generated. The company ultimately planned to achieve zero hazardous waste standards for all of its plants. DuPont also created DuPont Safety Resources, a new strategic business unit dedicated to managing "hazards" resulting from industrial activities throughout the world. This business unit contributed to the company's mission of developing useful products for consumers while preserving the environment and enhancing safety for industrial workers and communities located near production plants.

DuPont also continued to invest heavily in the development of improved replacements for its current product lines. In 1998, for example, DuPont introduced two new carpet fibers—the Antron Stainmaster and Antron Teflon SuperProtection brands—which improved the easy-care properties, durability, and aesthetic capabilities of the original Stainmaster carpet brands. Another example was DuPont's 1993 introduction of Suva, a chemical refrigerant replacement for Freon, which was invented by DuPont in 1931. R&D funding for Suva development spawned from a wave of protest from environmentalists who were concerned by the fact that Freon's use of chlorofluorocarbons contributed to ozone depletion.

By 2004, DuPont had over 75 R&D facilities globally, including 35 outside the United States. These sites were staffed by nearly 2,000 scientists and researches—including 600 with Ph.D.s—who worked to pursue science-based solutions for global markets (see Exhibit 2 for the number of annual patents secured as a result of DuPont R&D). When the company began to focus on revitalizing its R&D in early 2000, 40 percent of its technology resources and assets were dedicated to growth; the rest supported existing products and operations. By 2005, 65 percent of the company's research was focused on growth.[12]

DUPONT'S BRANDING EFFORTS INTO THE FUTURE

By the mid-1990s, DuPont had embarked on a massive reinvention of its business plan that dramatically transformed the focus of the company. DuPont would no longer simply remain a chemical and energy products corporation. Instead, the company would pursue a strategy that placed greater emphasis on developing products related to the biological sciences while retaining healthy business units that were connected to the company's traditional chemistry research. In 1998, DuPont's corporate branding team developed a marketing strategy that captured the dynamics of the company's new dual chemistry/biology focus. Branding executives at DuPont felt that "Better Things for Better Living," which the company had used since 1935, needed to be replaced by a more contemporary campaign that captured the company's focus on using pure scientific research to develop products that added convenience and safety to the lives of consumers. "Better Things for Better Living" was viewed as too product oriented. It conveyed an image that DuPont was solely concerned with using science to improve its current products while in reality the company had placed a great deal of emphasis on pure scientific research aimed at "breakthrough" products never conceived of before.

Research showed that consumers viewed DuPont as a leader in "smoke-stack science"—the materials and industrial sciences—because its research often led to products that had purely industrial applications. But consumers had not yet become aware of the company's competencies in biological research and ability to integrate strengths from a variety of scientific disciplines to develop revolutionary products. One DuPont marketing executive admitted that DuPont traditionally had difficulty relating its scientific endeavors to the lives of average consumers. DuPont needed a new image showing that the company "is not simply providing a playpen for scientists to cook up inventions, we want to help people." The "Better Things for Better Living" campaign also confused consumers because of its similarity to other corporate branding efforts such as BASF's "We don't make a lot of the products you buy, we make a lot of the products you buy better," Phillips Electronics' "We Make Good Things Better" and General Electric's "We Bring Good Things to Life."

Finding a New Tagline

In the fall of 1998, CEO Charles Holliday informed the advertising agencies bidding for DuPont's global account that the company wanted to reinvent itself. In particular, Holliday felt the company needed to express to consumers how its chemicals and biotechnology businesses collaborate to create innovative products. Speaking on the need for a new name, Kathleen Forte, vice president of global corporate affairs said, "Clearly, we don't want to be seen as a chemical company. It's really limiting, and it doesn't describe who we are."[13] One ad executive saw a similar need for change, saying, "How many taglines can last for seven decades? It was time to move on to something new."[14] In developing its winning pitch, McCann-Erickson sought insights by analyzing DuPont's research and conducting its own research. McCann interviewed DuPont employees, who revealed that they viewed DuPont as a science company that applied discoveries to improve the quality of life for consumers. Nat Puccio, McCann's executive vice president-director of strategic planning, detailed how this insight reconciled DuPont's biotech and chemicals businesses, "If you think of DuPont as a science company, suddenly the material sciences and life sciences really become two flavors, if you will, of the larger mission."[15]

The task of summarizing this insight with a concise tagline, however, proved challenging. A few days before the final pitch, a McCann creative director came up with the succinct four-word phrase "The Miracles of Science." When the new concept was embraced by a committee of DuPont executives, as well as focus groups made of consumers and employees, the company went ahead with the change. The buy-in among employees was something DuPont was monitoring closely, and the "Miracles of Science" slogan immediately earned employee praise. Said one North American employee, "[the slogan] did a good job of tying together all of DuPont's businesses and…can last forever."[16]

In April 1999, DuPont introduced the "Miracles of Science" campaign with a twelve-page advertisement supplement in the *Wall Street Journal* that emphasized DuPont's ability to "make miracles happen in every field from fashion to pharmaceuticals to agriculture to aerospace." The ad indicated that DuPont scientists developed some of the major breakthroughs that influenced life in the twentieth century. These breakthrough products included Mylar, which aided the space program's quest to put a man on the moon, and Teflon, which helped make the computer chip possible. The campaign, which cost an estimated $50 million, appeared in popular magazines, newspapers, trade publications, and television. According to one DuPont marketing executive, the "Miracles of Science" campaign "[set] the record straight on what kind of company we are and what we are becoming"—that is, it emphasized DuPont's use of pure scientific research to develop new-age products that had wider applications than the company's previous product portfolio. Accordingly, Holliday commented, "Over two centuries, we have delivered big miracles and small miracles. . .Going forward, our common focus will be to leverage our collective scientific knowledge and competencies to innovate, originate, and realize many more miracles."[17]

By changing the marketing campaign focus from "Better Things for Better Living" to the "Miracles of Science," DuPont attempted to show consumers that it was essentially a new company with a new look and feel. The "miracles" came from the company's ability to take the best research from a wide variety of scientific disciplines and generate innovations. The marketing campaign helped clarify consumer and investor confusion concerning the direction of DuPont, making clear that DuPont was neither solely a chemical nor biological research company, but rather was dedicated to science in general. DuPont's branding team also viewed the "Miracles of Science" tagline as a way to change consumer perceptions of DuPont as stodgy and old-fashioned. The campaign captured a more humane image for DuPont and showed consumers that the company is concerned with developing innovations that "improve the quality of human life."

In September 1999, DuPont launched its first-ever global advertising campaign. The campaign, themed "To Do List for the Planet," launched simultaneously with regional and national television and print ads in North America, South America, Europe, and Asia. On the "to do list" featured in the ads was a number of health and safety issues including: find food that helps prevent osteoporosis; turn ocean water into drinking water; invent fabric that knows to either cool or warm you; develop medicines that fight HIV; and humorously, add Lycra to leather.

DUPONT BUSINESS DEVELOPMENTS

Biological Research and Development
As DuPont launched its Miracles of Science campaign, CEO Chad Holliday commented that biological research was to become "the centerpiece of DuPont in the future."[18] Accordingly, the company focused some of its R&D considerable resources on new biological sciences initiatives.

DuPont had recently created a strong presence in the biotechnology sector with the introduction of environmentally friendly herbicides and processes that incorporated biotechnology in agricultural production. Furthermore, in 1997 DuPont invested more than $3.2 billion in partner Ralston Purina's Protein Technologies International in an effort to facilitate greater involvement in biotech agriculture. Perhaps the most significant progress DuPont made in pursuing revenue growth of its biological research business was its $7.7 billion purchase in 1999 of Pioneer Hi-Bred International, the world's largest seed company. DuPont used seeds from Pioneer to grow corn capable of producing bioengineered chemicals that then served as the basis of the various chemicals, polymers, and fibers produced by the company. Instead of relying on nonrenewable petroleum sources as the base for chemicals vital to DuPont's product lines, the company will use renewable crop resources to satisfy its raw material needs.

DuPont's new focus on biological sciences led to the channeling of more R&D funds toward drug development and medical imaging chemical agents. DuPont investigated possible partnerships with various pharmaceutical companies, but the pace of these potential deals was criticized by industry analysts for proceeding too slowly. Total prescription drug sales for DuPont fell 6 percent in 2000, to $1.5 billion. At the time, DuPont had a number of experimental drugs in development, including cancer, blood clot, and depression treatments, but these would not be market-ready for years. In 2001, DuPont sought a buyer for its pharmaceuticals unit. Bristol-Myers Squibb, the world's fifth largest drug maker, agreed to purchase DuPont Pharmaceuticals for $7.8 billion.

Fine-Tuning DuPont's Positioning
With the advent of genetically modified foods, and the subsequent boycotting of them by activists, DuPont backed away from its biological research positioning somewhat. By 2000, less than 3 percent of DuPont's revenues came from genetically modified seeds. Holliday revealed that the company would wait to gauge consumer opinion before releasing a number of genetically modified products that were otherwise ready for the market. While DuPont continued to develop biotechnology products, or "biosolutions," the company aimed to use these products in polymers, rather than in foods. Its exit from the pharma business in 2001 was also indicative of a shift away from its biological research positioning.

As it distanced itself somewhat from the biological sciences positioning, DuPont placed added emphasis on developing materials and chemicals useful for use in electronic devices and the information industry. The company renamed its Electronic & Communication unit, calling it DuPont iTechnologies, and established itself as a leader in lightweight and energy-efficient polymer displays. These displays were designed for use in electronic devices such as cell phones, personal digital assistants, notebooks, and high definition television. In 2000, DuPont acquired UNIAX Corporation, a California company that produced the first polymer-based plastic display.

Also in 2000, DuPont unveiled another innovation called Sorona, the first product from the company to come from the integration of biology and chemical research. Sorona was a bio-based material with applications in the textile fiber business. Sorona bore properties similar to polyester: stretch, softness, dye-ability, and ease-of-care. The product also illustrated DuPont's focus on "sustainable growth," since Sorona was made from renewable biological resources.

Sorona represented a new aspect of DuPont's sustainable growth mission. In 2001, DuPont set a target to get 10 percent of its energy and 25 percent of its revenue from renewable—or "non-depletable"—resources by 2010. The company's efforts to improve its environmental record since the 1990s were largely successful. Across its global operations, DuPont reduced greenhouse gas emissions 60 percent, air toxins dropped 70 percent, and air carcinogens fell 90 percent between 1992 and 2000. Dr. Paul Tebo, vice-president for health, safety, and the environment, spoke in 2001 of sustainability as DuPont's next step:

> If you effect the environment the right way, you can grow your business. It then becomes fundamental not having waste in your corporation and so the whole concept of sustainability begins to make sense to business people.[19]

In 2001, Holliday stated that DuPont was still striving toward a goal of "zero waste and zero emissions" in its manufacturing.[20]

Focusing on the Core Business

Due to challenging conditions in the textile and apparel markets, DuPont's fabric brands had suffered financially in the fourth quarter of 2001. Earnings from nylon products dropped 73 percent compared with the same quarter a year earlier, and the company's polyester business lost $29 million in the quarter. In 2002, DuPont announced that it planned to spin off or sell its fabrics businesses. This plan was finalized in April of 2004, when DuPont Textiles & Interiors was sold to privately held Koch Industries for $4.2 billion. With this move, DuPont sold valuable brands such as Lycra, Stainmaster, CoolMax, and ThermoLite, ending its 70-year run as an innovator and leader in nylon, spandex, and other textile fibers.

Holliday commented, "With the separation of INVISTA [the name of the new company], DuPont enters the next chapter of its transformation. In essence, we are launching a new DuPont."[21] This divestiture was part of a larger plan to accelerate the company's transition from a chemical company to a materials science company.

Analysts applauded this move to reshape the company and its asset base. With the sale of its textiles business, DuPont was then organized into five strategic business units: 1) Electronic & Communication Technologies; 2) Performance Materials; 3) Coatings & Color Technologies; 4) Safety & Protection; 5) Agriculture & Nutrition (see Exhibit 3 for 2005 sales by business segment). In another move that signaled a shift in the company's direction, DuPont announced that Ogilvy & Mather had been selected as its lead global communications agency. This was the first time in its 200-year history that DuPont had consolidated marketing and communications across its businesses and the corporate brand with a single lead agency.

In 2002, DuPont stated that new products would contribute 35 percent of revenue by 2007, up from 20 percent at the time. This statement indicated that DuPont would continue to dedicate itself to discovering new innovations that had consumer applications. By 2004, the company had achieved 30 percent of revenues from new products, and expected to reach 33 percent in 2005. In order to reach this goal, DuPont had started an initiative to revitalize its R&D process to allocate capital to growth opportunities rather than sustaining existing platforms. The company also committed itself to strengthening its position in emerging markets, beginning with China and then moving to Central and Eastern Europe and Brazil.

This renewed focus on the core business helped DuPont's net income rise 15 percent to $2.1 billion, even as revenues decreased by 3 percent to $26.6 billion due to the spin-off of INVISTA (see Exhibit 4 for DuPont's net sales compared with net income by year).

Marketing the New DuPont

DuPont continued its marketing efforts with a variety of new initiatives. When the company learned that a single mother with two children lost her home during Hurricane Charlie in 2004, DuPont stepped in and pledged $80,000 to help her rebuild her home. The new home was to be outfitted with Corian surfaces, Tyvek house wrap, and a StormRoom. In 2005, the company announced that it would serve as the premier sponsor of the XVII World Congress on Safety and Health at Work, to be held in Orlando later that year. This would be the first time the global event was to be held in the United States. DuPont partnered with another event in 2005 when it announced its sponsorship of the World Police and Fire Games. This event, held once every two years, attracted 10,000 participants from 60 countries. It was the second largest international sporting event after the Olympics. DuPont used the event to showcase new Kevlar vests, and a new Tychem ThermoPro suit that offered first responders protection from heat as well as chemical and biological agents.

DuPont also embraced new marketing techniques, as it did when it joined Dell, Kraft Foods, and Harvard Business School when it became a member of the Word of Mouth Marketing Association (WOMMA). WOMMA was the official trade organization of the word-of-mouth marketing industry. Its mission was to promote and improve word-of-mouth marketing by protecting consumers and industry with strong ethical guidelines as well as promoting word-of-mouth marketing as an effective tool.

CONCLUSION

Since its inception in 1802, DuPont had grown into a global powerhouse with 60,000 employees and revenues of over $26 billion in 2005. Profits had increased for three consecutive years. It had a portfolio of over 100 businesses and 26 business units organized into five strategic business units. By the early twenty-first century the company had determined that its traditional focus on chemicals would limit its growth. The company faced the challenge of finding new ways to reinvent itself while remaining relevant to modern consumers.

After repositioning itself with the "Miracles of Science" tagline in 1999, the company initially made aggressive moves into biotechnology. These moves became more hesitant, however, as public opinion made biotechnology—particularly biofoods—a less-then-favorable business focus. With the spin-offs of its Textiles and Interiors and its pharmaceutical unit, DuPont neared the end of its third metamorphosis in two centuries. First recognized as the leading explosives company in the nineteenth century, then as a leading diversified chemical company in the twentieth century, DuPont reshaped itself into a materials science company that integrated classical chemistry, biology, information science, and the emerging fields of bioengineering and nanotechnology.

DuPont felt confident that its tradition of innovation and scientific discovery would enable the company to successfully transition to a new era of growth as a materials sciences company. It remained to be seen, though, how successful this transition would be.

DISCUSSION QUESTIONS

1. How would you characterize DuPont's brand equity? What factors contribute to the company's equity? How can DuPont best preserve that equity?
2. Compare the benefits and drawbacks of a corporate brand strategy with that of an ingredient brand strategy. Do you think DuPont should emphasize one strategy more in the future?
3. Evaluate the "Miracles of Science" tagline. Do you think this effectively communicates DuPont's positioning as a premier science company? Does it support DuPont's ingredient branding strategy? Do you think it has potential to last as long as the "Better Things for Better Living" tagline?
4. DuPont does not make many finished goods, instead supplying ingredient components to manufacturers through licensing agreements. What are the risks in a business model such as this? Can DuPont mitigate these risks?

Exhibit 1: Timeline of Major DuPont Innovations

Year	Innovation
1924	Duco
1930	Neoprene
1935	Nylon
1938	Teflon
1950	Dacron
1952	Mylar
1962	Lycra
1965	Kevlar
1966	Tyvek
1986	Stainmaster
1990	Suva
2000	Sorona

Exhibit 2: Global Patent Filing by DuPont's R&D Department

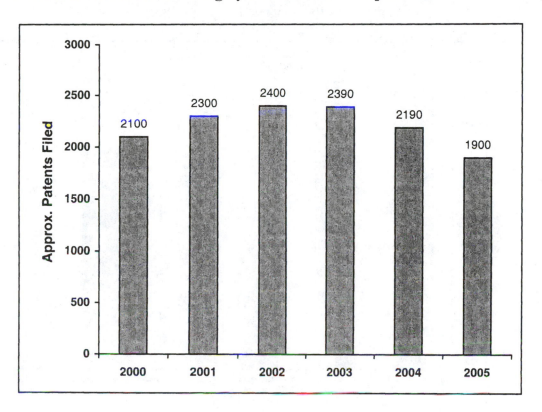

Source: Company Reports

Exhibit 3: 2005 Revenues by Business Segment
(as a percent of the total company revenues)

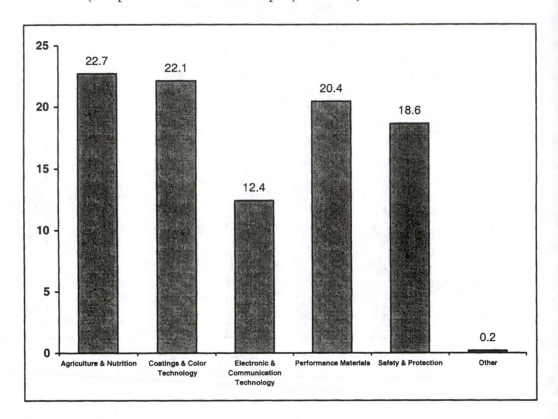

Source: Company Reports

Exhibit 4: Net Sales and Net Income by Year

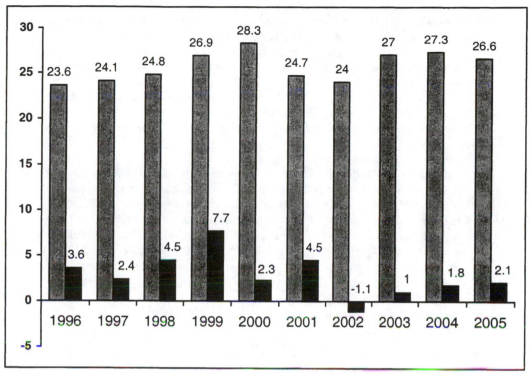

Source: Company Reports

REFERENCES

[1] This case was made possible through the cooperation of DuPont and the assistance of Barbara Pandos, Scott Nelson, Jamie Murray, and Cheryl Gee. Keith Richey prepared this case, which was revised and updated by Jonathan Michaels, under the supervision of Professor Kevin Lane Keller as the basis for class discussion.

[2] The proceeding two examples were described in www.heritage.dupont.com

[3] www.dupont.com

[4] Gail S. Bower. "How Corporations Pay Their Dues." *Focus*, September 30, 1987, p. 23.

[5] NASCAR Brand and Consumer Marketing Memo

[6] Barbara Hagenbaugh, "5 Cities Gun to Win Race for NASCAR Hall of Fame." *USA Today*, May 26, 2005.

[7] DuPont video, April 13, 1998.

[8] Sandra Dolbow. "Teflon: We 'Let Life Happen.' " *Brandweek*, January 29, 2001, p. 5.

[9] The following examples come from: Bette Collins and Paul Farris, "Stainmaster." UVA-M-357, Darden Graduate School of Business, University of Virginia, Charlottesville, VA and Paul Farris, :Stainmaster Teaching Note." UVA-M-357TN, Darden Graduate School of Business, University of Virginia, Charlottesville, VA.

[10] Sandra Dolbow. "Teflon: We 'Let Life Happen.'" *Brandweek*, January 29, 2001, p. 5.

[11] www.dupont.com

[12] Sasha Planting, DuPont Company Overview, www.financialmail.co.za, June 17, 2005.

[13] Sean Callahan. "Marketing Miracles: DuPont Replaces 1935 Tagline To Reflect Corporate Change." *Business Marketing*, June 1, 1999, p. 1.

[14] Ibid.

[15] Ibid.

[16] Ibid.

[17] *DuPont* magazine No. 2, 1999.

[18] *Fortune* April 26, 1999.

[19] Jennifer Hewet. "DuPont Turns Into a Green Crusader." *Sydney Morning Herald*, June 4, 2001, p. 33.

[20] "Chemicals: DuPont's Punt." *The Economist*, October 2, 1999, p. 75.

[21] Company press release, "DuPont Takes Action to Achieve $900 Million Annualized Cost Improvement in 2005." December 1, 2003.

DOCKERS:
CREATING A SUB-BRAND[1]

INTRODUCTION

In the spring of 1985, Levi Strauss & Co. (LS&Co.) was flush with its success in the blue jeans market. The company's star campaign, called "501 Blues," had recently brought new vitality to the company after several failed expansions into other apparel market segments in the earlier part of the decade. Confident in the wake of 501's success, the company was contemplating its next steps when research revealed a decline in jeans purchases by LS&Co.'s core customer base of baby boomers. In short, the company's "bread and butter" customer for the last 30 years—the American male teenager—was now 25–49 and was moving out of the jeans market at an alarming rate. To retain these customers even as their jeans purchases slowed or stopped, the company introduced Levi's Dockers casual pants. Dockers, as the name was later shortened to, was one of the most successful new product introductions of the 1980s in the clothing industry. Consumers responded to the product design, which utilized the comfort and casual feel of cotton, and likeable advertising by purchasing enough Dockers to make it a billion-dollar brand by 1993.

Over the course of the 1990s, LS&Co. enjoyed phenomenal success from its Dockers sub-brand. The Dockers brand achieved record sales growth in 1998 and *Fortune* magazine estimated in 1999 that 75 percent of American men owned a pair of Dockers and that the average customer owned 3.8 pairs. That year, the total number of Dockers owners exceeded 40 million. The company noticed at this time that younger consumers began to lose interest in Dockers, however, with many dismissing the pants as something "their fathers wore." In the late 1990s, Levi Strauss developed new advertising campaigns and introduced new Dockers sub-brands to counteract this trend. Sales of Dockers remained over $1 billion through 2000, but sales growth continued to slow. Many questioned the brand's long-term relevance. Would Dockers be able to keep up with changing consumer tastes and shifting fashion standards? Could the brand maintain a loyal customer base while adapting to new styles?

THE ORIGINS OF LEVI STRAUSS & CO. AND LEVI'S 501 JEANS

In 1849, a poor Bavarian immigrant named Levi Strauss landed in San Francisco, California at the invitation of his brother-in-law, the owner of a dry goods business. This dry goods business would later become known as Levi Strauss & Co. Strauss quickly learned that the gold miners were seeking a durable pair of pants that could withstand their rugged lifestyle. To meet their needs, Strauss designed a pair of pants from a heavy brown canvas-like material—the world's first pair of "jeans." Levi's pants quickly became an indispensable part of the miner's uniform, gaining a reputation for being as tough and rugged as the people who wore them. Strauss called his pants "waist high overalls"—the miners called them "those pants of Levi."

Strauss soon switched to a sturdier fabric called "serge de Nimes," made in Nimes, France, to make his pants. The fabric name was later shortened to "denim," and indigo dye was added to give the jeans their blue color. In 1873, rivets were added to strengthen pockets, which had been unable to hold up under the weight of the miners' gold nuggets, along with the patented double arcuate pattern sewn into the back hip pocket—America's first apparel trademark—and the "Two Horse Brand" leather patch. By the 1890s, the popularity of their jeans and other dry goods had spread, and to keep better track of the expanding product line, LS&Co. adopted a new inventory system. Levi's jeans were assigned the lot number "501" and given that number as their name.

Sales of Levi's 501 jeans grew through the 1900s. During the 1930s, the jeans' popularity burgeoned as Western movies began to glamorize blue jeans, establishing 501's Western mystique. Levi's jeans became an even more valuable product during World War II, when the government declared them an essential commodity available primarily to defense workers. In the 1950s, appearances by teen-age idols James Dean and Marlon Brando wearing jeans in the motion pictures *Rebel Without a Cause* and *The Wild Ones*, respectively, captivated an entire post-war baby boom generation. LS&Co. abandoned the wholesale dry goods business and concentrated exclusively on selling their own brand of clothes to a generation that represented millions of potential customers. By 1959, Levi's sales volume totaled $46 million. The love affair with Levi's jeans continued into the 1960s as students started to wear 501's as a form of self-expression. By the time of the Woodstock rock festival in 1969, Levi's jeans were the essential fashion for the emerging baby boom generation. What had originally been a tough pair of pants had become a symbol of freedom, adventure, and independence. Levi's 501 jeans were now an icon, and the Levi's brand name became synonymous with jeans.

DIVERSIFICATION: 1970–1984

For nearly 30 years since World War II, LS&Co. had serviced a seemingly "bottomless" jeans market. Through the 1950s and 1960s, the company doubled sales every three to four years. By the end of the 1960s, the company's operations included jeans, cords, slacks, and sportswear for men, as well as a range of apparel for women and children. In 1968, new divisions for youthwear, sportswear, and accessories were created. The Levi's for Gals marketing unit was expanded into a full-fledged women's wear division. In addition, Levi Strauss International was formed as a subsidiary, enabling the company to parlay its legendary All-American image to foreign consumers eager to own a piece of Americana. With all this growth activity, LS&Co.'s worldwide sales in 1969 totaled $251 million.

The rapid expansion necessitated further capital. In 1971, the company was taken public with an initial public offering of $47.50 per share. Sales continued to experience rapid growth as baby boomer teens entered college. By 1975, sales had reached $1 billion, and rose to $2 billion in 1979. During this time the company's flagship product, 501 jeans, remained its top-selling product, and LS&Co. continued to hold nearly a third of the U.S. jeans market. Production expanded locally and abroad to meet continuing demand. Nonetheless, given the slow growth among its primary market, 12–24 year olds, cash-rich LS&Co. considered alternative actions to hedge against an expected decline in the jeans market in the 1980s.

In the early 1980s, LS&Co. adopted a strategy to expand beyond the core jeans lines to utilize the Levi's name on non-jeans. "We are not going to forget the gal we brought to the dance," explained Robert Haas, then the company's Executive Vice President and COO and great-great grand-nephew of the company's founder. "We want to reemphasize our central nature. But we want to bring out flanking products in our basic industries, to make them more exciting."[2] The company introduced new product lines, covering a broad range of family clothing needs. Many of these came from within the company's existing divisions. Product lines included denim and corduroy jeans for men, women, and children; Action Suits and Tailored Classic blazers and slacks for professional men; and Activewear for sports participants—skiers, tennis players, and the general outdoors person. Counting colors, styles, and sizes, the company offered thousands of different pants, skirts, vests, shirts, blazers, shorts, and blouses—even maternity jeans and jumpers.

An acquisition strategy was implemented to provide for further growth. LS&Co.'s 1979 acquisition of Koracorp Industries, a $185 million California clothing manufacturer, immediately doubled Levi's women's wear sales. Koracorp businesses included: Koret of North America women's wear, Byer-Rolnick hats, Oxford men's suits, and a European-based children's wear division. Other acquisitions included Resistol hats, Rainfair industrial clothing, and Frank Shorter running gear. The company also established numerous licensing agreements for products including casual shoes and socks bearing the Levi's brand, as well as with designers, including Perry Ellis America, Alexander Julian, and Andrew Fezza to broaden LS&Co.'s scope of business into more fashionable clothing segments. As a result of this vigorous diversification and acquisition strategy, LS&Co. owned apparel businesses that offered products to suit almost any lifestyle.

COMMUNICATIONS STRATEGY

Historically, company advertisements had focused almost exclusively on the quality of Levi's jeans for men. The ads, whether print or television, emphasized the quality, durability, and timeless nature of Levi's jeans for men. Western gold miner themes dominated the tone of the early ads. Beginning in the 1970s, LS&Co. shifted its advertising strategy to reflect the company's change in product focus. The company largely replaced its traditional western, miner or prospector image with more contemporary, psychedelic, and "hip" imagery of the day. Ad tag lines included: "Levi's don't have to be blue—they just have to be good"; "Quality never goes out of style"; and "We put a little blue jean in everything we make." At the same time, even though it was diversifying dramatically, the company also wanted to ensure that American men understood that LS&Co. still sold its traditional jeans as work clothes for men. Consequently, the company produced some ads that focused exclusively on men's jeans, retaining the traditional emphasis on jeans as the quality, good-value pant for hard-working American men.

When LS&Co. reorganized its corporate structure in the early 1980s, each division became responsible for its own advertising strategy. As a result, the focus of the company's ads shifted to target specific groups rather than selling products across divisions. Although LS&Co.'s advertising focused primarily on selling to men, expansion of its women's wear and youth apparel lines resulted in more advertising dollars being allocated to these two consumer groups. To sell its array of new apparel lines, LS&Co. expanded its advertising budget dramatically beginning in 1978. By 1982, the advertising budget had grown to $100 million[3], with much of that growth coming from increased television spending.

BACK TO BASICS

Initial diversification efforts produced promising results. Starting in 1980, however, LS&Co. began a three-year earnings decline. Between 1980 and 1982, sales fell 10 percent and net income dropped 76 percent. Although sales and earnings rebounded in 1983 as a result of expanding retail distribution to include Sears and JCPenney, they slipped again in 1984.

Many of the company's non-jeans lines struggled in the face of more established competition. Concern arose that the failure of a number of non-jeans products could adversely impact the cachet associated with its jeans. Management had learned that while the Levi's brand was the company's most powerful asset, it also had its limitations in terms of the products with which it could be identified. With the decline in sales, the company began to consider further expanding its distribution to accounts like Wal-Mart and K-Mart. Reflecting back on the years, Robert Haas described the situation as follows:

> We had diversified too much. We produced everything from hats to $2000 suits, but we no longer stood for anything. We had lost our focus on our core products. Our retail relations had sunk to a point of hostility.[4]

In October 1984, Tom Tusher, president of Levi Strauss International, was named Executive Vice President and Chief Operating Officer. At the employee meeting in which his appointment was announced, he indicated his first decision— LS&Co. would not expand its distribution but would rather concentrate on changing product focus and rebuilding relations with its department and specialty store accounts. Under Tusher's direction, the company instituted plans to improve relations with its retailers and re-focus the Levi's brand name and image to bolster sagging sales.

For Tusher and Haas, LS&Co.'s main objective was to preserve the company's "important values and traditions." To achieve this objective, LS&Co. planned to move away from non-core products and re-emphasize its basic jeans and corduroy lines, which comprised almost two-thirds of revenues, and to "grow the company from the bottom line—through greater efficiency, penetrating market segments more effectively and through cost savings."[5]

STRENGTHENING THE BRAND IMAGE

LS&Co. next focused its marketing efforts on strengthening the Levi's brand. In mid-1985, after reporting a $114 million loss, the company was taken private through a $1.65 billion leveraged buyout, the largest LBO ever at the time. Levi's then began to implement the strategic direction outlined by Tusher in late 1984—shifting focus back to the core product businesses. Consistent with the core product focus and as a means to pay down debt, non-core businesses were sold or discontinued: Rainfair in 1984, Resistol in 1985, Koret of North America, Oxford, and Frank Shorter in 1987. LS&Co. also discontinued its licensing arrangements with Perry Ellis America and Andrew Fezza in 1986. The company closed 40 factories and streamlined staff, reducing payroll from 48,000 employees in 1980 to 36,000 employees by 1986.

LS&Co. also set out to reinvigorate the company's core products. At this time, the company faced both increased competition and shifts in fashion trends. In the early 1980s, there had been a proliferation of new products in the apparel market. Within the jeans market, competition had intensified at the same time that consumer demand began to fall. The well-defined urban image of Lee jeans and western image of Wrangler's jeans, in addition to the high priced, fashion image of Calvin Klein, Bill Blass, and Gloria Vanderbilt designer jeans, posed a serious threat to the loyalty of the traditional Levi's 501 jeans buyer. Moreover, LS&Co., whose historic franchise had been in the Western United States, found its sales failing to meet expectations in the Eastern United States, particularly in major metropolitan areas and among its key target market of 12–24 year olds. This slump in sales was due, in part, to the company's failure to keep pace with product changes in the jeans market. LS&Co.'s products remained "non-washed" long after designer jeans and LS&Co.'s own international markets had begun to rinse and bleach products to appeal to more fashion-conscious consumers.

501 Blues

The $36 million "501 Blues" advertising campaign set out to create an image for 501 jeans consistent with LS&Co.'s corporate philosophy and values. The ads featured a variety of real people "being themselves" by wearing 501s as part of everyday life in a series of urban East Coast settings. The ads' audio focused on Levi's unique, personal "shrink-to-fit" and "button-fly" attributes and blended blues-style music with free association verbiage. The hope was that the campaign would remind existing customers of the uniqueness of 501 jeans and how comfortably they fit into their everyday lives, both in a physical and social sense, as well as introduce the company's flagship product to a new generation of adults. The award-winning campaign helped 501 sales double in 1985, despite the fact that overall U.S. denim sales for the year declined, and placed 501 jeans of a firmer footing nationally.

NEW CHALLENGES

By the beginning of 1986, management was confident it was on the right track. The 501 jeans campaign had proved extremely successful among its target 12–24 year old urban audience. Not only had it re-invigorated jeans sales, but also had brought the Levi's brand back to its core values. Plans were to continue with the "Blues" campaign for the near future.

A per-capita jeans purchases chart prepared by the LS&Co. Menswear research department, however, revealed a troubling fact: 25–49 year old U.S. males purchased an average of 1 to 2 pairs of jeans annually, as compared to an average of 4 to 5 pairs for 15–24 year olds. In 1980, there were 36.8 million men in the U.S. between the ages of 25 and 49; by 1990, this figure was expected to be 47.5 million, nearly half of the adult male population. Although these baby boomers had grown up with Levi's jeans and had developed tremendous loyalty to the Levi's name, they now sought a different kind of pant. Baby boomers viewed themselves as distinct from their parents generation—as they had proven by adopting jeans as kids—and they wanted their clothes to be a break from tradition. Fashion assumed a far greater role for these males than for previous generations. Although these men had aged, they still had a driving need to be active, involved, fashionable, and comfortable. Rejecting the artificial fabrics traditional to the Menswear business in the past, they preferred more natural fibers. At the same time, in the traditionally formal work environment, many companies were relaxing their dress codes to allow employees to dress in more casual attire.

For these reasons, male baby boomers needed a pant that combined style, versatility, and comfort that would be appropriate for both professional and leisure activities. This need was reflected in the change of emphasis on 100 percent cotton and cotton blends in the product mix in men's departments at retailers was.

Developing a Market Strategy

LS&Co. recognized that the casual pant market represented an enormous opportunity. Between 1981 and 1985, jeans retail volume had decreased by 11 percent while slacks volume had increased by 19 percent. Slacks as a percentage of bottoms sales (jeans plus slacks) grew from 33 percent in 1981 to 40 percent in 1985, and the trend was certain to continue. Between the summer of 1985 and the summer of 1986 alone, slacks sales grew by 20 percent.[6] Yet merchandising of slacks was uninspired, and consumers found the slacks department one of the most boring areas in the store. Moreover, brand fragmentation was more prevalent in the dress slacks category than with jeans, and there was no dominant brand leader. LS&Co. had been in the dress slacks market since the mid-1950s (its first non-jeans diversification effort), but the top three dress slacks brands (Levi's, Haggar, and Farah) accounted for 25 percent of the U.S. market, and the top five brands accounted for only 35 percent of the market. In contrast, the top three jeans brands (Levi's, Wrangler, and Lee) accounted for 66 percent of the U.S. men's market, and the top five brands owned 75 percent.[7]

In addition, natural fibers and blends were replacing the traditional 100 percent polyester slacks. Certain designer menswear, such as Ralph Lauren (Polo), did offer full legged, tapered bottom trousers that were cotton/cotton blend.[8] Although these pants were often found in the main floor Men's department, they were sold as "Better Sportswear" with a price tag of $60 to $80.

LS&Co. was determined to maintain the brand loyalty of the "Levi's jeans generation"—who were about to enter into their peak earning years—even if they were no longer buying traditional jeans. These men had been the cornerstone of the company's success and key drivers of apparel trends for over 20 years. The company hoped to appeal to the traditional, older main floor Men's customer as well as to the new, younger crossovers. As the overwhelming brand leader in the men's jeans market, LS&Co. hoped to capitalize on the changing demographics and consumer tastes in two ways: a new line of casual slacks and a new line of re-styled, loose fitting jeans.

INTRODUCING "NEW CASUALS"

The Menswear division decided to first address opportunities in the casual slacks market because it was felt that existing product lines did not sufficiently satisfy the needs of the 25–49 year old male customers. LS&Co. identified its challenge as follows:

> To increase our slacks brand share, Levi's must aggressively market and support trend-right products to create a leadership position in a market that is growing and has no category owner.[9]

The image that the Levi's brand had earned from its jeans business was thought to have already contributed in a limited way to its current slacks image— namely, that Levi's slacks were considered to be more contemporary, less conservative, and more casual than other leading slacks. However, its Action Slacks line (made of 100 percent polyester) did not address the fabric shifts in the slacks market, nor did it reflect the core values that the recent 501 jeans campaign had so successfully established. As one LS&Co. executive explained:

> We feel as though we've got the power of the Levi's brand, which is significant and carries with it all the mystique to be influential in the marketplace. But we recognize that we need to segment from a marketing/advertising perspective because there are so many market types.[10]

LS&Co. needed a new product that motivated the customer to remain within the Levi's brand franchise but that was different from anything they had sold before. Perhaps with some reservations, LS&Co. was moving away from jeans again. In this case, however, rather than de-emphasize its jeans business, the company was determined to simultaneously continue its strong core jeans focus.

To meet the needs of its customers and to establish LS&Co. as the market leader, the Menswear team believed a bold strike was necessary. They decided to create a new product category—"new casuals"—that would position the new pants to men as more formal than jeans and less casual than dress slacks. To LS&Co.,

"new casuals" satisfied an unfilled need in the men's pants market. They were designed to appeal to the baby boomers' fashion demands: casual and comfortable, yet stylish; the right pant for a variety of occasions; and, of course, meeting LS&Co.'s high quality standards. The basic pants design was a 100 percent cotton, pleated, washed fabric with a "reverse silhouette" design—wider at the top and narrower at the leg opening—available in a variety of stylish colors. The company hoped that its new casuals, the first line to bring the full-leg, tapered-bottom trousers of "better sportswear" to the main floor of department stores, would give men a way to ask for a pair of loose, unfitted pants. LS&Co. wanted this new pant to become the standard for the "new casual" pant category. In an effort to make this new pant accessible and affordable, it was priced in the moderate to upper moderate price range, retailing on average for $32.

Branding New Casuals

To brand this new line of casual pants, the Menswear team needed to choose a name, logo, and other important brand elements. To attract the "baby boomer" shopper, the idea was to package the product with a memorable, trademarked name; a unique, permanent, on-garment logo; and a colorful pocket flasher. The team knew they could not simply call this new product "Levi's Pants." The strategic marketing positioning of the company's very successful 501 jeans campaign had defined Levi's as jeans. Somehow the name had to establish its independence and leverage the Levi's brand name in a way so as to maintain a link to the existing name and heritage but not detract from the core jeans focus.

At the time the team was contemplating a name for these new pants, Sue Kilgore, a Menswear merchandiser, returned from a trip to Japan with a pair of twill pants sold by Levi Strauss Japan named Levi Docker Pants. LS&Co.'s Japanese group had adopted the moniker from a Levi's pant sold in Argentina. Both Japan and Argentina had positioned the product to their younger age consumers, but with only limited success. The team liked the Docker name but knew Americans would never say "Levi Docker Pants." The question became how to shorten the name to something Americans would say. In the end, the team decided to add an "s" to Docker and shortening the name to Levi's Dockers. The team liked the Dockers name because although it did have some nautical connotations, for the most part it was considered a neutral empty basket that the company could fill with imagery that was relevant to its broad target audience.

The logo that was chosen blended the Argentine and Japanese logos and consisted of interlocked wings and anchors. The pocket flasher, attached to the back of all pants, consisted of a woman who was being led off a ship by a formally dressed man but whose attention was focused on a relaxed, casually dressed young man standing on the dock. Finally, to establish an understated association with the Levi's name, the Levi's moniker was incorporated in the Dockers winged logo.

Introducing Dockers to the Retail Trade

Levi's Dockers pants were marketed to the retail trade as a major fashion statement—an alternative to jeans—and the driving force in the "new casuals" category. Based on the changing demographics of the U.S. male population, Levi's projected "new casuals" to grow from 28 percent of the total bottoms business to 34 percent by 1989, with contemporary dress slacks increasing from 6 percent to 28 percent and traditional dress slacks decreasing from 38 percent to 21 percent over the same period.[11]

In an effort to establish its Dockers new casuals line, LS&Co. concentrated distribution in department stores and chains where the majority of 25–49 year old men did their shopping and where one-third of all slacks were sold. The company worked closely with retailers, from JCPenney to Bloomingdale's, to generate excitement and support for its new pants. The company courted retailers nationwide—including those department and specialty stores who had previously curtailed business with LS&Co. in the early 1980s—with extensive presentations, sell-in brochures, and swatch books. They provided sales support in a variety of ways including sales kits that provided a "road map" for retail-based marketing, cooperative advertising, and sales promotion programs. In addition, the company offered supplemental financial support for advertising and promotional activities to important high image department stores.

A critical component of the company's marketing effort was the establishment of Dockers shops within main floor Men's areas of major department stores. The traditional Men's department was changing, reducing emphasis on dress slacks and shifting to 100 percent cotton and cotton blends that were targeted to the more youthful customer. This trend was expected to continue as the baby boomer market segment increased as a percentage of the main floor customer base. Retailers were showing greater interest in innovative merchandise techniques.

In recognition of these trends, LS&Co. introduced the first in-store concept shop for the Men's department. A test version was constructed for display at MAGIC (Men's Apparel Guild in California), a key trade show, to introduce Dockers casual pants to retailers. The Dockers in-store shop sought to create a friendly, accessible environment, prominently displaying the sporty Dockers logo, linking consumer advertising with point-of-sale signage and posters, and making trial as easy as possible. Fixtures and tables were installed that allowed for displaying the pants folded, similar to the experience of buying jeans and distinctly different from the rows of hanging slacks. Testing proved very successful, generating twice the sales of pants that were just hung on racks. In stores where shops were not possible due to space or financial constraints, LS&Co. planned to establish point-of-sale displays.

The company's product positioning and marketing strategy were able to overcome the initial reluctance of retailers, and ultimately generated an exceptionally high level of pre-promotion excitement. The company successfully placed Levi's Dockers in all of the Menswear Division's top 50 accounts and in another 50 accounts across the country. Retailers saw Levi's Dockers as the leader in the new casuals category and moved the pants ahead of its primary competitors, including

Gallery by Haggar, Savane by Farah, and "M" by Bugle Boy. With the retail trade behind them, the Menswear Division turned its attention to the development of an effective communications program focused on the consumer.

Launching Dockers to the Consumer

It quickly became apparent to the LS&Co. Menswear Division that in order to establish Levi's Dockers as a major brand in men's casual sportswear, a focused and comprehensive consumer marketing effort beyond the available resources of the Menswear Division would be required. Given the market opportunity for casual pants, the Menswear Division believed that a high impact-marketing program would accelerate the growth of the Dockers line and generate consumer support that could be leveraged to effectively influence trade awareness and interest. The Menswear Division management team convinced Tom Tusher, who had established an advertising reserve for special marketing opportunities, that investment in the required marketing effort to launch Dockers would produce the requisite pay-back to the corporation in terms of revenues, profits, and long-term brand ownership of the crucial baby boomer segment. With the entire LS&Co. organization behind them, the Menswear Division set out to establish a clear proprietary position for Levi's Dockers.

Advertising Strategy

The advertising challenge was to build product and brand awareness for Levi's Dockers so that they would be seen as an unpretentious alternative to traditional dressing for almost every occasion. Thus, advertising had to achieve two goals: 1) because there was no consumer terminology for Dockers-type pants, the ads would have to educate its audience about the new product itself and create brand awareness; and 2) an image for the new product had to be created that leveraged the positive Levi's brand associations but also established a certain amount of autonomy or distance to signal the inherent product differences.

The target audience for the advertising was defined demographically as white collar working men between the ages of 25 and 49 who lived in major metropolitan areas in the United States[12] These target men were expanding their wardrobes to include more casual apparel made from natural fibers that were suitable for a range of informal occasions. LS&Co. conducted a series of focus groups with men in its target market. The men were shown pictures representing a variety of leisure situations and asked to select the pictures that best described when they were "most comfortable and relaxed." The most common scenes chosen included: a man sitting on top of a hill alone, two men walking together on a golf course, and a group of men hanging out and laughing on the beach. Even though many of the men said they did not tend to partake in these events once they were older and married, they still thought fondly in reminiscing about them.

Based on the results of the focus groups, LS&Co. decided that the ads should create an image for the brand based on an emotional appeal. The ads were to create a singular, appealing, and relevant image for the brand that elevated Dockers above all other possible alternatives. Given the target customer, the attitude of the advertising needed to be contemporary. It was important, however, to ensure that the styling of the pants be perceived as timeless and classic. The men wearing Dockers were to be real, approachable and attractive, but not fashion models. The ads were to show Dockers as appropriate attire for a variety of occasions—for work and for weekends. They wanted Dockers to be seen as a way to be comfortable and casual in any setting. Therefore, the advertising was to emphasize the sociability of men wearing the pants. It was also important for the ads to convey the high quality of the Dockers pants line and maintain the link to the Levi's brand name and heritage. The Levi's name would help give the new pant credibility and capitalize on the tremendous loyalty of the target group to the Levi's brand. Finally, the ads would use the "reality-based advertising" style and imagery begun with the 501 Blues ads that LS&Co. wanted to continue. Management hoped that men would view a Dockers commercial and say to themselves: "I like those guys. They're like me. And I like the way they look in those pants."

Advertising Executions

Based on this strategy, LS&Co. and its ad agency Foote, Cone & Belding developed a $4.5 million television campaign for Dockers consisting of three 30-second ads of men in their 20s, 30s, and 40s having informal conversations about life. The situations were varied to include both casual weekend and work-related settings. The audio in the ad consisted of natural, unscripted dialogue while the camera worked like an eye, moving around the group and using extreme close-ups. The ads carefully sought to exclude any "yuppie" talk or yuppie accessories (e.g., Rolex watches). The focus was on the waist down, and no faces were shown at any time. The tagline ran: "Levi's 100% Cotton Dockers. If You're Not Wearing Dockers, You're Just Wearing Pants." As Mike Koelker of Foote, Cone & Belding explained, "using '100% Cotton' provided a tangible bridge to the Levi's jeans heritage."

Media Strategy

The company planned to introduce Dockers through a multi-dimensional, high impact regional program aimed primarily at consumers and secondarily to the trade. The consumer advertising was to provide a positioning and image umbrella for both the consumer and trade markets. Dockers ads were slotted to run in fall 1987 and winter 1988 in 11 major regional markets where Dockers pants were sold. The markets were selected on the basis of retail placement of Dockers, potential for volume growth and geographical dispersion. The 11 markets were New York, Columbus, Cincinnati, Minneapolis, Houston, Washington, D.C., L.A., Miami, Dallas, Charlotte, and Denver.

The Dockers media strategy used spot television in all 11 targeted markets. Spot television was considered the most effective medium to communicate the Dockers "attitude" because it provided a means of delivering the message to a broad target audience quickly and efficiently. The company chose to air its commercials during selective "showcase" prime time, sports, and late night programs. To increase overall effectiveness of the effort, the company planned to show multiple commercials in a single program. In key late night shows, the commercials would be aired each night of the week. Commercials were aired in sports events that included local target market teams. In New York City, which was considered a key market because it could set trends for the entire country, television spots were supplemented with subway signs and mobile billboards located primarily in and around the city's garment district.

Additional Promotion Activities

In addition to television, LS&Co. targeted consumers through co-op advertising with retailers. Dockers Shops and point-of-sale displays provided in-store visibility. Sales promotions (i.e., gift with purchase programs), were planned during kick-off and key seasons to create in-store excitement.

Concurrent with the initial airing of the Dockers commercials, LS&Co. organized an advertising kick-off party in New York City for buying groups, trade press, and key retail executives. In addition, a publicity campaign targeted key market influencers with talk show fashion presentations and press kits. As a follow-up to its initial marketing to retailers, LS&Co. planned a series of visits to key retail accounts by designers, merchandisers, marketing personnel, and senior management.

Initial Results

Success for Dockers came almost overnight. Department stores ordered so much of the product during its first season in 1986 that LS&Co. experienced difficulty filling all the orders. Since other brands like VF Corporation's Lee Jeans chose not to introduce casual pant lines of their own, Dockers continued to draw customer and retailer demand. Following the success of the initial "butt-cam" advertisements, as they came to be known, LS&Co. updated the campaign to make it more stylish. The new ads showed Dockers pants being worn for specific occasions, either at work or at play. These spots featured the tagline "Relax. You're Among Friends" and ran from 1986 to 1990. By 1991, Dockers was a $500 million business and enjoyed 90 percent awareness in the target market of men between 25 and 44 years of age. From this group, 40 percent owned at least one pair of Dockers. The average Dockers customer owned 2.5 pairs of the pants.

Seeking to retain its current customer base while attracting new customers, LS&Co. devised a new advertising campaign in 1991 that attempted to broaden the Dockers image beyond plain khakis. The campaign, titled "Nobody Does Colors Like Dockers," used vibrant color schemes to convey this new image. Each ad in the series showcased a different color offered by Dockers. For example, one ad used only gray tones and featured the tagline: "Gray. What Black Would Look Like if It Lightened Up."

A BILLION-DOLLAR BRAND

By 1993, annual Dockers sales topped $1 billion. That year, Dockers accounted for 50 percent or more of casual pant volume in stores where the line was sold. During 1993, LS&Co. attempted to promote full-time casual office environments by mailing a four-page newsletter entitled "Casual Clothing in the Workplace News" to over 40,000 human resource managers at corporations nationwide. The newsletter contained information about implementing dress-down policies, as well as articles about corporations that adopted casual dress codes. According to the company, 19 percent of the corporations that received newsletters responded, including 81 of the *Fortune* 100 companies. The year 1993 also marked Dockers' move into European markets. LS&Co. established a Dockers Europe subsidiary in Amsterdam and launched the brand with pan-European advertising.

In the hopes of attracting a younger and more style-conscious breed of customer, the company unveiled its Dockers Authentics brand in the summer of 1993. LS&Co. applied the new Dockers Authentics label to pants and shirts cut more stylishly and made of more sophisticated fabrics than the 100 percent cotton used for Dockers. The company allocated about 20 percent of the overall Dockers advertising budget, or $5 million dollars, to a campaign for Authentics. Dockers Authentics occupied roughly 20 percent of Dockers' department store floor space. In addition to a 500,000-piece direct-mail introduction, Dockers Authentics received support from a series of print ads appearing in male-oriented magazines such as *Esquire* and *Outside.*

WRINKLE-FREE COMPETITION

LS&Co. also encountered a challenge to its market dominance in 1993. Companies like Haggar and Farah developed "wrinkle-free" cotton pants that looked like the standard Dockers khaki pant but contained a special fabric treatment that eliminated the need for ironing. Consumers responded positively to the wrinkle-free pants, but LS&Co. ignored the trend in the belief that the pants "[were] too formal for Dockers."[13] Other pants manufacturers gained ground on Dockers, causing the brand to experience slowed sales in 1993 and its first drop in sales in 1994. In the latter year, Dockers' share in the men's khakis market at department stores dropped to 29 percent from 42 percent the previous year, as a host of look-alike and wrinkle-free competitors drew consumers away from Dockers. Wrinkle-free pants had grown from 2 percent of all pants sales at the beginning of the decade to as much as 15 percent at some stores in 1994. Dockers' competitor Haggar held a staggering 73 percent share of the wrinkle-free segment. LS&Co. realized that in addition to losing current customers, the Dockers brand was failing to attract new customers: research showed that men in their 20s had little interest in the brand. The company needed to ensure that Dockers remained relevant to the existing customer base while attracting new customers.

"Nice Pants"

A first step in the domestic revival of Dockers was to catch up to the wrinkle-free trend, which LS&Co. did by launching wrinkle-free Dockers in November 1994.

The launch was supported by a $40 million advertising campaign that began in April. In addition to a new tagline—"Don't just get dressed. Get Dockers"—the campaign included four humorous television spots and a retail promotion linked with the U.S. Open golf tournament. The television ads showcased the wrinkle-free properties of the pants in scripts that sought to appeal to baby boomers. One ad, titled "The Red Eye," showed an airline passenger executing various contortions in order to get comfortable. Throughout the elaborate maneuvers, the pants remain free of wrinkles. LS&Co. continued to expand aggressively into this market, and by 1995 almost all Dockers pants were wrinkle-free.

Because many consumers had just assumed Dockers offered wrinkle-free pants before the line was launched, LS&Co. took a more noteworthy step that same year with the development of the sexed-up "Nice Pants" campaign. The focus of the ad series was a distinct departure from the male bonding scenes characteristic of the original Dockers ad series. The television spots turned up the sex appeal by featuring an ordinary-looking male actor—the Dockers-wearing archetype—pursued by a stunning female. A bout of somewhat awkward eye contact led up to the commercial's climax, when the woman admired the man's pants aloud by remarking, "Nice pants." The advent of Dockers Wrinkle-Free combined with "Nice Pants" campaign contributed to the reversal of Dockers' sales decline. In one major department store chain, sales of Dockers rose 10 to 15 percent per year in 1995 and 1996, compared with growth of less than 5 percent in 1994. By 1997, Dockers represented 80 percent of all men's casual pants sold at the chain.

CREATING ANOTHER SUB-BRAND

Levi's Moves Into Business Casuals

Office workers in the late 1980s witnessed the widespread acceptance of "casual Friday" by the corporate world. In the latter half of the decade, many companies relaxed their dress codes even further by instituting a "business casual" standard that banished suits for the duration of the work week. Just as Levi's Dockers capitalized on the surge in popularity of informal casual wear for Fridays and weekends, the company positioned its new Slates brand to capture what it predicted would be a burgeoning office casual market. At the time of the launch, however, the strategy seemed like a risk. LS&Co. introduced the Slates line in August 1996 into a market dominated by dress pants makers Haggar Clothing Co., which dwarfed Levi's 14 percent dress pants market share with 30 percent of the market. Additionally, the dress pants market had experienced a recent sales slide, from $2.0 billion in 1994 to $1.9 billion in 1995. In spite of the competition and the ailing category, LS&Co. executives felt that "there was room in a man's closet for a third brand."[14]

For the twelve months before the launch, LS&Co. conducted extensive market research to determine the "Slates" name, the pants' pre-tailored cut, the in-store shop style, and the advertising content. LS&Co. tested the name on mock clothing labels and in fake news and magazine articles to gauge customer reaction to the name in print. Consumer testing revealed that double pleated pants were the favored among men, as were hemmed and cuffed pants that did not require additional tailoring. Believing that odd-numbered waist sizes provided a better fit off the shelf, LS&Co. offered Slates in sizes such as 35 and 37. The company tested in-store displays with focus groups in New York and San Francisco. Over 240 retailers nationwide featured the mahogany-detailed Slates displays upon the launch. The company spent more advertising dollars launching Slates than it did on the Dockers' introduction, spending $20 million on a similar introductory campaign involving both extensive television and point-of-purchase advertising.

RETURN OF THE KHAKI

Accompanying this move into business casuals was an overall increase in demand for khakis. By the end of 1997, sales of men's khakis had risen 21 percent from 1995 to $2.8 billion. The success of khakis sharply contrasted a decline in the men's jeans market, which experienced a 6 percent decrease in growth rate from 1996 to 1997. Dockers began facing increased competition from the Gap in 1998, when that company introduced a $20 million television, print, and outdoor advertising campaign to promote their own khakis. According to figures released by LS&Co., the Gap had lots of ground to cover, however. Dockers claimed 26 percent of the khaki market in 1998, more than double its closest competitor. Additionally, Dockers more than doubled the Gap's ad expenditures that same year, launching a $50 million consumer marketing campaign. Dockers also expanded its product line in 1998 with its women's apparel collection, Dockers for Her.

A healthy portion of the 1998 marketing budget, 65 percent, went to Dockers' "urban networking" program. The program, begun in San Francisco, functioned as a sort of cultural outreach, where Dockers sponsored parties, dinners, film festivals, concert series, and khaki giveaways in urban centers across the country. In order to coordinate these efforts within a city, the company created the position of "urban networker." The Dockers urban networker worked from street level to promote the brand to the city's "visionaries." The networker's liberal expense account funded everything from intimate dinners at posh restaurants and rounds of drinks at popular nightspots to extravagant themed parties and independent film festivals. One reason for the large investment in the elaborate urban networking program was the fact that a sizeable portion of Dockers wearers lived in metropolitan areas; one-third of khaki sales came from the top 10 urban markets in the States. Believing also that the consumer public took their fashion cues from the trendsetting urban population, LS&Co. sought to establish Dockers as a desired brand among the urban "critical influencers."

FACING NEW CHALLENGES

Khaki Competition

As khakis climbed in popularity, so too did Dockers competitors. Khakis had been attracting a following in the youth market, and more youth-oriented brands such as the Gap, Polo, and Tommy Hilfiger appealed to teens and twentysomethings in a way Dockers, with its history of targeting aging baby boomers, could not. Research revealed that the young generation of khaki buyers was inclined to think of Dockers as pants that belonged in their fathers' closets. Companies like the Gap, with its $20 million ad campaign for its Gap Khakis, began massive marketing efforts to attract these younger buyers. The Gap Khakis television spots featured young khaki-wearers dancing, singing, and skateboarding to background music that varied depending on which of the themes from among "Khakis Rock," "Khakis Swing," or "Khakis Groove" was highlighted. Dockers countered the popular Gap ads with a youth-themed ad of its own, using the tagline "Khakis with a blue jeans soul" to connect Dockers with the Levi's brand. That same year, LS&Co. added another tagline to its advertising, dropping "Nice Pants" in favor of "One leg at a time."

In early 1999, LS&Co further modified its Dockers marketing approach to make the pants more appealing to young consumers. A first step was to make the link between the Dockers name and the popularity of khakis obvious by rebranding the line of pants "Dockers Khakis." Additionally, the company increased its mass media advertising budget 12 percent from the previous year. The centerpiece of the new Dockers Khakis campaign was a series of slick and sexy television commercials that were in complete contrast to the original Dockers spots featuring men relaxing amongst friends and "being themselves."

One ad, entitled "Nightclub," featured a Dockers-wearing man dancing at a stylish nightclub. Women everywhere are drawn as if by magnetism to him, or, more specifically, to his pants. Each time he finishes dancing with one, a different woman aggressively catches hold of his waistband and pulls him toward her for another dance. Upon leaving the club, the man enters a taxi driven by a woman, who leers suggestively at him. The spot ended with a shot of the man smiling while a female voiceover intones, "Durable, authentic khaki. You'll wear out before they do." The ad also marked the return of the "Nice Pants" tagline, which appeared at the end of the spot. LS&Co. also sought to attract the attention of retro fashion fans by introducing the classically influenced yet cutting-edge styled unisex Dockers K-1 Khakis. The K-1 Khakis were made from throwback fabrics styled after military-issue khakis from the early twentieth century.

Levi's Business Woes

The success of Dockers represented one of the few positive aspects of LS&Co.'s business in the late 1990s. As well as the company understood the tastes of its aging baby-boomer consumer base, it failed when it came to anticipating what the 12–24 year old segment of the market would demand. As jean designs for the youth market became increasingly dissimilar to the traditional straight-legged Levi's template, young buyers began abandoning the classic denim look in favor of baggy pants with big pockets fashioned from synthetic fabrics. LS&Co. resisted changing with the styles at first and subsequently fell out of favor with the teen market. The collective disfavor took its toll on the company's business. After achieving record sales in 1996 of $7.1 billion, the company experienced a sales slide and a market share drop for each of the next four years, a period in which the overall jeans market grew four percent annually.

The company ended its relationship with Foote, Cone & Belding, LS&Co.'s ad agency of 67 years. After a thorough review of its $90 million jeans ad account in late 1997, LS&Co. chose the agency TWBA/Chiat/Day. In spite of the fresh creative offered by TWBA/Chiat/Day, LS&Co.'s overall sales dropped 13 percent to $6 billion from 1997 to 1998. The company's market share dropped below 17 percent in 1998, nearly half of its 30 percent share at the beginning of the decade. By comparison, the Lee and Wrangler brands, owned by VF Corporation, combined market share rose from 17 percent in 1990 to 26 percent in 1998. Additionally, private-label jeans brands like JCPenney Co.'s Arizona label market segment climbed from a mere 3 percent of the market in 1990 to 20 percent in 1998.

Troubles at the company brought about significant changes, the greatest of which may have been in September 1999 when Robert Haas announced that he would leave his role as CEO. LS&Co. hired Phillip Marineau from PepsiCo to revive to company; Haas stayed on as Chairman of the Board. One month later, the company suffered another blow when Moody's Investors Service cut its rating on the company's $2.3 billion debt to junk status (this large amount of debt was incurred in 1996 when the company bought back close to one-third of its stock from family and employees).

LS&Co.'s string of losses prompted the company to drastically reduce its domestic work force by closing half of its remaining 22 North American manufacturing plants and laying off 30 percent of its 19,000 employees in 1999. Company spokeswoman Linda Butler explained at the time, "To maintain a large number of owned-and-operated plants is simply not feasible in this competitive market."[15] In 1999, LS&Co. lost $207 million as sales dropped 14 percent from the year before to $5.1 billion. More drastic was the 95 percent dive in LS&Co.'s net profits, which fell to $5.4 million from $102.5 million in 1998. Worse, Levi's jeans market share continued to hover near 17 percent.

E-commerce Troubles

Contributing to the company's woes was the fact that LS&Co. did not enjoy the same success with e-commerce that many other firms did. Reluctant at first to offer products for direct-order online for fear of angering retail partners, the company eventually allowed customers to purchase clothing from its websites beginning in November 1998. Each brand—Levi's, Dockers, and Slates—had a separate website with information about seasonal lines and retail locations as well as an online ordering feature. The Dockers site also featured an interactive fashion adviser that supplied ensembles for different occasions. The company touted its e-commerce venture with $5 million of web advertising on more than 20 prominent sites, including American Online and Yahoo! According to the company's director of e-commerce and retail marketing, Kevin McSpadden, the Internet advertising effort met with minimal success directing traffic to Levis.com. When the company abandoned its online advertising scheme, McSpadden lamented, "We dumped a lot of money into the Internet. It didn't pay out."[16]

Instead of online marketing, LS&Co. returned to the more traditional media mix of print, radio, and television ads to enliven sales at Levis.com, with similarly little success. The company operated the commercial site for 15 months, but it never turned a profit. Customers at the site typically spent between $56 and $120, but these revenues could not offset the costs of operating the site and delivering the products. At first, LS&Co. prohibited websites run by its retail partners from selling jeans and other LS&Co. products online. When the company repealed this restriction before the 1999 holiday season and allowed JCPenney.com and Macys.com to sell Levi's products, the retailers' sites sold 60 percent more merchandise than LS&Co. did at its own site. The e-commerce features of the company's websites were ultimately removed in January 2000.

DOCKERS TRIES TO REBOUND

The question remained whether Dockers could continue to stimulate growth in a nearly saturated market. With every major clothing brand offering its own interpretation of the classic khakis, Dockers no longer single-handedly filled the hole between jeans and formal pants. To expand outside the now-crowded khakis market by attracting more "fashion-forward" customers, LS&Co introduced the Dockers Recode brand extension in the spring of 2000. As a line of business-casual tops, bottoms, and outerwear offered in a range of colors and made from stretch fabrics, Dockers Recode bore a greater resemblance to Slates merchandise than the original "100% Cotton" Dockers. Both the Recode and Slates brands were eventually streamlined into the Dockers Premium sub-brand, which offered both high-fashion and high-tech styles.

In 2001, Levi Strauss introduced the Dockers Mobile Pant, a pair of fashion-forward Dockers that featured additional pockets for technological gadgets. An advertisement for the Mobile Pant displayed the pant's features using a spy movie premise. In the ad, a woman uses X-ray spectacles to spy on a Dockers-wearing man. She notes that his pants conceal mobile devices such as a cell phone and a PDA, which are invisible to the naked eye. The Mobile Pant was a high-volume seller for Dockers in 2001 and named a "Best Invention of 2001" by *Time* magazine. Though still a billion-dollar brand, Dockers sales in 2001 were hovering near the mark set in 1993.

Dockers Goes Hi-Tech

Dockers began to focus not just on product design, but on adding new features to the materials its clothes were made from. It created the Advanced Innovation Team, who researched materials and ways to make them better. One of the first innovations was Stain Defender technology. Stain Defender was designed using an exclusive DuPont Teflon formula that formed a barrier at the molecular level to defend against many liquid spills. In describing the product, Dockers noted that similar Teflon technology was used in the spacesuits worn during the Apollo moon flight, that Teflon was used in the case housing for the original Emancipation Proclamation.

Aside from fighting stains, Dockers also used technologies that affected fabrics in other ways. Color Bond was a technology that resisted fading during laundering with the help of dyes that formed covalent bonds on the molecular level with the cellulose polymer chains in the fabric. Using antimicrobial technology that eliminated the bacteria that caused odor, Refresh Action functioned on a micro-biological scale, disrupting the bacteria's ability to produce the enzymes that allow it to grow and reproduce. The company claimed this kept shirts fresher longer.

In an effort to make Dockers clothes more comfortable in varying temperatures, the Advanced Innovation Team created the Dockers Thermal Adapt Khaki. This khaki used Smart Fabric Technology that consisted of Thermocules (or "microencapsulated phase-change material") that absorbed excess body heat and released it as the body cooled. These pants were priced at $60.

While technologically advanced, these products did not receive significant media attention. Dockers reversed this trend and garnered media attention in the fall of 2004 when it proclaimed itself the "Unofficial Shirt Sponsor of the 2004 Presidential Campaign." Touting a survey that revealed almost half of Americans admitted to having a negative perception of a professional who had sweat marks on his or her clothes, Dockers advertised its new Perspiration Guard Shirts. These 100 percent cotton shirts wicked moisture away from the body, and then dried that moisture six to eight times faster than normal, eliminating the appearance of perspiration marks. The shirts also had the new Refresh Action technology. The company reminded people of the famous Nixon-Kennedy Presidential debate of 1960, when Vice President Nixon appeared sweaty and uncomfortable on screen, while Senator Kennedy did not show a drop of sweat and looked to be polished and prepared. Dockers sent one dozen shirts, which had a retail price of $50, to both George Bush and John Kerry. There was no official endorsement from either candidate, and it was not clear if the shirts were ever worn. Nonetheless, the move generated publicity for Dockers as its new product was mentioned in various magazines and newspaper articles.

Licensing Agreements

Dockers made aggressive use of licensing to expand its line of products. Dockers licensed its name to the Haddad Apparel Group in 2002, with Haddad designing, producing, and marketing a full line of clothing for boys, girls, infants, and toddlers under the Dockers brand. This collection included pants, tops, outerwear, school uniforms, footwear, and accessories. The next year, Dockers extended its agreement with Northern Cap Manufacturing, in which Northern Cap designed and produced a full range of men's headwear, gloves, and scarves under the Dockers name.

Dockers also entered into agreements with companies that expanded the Dockers brand to products outside the traditional apparel category. The company entered into a licensing agreement with American Pacific Enterprises in 2002. American Pacific designed and marketed a line of bedding ensembles, sheets, towels, and bath accessories known as the Dockers Home collection. This was followed in 2003 in an agreement with Olivet International to market luggage and travel accessories. In 2004, Lacy Mills, Inc. teamed up with Dockers to produce bedding and bath ensembles, as well as a new rug collection. Dockers' executives saw these agreements as natural extensions of the brand. In describing the association with American Pacific, Maureen Griffin, Dockers' consumer marketing director, commented, "Dockers Home makes perfect sense as an extension of the Dockers brand. Dockers is known as being *the* resource for stylish, comfortable, and versatile clothing. Now we can extend these same great features to the home."[17]

Dockers on the Auction Block

LS&Co. had debt of over $2.3 billion and the company continued to experience financial difficulty in the early 2000s. In 2003 the company reported revenues of $4.09 billion, marking seven consecutive years of decreasing revenue; revenue peaked in 1996 at $7.1 billion (see Exhibit 1). The company continued to close plants, and by 2003 it had shuttered all of its U.S. manufacturing plants, even its landmark Valencia Street plant in its hometown of San Francisco (a small amount of Levi's and Dockers manufacturing remained in the United States, through agreements with other firms). LS&Co. did provide for these workers; the company provided employee benefits for those laid off, and the Levi Strauss Foundation donated grants to communities affected by the plant closings.

The company reached a low point in May of 2004 when it announced that it was looking to sell off the Dockers brand. Some analysts estimated that LS&Co. could get close to $1.5 billion by selling Dockers. The company spent five months reviewing offers, and in October decided not to sell the brand. CEO Phil Marineau explained:

> After carefully considering the numerous sales offers and terms we received, and reflecting upon our improved financial performance this year, we have chosen to keep the Dockers business. We believe that we will create more value for LS&Co. and the Dockers brand by retaining the business and driving its continued development ourselves. Additionally, the comprehensive sales exploration process we've been through during the past several months has enabled us to identify a number of opportunities that we believe will make the brand more profitable and successful. We are incorporating these ideas into our business as we move full steam ahead with our retail customers to achieve our mutual goals.[18]

This announcement came one week after the company filed its third quarter 10-Q, the third consecutive quarter in which the company posted improved financial results (LS&Co. is a private company, but because some of its debt was publicly traded, Levi's filed quarterly earnings reports).

The final results for 2004 were encouraging for LS&Co. The company posted revenues of $4.07 billion, down 0.4 percent from the year before—but there were some bright spots. Reported revenues were driven by sales growth in the Asia Pacific Region and for the new Levi Strauss Signature brand, as well as stronger foreign currencies. Even though revenue was nearly flat, lower product sourcing costs and lower inventory markdowns led to an increase in gross profit of 13 percent. When all accounting measures were tallied, the company posted net income of $30 million, compared to a loss of $349 the year prior. This turn of events helped the company's bonds, as credit rating agencies Standard & Poor's and Moody's upgraded their ratings on Levi's long-term debt rating. Even with this good news, and the company's overall financial picture improving, the Dockers brand was still in trouble—the company reported that Dockers experienced lower net sales performance in 2004, down 20 percent to $649 million.

Dockers New Brand Direction

Following these disappointing results for Dockers, LS&Co. made a number of moves to try and revive the flagging brand. In May 2005, the company installed John Goodman, who was Kmart's chief apparel officer, as the new president of the Dockers brand. Soon after, Dockers introduced a new tagline, "Dress to Live" that replaced the long-standing "Nice Pants." The new tagline was designed to expand the brand's positioning beyond casual slacks to a "head-to-toe lifestyle brand."[19] Whereas "Nice Pants" only reinforced the brand's traditional product set, the new slogan encompassed Dockers recently expanded range of product lines, which research had indicated consumers were not aware of. Concurrently, Dockers launched a new brand identity and logo: Dockers San Francisco. The addition of the place-name "San Francisco" was intended to update the Dockers image from its "guys-club" heritage to a more inclusive brand persona offering "a feel-good, look-good approach rooted in the essence of San Francisco's stylish-but-not-stiff way of dressing." The brand's primary logo was updated with the words "San Francisco" replacing the anchor design that had been positioned under the word Dockers from the brand's inception. The brand still used the anchor design on clothing tags to provide continuity with the past. Launch ads featuring the new slogan and logo gave equal time to both male and female styles and took place in iconic San Francisco locations, such as on a cable car by the waterfront.

Additionally, Dockers reorganized its men's line into four occasion-based segments: Work, Weekend, Dress, and Golf. It supported this segmentation with a campaign called "Dockers Four Wearing Occasions" that illustrated the simple ways that Dockers could help men dress for all the activities that they engage in. Ads for the campaign showed a man moving seamlessly through these four activity segments, with overlaid text identifying the appropriate clothing segment for each. The own-brand Dockers stores and website were redesigned to enable customers to shop by occasion.

As a consequence of these moves, Dockers 2005 revenues held flat from 2004 that was a positive result given they had plummeted 20 percent the previous year. LS&Co.'s overall financial performance continued to improve in 2005 (see Exhibit 2). While revenues increased only slightly to $4.1 billion, net income rose by $126 million to $155.9 million. These results were driven by selling higher-margin premium products, such as the Levi Strauss Signature line. The results also reflected continued strong sales in the Asia-Pacific region and, for the first time in years, stable sales in the U.S. market.

THE LEVI STRAUSS & CO. PORTFOLIO OF BRANDS

By 2005, Dockers was one of three brands in the Levi Strauss portfolio. The company also managed the Levi's brand and the Levi Strauss Signature brand. In addition to being the home of the flagship "red tab" line of jeans, the Levi's brand encompassed many new products, such as Type One jeans and Levi's Vintage jeans. While the red tab line sold for about $35 in traditional department stores, Type One jeans were priced from $35 to $95 and sold in many upscale specialty retailers like Barneys New York. The Levi brand moved further upscale with its Vintage jeans. These products, sold in high-end stores like Neiman Marcus, carried a price tag of between $145 and $220.

Levi's introduced a new ad campaign in 2004, titled "A Style for Every Story," to promote the brand. These print ads featured real people and the personal connection they had with their jeans. Four months after its introduction, the campaign was expanded to include television spots. These ads featured the great lengths an owner would go to in order to reunite with a pair of Levi's jeans. In one ad, the lead male character shows up on his girlfriend's doorstep with a bouquet of flowers as an apparent peace offering. Once he charms his way back into her apartment, she leaves to place the flowers in a vase and he is seen snatching up the item he could *really* not say goodbye to—his favorite pair of Levi's jeans.

To capture the discount end of the jeans market, LS&Co. launched the Levi Strauss Signature brand in 2003. These jeans, priced at $21 to $23, were sold through large retailers such as Wal-Mart and Target. Levi Strauss Signature targeted the 160 million U.S. consumers who shopped at mass-channel stores (where 31 percent of all jeans in the United States were sold). This brand launched its inaugural print ad campaign in 2004, targeting the primary value channel shopper—females over the age of 35. Aside from women, the campaign, created by Foote, Cone & Belding, leveraged its relationship with NASCAR driver Jimmie Johnson to reach out to men as well.

CONCLUSION

In the years since the introduction of Dockers, the brand had experienced varying degrees of success. While the Levi's and Levi Strauss Signature brands helped the company back to profitability in 2004, the Dockers brand had experienced a significant drop in sales that year. Even with all the material and product innovation that Dockers contributed in the early 2000s, sales had been well off their peak, and analysts wondered if new styles would be enough to reinvigorate the brand in the coming years.

In spite of these difficulties, Dockers continued to innovate. In 2003, the company signed PGA Tour player Cliff Kresge to a multi-year apparel contract to promote its Dockers Tour line of golf apparel. Later that year, Dockers unveiled the next phase of its print ad campaign for its women's collection. Using the tagline, "Style that works," Dockers added its Individual Fit Waistband and Stain Defender technology to its women's line. In 2005, Dockers introduced its newest product innovation, Never Iron pants. These pants had a special fabric and finish that gave them a "straight from the dry-cleaner" look, including a permanent crease, right out of the dryer (in contrast, the company noted that "wrinkle free" pants often needed to be ironed to make them look crisp and clean).

In 2005, Dockers introduced a new brand identity, logo, slogan, and advertising campaign that helped it stem the losses from the previous fiscal year. Still, the apparel industry remained a difficult environment for Dockers. In addition to continued competition from Haggar and the Gap, new threats came from teen favorites Abercrombie & Fitch, and American Eagle Outfitters. Additionally, declines in world cotton production in 2004, combined with increased consumption, would likely impact the company's profitability. LS&Co. was faced with these challenges, as well as the task of finding new ways to make the Dockers brand relevant and interesting to consumers.

DISCUSSION QUESTIONS

1. How would you characterize Levi's branding strategy in general? What are the positive aspects? Are there any negative aspects?
2. Analyze Dockers' communication strategy at the time of the launch. How did it fit in with past Levi's advertising efforts? How did it contribute to brand equity?
3. How would you characterize the Dockers brand image? What makes up its brand equity? Evaluate the move to expand the line into the bedding, bath, and luggage markets.
4. Describe some of the changes in the Dockers marketing strategy from its debut. Has LS&Co. maintained a consistent enough marketing message? Is it well-positioned strategically and tactically to maintain its strong leadership status in the coming years?
5. Dockers missed out on the "wrinkle free" trend when it first surfaced. Not incorporating this technology into pants hurt the company. Years later, Dockers embraced technology in its products, creating the Thermal Adapt Kahki and Perspiration Guard shirt. Was adding this technology to their products the right move, or did Dockers "go too far" in adding these features to their clothes?
6. Evaluate Dockers' decision to stop selling products directly to consumers on its website. Dockers' main competitors (e.g., Gap, J.Crew, and Abercrombie & Fitch) are heavily involved in online retailing. Should Dockers reconsider their decision?
7. Imagine that you are John Goodman and have just been named as the head of the Dockers brand. What are your priorities? What do you do first?

Exhibit 1: Levi Strauss & Co. Net Revenues

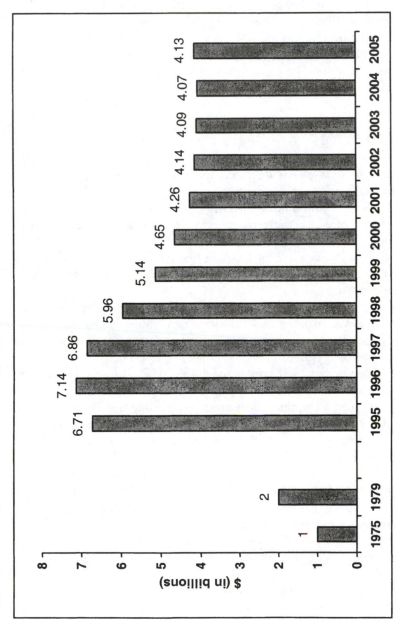

Source: Company Reports

220

Exhibit 2: Levi Strauss & Co. Revenue for 2005 (in millions)

U.S. Revenue By Division		Total Revenue By Region	
Levi's Brand	$ 1,259	North America	$ 2,455
Dockers Brand	647	Europe	981
Levi Strauss Signature Brand	361	Asia Pacific	689
Total	$ 2,267	Total	$ 4,125

Source: Company Reports

REFERENCES

[1] This case was made possible through the cooperation of Levi-Strauss and the assistance of Steve Goldstein, Director of Marketing, Men's Jeans, Levi-Strauss & Co. Leslie Kimerling and Gregory Tusher prepared this case, with research assistance from Keith Richey and updates and revisions by Jonathan Michaels, under the supervision of Professor Kevin Lane Keller as the basis for class discussion.

[2] *BusinessWeek*, October 23, 1983.

[3] *BusinessWeek*, March 8, 1982.

[4] *San Francisco Focus,* October 1993.

[5] *Forbes*, August 11, 1986.

[6] Internal Company Sources.

[7] Internal Company Sources.

[8] Internal Company Sources.

[9] Internal Company Sources.

[10] *Bobbin*, November 1990.

[11] *Daily News Record*, January 6, 1988.

[12] Internal Company Sources.

[13] As quoted in The *San Francisco Chronicle*, July 19, 1997

[14] as quoted in *Brandweek*, "Levi's New Dress Code," August 19, 1996

[15] As quoted in *Advertising Age*, June 1999

[16] As quoted in *Advertising Age*, June 1999

[17] Company press release, "New Dockers Home Collection to Debut in Spring 2003." May 10, 2002.

[18] Company press release, "Levi Strauss & Co. Announces Decision to Retain Dockers Business." October 18, 2004.

[19] Celeste Ward, "Dockers Dons a New Lifestyle Image, Logo," *Adweek*, September 12, 2005.

NIVEA:
MANAGING A MULTI-CATEGORY BRAND[1]

BACKGROUND

As 2005 drew to a close, executives at Beiersdorf's (BDF) Cosmed division reflected on the growth of their Nivea brand over the last decade and a half. Nivea, the largest cosmetics brand in the world, had successfully defended its position during intense competition in its major European markets. Additionally, the company had expanded into many new markets in South and Latin America, Eastern Europe, and Asia. Nivea had created a number of new sub-brands that broadened the company's product offerings, including the 1997 launch of a decorative cosmetics line, Nivea Beauté, and the aggressive expansion of Nivea for Men. Nivea also introduced a major scientific breakthrough—an anti-aging coenzyme called Q10—that became an unqualified success and was included in a number of sub-brand products. Nivea's growth during this time was reflected by its net sales. Sales in Beiersdorf's Cosmed division, primarily driven by Nivea, grew from €1.4 million billion in 1995 to €3.8 billion in 2005 (see Exhibit 1). In addition, Beiersdorf's share price grew from €25.69 in 1995 to €85.6 in 2004 after peaking at €127.50 in 2001.

As Nivea's product portfolio expanded, the company faced a new challenge: maintaining growth while preserving the established brand equity. During the 1970s and 1980s, BDF's Cosmed Division had successfully extended the Nivea brand from a limited range of products—Nivea Crème, Milk, Soap, and Sun—to a full range of skin care and personal care products. Over time, these different product lines had established their own identities as "sub-brands," independent of and yet still connected to the Nivea Crème core brand. Given the breadth of products sold under the Nivea name, however, there had been debates in the 1990s as to how to achieve the proper synergy between the Nivea Crème core brand and the sub-brands from other product classes. In planning new product developments, Cosmed management sought to ensure that the Nivea brand met the market needs while also remaining true to the heritage of Nivea, as exemplified by flagship moisturizer product Nivea Crème.

Nivea's marketing program in the 1990s and 2000s followed a "sub-brand strategy" where individual sub-brands received budget allocations for independent marketing communications activities, rather than an "umbrella brand" strategy where the Nivea corporate brand was promoted first and foremost. Internally, however, executives debated whether the Nivea Crème brand should continue to receive significant marketing dollars. Some felt that Nivea Crème was the core brand in the Nivea brand franchise and therefore played the most valuable role. Others worried about how the traditional Nivea Crème image could be maintained if the company also needed to innovate and modernize it. Now that the company had a broad spectrum of successful sub-brands, the big question going forward was how the company could best manage its brand hierarchy. Additionally, management wondered from where the next surge of growth would come and whether it would be crossing Nivea's brand "boundaries."

DEVELOPMENT OF THE NIVEA BRAND: 1912–1970

Nivea Crème was first introduced into the German market in 1912. In the early 1900s, industrialization led to the emergence of mass markets and branded articles. Society—women in particular—began to appreciate to a greater degree physical appearance and look for products to both care for and beautify the skin. Nivea Crème's unique water-in-oil emulsion was the first crème to offer both skin care and protection at a reasonable price. The Nivea name came from the Latin word, nives, meaning "snow"—reflecting the snow white color of Nivea Crème. As the world's first multi-purpose, "universal" skin crème, Nivea Crème was quickly adopted for use by the entire family. Nivea Crème was introduced throughout Europe in 1912; in the United States in 1922; and in South America and other parts of the world in 1926.[2]

Recognizing the value of Nivea Crème and the need for other reasonably priced skin care products, Beiersdorf introduced over forty-eight other skin care products under the Nivea brand name between 1911 and 1970. As BDF expanded its range of product offerings, it maintained a "mono-product" philosophy—typically offering one multi-purpose product in each skin care market segment and category it entered.

Throughout this period, Nivea Crème remained the company's primary product and the carrier of the Nivea brand name. The famous Nivea Crème blue tin with white lettering, standardized in 1925, was a familiar sight in millions of households worldwide. In addition to Nivea Crème, the brand's other primary products included body soap and powder and two sun care products—tanning lotion and oil.[3]

Nivea Crème Brand Identity and Values

Over the years, Nivea—primarily through Nivea Crème—had acquired a unique, widely-understood brand identity as a "caretaker" of skin. Throughout Europe, most users were first introduced to Nivea Crème during their childhood, learning that it was a product that could be used by the entire family to satisfy all kinds of needs. Because of consumers' own personal history with the brand and the company's advertising, Nivea had become strongly associated with shared family experiences and had a rich set of other brand associations such as "care," "mildness," "reliability," "gentleness," "protection," "high quality," "feeling good," and "reasonably priced." Over time, the Nivea name became synonymous with protection and care for the skin. By the 1960s, Nivea Crème could be found in almost every German household and in the majority of households across Europe and was the dominant multi-purpose skin crème worldwide.

Early Nivea Advertising

BDF first began advertising Nivea products—primarily Nivea Crème—in 1912. The company viewed advertising as a means of strengthening consumer perceptions of a quality product. For over 60 years, Nivea advertising promoted the basic themes of skin care and protection. Ads were always simple, plain, and informative. In the 1910s and 1920s, BDF advertised three main Nivea products—crème, soap, and powder. Early ads established the image of the Nivea woman as clean, fresh, and natural.

Over time, Nivea ads were altered to reflect changes in self-images and lifestyles. For example, in the 1920s, when German women were becoming more athletic and active, Nivea ads began to show women in more outdoor and active settings. In the 1930s, when tanning came into fashion, BDF responded by highlighting the skin protective qualities of Nivea crème and introducing a new product—Nivea oil—for sunburn. In the 1950s, following the end of World War II, Nivea ads reflected the German population's desire to enjoy life by showing Nivea products used in relaxed and happy settings.

While the settings of the ads changed, the clean, fresh, and natural image of the Nivea woman remained essentially unchanged. While she was modernized to reflect the styles of the time, she was always a face with whom the average woman could identify. Over time, Nivea ads sought to link the clean, fresh, and natural image of the Nivea user to related elements of nature—fresh air, light, and sunshine.

NIVEA'S FIRST COMPETITIVE CHALLENGE: THE 1970s

During Nivea Crème's first fifty years, the market for multi-purpose crème grew steadily. By 1970, Nivea held over 35 percent of the multi-purpose crème market in Germany and majority market share in Europe. In the late 1960s and early 1970s, the multi-purpose crème market changed substantially as BDF faced its first strong competition in 60 years. Henkel-Khasana, a small German toiletries company and subsidiary of Henkel, launched its own multi-purpose crème, Crème 21, in 1972. A direct copy of Nivea Crème, this product was backed by extensive advertising and a distribution strategy designed to take advantage of a broader, fundamental shift in consumer purchase habits for cosmetics from specialized outlets to mass market, self-service outlets such as food stores. Also at this time, a number of manufacturers—including Ponds, Unilever, and Lingner-Fisher (now part of Procter & Gamble)—introduced a variety of specialized crèmes into the market, particularly moisturizing crèmes, designed for specific skin care uses.

Concerned with this new competition, BDF performed a study of the Nivea brand image in the German market. The study found that the Nivea brand enjoyed a high degree of goodwill and represented reliability, quality, and honesty. Yet, the brand had an "older" image and was not viewed as young, dynamic, and modern, as was the case with many of the recently introduced competitive brands.

In recognition of these new competitive challenges and current consumer perceptions of the Nivea brand, BDF developed a "two-prong" strategy. First, BDF sought to stabilize the strong historical market position of Nivea Crème. Second, the company sought to exploit the strength of Nivea Crème by transferring the goodwill it had created for the Nivea brand to other product classes.

Revitalizing Nivea Crème

BDF introduced larger sized units, altered its distribution strategy by shifting from special-line outlets to food outlets, and increased its level of promotional activities with the trade and within stores. The primary means to revitalize Nivea Crème's brand image, however, was the introduction of a very aggressive ad campaign aimed directly at the competition.

The initial campaign launched in spring 1971, and used the tag line "Nivea, the Crème de la crème." A series of seven ads were developed around the slogan. After two years of the "Crème de la crème" campaign, Cosmed developed a new series of ads directly aimed at updating the "old" brand image. The "Only Me" campaign ran internationally and made a new brand promise: Nivea Crème meets all skin care needs.

The Nivea brand had been synonymous for the skin crème product category but new competition forced BDF to tell consumers directly about its actual product benefits. Each ad showed the blue and white Nivea tin being embraced by an element of nature and highlighted a specific purpose for the use of Nivea Crème. The objective was to negate competitors' claims for special crèmes by positioning Nivea Crème as the best crème for every kind of special need. Together, these ads reinforced caring and mildness as key consumer benefits and presented Nivea as the universal skin crème that embodied all the needs of consumers in one product.

Extending the Nivea Brand

In addition to strengthening the brand image of Nivea Crème, BDF's second objective was to use the recognition and reputation of the Nivea brand name to introduce new products—both in categories where Nivea products were sold currently as well as in related categories. While BDF had been selling a variety of different products under the Nivea name for years, Nivea Crème dominated company sales and was the primary image-maker for the Nivea brand. Since the market for multi-purpose crème was stagnating, BDF actively targeted new and growing market segments in which to extend the Nivea brand. The company's long-term objective was to evolve Nivea from a *skin crème* brand into a *skin care* brand by providing a range of new products that would both complement Nivea Crème and broaden the meaning of the Nivea brand name.

At this time, the Nivea family of products included: Nivea Crème, Nivea Milk, Nivea Baby (oil and powder), Nivea Sun oil and milk, and regular soap (sold only in Germany). To establish Nivea as a skin care brand, the company decided to create a family of products that symbolically could be represented as the "Nivea universe." At the center of the Nivea universe was the Nivea Crème core brand. Nivea products—some already existing, some new—would function as satellite sub-brands around this center.

Cosmed established a set of guidelines for Nivea brand extensions. All new products had to be compatible with the Nivea brand and be targeted to market segments with attractive, current, and potential size. The company had a "mono-product" philosophy, meaning that there would be only one product promising consumers universal application in each product category. A second version of a particular product could be introduced only if it satisfied a unique need not met by the current product(s) in its category. To clarify, the company established a set of guidelines that any possible new products had to satisfy:

1. Meet a basic need: clean and/or protect.
2. Offer the special care/mildness benefit of Nivea crème.
3. Be simple and uncomplicated.
4. Not offer to solve only a specific problem.
5. Maintain a leading position in terms of quality.
6. Offer the product at a reasonable price so the consumer perceives a balanced cost- benefit relationship.
7. Offer the broadest possible distribution.

All new products had to offer "continuity plus innovation" that is, maintain the essential Nivea core while offering something new. Additionally, existing products had to be continuously improved, reflecting the company's philosophy to respond to market trends and to innovate through research and development. As one long-time Cosmed executive explained:

> It was like taking a teaspoon of Nivea Crème and putting it into every new Nivea product as a special benefit—as an additional amount of care. In this way the new product was really a two-in-one product: satisfying a basic need plus offering the care of Nivea Crème as a symbol.

UNDERSTANDING THE NIVEA BRAND

By the early 1990s, it was clear that BDF had succeeded in extending the Nivea brand from skin crème to a skin care and personal care brand. In 1992, Nivea Crème accounted for only 22 percent of total Nivea brand sales. While Nivea Crème remained the largest single contributor to total revenues, the newer product lines each made significant contributions. Nivea products held strong market positions throughout Europe, especially in smaller volume markets where advertising costs were lower. BDF was a small company relative to its competition (e.g. Unilever, Procter & Gamble, and L'Oréal) and its advertising budget was substantially smaller. Nivea's highest percentage market penetration was in Belgium, Switzerland, and Austria. Germany—the largest skin and personal care market in Europe—however, remained BDF's largest volume market.

BDF's success in establishing Nivea as a broad skin care and personal care brand now presented the company with a new set of issues and challenges. In the process of establishing sub-brands, there was concern that the Nivea brand image—in particular, the Nivea Crème image—had been weakened through all the product introductions. Moreover, there was fear that continuing to develop sub-brands independent of one another would be complicated, risky, and send a confusing set of messages to consumers about what Nivea represented. At the time, ad campaigns were developed independently by three different ad agencies. Although there were similarities in the various campaigns, there was no consistent message strategy or standardized presentation. Cosmed management decided it was time to bring consistency to the marketing of the Nivea sub-brands.

At the same time, the Cosmed Division came under new leadership. Dr. Rolf Kunisch, head of Procter & Gamble's European Division for 22 years, joined BDF to head the Cosmed Division. Kunisch—who later became CEO and president of BDF's board in 1994—joined a task force to define the Nivea brand philosophy. Kunisch believed that in preparing to develop a new Nivea communications strategy, a formalized brand philosophy was necessary. Kunisch explained:

> Nivea is the most fascinating brand in the world, second only to Coca-Cola. The company had done a tremendous job over the last 50 years to keep the Nivea brand focused yet diversified in a very reasonable way. But at the same time there was a lack of conscientiousness of what it meant to be a brand. In the good old days, BDF had a brand relationship that was very personalized. Only three people knew how it had all been done—one retired, one left the company and one died. In addition, there were three advertising agencies that did not talk with one another. I began with the basics and asked: What is Nivea? The data was all there, the feeling was there, but no one had put it on a piece of paper.

While working internally on the Nivea brand philosophy, the company undertook a set of market research studies to provide consumer insight of their perceptions and associations with the Nivea brand. One study revealed that consumers associated the Nivea brand with traditional family values, communities, and nature. Another study analyzed consumers' socio-cultural values and compared them to Nivea's positioning. The studies revealed that Nivea's brand associations and needs, including mildness and care, fit well into consumer's values in the 1990s. The return to a more simplistic, holistic approach to life; the desire for fairness, authenticity, openness and belonging, and an integration of the past with the present were all values that were also associated with the Nivea brand and particularly Nivea Creme. The results of this research clearly suggested that the 1990s presented an opportunity to grow and expand the Nivea brand.

Developing Cosmed's Corporate Strategy
Combining the results of the external research with their own internal research and discussions, the Cosmed task force developed a common brand philosophy for Nivea to be adopted by the entire company and become the basis for developing a corporate strategy that the Cosmed Division could implement at the product level.

The brand philosophy centered on maintaining the association of "universality" for Nivea products. Now that the Nivea brand represented comprehensive skin care and personal care, the company wanted to develop a marketing strategy that would continue to nurture core Nivea associations while widening their applicability and enhancing their meaning via sub-brands. Kunisch explained, "We want to build on the image of the blue tin where we are number one almost everywhere in Europe." Nivea Creme continued to represent the heart of the Nivea image, evoking the most trust and sympathy of the consumer. Even as Nivea's sub-brands continued to expand in the 1990s, Nivea Crème was to remain the primary representative of the brand's history and myth. Though its sales share had declined over the years, Nivea Crème was still considered the company's most important product for its role in establishing and renewing basic trust in the Nivea brand. The company wanted to develop a marketing strategy that would continue to nurture core Nivea associations while widening their applicability and enhancing their meaning via sub-brands.

The role of the other sub-brands was to continue to cater to the specific skin care and personal care needs of their target market segments and contribute back their particular product class associations to reinforce and elaborate on the image of Nivea as a skin care specialist. Because facial skin care represented 75 percent of the European skin care market and was very closely related to Nivea's strong association of "general skin care" from Nivea Creme, Nivea Visage was considered the primary sub-brand to upgrade Nivea's image into the 1990s. Nivea Visage, the company's face care brand, had the most sophisticated, contemporary and specialist brand image of all Nivea sub-brands. At the same time, it benefited from the "halo" of the Nivea name that represented trust, care, mildness and fair price. The primary challenge facing Nivea Visage was how to effectively upgrade the Nivea image as a skin care specialist while continuing to represent the universality and accessibility of the Nivea brand. As with Visage, other sub-brands were expected to offer something back to the Nivea brand. Through this combination, BDF sought to maintain Nivea's leading position in the mass-market segment of the European skin care market.

While the Nivea brand was BDF's leading skin and personal care brand, the company sold other skin and personal care products under different brand names, including 8x4 deodorant and bath products, Labello lip balm, and Atrix lotion.[4] In total, these other brands represented nearly 40 percent of Cosmed's sales in 1991. Although these brands would continue to be part of BDF's product offerings, the company decided that the company's primary focus in the future would be the further development of the Nivea brand through the introduction of new products. Only "extra" efforts and investments would be devoted to the development of these other brands.

EXECUTING THE NIVEA BRAND PHILOSOPHY

Having established corporate objectives, Cosmed now needed to design a communications strategy. Cosmed worked with its advertising agency, TBWA, to develop a set of guidelines that would communicate a certain "Niveaness" in all ads and promotions. This "Niveaness" was to be represented in the layout, message, and image of the ads. Any campaign for Nivea Crème would have to incorporate the brand's values: timeless and ageless; motherhood and a happy family; honesty and trustworthiness; and the product benefits of mildness and quality. Any campaign for a sub-brand would have to reflect elements of these values.

Cosmed was able to establish additional guidelines for the ad agency to follow. These guidelines included: using common emotion in all ads, a uniform

Nivea logo, consistent lettering and typeface, real, inspirational people in the ads, and understandable copy about the product.

Expansion of Nivea Sub-Brands

During the 1980s, the Nivea category extensions grew into distinct sub-brands and adopted separate ad campaigns for each sub-brand. Consequently, each sub-brand had built its own personality and developed its own set of brand associations that were consistent with, but independent of, the Nivea Crème core brand image. Through advertising, each sub-brand promoted specific product attributes and benefits that best satisfied the needs of its target market, and contained a common "Nivea" message of quality and care.

By 2005, the Nivea brand portfolio had grown from six product groups in 1993 to fifteen, including:

- Skin Care—Nivea Body, Nivea Visage, Nivea for Men, Nivea Sun, Nivea Baby, Nivea Crème, Nivea Vital, Nivea Soft, Nivea Hand, and Nivea Lip.
- Personal Care—Nivea Deo, Nivea Beaute, Nivea Hair Care, Nivea Bath Care, and Nivea Intimate Care.

SKIN CARE

Nivea Crème

Nivea Crème, Nivea's first product, was introduced in 1911 and was the first stable water-in-oil emulsion available in the world. Original Nivea Crème tins were pale yellow with "Nivea Crème" in blue print in the center and a red and blue Art Nouveau border, but were changed in 1926 to the now-familiar blue and white design. The tin design and advertising style evolved over the years, but both always reflected the simplicity and caring embodied by the brand.

Historically, most Nivea ad campaigns had been developed from a predominantly German perspective, largely because BDF had built the Nivea brand around the local needs of the German market. With the increasing internationalization of the cosmetics and toiletries market and the international strength of its main competitors, BDF felt that it was very important in going forward to build the Nivea brand through a strong European base. Consequently, in the 1990s, the company developed a true international ad campaign that presented a common brand image for Nivea Crème.

The "Blue Harmony" campaign, introduced in January 1992, included a series of television and print ads highlighting Nivea Crème. Because Nivea Creme was still the company's most important image carrier, but was plagued by stagnating sales, Cosmed decided first to develop a worldwide ad campaign that presented a common brand image for Nivea Creme. The first ad showed a group of seagulls flying together through the air as circus music played in the background. The headline read: "Harmony in Blue." "Harmony" was written in the Nivea logo lettering while "in Blue" was written in white cursive letters. At the end of the ad a picture of a tin of Nivea Creme flashed on the screen with the tagline " All that skin needs to live."

Nivea Soft

Nivea Soft, a lighter skin cream distinct from Nivea Crème, was first introduced in Europe in 1994. The Nivea Soft formula was designed to be lighter than the heavier, greasier feeling of Nivea Crème's Oil and Water formulation. The company was careful to position Nivea Soft as a separate identity so not to cannibalize sales from Nivea Crème. Nivea Soft initially launched in the United Kingdom with an innovative marketing strategy called "fast marketing" internally. The fast marketing strategy collapsed the annual marketing budget into a single week of intensive television and print advertising, sampling, and promotion. After the fast marketing was deemed successful in the United Kingdom. Nivea employed the strategy for Nivea Soft introductions in other markets. Following the European launch, Nivea Soft expanded to South America, Asia, Africa, Canada, and Mexico during the 1990s.

Awareness for Nivea Soft was low initially, but sales continued to climb. By 2001, Nivea Soft was the number two product in its category throughout most of Europe. Despite the fact that Nivea Soft and Nivea Crème were similarly positioned as all-purpose creams, there was little cannibalization of sales. Nivea Crème sales held steady while Nivea Soft grew and many consumers started purchasing both products. In 2004, Nivea Soft launched in the United States in two sizes and revolved around extensive sampling targeting women ages 18–49. The campaign also included couponing, an online sweepstakes, and radio spots. Nivea Soft's launch in the United States was very successful and by February 2005 Nivea (Soft and Crème sub-brands combined) had moved to the number one position in the U.S. hand and body lotion market in terms of dollar sales.[5] That same year, Nivea Soft also introduced three new sizes in Europe, including a mini tube for traveling.

Nivea Visage

In 1982, Cosmed introduced in Europe its first set of face care products for women, called Nivea Visage after a line of products sold in France since the early 1970s. Early Visage ads stressed the mildness of Nivea products in caring for the face. Within one year, Visage became a leading face cleanser in many European countries.

For the next five years, Nivea Visage's message focused on mildness. In 1987, BDF introduced a beauty fluid (liquid moisturizer) to try and established itself as a face care specialist. The product performed poorly and BDF learned that the benefit of "mildness" which had been such a successful point of difference in the cleansing segment of the market was not as unique in the moisturizing segment of the market. Rather, consumers in this market segment were looking for proof of a product's effectiveness.

Cosmed upgraded Nivea Visage's image through a series of actions. First, Cosmed changed the packaging of its products from plastic to glass. Second, the company altered the logo for Nivea Visage. Third, the company improved its product offerings, including the introduction of a moisturizing day crème and night crème in 1989. Finally, Cosmed introduced a new series of ads that focused on highlighting specific benefits of Nivea Visage products. The ads moved away from Nivea's traditional codes of simplicity and universality to develop a more sophisticated specialty image.

With the addition of its first "anti-age" products in 1991, BDF introduced a third ad campaign, "Science in all confidence" that sought to blend the image of the best in face care science with the trust historically attached to the Nivea brand name.

By 1996, Nivea had passed L'Oréal to become the number one face care brand in Europe, with an 18 percent market share compared to 13 percent for L'Oréal. In 1998, Nivea introduced a scientific breakthrough called Q10 that would soon become one of the company's best-selling products. Q10 is a coenzyme produced naturally by the skin that helps reduce wrinkles. In scientific tests conducted by the company, usage of Q10 visibly reduced wrinkles after six weeks. Q10 was first used in the Nivea Visage line, in a product named Nivea Visage Anti-Wrinkle Q10 Day Cream. The Q10 coenzyme was used in other products, including products in the Nivea Body, Nivea Vital, and Nivea Beauté sub-brands.

Between 1998 and 2001, Q10 products achieved 20 percent growth, making the product, according to Nivea's current Vice President of International Brand Management Franziska Schmiedebach, "the biggest success story in the last 20 years." In the three top-selling markets, Q10 products represented one quarter of all Nivea Visage sales. The success of Q10 enabled the Nivea Visage sub-brand to become the number one face care brand in the world, with a 13 percent global market share in 2000.

By 2004, Niveage Visage led the German market with 24.4 percent market share and the United Kingdom. with 12.9 percent market share. Nivea Visage sales in the United States hit 2.5 percent share in 2005, a 144 percent increase over the previous year. Experts forecasted skin care growth over the next five years to come from firming, anti-cellulite, and anti-aging products. As a result, Nivea reformulated and improved its Q10 and renamed it Q10 Plus. Q10 Plus contained Q10 and creatine, ingredients that not only reduced the appearance of wrinkles but also helped prevent wrinkles. Q10 Plus became the active ingredient in many of Nivea's Visage product lines, especially those targeting women over 40 years of age.

Nivea Vital

Nivea Vital was introduced in 1994 in order to address the different skin care needs of women over the age of 50. Nivea chose to advertise using older models so these mature, educated and critical consumers would be able to identify with the brand. By using a 52-year-old German model in the introductory campaign, Nivea broke the unwritten rule of the cosmetics category that mature women should not be depicted in advertising. A television spot developed for European countries depicted the model and detailed the product benefits. The tagline stated, "Activating day cream from Nivea Vital. For more elasticity . . . that you can even feel!"

Nivea redesigned its packaging and logo for Nivea Vital in 1999. The new design, which incorporated the color red and curved gold bands, was intended to suggest energy and femininity. In 2000, the Nivea Vital range included cleansing, day and night creams, body lotion, and intensive special products that support the cell renewal process. Nivea Vital continued to grow with innovation. In 2003, Nivea Vital launched Comfort Cleansing Wipes, leaving mature skin with "a fresh, healthy glow and a pleasantly smooth feel." New versions of Nivea Vital products came from specific ingredients like soy proteins and primrose oil, which were added in the mid-2000s to give the consumer specific anti-aging benefits. Often grouped with Nivea Visage, the two sub-brands together held the number two global market share position for skin care.

Nivea Body

The Nivea Body sub-brand, one of BDF's smallest product groups, consisted of Nivea Milk and Nivea Lotion. Nivea Milk, like Nivea Crème, was a water-in-oil emulsion but in liquid form to provide long-term storage of moisture for dry skin. Nivea Lotion was an oil-in-water emulsion designed for daily care of normal skin. By offering liquid skin care for dry and normal skin in addition to the classic Nivea Crème, BDF sought to provide a comprehensive range of products that met the specialized skin care needs of different skin types. [6]

In 1996, Nivea developed the first special care product for the Nivea Body line. Called the Skin-Firming Complex, it produced "noticeably firmer skin and increased elasticity."[7] Other innovative products introduced by Nivea Body included Nivea Whitening Cream, which targeted the Asia-Pacific region where white skin is considered fashionable. The company also produced a Body Spray (called Sheer Moisturizing Spray in the United States) and a Shimmer Lotion with reflective properties that made skin appear to shine. In 2000, the company introduced Nivea Body Firming Lotion with Q10.

With the expansive growth in anti-firming products, Nivea body positioned its body care products in three categories: Essential, Performance, and Pleasure. The company used Nivea.com to help explain the benefits of each category. The Essential line was developed to moisturize, soften, and protect skin in various forms such as oil, milk, and lotion. The Performance line focused on shaving, exfoliating, night time, and skin firming products using Q10 plus. The Pleasure line focused on senses to relax, re-energize or refresh consumers and included products like, Body Lotion Rice & Lotus, Ocean Breeze Spray, Skin Oil, and Caring Water.

In 2004, the global body care market hit $8.7 billion. Nivea Body was the sixth largest skin care brand in the world in 2004 with a 2.4 percent market share overall. In Germany and the United Kingdom, Nivea Body maintained its market share leadership. Firming and anti-cellulite products, in general, had increased over 14 percent in one year. Most of Nivea's growth that year came from this "slimming phenomenon."

Nivea for Men

In 1980, Nivea introduced its first product specifically designed for the men's skin care market—an after-shave balsam. The product embodied the Nivea brand extension requirements of product innovation with brand continuity. It was the first after-shave product to provide both an alcohol cleanser and a moisturizer to care for the face. From the beginning, the Nivea for Men ads emphasized the mildness and caring of Nivea as their distinguishing customer benefits. The first print ad for the after-shave balm carried the tag line, "Less alcohol, more care."

The Nivea for Men sub-brand grew into a full line of men's skin care products by 1986 but launched many more products in the 1990s and early 2000s. In 1993, Nivea Men launched the Sensitive line for men who suffered from skin irritation. In 1998, Nivea developed the Philishave Cool Skin electric razor with Nivea for Men shaving emulsion. The razor emitted Nivea for Men lotion during shaving. Nivea also introduced its Q10 formulation to men in a face and eye cream. A number of products previously unavailable in the men's skin care category were launched from 2000–2003, including a face scrub, facemask, toner, and oil control. By 2005, Nivea for Men had three product lines—Normal, Sensitive, and Fresh—which offered foams, creams, and balms. The latest product launch, Men's Active Firming Lotion, was specifically designed to firm and tighten skin in the cheeks, neck, and chin.

The growth of men's skin care exploded in the early 2000s with the emergence of the "metrosexual" male, an urban-dwelling man who embraced products that helped with his overall appearance and health. In 2003, sales of men's shaving, skin, and hair care products hit $3.8 billion in the United States, $1.1 billion in the United Kingdom, and $863 million in Germany. Researchers forecasted future growth to come from after-shave and skin care products. This trend in men's care led competitor Procter & Gamble to purchase the Gillette Co. in 2004 for $54 billion in cash and stock. L'Oréal and Neutrogena also followed suit and launched a men's skin care line. As Joanne Mintz, marketing manager for Nivea for Men U.K. explains: "Our real long term challenge is to make this sector of male skin care as big as it is currently for women."

As of 2003, Nivea for Men held a 14.9 percent market share in Germany, third in the country. In the United Kingdom Nivea for Men had a 3.7 percent market share and ranked sixth. It moved up three places by 2006 by increasing its market share to 10 percent. Nivea for Men had a 17 percent global market share in 2006.

Nivea Sun

After Nivea Crème, Nivea Sun is one of the oldest Nivea products. Nivea sun care products had a long advertising history dating back to the 1930s. Only in the early 1970s, however, did BDF consciously begin to develop Nivea Sun as an independent sub-brand. A unique logo and design was developed to create a Nivea Sun "world" where people were happy under the care and protection of Nivea Sun products.

In the 1980s, it had the most extensive product range of any Nivea sub-brand, having expanded its oil and crème products to include lotions in a variety of SPF factors and after-sun products, among others. In the late 1980s and early 1990s, BDF extended the Nivea Sun line to include more specialized sun care products, including a line of sensitive skin and after-sun products, further demonstrating Nivea Sun's ability to fulfill specialized needs.

In 1997, Nivea introduced a line of moisturizing sun cream that were co-branded with Nivea Visage called Nivea Sun Visage. These products offered "active cell protection and vitamin E-plus to prevent sun wrinkles" as well as high UVA and UVB protection levels. In 1999, Nivea launched the successful Nivea Sun Spray line. Another innovative product was Nivea Sun Kids Sun Spray that appeared green when first applied to the skin and disappeared after a few minutes. Not only did it ensure parents that sun tan lotion covered the entire child, but it was fun for kids, too. An ad showed a young child with the product on his face, arms, and chest in a manner resembling warrior paint, while the copy read, "Where it's green, it won't be red."

The early 2000s marked a dynamic growth period for Nivea Sun, led with innovations in self-tanning and firming sun products. In 2000, Nivea Sun developed a product containing Q10, called Nivea Sun After Sun Cream with Q10. The product was designed to prevent the wrinkles and lines that result from repeated sun exposure. That innovation led to the creation of Nivea Firm Sun Lotion in 2002, designed to protect the skin from the sun and also increase the skin's firmness and elasticity. In 2004, Nivea Sun branched into hair care with a seasonal hair care product that combined UV protection from the sun's radiation, chlorine, and salt.

In 2004, Nivea Sun ranked first in Germany with a 24 percent market share. Nivea Sun was second to L'Oréal in the United Kingdom. with a 19.5 percent market share. By 2005, Nivea Sun had the number one global market share in sun protection but still had not yet entered the U.S. billion dollar sun protection market.[8]

Nivea Baby

The Nivea Baby line was introduced in Central Europe in the 1970s, but the products failed to meet sales targets in Austria, Germany, and Holland and were pulled within a few years. In 1996, Nivea relaunched the entire Nivea Baby line. By 2000, Nivea Baby had a total market share of 13 percent in Western Europe. Of the major baby care brands in this region, only Pampers had a higher market share at 17 percent.

In 2005, Nivea Baby developed Toddies, the first all-purpose wipe for babies and toilet training wipe for toddlers. Toddies launched in Austria, Switzerland, Ireland, Poland, France and Belgium. Nivea Baby also introduced Soft-Crème Wipes—wipes soaked in baby soft cream to care for the baby's sensitive bottoms. By 2005, Nivea Baby had a complete baby care product line, including cleansing wipes, shampoos, conditioners, bathing soaps, lotions, powders, crèmes, oils, and sun protection and was achieving particularly strong growth in developing countries such as Hungary and Thailand.

Nivea Hand

Nivea Hand was launched in 1998 with a hand cream named Nivea Hand Age Control Lotion designed to counteract skin aging. An introductory print ad showed a close-up of a smooth set of hands, and the copy read "Apparently, you can tell a woman's age by her hands . . . Now you can lie a little." The ad indicated that women could essentially "cheat time" with the new Nivea Hand lotion. Nivea Hand added anti-ageing ingredients in 2000 and introduced Nivea Hand Anti Age Q10 Plus, which contains Q10 and UV Filters to prevent and reduce signs of aging in the hands. The remaining products within Nivea Hand focused on moisturizing, nourishing, and night renewal.

Nivea Lip

Nivea Lip care sticks were first introduced in 1902 and known in Europe as the brand, Labello. Nivea Lip's product line focused on four areas—essential care, beauty care, sophisticated care, and performance care. By 2004, the global lip care market was just shy of $1 billion, and had increased 4.8 percent in the previous year. Nivea Lip continued to expand its distribution in the early 2000s including markets throughout Asia and North America.

PERSONAL CARE

Nivea Deo

In 1991, BDF extended Nivea's presence in the personal care area with a line of deodorant products called Nivea Deo. Though Cosmed had initially discussed introducing a deodorant product under the Nivea brand name since 1983, management was not convinced the time was right until 1991. Uwe Wolfer, Director of Cosmed Germany explained:

> In the deodorant field, there is demand today for mildness and caring that wasn't there before. Ten years ago, people wanted freshness, fragrance, efficacy and they wanted the product to be transparent. Today, even in the deodorant field, people want assurance of mildness. So we introduced a product with this caring and mildness image. If we had done the same operation ten years ago, we would not have succeeded.

The initial Deo line included aerosol, roll-on, pump-spray and crème products. In the advertising, Nivea Deo went beyond the traditional "efficacy" appeals to emphasize the additional dimension of "caring" through the introduction of a feather as a symbol of mildness and caring. The company introduced a sensitive-skin version of Nivea Deo in 1995 with Nivea Deo Sensitive Balsam. Nivea Deo for Men also launched in 1995.

In 2000, Nivea relaunched the Nivea Deo range using the new concept "Mild Care and Natural Freshness." That year, Nivea Deodorant was Nivea's third-largest sub-brand. Two innovative products developed for the Japanese market—Nivea Deo Wipes and Nivea Deo Compact—became key products in other markets. In 2000, Nivea launched Nivea Deo Wipes, a convenient and effective underarm cleanser in a wipe form. The Nivea Deo Compact, introduced in 2001, is a portable spray deodorant and claimed to be the smallest of its kind anywhere.

In 2004, Beiersdorf launched Nivea "Fresh" a 24-hour antiperspirant spray and roll-on. The next year, Nivea Deo launched Aqua Cool for men, which provided consumers with protection and a cool masculine scent. For women, Nivea Deo launched Pure—a clear and pure deodorant formula that does not leave white marks or residue. Innovation continued to be critical in the extremely competitive deodorant category and Nivea supported its new products with million dollar advertising campaigns.

As of 2004, sales of Nivea Deo reached $5.6 billion in Germany and led the German market with a 33 percent share. Success abroad was still elusive, as market share in the United Kingdom. only hit a 2 percent that same year.

Nivea Beauté

Nivea Beauté was the company's second-biggest brand launch, after the Q10 ingredient brand. In 1997, Nivea made its first appearance in the color cosmetics category with Nivea Beauté test markets in France and Belgium. The brand was positioned with primary focus on the skin-care attributes of the products by using the slogan "Colors that Care." Consumers felt that Nivea Beauté products were consistent with Nivea's core competency of caring. The products were packaged in stylish containers made in deep-blue hues that resonated with the Nivea Crème packaging. Nivea Beauté set price points at the top of the mass market in order to compete with entrenched competitors, Maybelline and L'Oréal. The sub-brand consisted of a full line of color cosmetics with more than 100 different SKUs. After successful launches in the test markets, Nivea Beauté expanded into Germany, Switzerland, and Austria in 1998, and Greece, Turkey, Portugal, Finland, Norway, Sweden, and Denmark in 1999.

Nivea spent lavishly marketing Nivea Beauté. Ads emphasized the caring aspects of the products as well as their high-fashion design. Early print ads for the sub-brand were primarily informational, with lots of copy text detailing product ingredients and benefits. Later ads contained more fashion and glamour than traditional decorative cosmetics advertising.

The first year for the Nivea Beauté sub-brand was not without difficulty. First, Beauté encountered intense competition from established color cosmetics companies like L'Oréal, which increased its ad spends and aggressively launched new products in order to stay a step ahead of Nivea Beauté. The company also discovered that seasonal colors, which they had not planned on developing, were imperative in the marketplace. So, by 2000, Nivea was developing products coordinated with seasonal color themes, such as Sahara Gold lipstick, foundation, nail polish, and eyeliner.

In 1999, the company combined its Q10 innovation with the Nivea Beauté line and developed Nivea Beauté Time Balance Q10 make-up. Over the next 5 years, Nivea Beauté innovated in the cosmetics category with products like: Mascara Optimal 3 in 1 in 1999, Color & Calcium Nailpolish in 2000, Velvet Mat Makeup in

2003, Lash Revolution Mascara with patented elastoflex brush in 2004, and Flex&Strong with Bamboo Nailpolish in 2005.

In 2004, Nivea Beaute's largest market was in Germany, where its 8.4 percent market share made it the fifth largest cosmetics brand in the country. In France, Nivea Beauté had a 6.9 percent share, which was sixth in the nation. Beiersdorf spent $800 million on advertising for Nivea Beauté in 2004, which was dwarfed by L'Oréal's $2.2 billion advertising budget for cosmetics. Nivea Beauté had not entered either the lucrative U.K. or the U.S. cosmetics markets by 2005.

Nivea considered the Nivea Beauté line to have a halo effect on the overall brand. Not only did having a product in the high-image cosmetics category give the brand more cachet, but the Beauté line also attracted new, younger consumers to the brand and Nivea's other products.

Nivea Bath Care

Nivea Shower and Bath (now called Nivea Bath Care) was Nivea's first sub-brand developed primarily for personal care, extending the Nivea brand into important skin-related personal care categories. Since their initial introduction, ads for Nivea shower and bath products have promoted the high-quality, mild, caring benefits of the Nivea brand while also emphasizing the added emotional benefit of pleasure.

In 1993, Nivea Bath Care became official introducing Nivea Shower Milk, a line of co-branded bath care products that combined the Nivea Body Milk lotion with Nivea Bath Care products. In 1995, Nivea developed Nivea Milk Bar, a bar soap form of Shower Milk. In 1997, Nivea Aroma Bath Care capitalized on the aromatherapy trend. In 1998, Nivea launched two products for children—Nivea Bath Care Shampoo & Shower for Kids and Nivea Bath Care Foam Bath for Kids. In 2000, Nivea Bath Care Shower Gel debuted with a line of shower gel products for the whole family. That same year, the Cosmed relaunched its Nivea Bath Care brand by changing the packaging, price, and formulas and sought to project a more feminine image. In 2002, Nivea introduced Nivea Shower Oil and won "Product of the Year" in France for outstanding innovation. Nivea introduced a shower massager with built-in shower gel in 2004. The massager was developed to stimulate blood circulation and encourage skin firming.

Total sales of bath and shower products had been declining in Germany and the United States from 2000–2005. While Nivea Bath Care remained relatively strong throughout Europe and held a dominant 14.3 percent market share in Germany, it did not benefit from a booming category. Nivea continued to innovate, though, as with its new 2005 "flavors"—Milk & Apricot Body Wash and the Rice & Lotus line.

Nivea Hair Care

Nivea Hair's first product, Nivea Milk was introduced in the 1920s but Nivea's first hair care product, shampoo plus conditioner, officially launched in 1991. The introduction of hair care products extended Nivea's presence even further in the personal care market. Unlike Nivea Bath and Shower, however, hair care was not viewed as a skin-related product line and hence was not to be closely aligned with

Nivea's key association as a skin care provider. To maintain a strong link to other aspects of Nivea's core brand image, the first two products were named (in German) "Pflege-Shampoo" and "Pflege-Spulung." By adding the word "Pflege" (Care) to the product names, it was clear that these products continued in the Nivea tradition of caring. Over the next few years, ads for Nivea Shampoo and Conditioner remained essentially unchanged and continued to emphasize its mildness and care qualities.

The biggest development in the Nivea Hair Care sub-brand was the launch of the all-new Nivea Hair Care Styling line in 1996. Nivea Hair Care Styling began with three hair sprays and three hair gels that catered to individual hairstyles. The styling products were gentle and effective, providing hold and promoting healthy hair. Sales for the first year of availability topped $11 million. In 1997, Nivea unveiled Ultra Strong Hair Lacque and by the end of that year, Nivea Hair Care Styling products sold $18 million.

Market research revealed that consumers perceived that Nivea Hair Care Styling did not provide long-lasting hold because its position as a mild styling product. Therefore, Nivea relaunched the entire product line with better focus on "hold." In 1998, the company developed new formulations for its range of hairspray and mousse and introduced a line extension with Ultra Strong Mousse. A new advertisement, "Powershopping," depicted a model in a shop busily trying on clothes. Though she pulls several tops on and off, her hairstyle never loses its form.

In 1999, the company launched Nivea Hair Care Shampoo for Men designed for frequent use. Nivea Hair Care Liquid Gel and Nivea Hair Care Aqua Gel were introduced in 2000 as the "wet look" became popular. Nivea Hair Care continued to expand the brand in the early 2000s with the launch of Color Shine shampoos, conditioners, and treatments. The company also introduced a line of Sun Hair Care products, including After-Sun Shampoo and Conditioner and Sun Protection Spray, which protected hair from UV rays, salt, and chlorine.

In the early 2000s, styling agents held the largest share of hair care products and Nivea Hair Care continued to prosper financially. By 2004, the German hair care market grew to $2.7 billion and Nivea Hair Care held the third position in the marketplace with a 6.2 U.K. share. Nivea continued to focus on and launch products not only for specific hair care needs, e.g. Nivea Locken for curly hair and Nivea After Sun, but also for specific consumer groups like men and children.[9]

Nivea Intimate Care

Nivea Intimate Care launched in 2004 with a series of feminine care wipes and lotions. Nivea Intimate Care included chamomile in its formula and emphasized the natural ingredient with a chamomile flower on the packaging. Like other Nivea sub-brands, the packaging was developed to communicate softness and care yet stay true to the Nivea brand image. The sub-brand only launched in Italy but exceeded sales in its first year.

NIVEA'S BRANDING STRATEGY

Marketing Guidelines

In the mid-1990s, Nivea began standardizing its advertising formats to establish a consistent look among its sub-brands. While the "Blue Manifesto" campaign was designed specifically for Nivea Crème, ads for other Nivea sub-brands adopted some of the design elements of the Nivea Crème ads, particularly in the use of the block and cursive combination in the Nivea logo lettering. The block letters were always used to identify the product and the cursive lettering was used to highlight specific product attributes.

Cosmed worked with agencies FCB and TBWA to develop the marketing concepts and ad executions. In each market, they implemented "perfect local execution" with local agency affiliates. For example, the models or language may change so the Nivea brand appears local but the content remains consistent. As Norbert Krapp, Nivea's vice president of skin care, stated, "Pictures travel, words don't."[10] In some Latin American, South American, and Asian Pacific markets, the ads used different models to reflect the local culture, but in almost all cases the advertising formats remained constant. Nivea distributed booklets with every product that detailed packaging and advertising guidelines.

The company also printed a booklet for internal use detailing its brand philosophy, called the "Blue Bible." The Blue Bible contained basic information about Nivea's brand identity, vision, mission, success factors, and the role of its sub-brands. The Blue Bible also gave guidelines for products, packaging, communication, promotion, public relations, direct marketing, and pricing. Norbert Krapp referred to the Blue Bible as "the best [branding step] we did in recent years," calling it the "key anchor" for all brand decisions.[11]

Direct Marketing

Nivea initiated a number of direct marketing programs around 1995, primarily for its Nivea Vital and Nivea Visage brands. Nivea's largest national direct marketing campaign, in France, involved a database with more than one million consumers. Consumers in France receive periodic mailings that contain product samples and information, coupons, and a survey. Another large effort was the development of Nivea magazines, which started in Germany. Nivea published a magazine with articles for the whole family, including ones specifically for men and younger adults. A total of more than 10 million of these magazines appear as inserts in other periodicals two times a year and were distributed throughout Europe. In addition to the latest Nivea advertising, they contain information about a wealth of Nivea products, beauty advice, decorating tips, feature articles related to beauty, and other content commonly found in fashion magazines.

Non-Traditional Marketing

In addition to its print and television advertising, Nivea engaged in numerous non-traditional advertising methods. One of Nivea's most enduring promotional tools was the blue Nivea beach ball that the company distributed at European beaches each summer. These balls had been standard issue for more than 30 years, and helped to reinforce Nivea's image as a caretaker of the skin in a fun way. Other unique promotional devices included a Blue Santa Claus giving away Nivea Crème in Germany during the holidays, a double-decker Nivea-branded blue promotional bus in Russia, and a "mega-poster" advertisement covering the outside of the Kremlin.

Nivea also built a Nivea Club in Austria in 1995. For an annual membership fee of about $10, members received a quarterly magazine, between four and six new product samplings, and a birthday gift. Similar to the Nivea Club, Nivea opened the Nivea Care Center in South Africa and planned to open its first "House of Nivea" store in Hamburg, Germany in 2006. The house will offer Nivea's product line and expert beauty advice. Similar to Tupperware parties, consumers in Austria could host the party in their home and Nivea would pay for a beautician to visit with an assortment of Nivea products. Nivea also organized "workshops for body & soul" in Germany, the United Kingdom and United States where small groups of women could attend a three-day conference at resort locations.

Nivea partnered with hospitals and sponsors young mothers in maternity wards by sending them "care packages" containing Nivea products. The company also provided free product samples and informational brochures for the mothers for one year after the birth of their child. Through the first three years following birth, Nivea provided important baby care information to mothers at regularly scheduled intervals that corresponded with stages in infant and toddler development.

Event Marketing

Nivea devoted a portion of its marketing budget to event marketing activities. Each country has an event manager that coordinates sub-brand marketing activities and is responsible for developing special events, such as sponsorship. Nivea sponsored various organizations in Europe, including beach lifesavers (lifeguards), children's sailing programs, and a beach volleyball tour. Nivea sponsored school education programs for safe sunbathing in several countries under the auspices of its Nivea Sun brand. And, Nivea sponsored beauty contests in diverse markets such as Poland, the United Kingdom, and Thailand.

Nivea created a branded double-decker bus that traveled to concerts and other youth-oriented events. The bus promoted such youthful products as Nivea Hair Care Styling and Nivea Beauté. Consumers could get a total hair and face makeover at the bus.

During 2000, Nivea developed a promotion for its Nivea Hand products in the Netherlands. Free with each tube of Nivea Hand Anti-Age Crème Q10 was a pair of metal relaxation balls. The balls, which are designed to stimulate circulation in the hands and calm the nervous system, came with instructions on use.

Nivea also worked with its retail partners to create Nivea shops in large German department stores. Nivea Shops included extensive point-of-sale display that integrated Nivea's sub-brands and had a beauty advisor in-house to help customers.

Nivea.com

Nivea.com is a global website with information about the company and its history, products, markets, beauty advice, and games. The website is designed with the popular Blue Harmony theme and each country has its own version—again to give the brand a local presence. Each sub-brand also has a website, with information about individual products and specialized beauty and skin care tips. Nivea.com has become an important information center, especially for new consumers like men.

In the early 2000s, Nivea experimented with viral marketing campaigns, including online sweepstakes, chat rooms, and promotions like the 2004 sponsorship of "Bridget Jones: the Edge of Reason" where consumers sent in 10-second video clips. However, while Nivea continued to interact more and more with its consumers online, as a whole, Nivea brand managers felt that traditional media like print and TV still best portrayed the Nivea image.[12]

Research and Development

Executives at Nivea believed that growth would continue to come from product innovation. In 2004, Beiersdorf spent €38 million on its new and improved research and development center in Germany, which made it the largest and most modern skin research center in the country and employed over 650 scientists.

New Market Rollout Guidelines

Nivea enters new markets first with its flagship product, Nivea Crème. As the company's most basic and all-purpose cosmetic product, Nivea Crème sells well in developing markets. Once the company establishes Nivea Crème as a market leader, it introduces Nivea Body, the sub-brand that shares the most common elements with Nivea Crème. Next, the company rolls out Nivea Visage, followed by Nivea Soft, then Nivea Deo. Once these sub-brands are established in a market, then Nivea introduces what it considers its most sophisticated sub-brand: Nivea Beauté. Nivea Visage must be a market leader before the company can launch Nivea Beauté in that market. Because the color cosmetics category is highly competitive and heavily developed, this hierarchical rollout strategy seeks to ensure that a national subsidiary has the expertise and experience necessary to give proper support to Nivea Beauté.

Geographic Growth Opportunities

Nivea has remained a small player in the U.S. market. In 2003, Nivea's U.S. retail sales hit $180 million, a small percentage of the U.S.'s $7 billion skin care market. In 2005, Nivea had five sub-brands in North America: Nivea for Men, Nivea Crème, Nivea Body, Nivea Soft, and Nivea Visage. Nivea launched an extensive marketing campaign for Nivea for Men throughout the United States and continued to see its expanding distribution in pharmacies, supermarkets, and club stores. In addition,

Nivea Visage Q10 and Nivea Firming Body Lotion were also gaining success as a result of the trends in anti-cellulite and firming products.

There was no dominant player in the U.S. skin care market, however companies with strong market share, such as L'Oréal, Estée Lauder, and Avon, also sold cosmetics. Nivea had not yet launched Nivea Beaute in the United States and this was seen as an opportunity for growth.

Emerging markets also provided Nivea with opportunity to grow. In 2001, emerging markets represented 86 percent of the world's population but only 23 percent of the world's cosmetic sales.[13] Analysts predicted this was an opportunity for Nivea to grow internationally without fierce competition like they would face in the United States.

OVERALL BRAND HEALTH

At the beginning of the 1990s, Nivea was already a global brand with a wide assortment of products catering to the full spectrum of consumer segments. The company had a widely recognized and respected brand, which it leveraged across a range of sub-brands. Throughout the decade, Nivea nurtured its existing sub-brands and moved into additional market segments by adding new sub-brands. The company's sub-brand strategy yielded remarkable results: between 1990 and 2000, every Nivea sub-brand experienced sales growth and gained market share. By 2005, Nivea was a leading international skin care company and voted the most trusted brand in Germany by *Reader's Digest* from 2001–2004 (see Exhibit 2 for Nivea market share in Germany and the United Kingdom). That same year, Nivea was also voted most trusted skin care company in eleven other European countries. Nivea management decided that the sub-brand strategy was effective. The company did, however, continue the "Blue Harmony" campaign for its flagship product, Nivea Crème.

Others at the company were less than enamored with the sub-brand strategy Nivea had followed during the 1990s. "We tried for 10 years to give the sub-brands a life of their own, and I think we more or less failed," said corporate vice president of skin care Norbert Krapp. According to Krapp, rather than thinking of a particular Nivea sub-brand when they are making a purchase, consumers are saying "I'd like to buy the blue bottle of Nivea" (meaning Nivea Body Milk) or "I'd like to buy the white cream" (meaning Nivea Soft). The problem with sub-brands, in Krapp's view, is that "Nobody is able to cope with 13 brand groups." Krapp did not believe a corporate image campaign would improve the state of the brand since Nivea Crème enjoyed such high awareness already—as much as 99 percent in many mature markets. Instead, Krapp wanted to see more marketing dollars devoted to the flagship product, Nivea Crème. Because he believed Nivea Crème to be central to the equity of the overall brand, Krapp maintained that "the image [of Nivea Crème] needs to be polished otherwise the core of the brand is losing strength."

Looking to the future, Nivea executives pondered how best to manage the Nivea hierarchy and from where the next surge of growth would come. There were many opportunities geographically, through product innovation and new target consumers. Geographically, Nivea could seek growth in either the United States where L'Oréal, P&G, and Estée Lauder held strong market share (see Exhibit 3) or emerging markets. Nivea could also focus more on product innovation, especially on the growing trends of skin firming and anti-cellulite products. There was also the booming sector of men's grooming—but more focus on men meant less focus on its core consumer base of women and families. And, Nivea had to consider whether Nivea Crème was still its flagship brand or whether consumers now preferred Nivea Soft with its gentler formulation.

Nivea had to be careful to manage these new developments and opportunities without spreading the Nivea brand too thin or harming its strong brand equity. Finally, the company had to decide whether the sub-brand strategy would continue to work or if the company should leverage the Nivea brand with an umbrella strategy.

DISCUSSION QUESTIONS

1. What is the brand image and sources of equity for the Nivea brand? Does it vary across product classes? How would you characterize their brand hierarchy?
2. What are the pros and cons of the sub-brand strategy? Should Nivea run a corporate brand or umbrella ad for all of their products? What is the role of the Nivea Crème advertising? Should it be changed?
3. Discuss the risks and benefits of Nivea's brand extension into new product categories and customers. How have Nivea's executives managed this extension? Have they missed opportunities such as perfume or foot care? Are there certain boundaries that Nivea should not cross?
4. Should Nivea pursue a Men's grooming category? Does the company risk alienating its core consumer base of families and women or is this a natural next brand extension?
5. What would you do now? What recommendations would you make to Nivea concerning next steps in their marketing program?

Exhibit 1: Beiersdorf Cosmed Division Sales (Euro Millions)

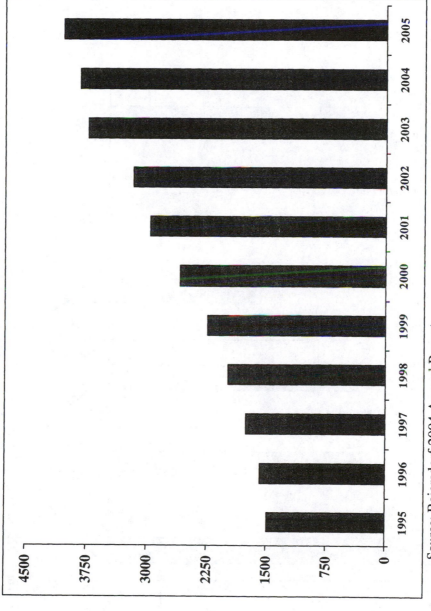

Source: Beiersdorf 2004 Annual Report

245

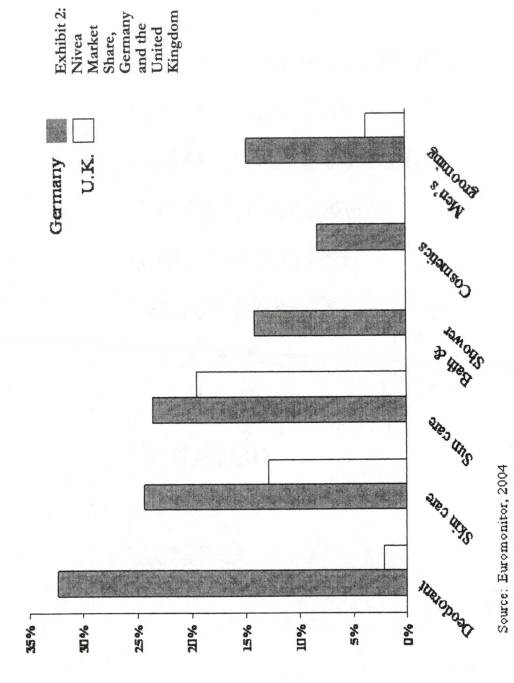

Exhibit 2: Nivea Market Share, Germany and the United Kingdom

Germany
U.K.

Men's grooming
Cosmetics
Bath & Shower
Sun care
Skin care
Deodorant

35%
30%
25%
20%
15%
10%
5%
0%

Source: Euromonitor, 2004

246

Exhibit 3: U.S. Market Share in Skin Care (Percents)

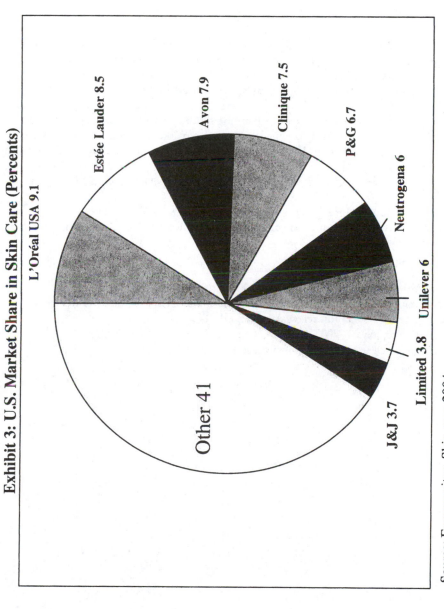

L'Oréal USA 9.1

Estée Lauder 8.5

Avon 7.9

Clinique 7.5

P&G 6.7

Neutrogena 6

Unilever 6

Limited 3.8

J&J 3.7

Other 41

Source: Euromonitor, Skin care 2004

247

REFERENCES

1 This case was made possible through the cooperation of Dr. Rolf Kunisch and Cosmed Division management, including Norbert Krapp, Franziska Schmiedebach, and Inken Hollmann-Peters for Beiersdorf AG in Hamburg, Germany. Leslie Kimerling and Keith Richey prepared this case under the supervision of Professor Kevin Lane Keller as the basis for class discussion.

2 While Nivea Skin and Personal Care products are sold in over 140 countries worldwide, this case study focuses primarily on Nivea's European market position and brand strategy.

3 Nivea oil was introduced in the 1930s. In the 1910s and 1920s, Nivea body powder was a popular product.

4 Other principal brands included Basis pH, Limara and Doppeldusch, Guhl, Azea, and Solea.

5 Information Resources Inc., 52 weeks ending February 20, 2005.

6 BDF also offered a line of problem-solving products called Nivea Body Specifics sold only in France, Belgium, and Italy.

7 *Nivea* book, 2001

8 Beiersdorf.com history.

9 Euromonitor, Haircare in Germany, June 2004.

10 Norbert Krapp. Personal Interview, August 2001.

11 Norbert Krapp. Personal Interview, August 2001.

12 New Media Age, July 31, 2005.

13 Morgan Stanley Dean Whitter Equity Research, April 9. 2001.

YAHOO!:
MANAGING AN ONLINE BRAND[1]

INTRODUCTION

In the second half of the 1990s, Yahoo! grew from a tiny upstart surrounded by Silicon Valley heavyweights into a major force in Internet media. The company expanded rapidly from its humble roots by making acquisitions, adding a vast assortment of content and services, expanding into foreign markets, and attracting the biggest dot-com advertisers to pay premium prices for ads on Yahoo! sites. By 2000, what began as a mere search engine had become an Internet giant, with a meteoric rise in stock value to match its new economy renown. Soon after Yahoo! hit its peak on the stock market, however, the dot-com frenzy began to lose momentum and the economy began a slide into recession. As dot-coms either went bankrupt or were forced to cut back on spending, Yahoo!'s advertiser base began to shrink. As the economy gradually worsened in 2001, Yahoo!'s once-lofty stock lost more than 90 percent of its value, and industry analysts wondered if the company was ripe for a takeover by a large media company.

Determined to remain independent, Yahoo! made a number of personnel changes, including hiring a new CEO, and redesigned its business plan to emphasize selling services in addition to advertising space. Through it all, Yahoo! remained one of the most popular destinations for web surfers—attracting over 430 million visitors worldwide every month—and therefore was one of the premier properties on the Internet. The challenge for Yahoo! was to develop new ways to translate this strong brand equity into strong financial results.

YAHOO!'S EARLY DAYS

Starting the Company

David Filo and Jerry Yang, two computer science Ph.D. students at Stanford University, created the Yahoo! search engine in 1994. Using a homespun filing system, the pair catalogued various websites and published the directory for free on the Internet. The original version was called Jerry and David's Guide to the World Wide Web, which was renamed Yahoo! once Filo and Yang left their studies to devote serious attention to the search engine. The name Yahoo! was an acronym for "Yet Another Hierarchical Officious Oracle,"—a tongue-in-cheek definition of the search engine in technology jargon. Yang discussed the various meanings inherent in the Yahoo! name: "For us, it had the meaning of being kind of a bunch of Yahoo!s, and that was fine. But I think for a lot of people, it was kind of like, 'Wow, this is great. Wow, I'm getting excited. I'm really getting used to the Internet. I can really do stuff on the Internet.' "[2] The humorous name caused some confusion among consumers early on, but it worked in setting Yahoo! apart from traditional companies. Vice President of Brand Marketing Karen Edwards recalled:

I remember when we first started doing some of this stuff, people would say, 'Oh, is that the chocolate drink?' Our goal really was just to get awareness. We knew that the name was really catchy, and we knew that people would respond just to the name. If they just knew the Yahoo! name, we had a pretty good shot at hooking them.[3]

Yang added, "[The name] was easy for people to remember. People could tell other people [about it] very easily, and they had an emotional attachment to it."[4]

The company's search engine was unique because in addition to the standard word search features, Yahoo! offered its users a massive searchable index. Surfers could search for sites in generic categories like Business and Economy, Arts and Humanities, and Entertainment, organize the results by country or region, and search within a category.

Because Yahoo! was among the very first searchable guides of the Internet, the site attracted hundreds of thousands of web surfers within a year of its introduction. The dissemination of Yahoo!'s product was fueled by Netscape founder Marc Andreessen's decision in January 1995 to make Yahoo! the default search engine of his browser. Whenever Netscape users clicked on the Internet Search icon, they were brought to the Yahoo! homepage. This early attention attracted investors, and in April 1995, Filo and Yang raised $1 million in first-round venture capital. The company also hired Tim Koogle, a veteran technology industry executive to serve as its CEO. Later that month, Japanese media conglomerate Softbank paid $106 million for a 37 percent stake in Yahoo!

Online Advertising

Yahoo! announced plans to generate revenues through advertiser support in July 1995. To test the effectiveness of this plan, five different advertisers rotated ad placements on the top five most visited pages in the Yahoo! directory. The ads were typically rectangular boxes, called "banners," placed in prominent locations at the top or bottom of a web page. These five charter sponsors were MCI Communications, MasterCard, the Internet Shopping Network, NECX (an online retailer), and Worlds (a web software developer). Advertisers typically paid a preset fee for every 1,000 "impressions," which occurred whenever an Internet surfer loaded a page with an advertisement on it. Yahoo! charged a fee of about $200 per 1,000 impressions. One of the advantages of online advertising was the ability to target consumers based on their web surfing behavior. For example, an advertiser like E*Trade could target its banner ads so that when an Internet user input a certain keyword such as "stock market" into the Yahoo! search engine, he or she was shown an E*Trade advertisement. The percentage of visitors to an ad-sponsored site who clicked on the advertisement to follow its link was called the "click-through rate." When Internet advertising first emerged, click-through rates were above 20 percent, but rapidly fell to 2 or 3 percent in 1996.

Yahoo! could deliver a large number of web surfers to its advertisers because of the nature of a search engine. Search engines were among the most heavily trafficked sites on the Internet because they offered services that could be accessed by anyone and were essential to gathering information on the web. As traffic to the Yahoo! site increased, so too did its advertiser base. Between the second quarter of 1996 and the second quarter of 1997, the average number of times people viewed Yahoo!'s homepage per day grew from 9 million to 38 million. Over that same period, the number of Yahoo! advertisers grew from 230 to 900. By the fourth quarter of 1997, the company averaged 65 million page views daily and had 1,700 advertisers buying space on its sites. As the top-rated search engine, Yahoo! was able to charge premium rates for ad space. Between 1996 and 1997, average monthly ad rates grew from $6,000 to $20,000.

Yahoo! Marketing Strategy

From its start, Yahoo! sought to convey an irreverent and fun attitude. This attitude originated from the top of the corporate ladder, in the personalities of founders Filo and Yang. The two had conceived of Yahoo! while housed "in a trailer full of empty pizza boxes,"[5] and each of their business cards bore the title "Chief Yahoo!"

The company went public in April 1996. Yahoo! was priced at $13, and jumped 154 percent by the end of the day to close at $34. In order to capitalize on this momentum, Yahoo! hired Black Rocket, a small Bay Area advertising agency, to develop a $10 million awareness-building campaign. Black Rocket worked to position Yahoo! as a consumer brand rather than a technology company. Yahoo's marketing director at the time, Karen Edwards, explained that this positioning emerged because "It's all happened so fast; search engines are no longer [just] search engines. We feel a lot more like media companies, providing information via various formats."[6]

The Black Rocket agency created the tagline "Do You Yahoo!?" Black Rocket also created the "Yahoo! yodel," the audio cue designed to reinforce customer recall of the brand. A partner with Yahoo!'s advertising firm remembered that while other tech companies were aiming above most consumers "with talk about the global, complex power of technology, putting their products on a pedestal," Yahoo!'s initial advertising "position[ed] itself as a familiar face people could trust when they got online."[7] Another partner added, "We knew the message had to be simple—what you would tell your dad or grandpa at Thanksgiving."[8]

To introduce the "Do You Yahoo!?" slogan, Yahoo! began traditional media advertising in April 1996 with a television campaign that was followed by print and radio ads. Yahoo! was one of the first Internet portals to realize that mainstream media buys were important in generating new customers that had yet to spend time on the Internet. Up until that point, most advertising was done either online or in industry magazines, an approach that targeted people who were already online. For this reason, the new marketing effort targeted consumers who intended to use the Internet for the first time within a year, referred to as "near surfers." Edwards explained "Near surfers are more brand loyal. People who tend to be brand sensitive tend to be more brand loyal…By going after the mainstream, it was a means to brand the category and ourselves."[9]

Acclaim for Yahoo! Marketing

Yahoo!'s integrated marketing program projected a targeted image to different audiences. An article in *Fortune* had high praise for the company's brand building:

251

Yahoo! is an awesome marketing machine targeting three different audiences with three distinct message: consumers who might use Yahoo! ("We're fun, wacky, and easy to use"); the press and financial analysts ("We're professional and well run"); and media buyers ("We're the market leader and experts in online advertising").[10]

The marketing program measurably increased consumer knowledge of Yahoo!. According to a report released by IntelliQuest, 82 percent of Internet users and 23 percent of prospective users recognized the Yahoo! name by the end of 1997 (compared to 64 percent and 8 percent, respectively, the prior year). When Yahoo! first began operating, America Online maintained significantly higher public awareness than any other Internet company. This changed by 2000, when Yahoo! had aided awareness levels of 90 percent, compared with AOL and MSN levels of 81 percent and 51 percent, respectively (see Exhibit 1).

Many felt that a key to Yahoo!'s success was the consistency of its advertising. Edwards commented, "In this industry, where others are always changing their names, their taglines and their positioning, we've stood out from the chaos by sticking to the same brand image."[11]

YAHOO! ACHIEVES SUCCESS

Transformation to a Destination

Yahoo! executives realized early on that the key to long-term success was to transform the site from a portal to a destination site where web surfers lingered and perhaps stayed. The key to retaining an audience was developing a "sticky" site with appealing content that kept consumer "eyeballs" glued to the site's page. Yahoo! offered content besides the original searchable directory, but these satellite sites were not visited often. In 1996, Jerry Yang said, "Most of our users today approach Yahoo! and type in a keyword and go from there. They do not stop at our other sites."[12] This behavior, while consistent with the function that portals originally performed, did not appeal to advertisers on Yahoo!, who naturally wanted their advertising to be seen often. As the need to expand beyond a search engine portal increased, executives looked to boost the time spent at the site per user in a variety of ways. This required the addition of homegrown content and vastly expanded onsite offerings, such as Yahoo! Finance, Yahoo! Travel, or the Yahoo!ligans kids directory, which would attract new users and keep them on Yahoo! pages. Yang professed the following vision for Yahoo!'s future with its users:

> As we continue to make Yahoo! a bigger part of our users' lives, our goal is to build the Yahoo! brand to be something that makes users feel empowered on the Internet and, ultimately, form a long-lasting relationship that our users trust.[13]

To bolster its content offerings, Yahoo! began acquiring companies with expertise in other Internet services aside from web searches. One of Yahoo!'s first acquisition was its purchase of free e-mail provider and directory service Four 11 Corp in October 1997. This acquisition enabled the company to offer its users Yahoo! Mail, a free e-mail service. The company's June 1998 acquisition of Viaweb, a provider of software and services for hosting online stores, enabled Yahoo! to develop more e-commerce capabilities. By acquiring online direct marketing firm Yoyodyne in October 1998, Yahoo! improved its marketing services for ad buyers.

Early Financial Success

After two years in a tightly contested portal market, Yahoo! eventually achieved separation from its competitors. Yahoo! attracted a much larger audience than competitor portals, as much as 8 million more than second ranked Web Crawler per day in 1997. As Yahoo! became one of the leading Internet portals, ad dollars began pouring in. By mid-1997, the company was selling ad space to over 900 advertisers. These ad sales contributed about $13 million to revenues, more than four times the previous year's sales. Karen Edwards credited Yahoo!'s success partly to its early entry into the search engine category:

> When there's a lot of clutter and noise, it bodes well for the brands that people trust and know. Unestablished brands will have a very difficult time stealing loyal users away from services that have critical mass.[14]

Among the most abundant Yahoo! advertisers were burgeoning dot-coms. As one analyst said, "Yahoo! brings eyeballs and that's what matters. Because of Yahoo!'s powerful brand position, they've become the first choice for other companies that want to get into the Internet."[15]

The most remarkable story about Yahoo! may have been its stock, which skyrocketed after the IPO. In fiscal 1997, the company's revenues grew by 242 percent to $125 million, while its stock rose 517 percent during the same period. By spring 1998, the stock had risen 745 percent from its IPO. Its price/earnings ratio in May was a lofty 1,062—compared with Microsoft's P/E ratio of 55 that month— yet it was considered a blue chip stock by many. Yahoo! garnered additional media attention when *Business Week* featured the company on the cover of its September 7, 1998 issue.

Joining the E-Commerce World

Yahoo! made its first move into e-commerce in February 1998 with the debut of a Yahoo! branded Visa card. Cardholders could use the Yahoo! Visa site to view card balances, make purchases from an online catalogue featuring various merchants, and redeem points earned on the card. This initiative was followed by a full-blown online shopping mall, called Yahoo! Shopping. In keeping with its roots as a web directory, the Yahoo! Shopping area enabled users to search for items from a variety of retailers that the site catalogued. Karen Edwards explained, "We think the brand needs to stand for commerce."[16]

For merchants, Yahoo! developed its Yahoo! Store site where merchants could pay to have their products listed in the Yahoo! Shopping directory. Yahoo! Store also offered merchants the opportunity to create and manage their own secure online stores. Additionally, Yahoo! Store included a service where merchants could apply online to set up payment accounts and credit card processing with third-party providers. The Yahoo! Store site appealed to small business that lacked the means to sustain an independent website, but still wanted an e-commerce presence.

An effort aimed at retaining users for more than a few clicks was the Yahoo! city guide. The company launched the inaugural city edition, Yahoo! San Francisco, in June 1996. Yahoo! New York and Yahoo! Los Angeles followed in August. The city editions contained such vital information as local movie listings, restaurant guides, entertainment calendars, and even pizza delivery numbers. The sites also contained information useful to visitors, like hotel and rental car information. Yahoo! designed the city guides with the intention of making the site more relevant to local consumers in those locations.

Among the services Yahoo! added in 1998 were Yahoo! Clubs, an online community, Yahoo! Calendar, an online calendar, and Yahoo! Small Business, with content and services aimed at small business proprietors. The new business site featured package tracking services from a variety of shipping companies, as well as editorial content from publications such as *Fast Company*, *Entrepreneur* magazine, and *Inc.*

Advertising Developments

Compared with other dot-coms, Yahoo!'s media spending was restrained. In 1998, Yahoo!'s total television spending was $7.2 million, compared with $31.4 million by AOL, $26.7 by Internet holding company CMGI, and $18.8 million by E*Trade. Though Yahoo!'s TV spending tripled to $21.7 million in 1999, this outlay was dwarfed by E*Trade ($96.9 million), Ameritrade ($79.4 million), and AOL ($45.8 million).

Despite its comparatively small marketing budget, Yahoo! earned honors from *Advertising Age* as the top marketer in the portal category for 1999. In the first nine months of 1998, Yahoo! led all other web publishers in advertising revenue, with $88 million. Despite leading the ad revenue category, Yahoo! was not among the top 25 Internet advertising spenders, preferring to execute much of its marketing strategy offline. Yahoo! paid for its logo to appear in affiliation with Bay Area sports teams. The San Jose Shark's Zamboni bore the Yahoo! logo, as did the scoreboard at 3Com Park—home to the San Francisco Giants and 49ers.

Yahoo! added to its set of sports marketing opportunities in 1998 by signing on to be an official sponsor of Major League Soccer through 2002 in a multimillion-dollar deal. In September 2000, Yahoo! signed a deal with the NBA and WNBA to become a global sponsor. Yahoo! would provide online coverage of league games and other events in return for event sponsorship and television time. As a result of the agreement, Yahoo! Sports offered content such as video highlights, real-time game statistics, and live audio broadcasts.

In 1999, Yahoo! inked a $20 million cross-promotional advertising deal with the Fox television network. Yahoo! became a sponsor of the Super Bowl pregame show and of the animated sitcom "Family Guy." Yahoo! also garnered prime time and late night advertising slots on Fox's news and sports channels for nine months. In return, Yahoo! provided extensive coverage of the Super Bowl on its website and promoted "Family Guy" for a six-week period. Ultimately, the deal involved cross-promotions in Fox Films, Fox Music, Fox Interactive, Fox Broadcasting, and Fox cable channels. The promotional partnership resembled earlier deals between Internet portals and media companies such as the AOL/Time Warner merger and Walt Disney Co.'s equity investment in Infoseek Corp, except in the case of Yahoo! and Fox, neither company invested in the other. Rupert Murdoch, chairman of Fox parent company News Corp., said that while he saw "enormous potential [in the Internet]," he could not "see the profits coming soon enough" to warrant a merger.[17]

Though it did not merge with an "old media" company, Yahoo! forged partnerships with print outfits such as Fodor's and the *Village Voice*. It also licensed its name in unconventional ways. The company partnered with Ziff-Davis to create the Yahoo! Internet Life magazine, and backpack manufacturer Gregory Mountain Sports produced a Yahoo! branded computer bag. Other licensed products included Yahoo! baseballs, sunglasses, yo-yos, kazoos, surfboards, shoes, stationary, and a compilation CD. Yahoo! benefited from high-profile product placements on popular television shows and movies, such as NBC's primetime drama *ER*, which were often provided free of charge by studios.

THINKING GLOBALLY

Yahoo! stock opened in January 2000 trading above $230. That year, awareness of the brand in the United States among Internet users reached 90 percent. Yahoo! had achieved a place among the best of the dot-coms, and now had global aspirations. In October 1999 Yahoo! was still trailing AOL in terms of unique users domestically, by a 53 million to 40 million margin. Abroad, however, Yahoo! was almost always ranked either first or second in every market it entered, while AOL often failed to rank among the top three. Yahoo! maintained specialized sites in 20 foreign countries, whereas AOL was present in 15 countries. Roughly one-third of Yahoo!'s registered users came from abroad. The two main areas for Yahoo!'s global growth where Europe and Asia.

Yahoo! Europe

Yahoo! first moved into Europe in summer 1996, when it partnered with Ziff-Davis International Media Group to form Yahoo! Europe. Initially, Yahoo! Europe offered home pages with specialized content for the United Kingdom, Germany, and France. By 2000, Yahoo! was the portal with the largest audience in Europe, where 42 percent of all Internet users visited the site. In addition to city guides for major cities like London, Yahoo! had pages for eight individual countries.

Yahoo! biggest competitor domestically, AOL, also maintained a significant presence in Europe as the top Internet service provider (ISP). Aside from AOL, Yahoo!'s primary competition came from European media and telecom companies. In 2000, German ISP T-Online was the top ISP in Europe, and ranked second globally behind AOL with 5.2 million European subscribers. France Telecom offered an ISP called Wanadoo, while Spain's leader was Tera Networks. In this highly competitive atmosphere, Yahoo! emerged as one of the top three portals in every market it entered. In 1999, Yahoo! was the top portal in Great Britain, the second-ranked portal in Germany and France, and in the top three in Italy, Spain, Norway, Sweden, and Denmark. This broad audience attracted advertisers, which numbered 1,500 by mid-2000. In 2000, ad sales in Europe contributed about $20 million, or about 10 percent, to Yahoo!'s total.

Yahoo! in Asia

Yahoo! Japan was launched in April 1996 and soon attracted a significantly greater share of Internet traffic than any other Japanese directory. In November 1997, Yahoo! Japan became the youngest company ever to go public and saw its share price nearly triple in the first day, despite the sagging Japanese economy. This success came partly from the fact that competition in Japan was almost nonexistent. Neither AOL nor MSN had any presence in the country, and web efforts from Sony and Nippon Telegraph & Telephone had met with consumer disdain. This left Yahoo! "virtually alone"[18] in a major market.

After its success in Japan, Yahoo! looked to provide specialized sites for other countries in Asia. The Asian region held enormous possibilities for a large Internet audience, which had already exploded from 3 million users in 1996 to 10 million in 1997. The company introduced native-language Yahoo! Korea in September 1997. Yahoo! also offered an English-based site called Yahoo! Asia, which mirrored the U.S. home site but afforded Asian users faster content retrieval by being based in Singapore. The company also added a Chinese-language site in early 1998, targeting web surfers in China, Taiwan, Hong-Kong, and Singapore.

In the first quarter of 1999, Yahoo! opened Yahoo! Hong Kong and Yahoo! Taiwan, followed by Yahoo! China during the third quarter. As it had in North America and Europe, Yahoo! became wildly popular among Asian Internet users. A survey of 30,000 people from nine Asian countries conducted in December 1999 by online survey company Consult.com revealed that respondents cited Yahoo! as their favorite Internet directory.

Following print and television campaigns in Asian markets, Yahoo! added grass roots marketing efforts in several key markets. This grass roots approach was prompted by research that revealed word-of-mouth to be an especially important decision variable for portal use in Asia. In Hong Kong, Yahoo! teamed with a local radio station in May 2000 and held a contest that challenged university students to invent creative means of linking campuses online. The contest drew 25,000 entries, and the winner was invited to implement the strategy. In June, Yahoo! sponsored a computer camp in Singapore that was attended by 150 schoolchildren. The company also sought to reach other audiences in Singapore by holding an Internet workshop for readers of a women's magazine and planning outreach to "country clubs and senior citizens."[19] In China, Yahoo! distributed 15,000 free Yahoo! Messenger CDs containing software for instant messaging, e-mail, and news alerts among eight universities in Beijing.

YAHOO! BROADENS ITS OFFERINGS

Going Wireless

In Europe and Asia, wireless technology gained an even stronger foothold than it had in the U.S. cell phone use in Western Europe when it rose to 41 percent in 2000, compared to 31 percent in the United States. As wireless and mobile technologies emerged, Yahoo! sought ways to provide service for its customers on platforms beyond the desktop computer, such as cell phones, pagers, and personal digital assistants. The company formed a business division, called Yahoo! Everywhere, to develop applications for the wireless web. After spending $80 million to acquire wireless software start-up Online Anywhere, Yahoo! was able to offer content and services formatted for non-PC devices. Mohan Vishwanath, the former CEO of Online Anywhere who became vice president of Yahoo! Everywhere, characterized the project as a logical growth mechanism:

> The Yahoo! Everywhere strategy is to extend the Yahoo! brand and services beyond the desktop...It is a way for us to increase the number of touch points with our users in markets where we already have a strong presence. And in newer markets, it is a way for us to acquire new customers.[20]

Since an equal number of web surfers were predicted to use wireless connections to access the Internet as would use home connections (300 million), one analyst described the mobile market as a "potential goldmine for Yahoo!"[21] The company soon began developing voice ads and geographically targeted advertising for wireless users. The company employed non-traditional media to promote its Yahoo! Everywhere strategy as well. In September 1999 the company unveiled a convoy of 10 Yahoo! branded taxis in San Francisco. The taxis were completely "wrapped" with the purple and yellow logo, so that even the side and rear windows contributed to the branded look. The taxis came equipped with Palm handheld computers that enabled passengers to access the Internet via wireless connection and Yahoo! software. The promotion ran in San Francisco through March 2000, and was followed by a similar campaign in New York City the following September.

New Acquisitions

Yahoo! purchased Internet service provider GeoCities for almost $5 billion in stock—more than a 50 percent premium—in January 1999. The deal gave Yahoo! an additional 18 million unique users. In April 1999, Yahoo! purchased streaming audio and video site Broadcast.com for about $5 billion. Yahoo! added group e-mail and bulletin board services to its free Yahoo! Mail services when it acquired eGroups for $420 million in stock in June 2000. Yahoo!'s plan for the group e-mail services would complement some of its other offerings, such as Yahoo! Auctions and Yahoo! Clubs, by facilitating communication between groups of people with similar interests.

CHALLENGES FOR YAHOO!

Economic Troubles

By mid-2000, the economy had begun to falter and even an Internet blue chip like Yahoo! was not immune to the effects of the dot-com crash. Analysts who considered Yahoo!'s stock overvalued (citing its high P/E ratio) saw their suspicions confirmed as the price fell 80 percent during the year. Because Yahoo! derived over 80 percent of its revenue from online advertising sales, and the bulk of its advertisers were Internet companies, their collective struggles would affect Yahoo!'s revenues. "It's only a matter of time before we see the impact on Yahoo!'s results," said one analyst in September 2000. "We continue to look for signs that traditional advertisers are embracing online advertising, but we are receiving little comfort."[22] A combination of fewer advertisers and the fact that growth in advertiser spending decreased 6 percent hurt the company. Contributing to Yahoo!'s problems was a low click-through rate. Click-through rates plummeted from 2 percent in 1999 to below 1 percent, lower than the 2 percent response rate for junk mail delivered by normal mail.

Yahoo! was quick to reassure Wall Street that profits would continue, citing a reduction in the percentage of pure-play Internet advertisers and retention of 98 percent of its biggest advertisers. The company also pointed to the fact that its top 200 advertisers, most of which were so-called traditional advertisers, contributed 60 percent of Yahoo!'s total revenue.

Despite its plummeting stock, the company did benefit from several positive indicators during the latter half of 2000. Yahoo! Japan doubled its profits in the fourth quarter with the help of strong advertising revenues, but warned that a slowdown similar to that in America was expected. Domestically, though overall Internet spending by consumers during the holidays grew a disappointing 53 percent, Yahoo! managed to double the sales its shopping site directed to retailers. Yahoo! earned an estimated $30 million from its Yahoo! Shopping service during that period, when many other e-tailers failed to turn a profit. Yahoo!'s users also began spending more time online during the holiday season. AOL traditionally led the "user-minutes-online" category, but in December 2000 Yahoo! visitors spent an average of almost one-and-a-half hours on Yahoo! sites, better than second-place MSN by nearly 20 minutes.

Still, the forecast for 2001 was grim. The company's projected 2001 revenue of between $1.2 and $1.3 billion, which translated to 18 percent growth. Considering that Yahoo! grew 88 percent in 2000, the limited growth prospects in 2001 disappointed analysts and investors alike. Worse, actual revenue numbers came in much lower than predictions (see Exhibit 2). Since Yahoo! was the last major portal to remain independent, after Excite merged with the @Home Network, Snap.com with NBC, Lycos with CMGI, Infoseek with Disney, and AOL with Time Warner, speculation about a possible takeover increased as its stock price plunged. Analysts figured a major global media company, such as Viacom, would be the most likely to pursue Yahoo!.

Executive Changes at Yahoo!

By 2001, Yahoo! was reeling from the falloff in Internet advertising and was in need of a major overhaul—Jerry Yang realized it was time to make a change in the company's leadership. Terry Semel immediately came to mind. Yang had met Terry Semel at a media conference in 1999, and the two remained friends. After spending 21 years at Waner Brothers, first as COO and then as co-CEO, Semel retired in 1999. During his time at the company, Warner Bros. grew from a $750 million studio to a $11 billion behemoth. Semel had a formidable entertainment industry pedigree—he was responsible for major blockbusters like the *Batman* and *Lethal Weapon* franchises, and would bring valuable entertainment industry connections to Yahoo!. Yang approached Semel in 2001 and offered him the top job. Semel agreed to take the job, but with the provision that current CEO Koogle also step down as Chairman. Koogle was loved by Yahoo! employees, but many analysts were happy to see him go. Commenting on the new CEO, UBS Warburg analyst Christopher Dixon said, "This is a classic example of bringing in the adults in to mind the children."[23] Soon after taking the job, Semel expressed optimism for Yahoo!'s future:

> We are the Internet's most dominant brand. We have the largest and most loyal audience. When advertising spending picks up, Yahoo! will be well positioned to take a disproportionate share of the market...There are three major worldwide portals, and we don't see a fourth. And therein lies the opportunity. We have a global franchise that simply cannot be replicated.[24]

YAHOO! LOOKS FOR SOLUTIONS

Yahoo! Alters its Approach

Yahoo! changed its strategy in order to generate more income from non-advertising sources. Semel announced in November 2001 his intention to achieve a 50-50 split between revenue from advertising and revenue from other sources by 2004. In 2000, 90 percent of Yahoo!'s revenues came from advertising. This figure was reduced to 80 percent in 2001, but advertising revenues decreased by almost 40 percent that year. In order to find new revenue streams, the company began charging for some services that traditionally had been free, a move that irked many consumers. Yahoo! acknowledged the difficulty of getting consumers to pay for services they had come to expect would be free. "We have absolutely trained people to get things for free," said Yahoo! vice president of communication Geoff Ralston.

Revenues for Yahoo! could be broken down into two categories: marketing services and fees. Marketing service revenues came from growing the number of users and advertisers. As the user base increased and spent more time on the Yahoo! network, they viewed more pages, and conducted more searches, which resulted in a higher number of impressions and paid clicks. Fee-based services included Internet broadband and dial-up services, premium e-mail, music, personals, as well as services for small businesses. Though fee-based revenues had increased on an absolute basis, their percentage of total revenues continued to decrease (see Exhibit 3 for fee-based revenues and Exhibit 4 for subscription data).

To attract more consumer dollars, Yahoo! targeted customers with Internet ads offering services as diverse as extra home-page space, personal domain names, enhanced e-mail, additional bandwidth, financial research, real-time stock quotes, auction listings, and more, for a fee. Yahoo! also began charging players in its fantasy baseball league a $4.95 fee to be able to get their team results over a web phone.

Yahoo! kept segments of its traditionally free services out of this pricing scheme. For example, Internet personal ads cost nothing to post on Yahoo!, but consumers paid $19.95 a month to respond to an ad. The Yahoo! Mail e-mail service remained free, but starting in 2002 consumers had to pay for mail-forwarding features and extra storage space. In a controversial move, Yahoo! revised its privacy policy in March 2002 to allow the company to market its services and products and services of other companies unless users specifically told Yahoo! not to. Users received e-mails where they could check 16 boxes on a website and instruct Yahoo! not to send marketing materials via phone, postal mail, or e-mail. Additionally, the revised policy allowed Yahoo! to share consumer data with other marketers for specific marketing campaigns. The response rate to the e-mail was very low, but the company maintained that its "fundamental approach to privacy hasn't changed."[25]

Building Relationships with Advertisers

The web had the potential for reinventing and reinvigorating advertising. With its unique ability for measurement—tracking who clicked on an ad and how they interacted with it—the Internet promised to solve the classic problem stated by department-store pioneer John Wanamaker: "Half of the money I spend on advertising is wasted; the trouble is, I don't know which half."[26]

A problem for Yahoo! was that it had garnered a reputation for neglecting the needs of corporate marketers. The company had grown accustomed to owning some of the most sought-after advertising space on the Internet, and could afford to be expensive, inflexible, and even inattentive to potential advertisers. The shrinking of advertising budgets of the slowed economy forced Yahoo! to re-evaluate its attitude. Semel wanted to change Yahoo!'s relationships with advertisers and help them solve the dilemma posed by John Wanamaker.

Yang and Semel decided to take a new angle and recruited a decidedly non-tech advertising sales manager when they hired Wenda Millard in late 2001 to reorganize and run the North American sales force. Millard had spent 20 years in the magazine business, starting out by selling ads for *Ladies' Home Journal* and *New York* magazine before moving on to become publisher of *Family Circle*, *Adweek*, and co-founder of *Brandweek* and *Mediaweek*. Many wondered why a "new media" company would hire an "old media" executive, but Millard believed her prior experience was her greatest asset. "When you're asking a major marketer to spend hundreds of millions of dollars on a new medium, they want to trust you. If I didn't have a relationship with the presidents of all these Fortune 1,000 companies or the heads of all these agencies, why would they trust me?"[27]

Millard attempted to add more traditional marketers to its roster of Internet advertisers. The problem for Yahoo! was that many traditional marketers were still wary of large ad spends on the Internet. "Traditional marketers aren't really convinced that online advertising works," said an analyst with Forrester Research. "While they are spending money, it's still very slow and very tentative."[28] Yahoo! revamped its ad sales program by cutting prices, hiring more experienced marketing executives, and allowing new ad formats on its sites. An ad for the 2002 Ford Explorer was one such example of the new formats. The ad featured sound effects simulating an engine, animation that made the web browser appear to shake, and a full-sized picture of the new SUV when consumers clicked on the ad. The Ford Explorer ad was the first animated ad allowed by Yahoo!.

The trust and experience that Millard brought to Yahoo! eventually paid off, enabling her to bring new and larger accounts to Yahoo!. Executives such as Julie Roehm, Chrysler's director of marketing communications, had a $2 billion budget to spend in 2005, and was looking for the optimal place to spend it. Roehm spent the biggest chunk of her online dollars (18 percent of Chrysler's total ad budget in 2005) on Yahoo!. She believed that Yahoo! gave her the most information about how the advertising performed, allowing her to "manage the effectiveness of every dollar spent." Yahoo! provided Roehm with detailed demographic information about the people who clicked on her ads, but also predicted the probable response rate to the ads on each segment of the portal. Yahoo! was also able to predict what time of day the ads would be most effective, and spot potential buyers at various stages of the consideration process.

By looking at the billions of user clicks that flowed through their servers every day, Yahoo! could "observe" patterns in consumers' behavior. For example, Yahoo! could track a user who looked up football on Yahoo! Sports, checked out adventure movies on Yahoo! Entertainment, and compared truck prices on Yahoo! Autos. This might signify the browser was interested in a Jeep and was just beginning to think about a purchase. Another usage pattern might signify that the browser was only days away from making a purchase. This information was valuable to Roehm—once Yahoo! knew where a potential customer was in the car-buying process, it could serve up the appropriate Chrysler ad.[29]

Roehm was pleased with the level of information she could get from Yahoo! In a 2005 interview she commented:

> We marketers are much more obligated to tell our shareholders and our management what the real return on our spending is. Online provides us the opportunity to give a real answer to that question…It's measurable. It allows you to have a one-on-one, two-way dialogue with your customers.

Roehm said that almost every dollar she spent online generated $1.50 or more in sales for Chrysler. She did not have a comparable figure for the company's spending on television or print, but believed in "her gut" that online was much better.[30]

Changing Media Landscape

It was clear now that Internet usage was changing the way Americans interacted with media. In the early 1970s, when Americans turned on their televisions, they tuned into ABC, NBC, or CBS 80 percent of the time. By 2005, the Big Three's share had fallen to 33 percent, with cable, video games, DVDs, and the Internet occupying the space once filled with television. Forrester Research estimated that surfing the Internet accounted for 15 percent of all time Americans spent with all media (that was a conservative estimate, according to Forrester and many advertisers, who believed the number to be double that).[31] Aside from just having an Internet connection, up to 50 percent of those online had a broadband connection allowing them to access more information, faster. This enabled advertisers to move beyond banner ads and fashion more creative messages.

Yahoo! was able to take advantage of this shift in media consumption and use it to their advantage. The company had over 181 million active registered users, which meant that Yahoo! could tell advertisers it knew the habits or more users than any other portal—or traditional media company. In contrast, Google never "trained" its users to register and it wasn't until late 2004 that the company started asking them to begin signing up for services. This allowed Yahoo! a tremendous lead in attracting brand advertising. According to Morgan Stanley Internet analyst Mary Meeker, "If you are new to online advertising, Yahoo! is your first call because they do everything"[32] (see Exhibit 5).

Yahoo! Corporate Offerings.

Utilizing streaming media capabilities from its Broadcast.com acquisition, Yahoo! used its Yahoo! Broadcast division to host web conferences, online training, and virtual corporate meetings. The company also established a unit called Corporate Yahoo! (changed to Yahoo! Portal Solutions in 2001) that specialized in building website portals for corporations, including McDonald's, Pfizer, and the state of North Carolina. Following the leads of other technology companies, Yahoo! developed a corporate services division in June 2000. The division, called Yahoo! Enterprise Solutions (YES), enabled corporations to customize Yahoo!'s web portal with the help of a package of software tools. By offering enterprise services, Yahoo! hoped to lessen its dependence on online advertising sales.

Yahoo! also began hosting online conferences for large corporations such as Procter & Gamble and Samsung Electronics. In December 2000, Yahoo! teamed with wireless carrier Motient to allow users of two-way wireless messaging service to access Yahoo! e-mail accounts. A few weeks later, Yahoo! partnered with Internet appliance maker VTech Connect to introduce two co-branded e-mail appliances. As with the Motient deal, this partnership allowed users to access existing Yahoo! e-mail accounts. As of early January 2001, YES had attracted 18 clients, including McDonald's Corp., Bayer AG, and Janus Capital Corp. Still, this service contributed only 10 percent of the company's total revenue and only 32 corporations signed on by November of that year. In 2003, the company folded the YES division into other business units, for instance, the corporate instant message service became managed by executives responsible for the free consumer instant messaging service.

In January 2001, Yahoo! added another corporate service, called Yahoo! Industry Marketplaces, which enabled technology professionals to research and purchase electronics, software, and hardware from a variety of vendors. The format was similar to Yahoo! Shopping, where users could search for items and compare prices. Yahoo! Industry Marketplaces was ultimately merged with Yahoo! Small Business services.

New Acquisitions and Partnerships

Yahoo! continued to add content through acquisitions. In 2001, it completed a $12 million acquisition of Launch Media, the tenth-largest music website that also possessed the biggest music video collection on the Internet. In a break from its traditional umbrella advertising strategy, Yahoo! allowed Launch to retain its own sales staff and its own brand. Rather than changing the brand to "Yahoo! Launch," the site remained Launch, and was billed as "Your Yahoo! music experience." Yahoo! added to its music portfolio in 2004, when it purchased Musicmatch, a provider of personalized music software and services, such as music on demand and a music download store. In 2005, Yahoo! launched Yahoo! Music Unlimited, a subscription service that offered unlimited access to over one million songs for $4.99 per month. It announced plans to eventually merge Musicmatch into this service.

As search advertising became a lucrative source of income for search engines, topping $1 billion in total category sales in 2002, Yahoo! pursued growth in search by acquiring several companies with leading technology. In 2003, the company acquired algorithmic search provider—and Google competitor—Inktomi for $235 million. Four months later, Yahoo! purchased another search advertising services company called Overture for $1.63 billion. Like Google, Overture specialized in paid search, which is the selling of advertising links that accompany search results. These moves boosted Yahoo!'s sponsored search revenues to $2 billion in 2003. In 2005, Yahoo! renamed its Overture Services unit to Yahoo! Search Marketing.

Yahoo! made a number of other acquisitions between 2003 and 2005. In 2004, Yahoo! paid more that $500 million for European online shopping site Kelkoo. The company also made several acquisitions related to user-generated media services, including the March 2005 purchase of Ludicorp, which owned photo-sharing site Flickr, and the December 2005 purchase of online social tagging and content management site del.icio.us. In 2005 it also purchased online events listing and local information site Upcoming.org and Internet telephony company Dialpad.

Yahoo! teamed with a wide variety of organizations to add content to the multiple Yahoo! sites and draw new users. One company Yahoo! partnered with was Target, the Minneapolis-based retailer with 1,330 stores in 47 states. The two companies introduced a digital photo website called "Target Yahoo! Photos" that allowed users to store, share, and print photos. Yahoo! Photos was already the leading online photo sharing service worldwide,[33] but the new partnership allowed users added features like the ability to share photos in real-time with Yahoo! Messenger or a mobile phone, and offered the option of printing photos at home, having printed photos delivered to a home or office, or picking up the photos at a local Target store.

Yahoo! also established more partnerships with large media companies. In 2001, Yahoo! signed on to carry Pressplay, the online music service from Sony and Vivendi Universal. Yahoo! also partnered with Sony to jointly develop an Internet site. "More entertainment companies are coming to Yahoo! to make sure their content is distributed," said David Mandelbrot, Yahoo!'s vice president and general manager of entertainment. "We're becoming more of a marketing partner rather than a company that takes dollars for our advertising." In addition to accepting marketing campaigns for movies, such as Disney's 2001 blockbuster *Pearl Harbor*, Yahoo! used its integrated marketing programs to post movie show times at local venues, shows animated commercials, and annotates Yahoo! users' Internet calendars with movie opening dates.

In an effort to integrate different types of media, Yahoo! entered a partnership with Mark Burnett Productions, one of the driving forces behind reality television with "unscripted" series such as "Survivor." This agreement made Yahoo! the official website for "The Apprentice" with Donald Trump and "The Apprentice" with Martha Stewart. The website had video clips produced exclusively for Yahoo!, extended versions of integral moments from each week's show, mobile content for phones, and special Yahoo! Messenger IMVironments (Instant Messaging environments) featuring Trump and Stewart. Advertising for the past two "Apprentice" sites had been very popular with marketers, allowing them to have 10- to 30-second video ads at the opening of exclusive video clips, display ads across the many pages of the shows' sites, and sponsorship of polls, interactive elements, and custom sweepstakes. "Yahoo! has an amazing ability to seamlessly integrate our televised programming into an interactive format that not only accurately reflects the content of each show, but enhances it in new and exciting ways," said Mark Burnett. "Yahoo!'s unique grasp of the entertainment world combined with its massive online audience makes it the perfect partner and an integral element in keeping shows like "The Apprentice" at the top of the ratings."[34]

RISK FACTORS FOR YAHOO!

As Yahoo! moved into the twenty-first century, it faced significant risks. Many analysts believed there were three primary threats to the company:

1. Competition from other Internet-related companies.
2. Potential exposure to concerns over aggressive industry online advertising practices.
3. Weak growth in international markets.

Competitive Marketplace

As an Internet advertiser, Yahoo! competed for users, advertising dollars, and fees revenue against a very wide group of companies, including Google, Microsoft, Time Warner, Monster Worldwide, and CNET. One of the most important competitive situations was with Google in Internet search. Google, which started operating in 1998, quickly became synonymous with searching the Internet and maintained this lead. On a worldwide basis, it was estimated that Google accounted for 50 percent of all search queries, while Yahoo! was used about 25 percent of the time (Microsoft held the third position).[35] This enabled Google to garner 400,000 paying advertisers, nearly twice as many as Yahoo![36]

Yahoo! responded by developing a revamped search advertising tool, codenamed "Panama," beginning in 2004. Panama promised to deliver more relevant advertising links to search users, as well as enable advertisers to better gauge ad effectiveness and make improvements. As a result, Yahoo! could charge more for its ads. The new search platform was expected to raise revenues by at least 20 percent immediately following its launch.[37] This would enable Yahoo! to close the gap with Google, which made an estimated 40 percent more per search. When the company announced in July 2006 that the system would be delayed three months, investor reaction was swift and severe: the stock dropped 22 percent in one day.[38] The company eventually delayed the release until 2007.

While Yahoo! was the runner-up in search, the company did hold a lead in overall page views. In May 2005, Yahoo! had 178 million page views, compared with MSN, which had 96 million page views, Google with 68 million, and AOL at 39 million.[39] It also was the leader in web-based e-mail service. By 2005, Yahoo! had 64 million users of its e-mail service, accounting for 30 percent of the market. Microsoft's Hotmail and MSN accounted for 25 percent, while AOL boasted a 23.4 percent share. Google entered the fray in 2004 with Gmail. Gmail was still officially in testing mode and held a 1.8 percent share. This share earned it eighth place in e-mail service provision, but many believed it to be strong competitor of Yahoo!'s in the future.[40]

Potential Fallout From Aggressive Online Advertising Practices

For users, one negative development of the Internet was the rise of aggressive advertising practices, such as spam, click fraud, spyware, and adware. Some analysts believed that when combined, these practices could reduce users' interest in the Internet and hinder the willingness of marketers to shift more of their advertising budgets online. Another concern was negative backlash surrounding spyware and adware. Yahoo! did not directly generate revenue from these sources, but it was believed that the company might suffer some damage to its reputation by consumers thinking that Yahoo! was associated with these practices.[41]

International Push

Yahoo! had established a presence in Europe and Asia as early as 1996, and international revenues continued to grow (from $59 million, or 10 percent of total revenues, in 1999 to $921 million, or 26 percent of total revenues, by 2004), but this still only accounted for 26 percent of the company's total revenue. Other Internet companies such as eBay and Amazon.com earned close to 50 percent of their revenues from international exposure, and analysts were looking for Yahoo! to make a bigger international push.

Yahoo!'s Chief Marketing Officer, Cammie Dunaway believed that in order to grow overseas, the company would have to extend its core brand by emanating the same wacky vibe that pervaded its yodel-filled domestic ads. The key, according to Dunaway, was to do things no one had ever done before, adding an edgy approach. In Taiwan, Yahoo! launched an ad campaign where users could get clues from the web and local billboards to discover who got a fictional supermodel pregnant. In France, the company hosted late night events at supermarkets where singles could pick up a purple Yahoo! shopping basket to demonstrate their willingness to meet another single. "You have to work hard…to engage [customers] in your marketing," said Dunaway.[42]

Aside from catchy marketing campaigns, Yahoo! had other plans for international growth. The company set its sights on China, where it had been trying since 1999 to attain a dominant position. China had the world's second-largest online population with 100 million users. Still, Internet penetration rates were below 10 percent and were expected to surge in the coming years and surpass the United States. To take advantage of this expected future growth, Yahoo! announced an agreement with local company Alibaba.com in August 2005 that gave Yahoo! a 40 percent stake in the Chinese company, in exchange for $1 billion in cash and turning over all of its Chinese operations to Alibaba.com. Despite some concerns, many saw this agreement as a positive step for Yahoo! "We don't see this as Yahoo! not being able to succeed on its own," said Daniel Rosenweig, Yahoo!'s Chief Operating Officer. "We look at this as an opportunity to get much bigger much faster, working with a great management team."[43]

YAHOO! DRIVES ON

Though the challenges faced by the company were real, Yahoo! continued to innovate and expand its services. The company's fundamental strategy, outlined by Semel, was to see "How broad can we build the audience by providing better products and services?"[44] Toward this end, Yahoo! worked to add to existing relationships with other firms and providing new services to both loyal and new users.

Yahoo! bolstered its ability to develop partnerships with Hollywood content creators in 2005 when it hired Lloyd Braun, a former entertainment lawyer, talent agent, and previously chairman of ABC Entertainment Television Network. Braun was able to leverage his stable of contacts to offer exclusive online content and coverage of "Survivor" producer Mark Burnett's reality boxing show "The Contender" and to extend Yahoo's contract with Burnett's "Apprentice" reality show, starring Donald Trump. Additionally, Braun worked with industry veterans to develop a site for the 2006 Olympics that featured exclusive editorial coverage and user-generated pictures posted on Yahoo's Flickr photo sharing site.

A developing issue for Yahoo! was the fact that many partners began withdrawing their content, preferring to develop their own online presence than partner with a company they perceived as a competitor. For example, the *New York Times* removed its stories from Yahoo! in order to focus traffic on its own site. Other Yahoo! content providers, such as Reuters, set up their own sites and began to charge more for its content. Said Braun, "There's no question that a lot of the other media companies out there are nervous about [us and wondering], Okay, are they friend or foe?"[45] The challenge for Yahoo! would be to convince content providers that the relationships would be mutually beneficial, given the fact that

Yahoo was able to deliver a vast younger-skewing audience that many traditional media companies coveted.

The company also looked to market its services to new customers in new areas. It announced a deal with Boeing in 2005 that provided their search services to the airplane maker's wireless-enabled fleet of planes, opening up the inflight market to the 100,000 advertisers who bought sponsored links through Yahoo!'s portal. The service worked much like a wireless connection one might use in a coffee shop. A Yahoo!-branded search box would appear after the user logged onto the Internet. The user could then go to any search engine or URL, but it "brings Yahoo! one click closer to the user," said Neils Steenstrup, director of product management at Connexion by Boeing.

Yahoo! also sought to improve its user experience by adding new services and upgrading existing ones. In 2005, Yahoo! launched a new social networking website called Yahoo! 360, which combined elements of blogs, familiar social networks like MySpace.com or Friendster.com, and proprietary Yahoo! offerings such as Yahoo! Messenger, Flickr, Launch, Yahoo! Local, Yahoo! Address Book, and many others. By July 2006, Yahoo! 360 had attracted 4.7 million users, a significant number but still small compared with 52 million MySpace users.[46]

In December 2005, Yahoo! responded to the growing trend of "social search"—epitomized by the popularity of the online collaborative encyclopedia Wikipedia and the video-sharing site YouTube—by launching Yahoo! Answers. The site enabled anyone to post a question, which any other user could offer an answer to, which made it more like a chat room than a traditional encyclopedia. Questions ranged from the technical ("What is the best PDA on the market and how much does it cost?") to the philosophical ("Do you believe in ghosts?") to the whimsical ("Should I race, or party?"). Within nine months, Yahoo! answers had attracted 50 million users who provided 75 million answers.[47] Additionally, in September 2006, Yahoo! launched a new version of its e-mail service offering enhanced features and better integration with other Yahoo! services. For example, users can post e-mails to their Yahoo! 360 blogs and send appointments and other information to their Yahoo! Calendars.

In spite of these efforts, Yahoo's financial performance suffered in 2005 and 2006. Revenues grew by 42 percent to $5.3 billion in 2005, which would be stunning for most companies but was disappointing for Yahoo!, following 77 percent revenue growth in 2004. In 2006, online advertising conditions worsened toward the end of the third quarter as many automotive and financial services advertisers slowed or stopped their online ad spending due to unfavorable conditions in their own industries. Yahoo! shares fell 34 percent from January to September 2006 to $25 per share as a result. The company predicted even lower revenue growth for the 2006 fiscal year of 29 percent. Yahoo! needed to find ways to deliver better growth or it risked a further decline in its market valuation.

CONCLUSION

Since taking the helm of Yahoo! on May 1, 2001, Terry Semel had turned the company around. As of September 2006, Yahoo! boasted more than 500 million unique users worldwide. More importantly, it had more than 8 million fee-paying customers, essential to increasing revenue streams. Semel streamlined the 44 business units he inherited to just five, and worked to bring other top executives with media experience to the company. He hired Lloyd Braun, a former entertainment lawyer, talent agent, and television executive with Hollywood connections to oversee content in entertainment, sports, and other areas of the media group. Braun's goal was to keep Yahoo!'s hundreds of millions of users coming back day after day.

Semel outlined aggressive goals for Yahoo! as the company moved forward. He wanted to focus on building deeper engagement with its users. As he wrote in the 2004 annual report, "Today's world is moving from mass media to 'my media,' a world in which the user is the programmer. Yahoo! aspires to be even more essential in people's lives. To achieve that, we know we must deliver what users want—when they want, how they want, and where they want." More than that, Semel wanted to take advantage of the continued convergence of broadband and wireless and play a greater role in people's connected lives. He continued, "We believe that in a connected world, users expect their Internet experience across all devices to be seamlessly integrated, and their content, such as games, photos or music, to be accessible and personalized." The challenge remained, though—how would Yahoo! accomplish these goals in an environment with increased competition from the likes of Google and an uncertain international market? As its revenue growth slowed and its stock slid in 2006, this challenge was more pressing than ever.

DISCUSSION QUESTIONS

1. Describe the sources of equity for the Yahoo! brand. Did these sources change during Yahoo!'s history? If so, how?
2. How did Yahoo!'s marketing program contribute to the company's success? What changes, if any, would you recommend for the future?
3. Evaluate Yahoo!'s strategy of selling services. What impact, if any, will it have on consumers' perceptions of the brand? How can Yahoo! get more people to pay for more of its services?
4. Should Yahoo! work more on growing its international presence, or should it focus on strengthening its domestic position?
5. What do you think is the biggest risk to Yahoo! at the time of the case? What should the company do about it?

Exhibit 1: Brand Awareness Measurement

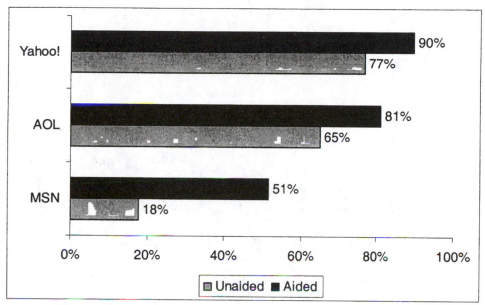

Source: IDC, Internet Portal Brands Image Survey, September 2000

Exhibit 2: Yahoo! Revenue

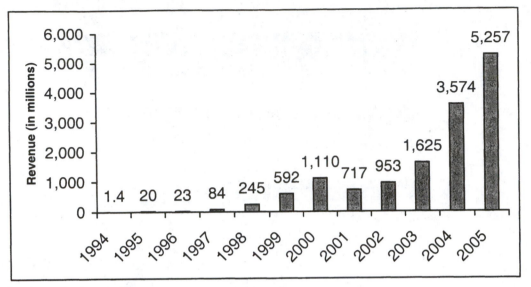

Source: Company Reports

Exhibit 3: Revenue by Groups of Similar Services (in millions)

	2003	% of total	2004	% of total	2005	% of to
Marketing Services	$ 1,327	82%	$ 3,149	88%	$ 4,594	87%
Fees	298	18%	426	12%	663	13%
Total	$ 1,625	100%	$ 3,575	100%	$ 5,257	100%

Source: Company Reports

Exhibit 4: Yahoo! Subscription Data

	2003	2004	2005E
Fee Paying Customers (000)	4,900	8,400	12,000
Y/Y Growth		71%	43%
Average Revenue per User (monthly)	$6.91	$5.61	$5.30
Active Registered Users (000)	133,000	165,000	201,000
Fee Paying % of Active	3.7%	5.1%	6.0%

Source: Company Reports, Smith Barney estimates

Exhibit 5: The 20 Most Visited Areas of Yahoo! (in millions)

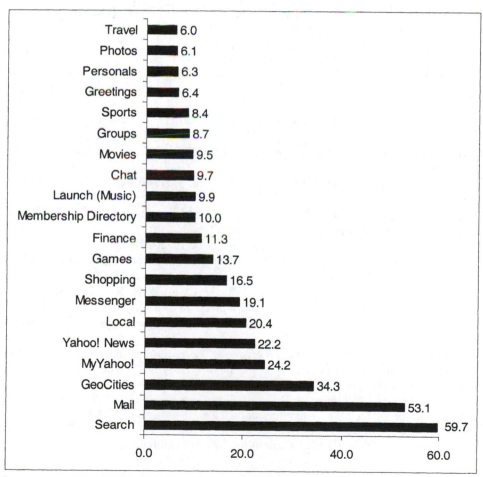

Source: comScore Media Metrix, March 2004

REFERENCES

[1] This case was prepared by Keith Richey, and revised and updated by Jonathan Michaels, under the supervision of Professor Kevin Lane Keller as the basis for class discussion.

[2] Kara Swisher. "Interview: Behind the Portal: What's Yahoo! Up To?" The *Wall Street Journal*, April 17, 2000, p. R74.

[3] Ibid.

[4] Ibid.

[5] Joseph Nocera. "Do You Believe? How Yahoo! Became a Blue Chip." *Fortune*, June 7, 1999, p. 76.

[6] "Directories Look For Ways to Build Brands." *Advertising Age*, June 1996.

[7] "Inside Yahoo! Search Party." *Adweek*, July 12, 1999.

[8] Ibid.

[9] As quoted in "Brandweek's Marketers of the Year: Yahoo!, Karen Edwards." *Adweek*, October 20, 1997.

[10] "What Is Yahoo!, Really?" *Fortune*, June 22, 1998.

[11] "Inside Yahoo! Search Party." *Adweek*, July 12, 1999.

[12] "Yahoo! Still Searching For Profits on the Internet." *Fortune*, December 9, 1996.

[13] Tobi Elkin, "The Interactive Future: Jerry Yang" *Advertising Age*, April 17, 2000, p. I56.

[14] "Yahoo! Informs the World It's Now an E-Mall." The *Wall Street Journal*, October 29, 1999.

[15] As quoted in "Brandweek's Marketers of the Year: Yahoo!, Karen Edwards." *Adweek*, October 20, 1997

[16] "Yahoo! TV Ads Connect the Brand With Shopping." *Advertising Age*, November 1, 1999

[17] "Yahoo! Inc. to Spend $20 Million In Campaign on News Corp.'s Fox." The *Wall Street Journal*, January 26, 1999

[18] "Yahoo! Japan Wins Hoorays." *Business Week*, June 19, 2000

[19] "Yahoo! Makes Grass-Roots Push in Asia." The *Wall Street Journal*, August 1, 2000

[20] "Interview: Wireless War." The *Wall Street Journal*, September 18, 2000

[21] "Yahoo! Everywhere Still Has to Find Its Way." *Business Week*, June 2, 2000

[22] As quoted in "Heard on the Street." The *Wall Street Journal*, September 1, 2000

[23] Daniel Roth, "Terry Semel thinks Yahoo should grow up already", *Fortune*, September 30,2002.

[24] Marc Gunther, "The Cheering Fades for Yahoo!" *Fortune*, November 12, 2001, p. 151.

[25] Mylene Mangalindan. "Users Flame New Yahoo! Privacy Plan." The *Wall Street Journal*, April 12, 2002, p. A16.

[26] Alan Deutschman, "Commercial Success." *Fast Company*, January 2005.

[27] Fred Vogelstein, "Yahoo's Brilliant Solution." *Fortune*, August 8, 2005.

[28] Marc Gunther, "The Cheering Fades for Yahoo!" *Fortune*, November 12, 2001.

[29] Fred Vogelstein, "Yahoo's Brilliant Solution." *Fortune*, August 8, 2005.

[30] Ibid.

[31] Ibid.

[32] Ibid.

[33] Yahoo! press release, "Target and Yahoo! Debut Full-Featured Digital Photo Resource." April 21, 2005.

[34] Yahoo! press release, "Mark Burnett Productions Says 'You're Hired' To Yahoo!" May 4, 2005.

[35] Smith Barney analyst report, "YHOO: Our Top Long Pick In The Internet Sector." June 8, 2005.

[36] Ben Elgin and Jay Greene, "The Counterattack on Google." *BusinessWeek*, May 8, 2006, p. 74.

[37] Saul Hansell, "Yahoo Is Unleashing a New Way to Turn Ad Clicks Into Ka-Ching." The *New York Times*, May 8, 2006, p. C1.

[38] Adam Lashinsky, "Yahoo Hangs Tough." *Fortune*, August 21, 2006, p. 123.

[39] Fred Vogelstein and Kate Bonamici, "Yahoo's Brilliant Solution." *Fortune*, August 8, 2005, p. 42

[40] Riva Richmond, "Yahoo to Beef Up Tools for Searching Its Web-Based Email." The *Wall Street Journal*, August 31, 2005.

[41] Smith Barney analyst report, "YHOO: Our Top Long Pick In The Internet Sector." June 8, 2005.

[42] Ben Elgin, "Exporting and Uber-Brand." *BusinessWeek*, April 4, 2005.

[43] Jason Dean, "Meet Jack Ma, Who Will Guide Yahoo in China." The *Wall Street Journal*, August 12, 2005.

[44] Adam Lashinsky, "Yahoo Hangs Tough." *Fortune*, August 21, 2006, p. 123.

[45] Fred Vogelstein and Kate Bonamici, "Yahoo's Brilliant Solution." *Fortune*, August 8, 2005, p. 42

[46] Saul Hansell, "In the Race With Google, It's Consistency vs. the 'Wow' Factor." The *New York Times*, July 24, 2006, p. C1.

[47] Richard Wray, "Yahoo! launches 'social search' in Britain with multimillion-pound ad campaign," The *Guardian*, September 4, 2006, p. 24.

AMERICAN EXPRESS:
MANAGING A FINANCIAL SERVICES BRAND[1]

INTRODUCTION

American Express, a well-known and respected global brand, was known worldwide for its charge cards, traveler's services, and financial services. As it grew from a nineteenth-century express shipping company into a travel services expert by the mid-1900s, American Express became associated in the minds of consumers with prestige, security, service, international acceptability, and leisure. Advertising for the company, which began in earnest in the 1960s, reinforced those associations. As the company grew, it expanded into a variety of financial categories, including brokerage services, banking, and insurance, and by the late 1980s, American Express was the largest diversified financial services firm in the world.

The company encountered difficulty integrating these broad financial services offerings, however, and this fact, combined with increased card competition from Visa and MasterCard, compelled American Express to divest many of its financial holdings in the early 1990s and focus on its core competencies of travel and cards. The company weathered a decrease in cardholders at this time by greatly increasing the number of merchants that accepted American Express cards and developing new card offerings, including co-branded cards and a genuine credit card that allowed customers to carry over the monthly balance. By the end of the 1990s, American Express was again seeking to broaden its brand to include select financial services in order to achieve growth. Beyond the challenge of integrating these services, American Express faced a number of issues in the 2000s, including a highly competitive credit card industry, a slowing economy, and a sluggish travel industry.

AMERICAN EXPRESS BUILDS A FINANCIAL EMPIRE

Early History of American Express

The American Express Company was formed in 1850 when two competing express companies merged. The express business, which was less than two decades old, specialized in shipping packages that were smaller than the bulk freight that railroads handled but were over the U.S. Postal Service size limits. Express companies also carried packages that required special handling or were particularly valuable. Bank transactions involving cash, securities, and gold gave express companies much of their business.

In response to losing business to express companies, the U.S. Postal Service created the money order, which allowed people to send a cash equivalent through the mail that could be cashed only by a specified recipient. The cash delivery service was traditionally the domain of express companies, because postal workers would often steal cash sent through regular mail. To counter the Postal Service's move into financial services, American Express created its own money order in 1881. The American Express money orders were easier to use than the Post Office money orders, and American Express extended the line to include orders in foreign currency that could be cashed internationally. The money order was a great success, selling 250,000 in its first year and more than half a million the next.

In the late 1880s, American Express president J. C. Fargo returned from a trip complaining about how difficult it was to use his letter of credit (used to obtain cash abroad) at foreign banks. To solve the problem of obtaining credit abroad, American Express employee Marcellus Berry designed the "Travelers Cheque" in 1890, intentionally using the British spelling of *check* to give it an international flair. The Travelers Cheque used the same signature security system still in use today and had exchange rates guaranteed by American Express printed on the front. American Express also gave foreign merchants commissions to encourage them to accept the check. Aided by the network of international financial relationships established for support of the American Express money order, sales of the Travelers Cheque quickly took off. From 1882 to 1896, Travelers Cheque sales quadrupled as travelers all over the world were using American Express products more and more to make their journeys easier.

Federal antitrust regulation led to the separation of American Express' express shipping business from its financial services and tourism businesses. By that time, American Express was already booking tours, hotel stays, and steamship and railway tickets. Money orders were still popular and Travelers Cheque sales were constantly increasing. American Express had also been investing the "float"—the money that remains in the company's account during the interval between when Travelers Cheques are bought and when they are cashed—and earning millions of dollars in interest. The Travelers Cheque fees and its float investments were responsible for most of American Express' earnings and almost all of its profits. The Travelers Cheque soon became the company's flagship product.

History of the Charge Card

In 1914, Western Union, another express company, issued the first "charge card" in the form of a metal plate given to preferred customers that enabled them to defer payment for services. Charge cards required that the balance be paid in full at regular intervals but did not charge interest on the balance. Soon, many different companies from department stores to oil companies issued charge cards that customers could use to purchase goods and services from the issuing company. In the 1940s, several U.S. banks began issuing a paper document—similar to a letter of credit—that customers could use like cash in local stores. Diners Club introduced the first modern charge card in 1950, when it issued a "Travel and Entertainment" card designed for use by business travelers. The card was accepted by a large variety of merchants, who paid a fee to Diners Club in compensation for the added business. The first bank card was issued by Franklin National Bank in Long Island, New York. The bank-issued card was accepted by local merchants only, unlike the Diners Club card. Shortly after the debut of the Franklin National Bank credit card, several other banks across the United States issued credit cards to their customers.

"The Card"

American Express actually had considered issuing a charge card on several occasions before Diners Club unveiled its card. This was as early as 1947, but then-president Ralph Reed refused because of security problems given the possibility of fraud. In

1956, when Diners Club card charges began to cut into American Express Travelers Cheque sales, American Express initiated negotiations to buy Diners Club. Talks lasted for two years, but Reed ultimately declined, citing concern about the dilution of American Express' prestige. In late 1957, American Express leadership decided that the company would issue its own card.

The public clamored to possess an American Express charge card. Even before the card was officially available, thousands of customers had written in or visited American Express offices to apply. By the launch date in October 1958, the company had issued more than 250,000 cards and signed on 17,500 merchants that would accept the cards. The card required the cardholder to pay off his or her entire balance monthly. The company also charged a $6.00 annual fee, which was $1.00 greater than the Diners Club fee, "for prestige." American Express' worldwide network of offices, travel agents, and associated banks helped it build the card's membership rapidly.

Because the American Express card was initially designed for the travel and entertainment expenses of businessmen and the upper class, it was known as a Travel and Entertainment (T&E) card. This classification put it in a category with such cards as Diners Club and Carte Blanche.

In 1958, Bank of America issued the first modern credit card, called the BankAmericard. The key feature of the BankAmericard and other credit cards was a "revolving" credit line, which allowed cardholders to pay their account balance in installments, with interest assessed on the remaining balance. The BankAmericard originally served the state of California, but within a decade Bank of America was licensing its card services to banks throughout the country. While American Express earned most of its card revenue from annual fees and discount rates (the percentage of a dollar transaction the merchant was required to pay to American Express in compensation for the business brought in by the card), credit cards earned revenues from interest charges and a lower merchant discount. Another important difference was that American Express issued its own cards while individual banks issued cards under license agreements from credit card companies.

Neither American Express management nor the accounting department had any experience with charge card operations. Rather than creating a separate accounting function for the card division, Reed had assigned American Express' existing comptroller's office to handle all of the card transactions. This proved an overwhelming amount of paperwork, and within a few months of the introduction, the comptroller's office was flooded with unprocessed transactions. Compounding the internal problems was the fact that customers were not paying on time, while American Express was required to pay merchants within ten days after a transaction. The card division had lost more than $4 million dollars in its first two years and an additional $14 million by 1962. One of Howard Clark's first moves after becoming American Express president in 1960 was to try to sell the card division, ironically enough, to Diners Club. The negotiations failed because of antitrust issues and American Express kept its card. In spite of the card problems, though, American Express as a whole was financially stable, with 1959 profits of $8.4 million from $69.6 million in revenue and Travelers Cheque volume of more than $1 billion.

Clark instituted measures to help the ailing card division, such as requiring cardholders to pay their balance within thirty days, raising the annual fee to $10.00, raising the discount rate, and imposing stricter credit requirements for cards issuance. The card division finally achieved profitability in 1962. By 1967, the card business yielded a net income of $6.5 million, or one-third of the company's total profit. The American Express card had surpassed the Travelers Cheque to become the most visible symbol of American Express.

Aggressive Acquisition Strategy

In the 1960s and 1970s, American Express executives looked for ways to grow the business beyond Travelers Cheques and charge cards. The competition from Master Charge (now MasterCard) and the BankAmericard (later to become Visa), who were issuing more charge and credit cards, raised fears that American Express would lose market share of its Travelers Cheques and see its cardholder base diminish. American Express also worried that the company's small size and high profits made it an attractive takeover target. A large acquisition would make a takeover less likely and give American Express a new source of income. Clark chose a company three times the size of American Express with the 1968 acquisition of Fund America Group. It included Fireman's Fund Insurance Company and four mutual funds that were later sold off.

Other changes by Clark included the acquisition of a magazine, which was later renamed *Travel & Leisure* and the creation of the Travel Related Services (TRS) division in 1971, which pooled the Travelers Cheque, the card, and other travel and tourism businesses. The company also organized its banking operations under the renamed American Express International Bank Corporation (AEIBC). When Clark left as president in 1977, American Express had $250 million in annual profits and 8 million cards generating $10 billion in charge volume.

The American Express Company had three divisions when James Robinson took over as CEO in 1977: Travel Related Services (TRS), American Express International Bank Corporation (AEIBC), and Fireman's Fund (FF). As CEO, Robinson pursued an aggressive acquisition strategy. In 1979, hoping to sell financial products through cable television, he entered into a programming partnership with Warner Communications for $175 million. A few months later in 1980, American Express bought First Data Resources for $50 million. First Data was a computerized billing operation that processed Visa and MasterCard transactions for banks. This was only a warm-up for Robinson, and in 1981 American Express merged with Shearson Loeb Rhoades Inc., the second largest public brokerage firm in the country behind Merrill Lynch.

American Express continued its expansion into a financial conglomerate by purchasing two additional brokerage houses and a real estate company. The international investment bank Trade Development Bank Holdings S.A. (TDB) was acquired in 1983 for $520 million to shore up AEIBC and focus its operations on trade finance and international private banking. That same year, American Express purchased Investors Diversified Services (IDS) for $773 million. IDS offered mutual funds, life insurance, annuities, and financial planning to middle-income consumers. The investment bank Lehman Brothers Kuhn Loeb Inc. was acquired in 1984 for $360 million, and American Express again added to its brokerage cache by acquiring E. F. Hutton & Co. in 1987 for almost $1 billion.

One Enterprise

Robinson and his top executives envisioned a transformed company structure called "One Enterprise." The One Enterprise vision would make American Express a one-stop financial and travel services powerhouse with each division cross-marketing its products to the others. Cardholders could obtain travel services from TRS; property and casualty, flight and travel, and life insurance from Fireman's Fund; financial advice and other products from IDS; and brokerage and investment banking services from Shearson Lehman Hutton; while the wealthier international clientele would be pampered by AEIBC (renamed American Express Bank Ltd. or AEB in 1986). Each division would in turn push American Express cards to any of their customers who weren't already cardholders or higher-end Gold or Platinum cards to those who were.

Due to the acquisition-based growth and cross-marketing concepts, which were fashionable corporate strategies in the 1980s, Robinson was hailed as a savvy CEO. By the end of 1984, American Express had developed $61 billion in assets and posted annual revenues of $13 million. The TRS division, which supplied American Express with almost three-quarters of its earnings, was selling $13 billion worth of Travelers Cheques, while 20 million cards were generating $45 billion in charges. American Express had name recognition of 75 percent and its services were used by 14 percent of the population, more than any other financial company.

MARKETING STRATEGY AND ADVERTISING

Howard Clark was the first American Express president to place a high priority on advertising. Before he took office in 1960, American Express' annual advertising budget was only $1 million. Clark increased it every year thereafter and in 1962 replaced its ad agency, Benton & Bowles, with Ogilvy & Mather. The new agency designed American Express' first modern ad campaign with the slogan "The Company for people who travel." This tag line promoted the company's travel and card products in a single campaign that conveyed its one-stop travel shopping expertise.

Early Campaigns

The now-famous tag line "Don't leave home without it" was developed by Ogilvy & Mather in the early 1970s. American Express wanted a "synergy tag line" like the other Ogilvy-produced line: "The Company for people who travel." Ogilvy also developed "Don't leave home without them" for Travelers Cheques, "Don't leave home without us" for travel services, and the "Don't leave home without it" tag line for charge cards. Ads for Travelers Cheques featured actor Karl Malden speaking the tagline and ran for 21 years. In 1974, the company debuted its now-familiar "blue-box logo," with the words *American Express* printed in white outline over a square blue background.

Ogilvy & Mather tried several conceptual approaches to use with this tag line and eventually hit upon the idea of replacing everyday and unknown actors in the ads with endorsers whose names were famous, but whose faces were not as familiar—this became the "Do You Know Me?" campaign. The ads typically began by showing the face of a moderately well-known celebrity, such as American playwright Neil Simon, and then showing a close-up of his or her American Express card to reveal his or her identity. The ads implied that using an American Express card would get the cardholder "recognized."

American Express advertising conveyed the prestige associated with the card. Cardholders were called "card members," and the year they became members was printed on their card—signaling membership to a club. American Express cards were perceived by many as status symbols, signifying success and achievement. American Express sought to maintain this elusive image through advertising, impeccable service, promotions, bonuses, and special events. The introduction of Gold and Platinum cards to the credit card industry further enhanced the cache associated with credit cards. By 1985, American Express was spending $500 million a year in marketing. "Marketing is our number one priority," said Robinson at the time.

Emphasizing Customer Service

Customer service was a key element of American Express' marketing program; as Robinson used to say, "Quality is our only form of patent protection." Before he became CEO, Robinson developed a comprehensive system for measuring service quality. His goal was to have customer service employees handle more than 99 percent of requests without any mistakes. The company measured the time it took a customer service representative to answer the phone and the time it took for a replacement card to arrive. It established a Quality University where customer service representatives and their managers were trained to deliver excellent service. In addition, American Express set up a committee of managers from throughout the corporation who met to discuss new ways of measuring and improving quality. "Quality Conferences" were held to disseminate and implement quality initiatives throughout the organization.

Besides internal monitoring, American Express constantly surveyed its customers and merchants by mail and by phone to ensure that the level of service remained consistent. American Express developed a database system, which was updated weekly, of customer information that tracked spending patterns, age, and 450 other customer characteristics. This database enabled the company to target specific marketing efforts to the customer segments most likely to respond. It also used this system to recruit new merchants by demonstrating what American Express could do for their businesses using real customer data, not projections.

In part due to these efforts, American Express earned a reputation for providing the highest level of customer service. One representative personally delivered a card in the middle of the night to a stranded cardholder at Boston's Logan airport. In another case, a company representative in New Delhi arranged for another representative's brother (a military helicopter pilot stationed close to the caller) to deliver cash to a Gold cardholder who was stranded in a remote village in the Himalayas.

Advertising in the 1980s

The company created the "Do you know me?" campaign to target older, successful, and affluent businessmen who traveled a great deal. Over the campaign's nine years, cardholders quadrupled to 12 million, a full 40 percent of that market segment.

Fearing that growth in this segment would soon level off, American Express looked to stimulate growth in other areas. In the 1980s, women were attaining more powerful business positions in large numbers. American Express targeted this segment of the population with ads tailored toward young urban professional women. In 1983, women comprised only 2.5 million American Express cardholders—the company thought it could achieve a number five times that.

Testing had shown that women did not respond positively to the existing ad campaign. Marketing data from the early 1980s showed that consumers thought that status and prestige came not necessarily from huge wealth or success, but from a varied and exciting life. Ogilvy & Mather came up with the "Interesting Lives" campaign that aimed to position American Express cards as symbols of people with interesting and multifaceted lives, people with unusual hobbies or who had unconventional careers. The American Express card, the ads indicated, gave its holders the opportunity to indulge in their varied interests, or be spontaneous by traveling the world. Rather than feature celebrities, the ads showed confident, independent women using the American Express card to take their husband to dinner or their kids to lunch, bantering with a flirtatious man in a bookstore, or leaving a sporting goods store with a briefcase and a lacrosse stick. "The American Express Card," the tag line says, "It's part of a lot of interesting lives." Soon the volume of female applicants was double that of men. By 1984, 27 percent of American Express cardholders were women, compared to 10 percent in the late 1970s.

Even though these campaigns did very well, American Express' marketing strategy for its core potential cardholders had become stale. It dropped the "Do you know me?" ads in 1987 and devised a new series of print ads called "Portraits." Renowned photographer Annie Leibovitz was recruited to photograph celebrities rarely shown in advertisements. The ads showed these celebrities in a more intimate, playful light, without the pomp and circumstance that celebrity ads usually employed. America's Cup yachtsman Dennis Connor played with a sailboat in his bathtub in one shot, while in another politician Tip O'Neill was shown at the beach under an umbrella. The only text was their names, the date they became "members," and the tag line that was to become one of American Express' most enduring: "Membership Has Its Privileges." The ads received much praise for their ingenuity and quirkiness.

By 1989, American Express was spending $250 million annually on advertising, more than twice as much as Visa and MasterCard combined. This expenditure reflected the numerous marketing initiatives underway to expand the company's cardholder base, including efforts to attract more women, students, senior citizens, and small companies. Additionally, the company developed a major ad campaign to get cardholders to use their cards at everyday retail shops, not just fine restaurants and boutiques. Research showed that the majority of card purchases were made with other credits cards while only high-ticket items were charged to American Express cards.

Cause Marketing

Since 1981, American Express had embarked on many cause-related advertising campaigns (where a percentage of the company's proceeds were donated to a specific charity). In fact, the company was credited with coining the phrase "cause-related marketing." Between 1981 and 1984, American Express donated to more than 45 different charitable organizations. Most of these donation drives occurred at the local level, such as when American Express donated $0.02 to the San Francisco Arts Festival each time Bay Area card members used their cards. By encouraging card members to spend more to support the cause, American Express profited from increased card usage. Similar campaigns around the country generated total donations in the tens of millions of dollars and increased card usage in locations where a cause-related marketing campaign was active by an average of 25 percent.

The company's first national cause-related marketing campaign was organized in 1983 to raise money for the Statue of Liberty Restoration Fund. To build awareness for the program, American Express developed a $4 million advertising campaign that included print, radio, and television advertising. Each time a card member used his or her card, a $0.01 donation was made to the fund. For every new account opened, American Express donated $1.00 to the fund. Donations were also made for Travelers Cheques and travel purchases. Between September and December 1983, American Express gave $1.7 million to the Statue of Liberty Restoration Fund. Card usage rose 28 percent nationally in the first month compared with the previous year, while new card applications increased 45 percent. Following its early success with cause-related marketing campaigns, American Express developed more than 90 programs in 17 countries.

One of American Express' best-known campaigns was the "Charge Against Hunger." The Charge Against Hunger, begun in 1993, was a charity effort in which the company donated a certain amount of money to hunger relief agency Share Our Strength every time a cardholder used an American Express card to make a purchase during the holiday season. The 1993 Charge Against Hunger raised $5.3 million. To raise awareness for the campaign, American Express produced a series of advertisements featuring information about the charity and detailing the specifics of the program. Between 1993 and the last year of the program in 1996, the Charge Against Hunger campaign raised more than $21 million. American Express also supported the arts at the local community level, publicizing its efforts with ads praising the charitable cause while underscoring the convenience of using the American Express card. In 2006, the company partnered with Bono—lead singer of the band U2—and his AIDS organization Project RED to introduce the American Express RED card, through which American Express contributes 1 percent of charges made with the card to fight AIDS in Africa.

CREDIT CARD COMPETITION HEATS UP

By 1985, American Express' 20 million cards that produced $45 billion in billings still lagged behind Visa's 115 million cards with $82 billion in billings and MasterCard's 103 million with $62 billion in billings. About 3.3 million of American Express' cards were Gold cards (first offered in 1966) and about 60,000 were Platinum (introduced in 1984). Visa had 3 million higher-end "Premier Visa" cards and MasterCard had 2.5 million "Preferred Customer" cards (both began issuing them in 1982) with annual fees of $55. In spite of their similar numbers of cardholders, American Express still had a clear advantage over Visa and MasterCard in the high-end market with Gold card charges totaling $13 billion while Visa and MasterCard had only $7.5 billion combined.

Although most credit cards had features similar to American Express' charge cards, prestige still seemed to win people over in terms of wanting American Express cards and in using them for their more expensive items. One analyst said, "If you want to buy an expensive car, you tend to buy a Mercedes or a Cadillac, not a souped-up Honda." For American Express customers, the fact that MasterCard and Visa were accepted at more than 4 million sites while American Express was accepted at only 1 million sites was mitigated by the fact that only American Express had offices in many remote locations capable of handling almost any travel emergency. Indeed, prestige seemed to be so important to consumers that they signed up at twice the expected rate for American Express' $250 annual fee Platinum Card and eventually numbered six times what the company expected.

In the 1980s, the standard American Express Green card had an annual fee of $35 and offered $1,000 check cashing at representative banks and American Express travel offices, the ability to withdraw $500 from ATMs, and $100,000 travel accident insurance. For a $65 annual fee, Gold Card members upgraded to $2,000 in checks cashed and a credit line of $2,000. The Platinum Card allows members to cash up to $10,000 in checks, get $1,000 from ATMs, $500,000 in travel insurance, and nonresident privileges in more than 25 private clubs around the world. American Express offered these cards to only about 5 percent of its U.S. cardholders who charged more than $10,000 a year and had good payment histories.

Higher-end credit cards (e.g., Gold, Platinum) proliferated in the mid-1980s as the market for standard cards became relatively saturated. Credit card delinquency rates increased due to banks' efforts to shore up profits by signing up more cardholders. The average cardholder possessed seven cards, forcing banks to find other ways to compete. Many consumers were frustrated with banks because they maintained high interest rates on their cards (around 19 percent) in spite of the fact that the prime lending rate had dropped 14 points since 1982. The banks defended their card rates, citing the cost of processing millions of card transactions every week. In order to appease their customers, banks offered special perks such as bonus points and cash back offers. They also began issuing Gold and Platinum cards to attract more customers. These "elite" cards were used 50 percent more often than regular cards, and the average purchase with them was 150 percent greater than with a normal card. Visa and MasterCard eventually gained enough Gold Card members, 12 and 11 million, respectively, to beat American Express' 6 million.

Optima Unveiled

American Express responded to the increasing popularity of credit cards by issuing its own credit card, called Optima, late in 1987. Not only did it compete head-to-head with the revolving credit bank-issued cards, but it also did so with a much lower interest rate and annual fee. Establishing Optima as a separate brand also allowed American Express to greatly expand its card base without damaging its upscale image. American Express initially offered the Optima only to current cardholders. Because these customers were accustomed to paying their balance monthly, they were considered the lowest-risk segment for this new "risky" product. Banks were worried that Optima cardholders would use the new credit card for regular purchases and the American Express charge cards for their T&E expenses, dropping regular and high-end bank cards from Visa and MasterCard in the process. Citicorp, at the time the nation's largest issuer of bank cards with close to 15 million, countered American Express' new card by lowering its rates to "preferred customers" to 16.8 percent from 19.8 percent. Visa USA Inc. even urged its issuing banks to stop selling American Express Travelers Cheques in protest. American Express replied with a Travelers Cheque ad that told consumers, "If your bank doesn't sell them, go to one that does!"

In order to compete, most charge and credit cards furiously began cutting prices and offering special incentives. Co-branded or "affinity" cards also became very popular. Visa had 768 affinity programs approved by the end of 1987. Most MasterCard and Visa Silver and Gold cardholders also got rebates on hotels and plane fares in addition to rental car discounts. Although American Express did not offer any affinity cards, it did continue to offer benefits and special offers. In addition to its Buyer's Assurance program, which doubled the manufacturer's warranty up to a year on items purchased with its cards, American Express also began its Purchase Protection program, which insured these items for ninety days against theft, loss, fire, or accidental damage up to $50,000. It also offered its Gold and Platinum members free rental car insurance.

By the end of 1988, having been offered for only 18 months, Optima ranked as one of the top ten credit cards in terms of cardholder volume. Optima had 2 million cardholders with more than $3 billion in outstanding balances. The interest and fees for Optima were nearly pure profit because American Express spent comparatively little—only $100 million—developing and launching it. American Express had the advantage of an established cardholder base to offer it to and merchants willing to accept it.

Due to the success of Optima and improved marketing to young men, women, and students, American Express' domestic share of the card market increased to 10 percent by 1989, totaling 22 million cards (30 million worldwide). Charge volume also increased to 27 percent or $69 billion, which led all card issuers. Visa meanwhile had 52 percent cardshare with 115 million cards, and MasterCard had 38 percent with 84 million. The remainder was primarily Sears' Discover card, which had about 28 million cardholders. Sears issued Discover in 1985 using its existing customer credit base of 40 million accounts, low interest, no fee, and a cash-back program as advantages. Nevertheless, American Express maintained that because consumers charged only 15 percent of the possible number of items that could be charged, its main competition was not the other card companies but cash.

American Express Applauded

Success continued through the late 1980s. Revenue and profits grew in every division and earnings topped the $1 billion mark in 1986. In 1989, American Express grossed more than $26 billion and netted $1.2 billion with a Travelers Cheque float of more than $4 billion to invest. Compounded earnings and sales over the decade had risen 9 percent and 13 percent every year, and American Express

had a return on shareholder equity of more than 15 percent a year. Its direct marketing department was the fifth largest in the nation selling electronics, furniture, jewelry, luggage, mutual funds, and
insurance. American Express' publishing arm included *Travel & Leisure* and *Food & Wine* magazines, with a combined circulation of more than 2 million. Analysts were recommending American Express stock, saying it was undervalued based on its future earnings potential with American Express being called "one of the great success stories of the last twenty years."

AMERICAN EXPRESS STUMBLES

Card Competition Continues

In 1991, American Express introduced its "Membership Miles" loyalty program, which gave customers one point for every dollar spent on the card. These points could be exchanged for credit in frequent flier airline miles. The program had the dual benefits of attracting more customers and increasing the spending volume of customers who wanted airline miles. The success of this program's introduction was offset, however, by problems with the Optima card.

Though Optima made the company one of the ten largest credit card issuers worldwide, American Express' first offering in the credit card category was fraught with problems. The company's decision to offer the card only to existing cardholders, meant to mitigate the risk inherent in offering a revolving line of credit, still exposed the company to risk and led to millions of dollars in bad debt. While it was true that existing cardholders were accustomed to paying their entire balances monthly, American Express failed to account for the fact that a significant portion of charges on their classic cards were business expenses for which the cardholder was reimbursed. Therefore, the majority of Optima cardholders used that card strictly as a credit device for purchases that were not reimbursed, and as a result only 5 percent of Optima accounts paid the full monthly balance. The resulting losses rose to 10 percent of outstanding balances in 1992, which was double the industry average. In its first three years, Optima cost American Express $2.3 billion. The company was forced to re-evaluate its Optima portfolio and relaunched the card in 1992 with a slightly different payment structure. In 1994, the company pared the number of Optima cardholders to 3 million from about 3.5 million. By 1996, Optima's 5.2 percent annual loss rate was only marginally higher than the 4.6 percent industry average.

As American Express struggled with its Optima card, other card companies were able to make up enormous ground on American Express by offering bonuses, service benefits, and cheaper fees to both merchants and consumers. Bank cards lacked the prestige factor, but, as one analyst noted, "Prestige is less of a Nineties concept than an Eighties concept." American Express' traditional points of difference were service and prestige, but 1990s consumers appeared to place greater value on "function [and] utility." Compounding problems was the launch of Visa's brilliant ad campaign, "Visa. It's Everywhere You Want to Be." That campaign highlighted desirable locations, resorts, events, and restaurants—none of which would accept American Express cards.

American Express was also under siege from a number of new competitors, such as Capital One, which in 1991 was the first company to issue so-called "teaser rate" cards with introductory rates well below the standard 19 percent. Other sources of competition came from co-branded or "affinity" cards, which became increasingly popular with consumers who wanted added value in the form of additional goods or services. American Express had the opportunity to issue one of the first co-branded cards back in 1985, when American Airlines approached the company with a proposal for a joint credit card that would offer frequent flier miles for dollars spent on the card. American Express rejected the offer and American Airlines inked a deal with Citibank instead, which attracted 4 million cardholders within a decade and set off an airline co-branding trend. American Express similarly declined to enter into a co-branding agreement with AT&T in 1990. Within five years, the AT&T card had more than 11 million cardholders.

Between 1990 and 1992, the number of American Express cards in circulation dropped by 1.6 million, or 6 percent. The company was in danger of seeing its competitive advantage disappear. Attempts to diversify into financial services had largely failed, and the company's flagship card business was faltering. These developments led American Express' board to force James Robinson to resign as CEO in 1993. Future CEO Kenneth Chenault later commented, "We were losing relevance with our customers. We were trying to be all things to all people with a few products."

RENEWED FOCUS

Back to Basics

After forcing Robinson's resignation, American Express selected Harvey Golub to succeed him as chairman and CEO in February 1993. Golub was a nine-year veteran of the company, having come to the IDS division from McKinsey & Co. consulting firm. He immediately initiated a series of divestitures to reduce American Express' holdings. Golub negotiated the sale of the Shearson brokerage operation and the Lehman Brothers investment bank. These sales, combined with other profit-saving cutbacks, eliminated 50,000 of the company's 114,000 workers. Following these moves, the now-leaner company was in a position to focus on its core competencies: charge and credit cards, Travelers Cheques and travel services, and select banking and financial services.

In the midst of these cutbacks, Golub pursued aggressive plans for high growth in the card sector. In mid-1994, he announced plans to introduce up to 15 different credit cards. Ready to improve on the company's first credit card offering, Optima, American Express introduced its next card, called Optima True Grace, in August 1994. The Optima True Grace Card featured a low introductory rate of 7.9 percent and came with an automatic "grace period" of twenty-five days after a purchase, during which time no interest would be charged to the cardholder.

The flexibility of Optima True Grace marked a departure from the company's card policies of the past. As bank-issued cards exploded in the 1980s by enticing customers with low annual fees, cash back offers, partnerships, point bonuses, and other special offers, American Express continued to charge high annual fees and declined to partner with other corporations for co-branded cards. The gap in market share between American Express and Visa and MasterCard only widened, and Golub reflected in 1995, "We should have seen what was happening...We were inflexible. We were arrogant. We were dreaming."

To spur growth in the card category, Golub sought to greatly increase merchant acceptance of American Express cards. In October 1996, responding to the requests of more than 14,000 card members, the company inked a deal with Wal-Mart stores to have its cards accepted at more than 2,300 Wal-Mart locations. During 1995, other retailers such as Laura Ashley, ShopRite, Service Merchandise, and Vons Supermarkets signed on to accept the cards. That year, research by the company showed that based on card member purchasing patterns, American Express customers charged 86 percent of their spending to their cards. Future CEO Ken Chenault later commented, "If our customer wants to use the American Express card at a hot dog stand, we want to be there."

In addition to adding merchants that would accept the cards, Golub worked to improve relations with the existing merchant roster. In the past, American Express was able to demonstrate to merchants that its cardholders charged a higher volume with their cards. For many merchants, this mitigated the fact that American Express' merchant discount was considerably higher than Visa or MasterCard's. Purchases by American Express cardholders carried discount fees of more than 3.5 percent, compared to merchant discounts lower than 2 percent for Visa and MasterCard.

As the number of Visa and MasterCard Gold cardholders continued to rise, nearly 90 percent of all American Express customers also carried these cards in addition to their American Express cards. The company needed to retain as many merchants as possible, because more than half of its annual revenues came from the merchant discount fees. The turning point came in 1991, with the so-called "Boston Fee Party." A group of Boston restaurant owners coordinated a boycott of the American Express card because they believed the discount rate to be too high. American Express worked rapidly to repair relationships with these and other merchants. By 1996, the discount rate for purchases was less than 3 percent and all the Boston Fee Party boycotters had been re-signed.

Golub also attempted to better relations with current cardholders. In October 1995, the company expanded its Membership Miles program to include point bonuses for retail merchandise and gourmet gifts, as well as more travel offerings such as car rentals, hotel stays, and vacation packages. This revised program was named Membership Rewards, and points earned through the program had no limit or expiration date. In 1995, American Express also launched its first co-branded card with Delta Air Lines. The airline miles card was called the Delta SkyMiles Optima, and within two years of its introduction it was the number-two airline affinity card with more than 1 million cardholders. American Express forged co-branding relationships with other partners, including Hilton Hotels, ITT Sheraton, and the New York Knicks.

New Initiatives

The renewed focus on American Express' core business led to the first new campaign for Travelers Cheques in twenty years. Though it still dominated the

Travelers Cheques category with $64 billion in annual worldwide sales and a 45 percent market share, American Express wanted to protect its lead against competitors like Visa. In 1994, a new $15 million advertising campaign updated the classic Travelers Cheques commercial, which traditionally featured hapless travelers falling prey to criminals while abroad and then experiencing firsthand the safety and security features of the Travelers Cheques. The new crop of ads focused on the "Cheques for two" feature, which enabled the same checks to be shared between two parties. Instead of getting stolen, the Travelers Cheques in the new ads were only lost, and featured lost-and-found employees in travel destinations describing the quirky items they encountered in the line of duty. The ads were intended to illustrate in a more lighthearted fashion the benefits of Travelers Cheques.

In 1995, the company renamed its IDS division "American Express Financial Advisors" (AEFA) in an effort to present a more uniform brand image to its customers. AEFA, which provided financial and estate planning, annuities, mutual funds, life insurance, pension plans, 401(k) plans, and loans and accounting services to businesses and individuals, was part of the "select financial services" that contributed to American Express' core competencies. One-third of the company's net income in 1996 came from AEFA, which controlled $130 billion in assets.

After dropping Chiat/Day and its "The Card" campaign, American Express re-hired Ogilvy & Mather, who in 1996 introduced a corporate ad campaign themed "Do More." This global ad campaign extended the company's advertising to include financial services and travel in addition to its card businesses. The purpose of the campaign was to underscore the transformation that had taken place at American Express during the previous several years, given that the company had:

1. Sold or spun off subsidiaries and refocused on businesses operating under the American Express brand;
2. Broadened its traditional charge card business to include revolving credit, co-branded cards and other products aimed at specific customer segments, such as students and women;
3. Expanded its global travel network;
4. Begun a major expansion of its financial services businesses; and
5. Introduced new products to its corporate services customers.

"For much of our history, our company's brand was defined by our card and Travelers Cheques businesses," said John Hayes, Chief Marketing Officer of American Express. "Now we are extending our brand to a variety of other products and services to mirror both where our company is and where it is going. What will remain consistent is our vision—to become the world's most respected service brand." The new advertising campaign was designed to capitalize on several of the company's historical brand attributes: trust, customer focus, travel, and financial insight. "American Express is one of the very few global brands in the financial services arena," Hayes added. "All over the world, people's experiences with our travel services, card products, and financial advice have defined our brand's characteristics, reflecting the reasons that both corporations and consumers are loyal to American Express."

Themed "American Express Helps You Do More," the campaign attempted to bridge the company's historic strengths with its newer initiatives. The pool of advertisements included commercials that featured a range of products and services as well as those designed to focus on individual businesses, such as American Express Financial Advisors. It also included ads for American Express charge cards. The spots ran on network and cable television, and were supported by newspaper and magazine ads in a variety of publications including *USA Today*, the *Wall Street Journal*, the *New York Times*, and *Newsweek*.

New Crop of Celebrity Endorsers

Beginning in 1992, American Express used comedian Jerry Seinfeld in advertising that emphasized the card's flexibility and added humor to the personality of the brand. In 1997, as part of the "Do More" campaign, ads featured Seinfeld and emphasized the card's acceptability in locations such as supermarkets and gas stations. In one ad, Seinfeld stops at a gas station to fill up. The premise was that he aimed to put an even dollar amount into the car, presumably so he could pay with cash without breaking change. Upon reaching the target amount, he gave the pump an extra squeeze that pushed the total a few cents over. Onlookers gasped in dismay, until he pulled out his American Express card in dramatic fashion and paid at the pump.

American Express signed one of the leading athletes in the world in 1997 when it inked a five-year, $30 million endorsement contract with Tiger Woods. That year, Woods appeared in print ads and television commercials that promoted American Express Financial Advisors. In one television spot titled "Tiger Wants," the golfer discussed personal aspirations, which included "tak[ing] care of the ones who took care of me" and "help[ing] people who need help." The campaign also featured Tiger's father, Earl, who explained that with the help of an American Express Financial Advisor, he was able to retire early and dedicate himself to helping Tiger reach his goals. John Hayes characterized the endorsement deal as follows:

> The appeal of Tiger Woods—and, indeed, of his father, Earl—transcends the world of golf. While Tiger's tenacity, work ethic, and abilities are outstanding, we also recognize him as a person whose achievements are the result of perseverance and an incredible focus on a goal. That kind of earned success is a hallmark of financial success as well.

In appraising American Express' position, Hayes also noted:

> The market became very segmented, and we needed to catch up with that to become more relevant to more segments. So now we've gone from a brand that was basically represented by one card product to one that has 25 products. That's a drastic change.

> Our toughest balancing act is not to lose our traditional core customers and our reputation for premium quality and service while we enact new initiatives to expand against other segments.

We're tracking that on a quarterly basis to make sure we don't go too far in one direction or the other.

New Card Products

In 1999, American Express unveiled the biggest new card launch since Optima with the Blue card. Blue, which was launched with a $45 million advertising campaign, was labeled a "smart card" because it contained an embedded chip that enhanced security for Internet purchases using a home-encryption system. American Express issued Blue cardholders a home card-swiper free of charge, which could be used for Internet transactions. The card targeted the 25 percent of Americans that owned computers and used sophisticated consumer technology, as well as another 25 percent of the population learning to use such technology. Unlike other American Express cards, Blue carried no annual fee. One perceived risk of the Blue marketing campaign was the implication that the company's other cards were not secure for use with Internet purchases and that this would prompt Internet-savvy cardholders to switch to Blue. Said Alfred Kelly, president of the American Express Consumer Card Services Group, "I would rather be cannibalizing myself than have the competition do it."

Launch advertising involved television, print, and subway advertising, as well as event marketing. The introductory television ads focused on the technology aspect of Blue. One ad showed a sea of amoeba dancing and multiplying over a rock-and-roll soundtrack. This ad was intended to demonstrate the "evolving credit" aspect of the card, which meant that Blue would improve as the company added new features to it. Another ad emphasized Blue's payment flexibility—unlike other American Express cards, monthly balances could be carried into the next month—by showing the card bent, pulled, and reshaped by robotic arms to the sounds of a classical score. In addition to major network broadcasts, these ads ran during television programs targeting young people, such as Fox's *The X-Files* and *Futurama*. Print ads appeared in newspapers and magazines, as well as in sports clubs and on restaurant table-top menus.

The ads did not use the familiar Roman Centurion soldier logo associated with other cards, choosing a new look that suggested a compact disc with blue concentric circles bordered by white. American Express also sponsored a concert in New York called "Central Park in Blue." The concert was promoted by a "street team" of sharply dressed scooter riders, who used handheld "swipers" to enable cardholders to pick up free tickets at nearby Blue information kiosks. These marketing activities were designed to give the card "a different, modern, more hip feel," said Alfred Kelly. "We wanted to break out." Blue was heralded as a success for American Express, reaching its 2000 target of 2 million cardholders in by the end of the first quarter of 2000.

At the same it introduced the non-traditional Blue card, American Express continued to market cards based on prestige. In 1998, it introduced the black Centurion Card—otherwise known as the "Black Card"—for elite clients. To obtain an invitation-only Centurion Card, current American Express cardholders had to satisfy minimum requirements such as $150,000 in annual spending on an existing American Express card and pay a $1,000 annual fee (later raised to $2,500). Services offered with the card included a 24-hour personal concierge service, first-class airline upgrades and bonus miles, and hotel upgrades. Another benefit was the perceived prestige of having the exclusive card. Even though American Express did not spend any money marketing the card, demand outstripped supply, and some clients went to great lengths to obtain the Centurion Card. One Denver executive got multiple Platinum cards and gave them to his friends, agreeing to pay their annual fees while they helped him reach the $150,000 spending limit. Another person in Connecticut filed a complaint with the Federal Deposit Insurance Corporation (FDIC) claiming American Express had discriminated against him by declining his Centurion Card application. After he eventually received a card, his complaint was dismissed.

American Express did not release any information about how many of the cards had been issued or details of the users' spending habits. The Centurion Card was a way to combat the glut of Platinum Cards, estimated at 100 million in 2002, and other premium cards bearing names such as Titanium and Diamond. It also enabled American Express to compete with other "elite" cards such as Visa's Infinite card and MBNA's Quantum card.

AMERICAN EXPRESS IN THE NEW MILLENNIUM

Challenges for the New CEO

When Ken Chenault became CEO of American Express in January 2001 after Harvey Golub's retirement, he was immediately tested with several challenges. Four months after he took the helm, the company was rocked by revelations that $1 billion had been lost by AEFA on junk-bond speculation. Only a few months later, the terrorist attacks of September 11, 2001 not only dislodged the company from its Lower Manhattan headquarters, but also severely crippled American Express' core corporate travel and entertainment business. The company's stock fell 27 percent in the week after the attacks, and profits fell 54 percent for the year. The company's future looked so bleak that rumors circulated that the company might be the target of a takeover by the likes of Citigroup or Morgan Stanley.

Further testing the company at this time was the ongoing struggle with Visa and MasterCard. Check cards—a debit card that subtracted money directly from a cardholders' bank account—were becoming increasingly popular, and Visa was taking advantage of this trend. To encourage growth, Visa spent close to $100 million on check card advertising in 2002. This concentrated ad campaign,—featuring the likes of Bob Dole, Deion Sanders, Kevin Bacon, and Pierce Brosnan—helped to make check transactions account for more than one-third of the $989 billion in gross dollar volume that ran through the Visa network.

MasterCard surged in popularity when it created the "Priceless" ad campaign that soon became a ubiquitous pop culture reference point. The campaign, created by McCann-Erickson Worldwide, consisted of 150 spots that had aired in 90 countries. The ads captured the attention of viewers, who began to imitate the ads' format and wording in everyday life. From the campaign's inception in 1997 through 2001, MasterCard's total gross dollar volume increased more than 62 percent to $986 billion, the number of cards rose to 52 percent to 520 million, and the number of acceptance locations climbed 61 percent, with over 24 million added.

As the travel business dried up and spending dropped in the wake of September 11th, and Visa and MasterCard strengthened their positions, Chenault faced difficult decisions. To control costs, he cut 14,500 jobs—16 percent of the workforce. He also outsourced 2,000 technology-related jobs to IBM. By 2004, his actions had cut costs by $4 billion. In 2002, while corporations were cutting spending, Chenault noticed that consumers were starting to spend again. The company quickly increased its promotions and rewards program for its consumer cards. American Express then expanded its corporate card offerings by courting small and medium-sized business owners, helping to expand its share of the corporate spending market (see Exhibit 1).

The company's efforts to engage small- and medium-sized businesses were bolstered by rebranding its Small Business Services division as "Open: The Small Business Network." The rebranding included a new logo with "Open" written in white capital letters on a blue rectangle background, which appeared on the back of American Express cards affiliated with the Open network and on all communication with cardholders. The benefits of the Open network included flexible payments, online account management, an Internet repository of information and resources to help small business owners, and discounts with companies such as Dell, Hilton, and FedEx. John Hayes explained the rationale behind developing a separate small business brand:

> Small business owners are fundamentally different from people who work for large companies. They're characterized by a shared mindset; they live and breathe the business they're in. We think it's important for this area to have its own identity.

American Express promoted Open with an aggressive online advertising campaign. The company generated more than 2 billion ad impressions in 2004 for its Open brand through its online advertising. It also launched a microsite devoted to helping small business owners share strategies, suggestions, and expertise. This online campaign for Open was part of a broader embrace of the Internet as a marketing vehicle by American Express. After American Express spent 10 percent more ($22 million in total) on online media during the first 7 months of 2004 than it did during all of 2003, John Hayes stated "You can count on us being even more active in the interactive space. There's no question about it."

Chenault's strategies yielded results: in 2003 and 2004, American Express posted record earnings of $3 billion and $3.4 billion, respectively. With these moves, Chenault turned American Express' business model on its head. Before September 11th, 2001, two-thirds of its card billings came from corporate T&E and a third came from regular spending. By 2003, those ratios were reversed.

Although the company had less than 5 percent of the total number of cards in circulation globally (see Exhibit 2), American Express users accounted for over 14 percent of total dollars spent domestically (see Exhibit 3). This disparity was due to the fact that American Express cardholders typically charged four times as much as a Visa or MasterCard customer (see Exhibit 4). This was Chenault's "ace in the hole" when it came time to negotiate with new merchants—if they balked at American Express' higher discount rates, he could show them that by accepting American Express cards, they were opening themselves to a new breed of customer. "I didn't know whether I would be able to see the value of the AmEx brand when we signed up with the company last year," said Steve O'Neil, CEO of CitationShares, which sold shares on private jets. "But the power of the card has been extraordinary." In 2004, one customer paid for 150 hours of flight time on his Centurion Card—at a cost of $645,000. American Express now needed a way to maintain this momentum and preserve the relationship it had built with consumers.

My Life. My Card.

American Express had a history of partnering with celebrities to promote its products. The "Portraits" campaign of 1987 was an example of this, but those ads did not allow the public to get an intimate look at the celebrity endorser. American Express addressed this issue when it announced the "My life. My card." campaign in 2004. These ads initially featured actor Robert DeNiro, television show host Ellen DeGeneres, golfer Tiger Woods, and professional surfer Laird Hamilton providing intimate narratives about the places, causes, achievements, and avocations that were meaningful to them. One ad showed DeNiro walking around lower Manhattan, an area that was devastated after the terrorist attacks of September 11th. As people went about their daily lives, DeNiro narrated, "My oldest friend. My first love. My heartbreak." As the music reached a dramatic crescendo and we see active people from all walks of life, DeNiro finished, "My life happens here. My card is American Express." Another ad showed the inside of Tiger Woods' home on a rainy day. As we see shots of his living room, desk, and TV room, Woods commented, "A rainy day is my chance to be home. Be a fan. Be lazy." The next shot is of Woods in his backyard, hitting golf balls in the driving rain. He narrated, "Problem is…there are no rainy days. My life is about never settling. That's why my card is American Express."

Design touches like handwriting, signatures, and snapshots lent a personal feeling to the campaign, in addition to each individual's customization of the "My life. My card." tagline for the closing frame of their ad. The television spots were directed by acclaimed filmmaker Martin Scorsese, while the print ads were shot by photographer Annie Leibovitz. The ads featured the familiar American Express blue box logo, but no visuals of any individual card products. "The 'My life. My card.' campaign portrays an emotional connection that is based on a commitment American Express makes to every Cardmember," said John Hayes. "By revealing snapshots of the lives of these incredible individuals, we demonstrate our belief that our Cardmembers are exceptional people no matter where they live or what they do."

To create buzz and attract people to the Mylifemycard.com website, American Express started a promotion that December called "My WishList." This promotion offered extraordinary items at unheard of prices. Each day for 30 days, a limited quantity of that day's featured item was made available on the website at three different times (noon, 4 p.m. and 9 p.m.). The first card member to click on the "I want it" button had the opportunity to purchase the item. Featured items included BMW Roadsters for $5,000 and Vespa scooters for $800.

The company continued to draw visitors to the website with new content. Ellen DeGeneres created a short film—aptly titled, "Making My First Short Film"—that was only viewable on the Mylifemycard.com website. The site also featured ways for users to "connect" with DeGeneres. There were video clips of her dancing, talking about her show, lists of her favorite songs, and random thoughts from her journal.

Legal Victory Over Visa and MasterCard

One of the reasons Visa and MasterCard had such strong market positions was that due to legal technicalities, American Express had been prevented by Visa and MasterCard from issuing American Express cards through banks. That changed in 2004 when the Supreme Court ruled against Visa and MasterCard in their anti-trust case against American Express. American Express was then free to pursue relationships with any and all banks. The first agreement the company reached was with MBNA, who had 50 million cardholders. American Express then reached an agreement with Citigroup, the largest U.S. credit-card issuer, with 105 million cards in circulation. Deals with UBS and USAA Federal Savings Bank soon followed. Before the court ruling, American Express had 40 million U.S. card accounts and about 65 million worldwide (see Exhibit 5). Partnerships with banks gave the company access to over 200 million new accounts (see Exhibit 6 for ranking of top credit card issuers). Analysts believed American Express would be able to double its U.S. card market share.

When issuing cards through banks, American Express specifically targeted the affluent investor class, who earned between $100,000 and $1 million a year. Once it had attracted these new cardholders, the company then hoped to leverage its 12,000 financial advisors to sell financial planning services to cardholders. Even before American Express issued its first card through a U.S. bank, competitors began fighting back, heavily promoting gold and platinum cards aimed at American Express' high-end customers. Visa launched a media blitz for its redesigned Signature Card, while MasterCard revamped its World MasterCard.

American Express was very selective about which banks it entered into agreements with. Aside from wanting to know that new card users would spend enough to maintain American Express' averages, Chenault also insisted that partner banks use some of the extra money they earned from American Express to develop their own customized reward programs. If a bank failed to deliver, "We absolutely pull the plug," says Chenault. For example, the company ended a card deal with Canadian Imperial Bank of Commerce in June 2004, after just 18 months of disappointing results.

CEO Ken Chenault hoped his effort to get banks to issue American Express cards would pay off, and he had many factors in his favor. Because American Express charged merchants a higher discount rate (about 0.5% higher than Visa and MasterCard), it could afford to give member banks a bigger percentage of its fees. Also, the banks issuing American Express cards would not bear any cost if customers failed to pay their bills (American Express assumed these charges on cards it issued). Finally, with more cards in circulation, Chenault hoped the company would extract economies of scale from its network linking merchants, banks, and customers. There was still pressure for American Express to lower its discount rate, but the company was reluctant to do so for another reason. Some analysts estimated that for every 0.05 percent drop in its discount rate, the company would suffer a 2 percent decline in earnings.

Expanding the Product Line

While it waged this legal battle against Visa and MasterCard, American Express continued to offer new products to its members. One of the most innovative was the ExpressPay feature added to the Blue line of cards. At checkout, having ExpressPay allowed a cardholder to simply place his or her card next to a special reader, collect the receipt, and then walk away. Test results showed that, on average, ExpressPay transactions were 63 percent faster than using cash. Important merchant benefits include reduced transaction time and increased spending relative to cash. Cardmembers were not liable for fraudulent charges if the card was lost or stolen. The first national merchant to accept ExpressPay was CVS, who had the special readers in 485 stores, but planned to expand the service to all of its 5,000 U.S. locations. Convenience store 7-Eleven signed on in 2005, with plans to offer the service in all of its 5,300 locations by the end of 2006. "We're continually looking for new ways to deliver more speed and service for our customers," said Rich Updyke, vice president of business development for 7-Eleven, Inc. "ExpressPay will allow us to provide a faster, more convenient and secure payment experience."

Looking to continue its reach to younger consumers, American Express launched the IN:NYC card in 2004. The company billed this new card as a "fee-free, rewards-rich credit card designed for younger-minded, active New York adults who want to party at special events, dine at hot restaurants, jam to top music acts at concert venues and experience some of the best that New York City has to offer." The card had a rewards program specially designed for New Yorkers that offered VIP access to concerts, advance ticket purchases to select events, and gift certificates to stylish restaurants. Other city-specific cards included the IN:CHICAGO and IN:LA cards.

American Express had a long-standing relationship with Delta Airlines, but wanted to expand its airline miles program to one of the increasingly popular low-cost airlines. It announced a partnership with JetBlue in 2005 and began offering the JetBlue Card from American Express. This card allowed users to earn points that were credited to their JetBlue TrueBlue awards account. Jet Blue was also part of American Express' Membership Rewards program—this allowed users to transfer points earned on any American Express card directly to a TrueBlue account. In 2005, American Express launched a travel rewards version of its Blue card called Sky Blue, which enabled cardholders to redeem points gained through purchases for travel items such as plane tickets, hotel stays, cruises, and car rentals. The rewards were valid for any company in these categories, and were not subject to blackout dates, minimum stay requirements or seat restrictions.

Aside from new cards, the company continued to innovate in other ways. In 2003 it announced the creation of the "Your Reward" program. This was an addition to the existing Membership Rewards program that allowed cardholders to redeem points for travel, entertainment, gift certificates, and other predetermined offerings. The Membership Rewards program was the world's largest card-based rewards program, with more than 4 million U.S. enrollees and more than 9 million worldwide. The Your Reward program offered unique redemption packages, like private rock climbing instruction in Colorado or three days of polo instruction from a world-renowned player in Palm Springs, California. The program also allowed users to create their own unique redemption packages. Cardmembers could call a concierge specialist, who would make suggestions, provide advice, research options, and even make all the necessary arrangements for a reward that fit the cardmembers' point balance.

During this time, American Express shifted its spending on traditional television advertising toward more interactive forms of communication; in the mid-1990s it spent 80 percent of its annual ad budget on television spots, but by 2004 that number had dropped to 35 percent. Much of the former TV budget was redirected to online advertising.

An example of this type of advertising came in 2004, The company leveraged its relationship with Jerry Seinfeld for a four-minute "webisode" that chronicled the exploits of Seinfeld and an animated Superman as they went about a day in New York City. The two discussed their views on reality television, ate a local diner, and saw a Broadway show. In two weeks, over 500,000 people had visited the company's website and viewed the clip. A second webisode followed two months later. John Hayes commented, "We are continually looking for innovative ways to engage consumers and introduce new customers to the brand, and the Internet has already proven to be an exciting channel for us." Overall, American Express' marketing budget in 2005 was nearly double that of both MasterCard and Visa (See Exhibit 7).

Improved Results

In 2004, American Express was named the "World's Leading Travel Company" for business and leisure travel by the independent *World Travel Awards*. The company was also recognized by *Business Traveler* magazine as having the best card for corporate travel, as well as the premier rewards program. This was the eighth year in a row that the magazine's readers chose American Express' Membership Rewards program as their favorite.

These honors coincided with continued positive developments in American Express' financial health. After the company experienced a 5 percent decline in revenues and an even more dramatic 54 percent drop in profits from 2000 to 2001, the company posted increased revenues and profits each of the next four years, after accounting for the divestment of American Express Financial Advisors (see Exhibit 8). After a period of difficulty following the 9/11 attacks, American Express was once again exhibiting consistent growth.

Performance in 2005 was particularly strong, with a 9 percent rise in total cardholders to 71 million helping push revenues up 10 percent to $24.3 billion and profits up 9 percent to $3.7 billion from the year prior. These improved results led to a recovery in the company's stock, which by February 2004 had risen more than 20 points from its post-9/11 low of $25 per share. In late 2006, the stock was trading within a few points of its pre-9/11 peak of $60 per share.

CONCLUSION

In its 155 year history, American Express had grown from a small delivery business to a multi-national firm that provided a variety of travel and financial services to millions of customers around the globe. According to the *BusinessWeek*/Interbrand 2005 ranking, American Express was the fourteenth most valuable brand in the world, three points higher than its 2001 ranking. This brand value was a testament to not only the company's product and marketing innovation, but also its commitment to providing its customers with outstanding service at any location in the world at any time of day.

American Express continued to look for new ways to grow its business. Chenault decided it would be best to spin off the Financial Advisors Group (AEFA) into a separate company. He believed that without AEFA, American Express would be able to focus on its card business and, to a lesser extent, its travel business, which would spur growth and profitability. One of the company's next moves continued its quest to expand the range of merchants that accepted American Express cards, as the company began signing up luxury apartment buildings in New York City to allow cardholders to charge their monthly rent. Additionally, in an effort to allay traveler's concerns about theft while abroad, American Express announced a modernized version of its Travelers Cheques—a prepaid, reloadable card that could be used at merchants and ATMs worldwide that accept American Express. Furthering its travel offerings, the company revamped its website to make it easier to use, and partnered with the American Association of Retired Persons (AARP) to offer Travelers Cheques, the new Travelers Cheque Card, and foreign currency exchange options over the phone and on the AARP website.

The question remained if American Express would be able to consistently grow its base of consumers *and* merchants, as well as attract more corporate customers and encourage more spending by them. Ken Chenault was successful in turning the company around from the challenges it faced in the early 2000s, but there were still significant issues ahead for American Express: sustained competition from Visa and MasterCard, an unpredictable U.S. economy, shifting consumer preferences, a saturated domestic credit card market, and a constantly changing marketing environment. Finding innovative ways of answering these challenges was Chenault's next major undertaking.

DISCUSSION QUESTIONS

1. What elements and characteristics comprised the equity in the American Express brand in the 1960s? In the 1980s? How would you currently characterize the American Express brand?
2. Evaluate American Express in terms of its competitors. How well is it positioned? What are its points-of-parity and points-of-difference in its different business areas? How has it changed over time? In what segments of its business does American Express face the most competition?
3. Evaluate American Express' integration of its various businesses. What recommendations would you make in order to maximize the contribution

to equity of all of its businesses' units? At the same time, is the corporate brand sufficiently coherent?

4. Was it worth the time and effort to make the "webisode" with Jerry Seinfeld? The short film by Ellen DeGeneres? What are the advantages and disadvantages of using the Internet to advertise a service-related company?

5. Of the advertising campaigns described in the case, which would you say was the most effective? Why?

6. What is more important for American Express—expand its product line of new cards (such as the IN:NYC card), or focus on offering new services to its cardholders (such as offering statements in Braille or making its travel website easier to use)?

Exhibit 1: Share of Corporate Card Spending Market in 2004

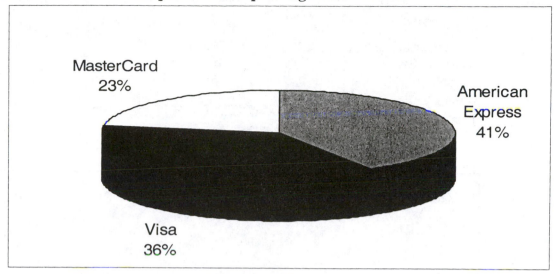

Source: The Nilson Report

**Exhibit 2: Global Share of Cards in Circulation, 2005
(of 2.5 billon total cards)**

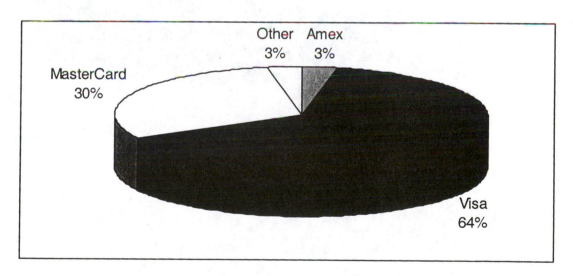

* Includes Diner's Club
Source: Visa USA Overview, UBS Global Financial Services
Conference, May 17, 2006.

Exhibit 3: Total U.S. Credit Card Charges in 2005 (in billions)

Visa	$ 1,225
MasterCard	590
American Express	353
Discover	82
Other	217
Total	$2,467

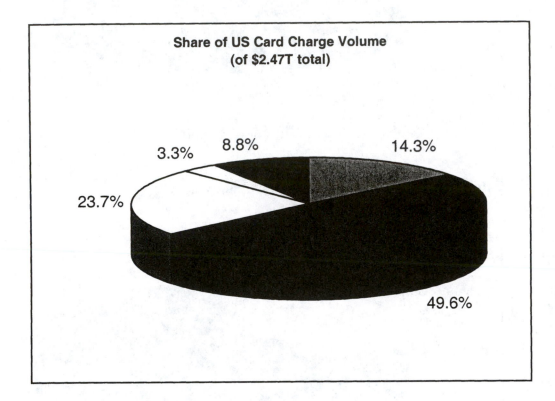

Source: Visa USA Overview, UBS Global Financial Services Conference, May 17, 2006.

Exhibit 4: Average Amount Charged per Card in 2004

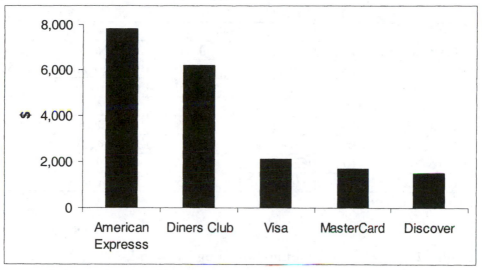

Source: Fortune Charts / The Nilson Report

Exhibit 5: American Express Worldwide Card in Circulation

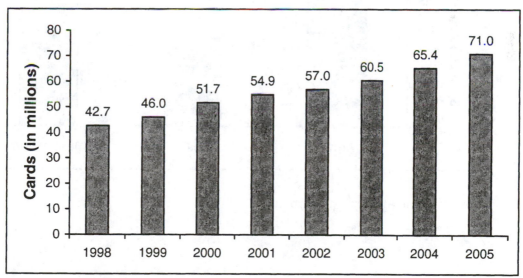

Source: Company Reports

Exhibit 6: Top Credit Card Issuers by Receivables
(loan amounts in $ billions)

Rank	1994		2000		2004	
	Company	Loans	Company	Loans	Company	Loans
1	Citibank	$39.0	CitiGroup	$103.5	JP Morgan Chase	$134.7
2	MBNA	$17.6	MBNA	$70.4	CitiGroup	$116.0
3	First Chicago	$12.3	First USA	$67.0	MBNA	$82.1
4	First USA	$12.2	Chase	$36.2	American Express	$63.7
5	Household	$11.0	Providian	$26.7	Bank of America	$61.1
6	Chase	$10.8	Capital One	$26.3	Capital One	$53.0
7	Chemical	$10.4	Household	$15.1	Discover	$45.7

Source: The Nilson Report

Exhibit 7   **Marketing Spending by Brand, 2005**

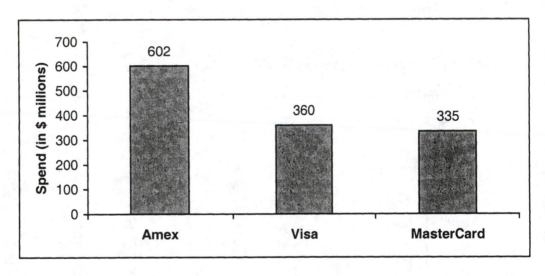

Source: Bank Marketing International, 2006

Exhibit 8: American Express Revenues and Net Income 1997–2005

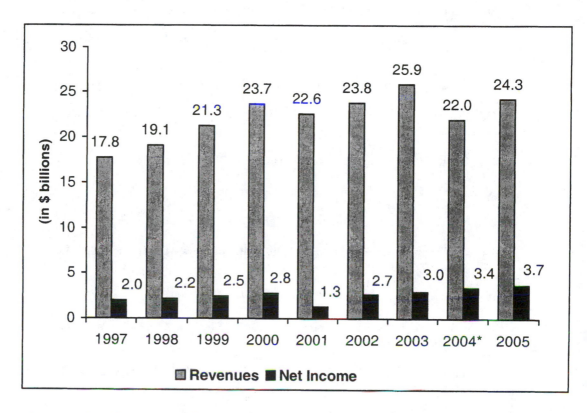

* 2004 results adjusted to reflect divestment of American Express Financial Advisors
Source: Company reports

REFERENCES

Susan Adkins. *Cause Related Marketing*. Butterworth Heineman, Oxford: 1999, p. 15.

Mercedes M. Cardona. "With Blue, Tiger as Stars, Amex Soars," *Advertising Age*, October 9, 2000, p. S10.

Hilary Cassidy. "Swiping Share at the Counter." *Brandweek*, May 19, 2003.

Hilary Cassidy. "Amex Has Big Plans; For Small Business Unit." *Brandweek*, January 21, 2002.

Julie Creswell."Ken Chenault Reshuffles His Cards." *Fortune*, April 18, 2005.

Mara Der Hovanesian. "Charge!" *BusinessWeek*, August 9, 2004.

Terry Lefton. "Widening the Expressway." *Brandweek*, September 7, 1998, pp. 32–38.

Larry Neumeister. "American Express Hurt Itself, Boss Says—But It Had Help." *Seattle Times*, June 30, 2000, C3.

Ann M. Mack. "Buddy Movies," *Brandweek*, November 22, 2004.

Jathon Sapsford. "American Express Moves to Net With Blue." The *Wall Street Journal*, September 24, 1999, p. B5.

Pamela Sherrid. "A New Class Act at AMEX," *U.S. News & World Report*, June 23, 1997, pp. 39–40.

Suzanne Vranica. "For Big Marketers Like AmEx, TV Ads Lose Starring Role." The *Wall Street Journal*, May 17, 2004, p.B1.

American Express Company Annual Report 2004.

CIBC World Markets Equity Research, American Express, March 17, 2005.

DataMonitor, American Express Company Profile, June 2005.

"MasterCard Seeks Ways to Keep Its 'Priceless' Effort on a Personal Note." *Brandweek*, October 7, 2002.

"The Bill is Due at American Express." *Fortune*, November 18, 1991.

"Tiger Woods Commercials for American Express Financial Advisors Features Tiger and Dad, Earl," *Business Wire*, September 8, 1997.

"Why Warren Buffett's Betting Big on American Express." *Fortune*, October 30, 1995.

www.americanexpress.com; www.mylifemycard.com

STARBUCKS:
MANAGING A HIGH GROWTH BRAND[1]

INTRODUCTION
In less than a decade, Starbucks was transformed from a fledgling whole-bean coffee retail chain into a globally recognized brand. From its IPO in 1992 to 2006, Starbucks grew to more than 10,500 stores located throughout North America, Latin America, the Pacific Rim, Europe, and the Middle East. Growth of the corporation's coffee retail business continued at the rapid pace of three store openings a day on average. With over 35 million customers each week, Starbucks recorded revenues of $6.4 billion in 2005 (see Exhibit 1 for revenue growth data). Moreover, joint ventures with some of the nation's strongest corporations, including Pepsi, Kraft, Dryer's, and Capitol Records, allowed Starbucks to launch a lucrative consumer products division to complement its cafe business. Licensing partnerships with other companies such as United Airlines, ITT Sheraton, and Host Marriott further added to the growth of the Starbucks brand. Indeed, Starbucks rose to become one of the most impressive high-growth brands of the 1990s and early twenty-first century.

Despite this remarkable growth, some questioned whether Starbucks began to lose focus as the company strove to constantly reinvent itself. Critics wondered if perhaps the brand grew too quickly to remain focused on its core values and business objectives. When James Donald took over as the company's third CEO in 2005, Starbucks had expanded its offerings to diverse interests such as credit cards, liquor, music, and was looking into the film industry. As the company added more components of a "lifestyle" brand to complement its core coffee offering, it needed to be careful that the coffeehouse concept responsible for its success retained its appeal with consumers.

COMPANY BACKGROUND
American coffee consumption had been on the decline for more than a decade when Seattle entrepreneurs Jerry Baldwin, Gordon Bowker, and Zev Siegl opened the first Starbucks in Seattle's Pike Place Market in 1971. By the 1970s, the country's major coffee brands were engaged in a bitter price war that forced them to use cheaper beans in their blends to reduce costs, resulting in a dramatic decline in the quality of America's most popular coffees. Accompanying this decline in quality was a decline in coffee consumption, which had peaked at 3.1 cups per day in 1961. As Americans gradually became disenchanted with the store brands, java enthusiasts—concentrated primarily on the West Coast—began experimenting with the finer coffees of Europe that offered richer, fuller flavors.

To harness the potential of the gourmet coffee trend in the Seattle area, the founders of Starbucks experimented with the new concept of a store dedicated to selling only the finest whole-bean coffee and coffee brewing equipment. At the time, Starbucks coffee was not brewed in-store, but rather by consumers themselves after they took the whole beans or grounds home. This emphasis on quality whole-bean coffee retail was fairly unique; only a handful of American cities had stores like

Starbucks up to that point. Such a store would satisfy the demand of Seattle's gourmet coffee enthusiasts for high-quality coffee products that could previously only be obtained through catalogs from companies in Europe. Starbucks also sought to convert Seattleites who had never experienced gourmet coffee to break away from traditional brands and integrate the finer European coffee blends into their daily lives.

From the start, Starbucks placed quality as its top priority. The Starbucks founders recognized that if they wanted to enhance Seattle's appreciation for fine coffee, they had to provide the best ingredients and brewing equipment to ensure that customers had the most enjoyable coffee experiences possible. The Starbucks management dedicated a great deal of their time and financial resources to establishing strong relationships with coffee growers from around the world. To distinguish their coffee from the bland and tasteless store brands, Starbucks only purchased Arabica beans from a carefully selected network of suppliers across the globe; including places like Sumatra, Kenya, Ethiopia, and Costa Rica. Arabica beans were selected because the bean's chemistry could withstand high roasting temperatures, resulting in a richer flavor. Starbucks also sought vendors who sold products that would protect, and even enhance, the Arabica's flavor. This required the formation of partnerships across the globe with coffee brewing equipment suppliers who provided products that captured the essence of the coffee brewing tradition. Simplicity was valued over advanced technology because the machines Europeans and others had been using to brew coffee for centuries often proved the most effective in delivering the richest flavors.

Starbucks Reinvented

It was not until Howard Schultz, current Chairman and Chief Global Strategist of Starbucks, came to the company in 1982 that a vision for expanding the scope and reach of the Starbucks brand came under serious consideration. Schultz realized the powerful business opportunities that lay ahead of the company if he could preserve Starbucks' core values while exposing a wider range of people to the brand. The fledgling company had seen great success in converting its small group of loyal Seattle customers into coffee enthusiasts, but Schultz recognized that the conservative business plans of early Starbucks management hindered the company from reaching other potential coffee lovers. Schultz saw that the next logical step for Starbucks was to begin serving freshly brewed coffee by the cup in every store. This realization came to Schultz following a trip to Italy, where he witnessed the bustling café culture where people stopped to socialize at various points throughout the day, always with a fresh cappuccino or espresso in hand. He reasoned that Americans would embrace the concept of consuming fresh coffee in a sociable coffeehouse atmosphere.

Transforming Starbucks from a coffee retailer into a café business resulted in several important competitive advantages. First, it increased quality control because the coffee was brewed by its own knowledgeable employees. Second, Starbucks captured the business of Seattle's business community who loved high quality coffee, but had hectic schedules. Starbucks made enjoying good coffee convenient, thereby enabling the entire community to enjoy all the brand had to offer. Lastly, incorporating a coffee service aspect into the business differentiated Starbucks from its coffee retail competitors, who were quickly growing in Seattle and in other major American cities.

With the coffeehouse model as the primary focus of the company's retailored business plan, Schultz began to concentrate on reshaping Starbucks' brand identity. As the company entered a period of explosive growth through market expansion it needed a reinvented image that captured the elegance of European coffeehouse culture, but was familiar enough to appeal to a broad range of Americans. Schultz's previous coffeehouse, Il Giornale, had acquired Starbucks in 1987, but Schultz recognized that keeping the Starbucks name was pivotal to the brand's success. It was already familiar to Seattleites, patrons of the nationwide mail order business and was more memorable than Il Giornale. The name was inspired by Starbuck, a deckhand in the classic American novel *Moby Dick*. For this reason, the logo included an image of a mermaid done in a woodcutting style. The Starbucks name captured all the aspects of Schultz's innovative coffeehouse concept; it was bold yet not overwhelming, mysterious yet not foreign, and romantic yet not impractical.

Creating a Look

Starbucks needed to shape the look and feel of the environment of its stores to reflect the synergy of Italian elegance and American informality that Schultz envisioned for his unique coffeehouse model. First, the original Starbucks logo was updated to appear more contemporary and the color was changed from the original earthen brown to the green used by Il Giornale. Next, each of the original Starbucks stores was redesigned so that they echoed the romantic atmosphere of Italian coffee bars.

Rich browns in the wooden fixtures and vibrant green logos on the detailing and packaging formed the primary color scheme of Starbucks store design. This palate was selected to represent the company's emphasis on European romance and elegance coupled with casual American warmth. In addition to selling only "best-of-class" coffee, Starbucks worked to fill its stores with only the highest quality of everything—from the coffee-making equipment to the fixtures and furnishings to the music and artwork. In Schultz's words, each Starbucks store "is carefully designed to enhance the quality of everything the customers see, touch, hear, smell or taste."[2] Schultz envisioned that the Starbucks store would become a "personal treat" for its customers, whether they saw it as a convenient stop on the way to work, a refreshing break in their day or a place to relax at night. Starbucks was to be, for its clientele, a "Third Place," a comfortable, sociable gathering spot bridging the workplace and the home. Designing a warm, inviting environment was essential to Schultz's objective of making Starbucks symbolize not just a coffeehouse, but a pleasurable coffee-centered experience.

Investing Ahead of the Growth Curve

This focus on developing creative solutions for solidifying a rich brand identity complemented the Starbucks executive team's philosophy of "investing ahead of the growth curve."[3] Constant reinvention—critical to developing a healthy Starbucks brand—could only be accomplished by making fundamental changes to the structure of Starbucks management and by investing in innovation. As Schultz assumed the role of CEO of the new Starbucks, he recognized that although he possessed keen entrepreneurial skills and vision to lead Starbucks in this period of immense growth and brand redevelopment, he would also need the support of experienced professionals to set his vision into motion. Schultz assembled a dynamic management team from some of the country's most successful and innovative corporations such as Nike, Deloitte & Touche, and Macy's. Each executive joining the Starbucks team brought years of experience and fresh creative perspectives.

Investments in Starbucks infrastructure and process efficiency were equally as crucial to building the brand. Schultz's team of executives identified the need for state-of-the-art facilities (namely roasting and packaging plants) that would allow Starbucks to continue producing the highest quality products on a nationwide, and eventually a global, scale. In 1989, Starbucks invested in high-speed coffee roaster and packaging equipment that would meet the needs of the growing business for at least 10 years. The company later implemented an advanced computer information system to keep track of sales across the hundreds of stores that would be opening within the first decade of expansion. Between 1990 and 1991 alone, Starbucks raised $18.5 million in venture capital to fund this expensive internal development.

Innovation to Support Growth of the Brand

As Starbucks began focusing on a nationwide growth strategy, the problem of how to protect the freshness and flavor of coffee during shipments to distant Starbucks locations became a pressing issue. In the time it took to ship fresh roasted beans thousands of miles across the country to store locations in Atlanta or New York, for example, the quality of the coffee would decline dramatically. Therefore, significant time and resources were invested to develop a vacuum packaging system that prevented harmful air and moisture from seeping into the coffee. After the roasting process, coffee would be sealed in "FlavorLock" bags that would remain unopened until ready for use in stores. Such an investment allowed Starbucks to preserve its quality, while saving the company from the significant costs entailed in building roasting plants in every new Starbucks market. Innovations such as the FlavorLock bags highlight the flexibility that Starbucks leveraged in order to adapt to new business climates.

Starbucks Core Values

The new Starbucks management strengthened many of the same core values that the company founders had established in the early years and reinvented others to meet the unique challenges it faced as a high growth brand. To communicate these core values, a diverse group of employees contributed to the development of the

Starbucks Mission Statement (see Exhibit 2). In drafting the mission statement, the Starbucks executive team listened to the views of employees at all levels and incorporated their beliefs into company policies. Consensus on company values among the diverse group of Starbucks employees was imperative for Schultz's vision of a unified team.

Pivotal to the values asserted in the mission statement was a continued commitment to investing in both Starbucks employees and customers. Schultz and his colleagues observed that the company had become too product oriented; Starbucks had to focus on people to achieve healthy organic growth. The key to the company's success and widespread appeal had always been the employees, whose knowledge and dedication attracted customers to continue returning to the store.

Schultz firmly believed that his business could not grow without the strongest team possible at all levels of the organization. Starbucks could only attract loyal customers if employees were skilled in delivering the highest quality service possible. The Starbucks work force deserved a disproportionate amount of company resources because they were essentially the key component in the revenue generating functions of the company. Therefore, under Schultz's leadership, Starbucks management adopted several policies that focused on recruiting and retaining a strong team of "partners"—the company's term for employees.

The first and most important policies concerning the development of a strong team of partners regarded the company's commitment to training. Starbucks spent more money on training than marketing, a fact that highlights the crucial role Schultz assigns to his employees—that of fostering positive customer relations so as to engender widespread word-of-mouth publicity. Starbucks also developed several policies regarding partner compensation and benefit packages to attract and retain a competent work force. These benefit packages included full health insurance coverage for all employees and the Bean Stock program, which awarded every partner between 12 percent and 14 percent of his or her annual base pay in Starbucks stock options. In extending equity to employees, Starbucks hoped to communicate that every employee would benefit as the company grew and performed well, providing an incentive for partners to work as a unified team toward achieving business objectives.

New philosophies were also adopted regarding Starbucks commitment to customers. The original company believed that they should educate the customer to appreciate coffee the way Starbucks liked it. Then-president Howard Behar and other top executives argued that the company needed to become more customer focused and serve coffee the way customers like it. Behar proposed a different model that called for Starbucks to "do whatever it takes to please the customer as long as it is moral, legal, and ethical."[4] Although the "customer is always right" philosophy made sense to Schultz, he also recognized that it posed a threat to the integrity of Starbucks products. Schultz wondered how much flexibility should be given to customer demands when they compromised the traditions that the company's products were based on.

When health conscious customers began to request skim milk as an option in place of the cream used in various coffees, Schultz was forced to tackle this issue of flexibility head on. While at first he remained steadfastly committed to preserving the authenticity of his coffees by forbidding the use of skim milk in recipes, Schultz finally conceded, recognizing that "a lost customer is the most powerful argument you can make to a retailer."[5] If Starbucks wanted to maintain its loyal following, it had to listen to customer feedback. Compromise had to be integrated into Schultz's decisions regarding product development. As long as Starbucks could continue to deliver the highest quality products possible, flexibility would be favored over dogmatic adherence to tradition.

GROWING THE BRAND

Geographical Market Expansion

Starbucks' carefully planned its expansion of specialty coffee stores into new markets throughout North America and eventually worldwide. The first phase of the expansion strategy secured a major foothold in the Pacific Northwest while experimenting in other key markets that were farther away such as Chicago, Los Angeles, San Francisco, New York, and Washington, D.C. Each of these new markets had its own strategic purpose for the company's market expansion program. In 1996, Starbucks International successfully launched Japan's first store in Tokyo's Ginza business district, proving that the coffeehouse concept even had cross-cultural appeal. Success with the original Starbucks in Tokyo led to 25 new stores in Japan by 1998.

The Starbucks management team agreed at the beginning of the company's massive expansion program that all stores would be owned and operated by the company instead of pursuing a franchise model like many other successful American food service companies. Although franchising offered advantages for some companies—a source of capital, an inexpensive means of rapid entry into new markets, and a guaranteed commitment by franchisees to the financial success of the business—it posed potentially negative consequences for brand development. In building a strong brand, Schultz recognized that he and his executive team needed complete control over the brand to cultivate an unparalleled image of quality. In too many other companies, franchisees did business their own way, which could potentially sacrifice Starbucks' commitment to excellence in order to turn higher profits. Schultz could not risk compromising the brand's image and kept the brand under the control of the Seattle headquarters to foster healthy growth.

The success of the expansion program rested on investment in extensive word-of-mouth publicity campaigns that created brand awareness even before the first Starbucks arrived to a new market. Local consumers were excited about welcoming Starbucks to their towns because of the attraction of having a trendy cafe environment for relaxation and personal enrichment. Grand openings became community events that encouraged local consumers to experience the new cultural dimension that Starbucks brought to their communities. Once a new Starbucks opened, highly skilled "baristas" (or servers) and managers would further strengthen the positive brand image by delivering the highest level of service possible.

Starbucks also employed a "hub" market strategy where its coffeehouses entered a new market in a clustered group. For each new region, a large city would serve as the hub where teams of professionals trained to support new stores were located. In the large hub market, the goal would be to rapidly open 20 or more stores within the first two years. From the established hub, Starbucks stores then spread to new "spoke" markets. These spoke markets consisted of smaller cities and suburban locations with demographics similar to the typical customer mix. This deliberate saturation strategy predictably resulted in cannibalization of almost 30 percent of own store sales by virtue of the introduction of a near-by store. This drop in revenue was offset, however, by efficiencies in marketing and distribution costs, and an enhanced image of convenience.

Joint Ventures and Partnerships

As Starbucks' geographical market expansion proceeded at a phenomenal rate, many companies across the country approached Schultz with partnership proposals. While partnerships with some organizations would likely strengthen the Starbucks brand by broadening its exposure and leading to new product innovations, Schultz was wary of any business opportunity that involved compromising his executive team's control of the brand. Therefore, Schultz decided from the beginning that Starbucks would only enter into partnerships with companies who maintained the same commitments to quality and people that Starbucks had as the foundation of its business.

Joint venture partners had to respect the integrity of the Starbucks brand, expose the brand to a broader range of consumers, and maintain a commitment to preserving the authenticity of Starbucks products. Ultimately, these partnerships had to present a clear benefit for the brand. Moreover, partnerships had to allow Starbucks to play a hands-on role in all aspects of the joint venture, especially with the product development aspect since Schultz was concerned that potential partner companies would seek to leverage the Starbucks name, but develop a product that clashed with Starbucks' commitment to highest quality and authenticity.

Host Marriott Partnership

In 1991, Starbucks engaged a partnership opportunity with Host Marriott in 1991 that allowed for Starbucks coffee to be brewed and served at concession stands in airports across the country. The opportunity provided a chance to expose the Starbucks brand to a large group of potential consumers—airline travelers. While in theory exposing more consumers to the brand through licensing agreements with vendors seemed to be the next logical step for Starbucks, Schultz was concerned about how the quality of the coffee would be affected if it were not to be brewed by Starbucks. Schultz's concerns were realized and consumers did not encounter the same quality of customer service at airport concessions stands as in Starbucks coffeehouses. The frenzied environment of most airports accounted for most of the customer service problems. Customers were not willing to learn about Starbucks coffee as they dashed off to catch a flight. Moreover, Host Marriott's staff was not as educated about coffee as the baristas in Starbucks stores and did not set the highest standards possible for how Starbucks coffee should be brewed.

Fortunately, Host Marriott and Starbucks were able to collaborate effectively to solve some of the most pressing customer service problems so that Starbucks' brand image would not be harmed in the partnership. Host Marriott funded a program that gave new concessions employees the same level of training as new hires at Starbucks. Moreover, Host Marriott agreed to devise ways to improve operations at concessions stands by adding more staff and cash registers during peak travel times to ensure that customers received their Starbucks coffee in the same efficient manner as in the company's coffeehouse locations. These improvements—which were only possible as a result of the positive relations and similar philosophies maintained between both companies—ensured that customers did not wait in long lines, that the coffee was brewed with the highest flavor standards, and that customers would be educated about the brand by knowledgeable employees.

United Airlines Partnership

The Starbucks partnership with United Airlines, started in 1996, presented similar benefits and potential problems as with the Host Marriott joint venture. With United's adoption of Starbucks as the official coffee served on all of its 2,200 daily flights, the brand stood to gain a tremendous advantage in generating awareness. United clearly benefited from the partnership as well. Serving high quality Starbucks coffee to passengers was yet another way that the airline could differentiate itself as a carrier dedicated to providing passengers with the best service possible. However, Starbucks once again encountered a situation where the coffee's quality would be risked because Starbucks was allowing an outside source to brew its coffee. Like Host Marriott, United was quick to remedy coffee quality problems by working with Starbucks to install more effective filtering devices in aircraft brewing equipment, and to better educate flight crews on how to protect the quality of the coffee. The partnership with United did reap some benefits for Starbucks—14 percent of Starbucks' loyal customers had their first cup of the brand's coffee on a United Airlines flight, prompting them to try Starbucks coffees in stores.

Other Retail and Service Partnerships

Based on the success of these early deals, partnerships were later set up between Starbucks and companies such as Nordstrom, ITT/Sheraton, Westin, Holland America Cruiselines, Barnes & Noble, and Albertson's (retail food-drug chain) as a further attempt to increase brand awareness and encourage consumers to regard Starbucks as a world-class brand.

Pepsi and Dryer's Joint Ventures

Although Starbucks always viewed coffee as its central focus, Schultz recognized that the development of new products was essential to the company's quest for continual reinvention. As long as the newly developed products did not destroy the integrity of Starbucks coffee, then Schultz and his executive team viewed them as viable means to promote the Starbucks brand to people who may have never tried coffee in Starbucks stores.

A partnership with Pepsi, started in 1997, led to the creation of Frappuccino, a popular bottled cold coffee beverage using extracts from Starbucks' famous Arabica beans. Frappuccino put the Starbucks brand into supermarkets for the first time, an environment Schultz had never dared to bring his coffee products before for fear that the quality of the coffees could not be protected. Although Starbucks was one of the least advertised major brands in the United States, an advertising campaign was launched to support Frappuccino that was intended to reinforce and enhance Starbucks core values of humility, humor, a "homey" feeling and rich, sensory experiences.

The Dryer's joint venture with Starbucks led to the creation of six popular Starbucks coffee ice cream flavors that were marketed under the Starbucks name, but produced and distributed by Dryer's. Sales of Starbucks ice cream surpassed even the most skeptical industry analyst's predictions, beating sales of Häagen-Dazs within the first month of its introduction into supermarkets and increasing category sales 54 percent in the year that it was launched, all while becoming the market leader.

Kraft and Supermarket Sales

In 1998, Starbucks initiated a large-scale supermarket sales effort and introduced Starbucks packaged whole coffee beans to 3,500 stores across 12 western states. This move strengthened the agreement with Kraft who then marketed and distributed the Starbucks coffee brand to more than 25,000 grocery, warehouse club, and mass merchandise stores across the United States

By partnering with Kraft, the second largest packaged-foods company in North America, Starbucks was able to benefit from Kraft's extensive distribution network as well as the company's 4,000-member sales team. Kraft marketed Starbucks coffees in 12-ounce bags as a super-premium brand. By marketing Starbucks coffee as "super-premium," Kraft aimed at preventing the Starbucks line from biting into sales of its Maxwell House brand, which has traditionally been marketed as a middle-priced brand. The Kraft partnership also left the door open for Starbucks to explore the possibility of marketing food products with the help of Kraft's distribution and marketing expertise.

Other Partnerships

During these same years, Starbucks formed many partnerships that did not involve major national corporations. In 1998, Starbucks inked a deal with famous NBA star Magic Johnson and his company, Johnson Development Corporation, to bring Starbucks to inner city America. The new enterprise was called Urban Coffee Opportunities. Under the agreement, Johnson's company developed the store locations and Starbucks operated them, and the two companies split the profits evenly. The stores contained visual cues, in the form of wall murals, signaling Johnson's involvement in the enterprise. Within a year, Starbucks and Johnson had opened three locations on the West Coast, and expanded to other major cities such as New York. By 2005, there were 25 stores in the greater Los Angeles area and a total of 75 stores located in 12 states and the District of Columbia. Johnson Development Corporation planned to open 20 more locations by 2006.

Starbucks also developed some partnerships with environmental agencies. In 1996, Starbucks teamed with the Alliance for Environmental Innovation to develop a less wasteful carryout coffee cup. While a single-cup solution was not achieved, the partnership did formulate a design that reduced waste—the single cup wrapped by a cardboard sleeve. As a result of another partnership, formed between Starbucks and Conservation International in 1999, Starbucks offered Shade Grown Mexican coffee in its stores. This type of coffee was grown exclusively on farms in the El Triunfo Biosphere Reserve in Chiapas, Mexico using environmentally sound agricultural methods that helped protect tropical forests in the surrounding area.

In April of 2000, Starbucks endured pressure from a national protest organized by human-rights group Global Exchange called "Roast Starbucks!" to offer Fair Trade certified coffee. Although most growers sold coffee for $0.50 a pound, Fair Trade certification required coffee to be sold at $1.26 a pound through small farm cooperatives in the hopes that the farm workers would see some of the extra profit. Starbucks agreed to work with the TransFair USA nonprofit organization to obtain and sell Fair Trade coffee in its stores and on its website. "Roast Starbucks!" campaigners had expected the protest to last as much as a month, and were caught completely by surprise when Starbucks agreed within a week to offer the certified coffee.

In addition to environmental work, Starbucks formed several partnerships that contributed to its Starbucks Foundation charity efforts. Starbucks entered into a licensing agreement with Garry Trudeau in 1998 to offer Doonesbury-themed products in its stores and online, with all net proceeds going to literacy programs across the country. Within a year, the partnership had raised over $300,000. The Starbucks Foundation used these funds to support programs that were dedicated to enriching the lives of youth in underserved communities. Examples included Jumpstart, an organization that provided one-on-one tutoring to at-risk preschoolers, and America SCORES, a program that combined soccer and creative writing to inspire teamwork in a safe, after-school setting.

Complementary Products

Starbucks also developed other coffee-related products. One of their first offerings was the Starbucks Barista Aroma thermal coffeemaker, which was positioned as a "durable, convenient and consistent" way to brew coffee. The company continually developed new products, eventually adding coffee presses, a variety of grinders, and a $449. Starbucks Barista Stainless Steel Espresso Machine. These items were sold on the company website, as well as in most retail stores.

MAINTAINING THE GROWTH

Initial Results

Looking back, Starbucks' early success was due in large part to a recognition that, fundamentally, what America needed was "a really good cup of coffee." Starbucks delivered a superior product via its extreme vertical integration and personal involvement from start to finish. Starbucks company-owned coffeehouses became a "Third Place"—not work and not home—where Starbucks could reward customers with a rich sensory experience by appealing to all five senses: through the rich aroma of the beans, the premium taste of the coffee, the product displays and attractive art work adorning the walls, the contemporary music playing in the background and even the cozy, clean feel of the tables and chairs. The "Starbucks experience" created stores with an "inviting, enriching environment that is comfortable and accessible yet also stylish and elegant."

The startling success of Starbucks was evidenced by the fact that by the late 1990s, an average customer visited a Starbucks store six times a month, while their most loyal customers averaged 18 store visits a month, with an expenditure of over $3.50 a visit. A one-a-day "latte plus scone" habit could add up to over $1,400 a year. Given that 50 percent of the American public drank at least one cup of coffee a day (averaging 3.4 cups per day), there was an opportunity for Starbucks to create an enormously profitable customer franchise. Moreover, Starbucks introduced new products leveraging their coffee reputation such as Frappuccino iced coffee and premium coffee ice cream. This high level of consumer involvement and aggressive product development resulted in Starbucks realizing an annual growth rate of sales and profits exceeding 50 percent through much of the 1990s.

Starbucks' purchased Tazo Tea, an Oregon tea retailer, in 1999. This indicated a potential new trend for Starbucks to acquire companies as a means of extending product lines. Starbucks planned to replace its in-house Infusia brand of tea with Tazo Tea, a move that would likely attract new customers who were looking for alternatives to coffee. Tazo Tea, once expected to become the "Starbucks of the tea market," produced authentic, premium tea with a quirky image—each tea bag promoted that it contained "the mumbled chantings of a certified tea shaman" as part of its ingredients. With the wish to reinvent the tea culture in the same way as it reinvented coffee culture, Starbucks expected this acquisition to lead the company into growth opportunities by attracting new consumers. This new line of premium product, priced at an 80 percent premium of a typical competitor's loose tea, was distributed in Starbucks coffee shops, as well as restaurants and supermarkets by year end.

Starbucks planned to strengthen its in-store and catalog product sales of CDs and books. Since 1995, Starbucks sold special mix CDs in their stores custom-made for the company by Capitol Records. The CDs were released seasonally, and were available online, as well as inside store locations. Another highly success venture started in 1998 when Starbucks partnered with Oprah Winfrey and sold the books her book club recommended.

Market Expansion into the Next Century

In 1987, Starbucks had only two coffee bars in Seattle and one in Vancouver, British Columbia. Starbucks' growth strategy at the time aimed at increasing market share in existing markets while continuing to explore new areas in which the company could become the leading coffee retailer. Store designs were seen as flexible enough to be tailored to a variety of location types including office buildings, malls, airports, and supermarkets, allowing the company to expose the brand to diverse market segments.

A minimum of a half million dollars needed to be invested in each new site to lease the property and tailor the building to meet Starbucks' uncompromising specifications for store interior design. Store locations were typically selected based on anticipated customer traffic volume, store visibility, and access to pedestrian street traffic. With so much money invested in each new market, however, Starbucks could not afford to make location selection errors. Starbucks specialty coffee retail stores were the core focus of the business, generating over 80 percent of the company's revenues. Because the coffee store business was so crucial to the company's success, precise calculations concerning the timing and location of new store openings were essential for the company to remain profitable.

Starbucks only deviated from the high-traffic, high-visibility equation for store site selection in a small number of cases such as its experimentation with drive-thru Starbucks locations. Drive-thru Starbucks locations targeted commuters who wanted their morning jolt as they battled traffic on the way to work instead of waiting until they reached the downtowns and business centers where Starbucks had typically been located. These drive-thru locations were conveniently placed on common commute routes in and around urban centers and targeted drivers instead of pedestrian customers. As of 2004, the company had increased its focus on drive-thru retail stores, operating 700 such locations.

Acquisitions

Starbucks used acquisitions to expand its international network beyond its 300 plus stores. In September 1998, Starbucks acquired London-based Seattle Coffee Company for $84.5 million in equities, effectively establishing a foothold in the growing British coffee market, as well as a jumping-off point for future European expansion. Seattle Coffee Company, started by two enterprising American coffee connoisseurs in 1990, had much the same feel as Starbucks with its emphasis on serving gourmet coffees and offering a Euro-American style coffeehouse atmosphere. Betting on a dynamic coffee bar culture trend, Starbucks publicly announced its wish to implement its core concept in the United Kingdom as fast as possible. In 1998, Starbucks opened 40 coffee stores, in addition to transforming all of the Seattle Coffee Company's 56 locations across Britain, as well as its two stores in South Africa and one store in Kuwait.

Later that year, Starbucks acquired Pasqua Coffee Company, a California-based coffee retailer that operated more than 50 locations in the San Francisco Bay Area and Los Angeles, including eight California airports. The Pasqua acquisition gave Starbucks the opportunity to further saturate the critical California markets and gave Starbucks desirable exposure to business travelers.

Strong Growth Continues

Nearly two decades of continuous and spectacular growth (1982–1999) built the Starbucks success story. In that time, Starbucks added about 30,000 employees, and as of 1998 the company added another 500 employees each month. In 1999, they opened 612 stores worldwide and posted revenues of $1.7 billion. As a result of the remarkable growth rate of Starbucks' sales and profits, its market capitalization rose dramatically. This culminated in the company's addition to the S&P 500 in 1999.

Nevertheless, in 1999, sales slowed down significantly. First, the pace of the opening of new coffeehouses fell behind schedule and same-store revenue growth flattened. Additionally, the initial high growth of Starbucks ice cream tapered considerably, and the supermarket launch of Frappuccino failed to meet sales expectations. To keep the brand on track, Starbucks continued to pursue strategies to push Starbucks beyond coffee shops to find growth areas. The challenge for Starbucks, however, was to manage growth and diversification while strengthening Starbucks core values and keeping customers trustful and loyal to the brand.

VENTURES INTO NEW AREAS

Starbucks introduced its first full-fledged restaurant in Seattle under the name of Café Starbucks in 1998. The restaurant served light entrees to complement a full menu of coffee beverages. The thought behind opening a restaurant division was that almost 85 percent of Starbucks' sales were completed by 3 p.m., with the majority of daytime purchases occurring in the morning. In 1999, Starbucks opened its first cybercafé—a coffeehouse/restaurant that provided web access along with food and beverages—in San Francisco, called Circadia.

Joe magazine, the result of a partnership with Time, Inc., was a major innovation launched in 1999. Starbucks aimed to tighten the relationship the brand had with consumers by creating an original, warm, and conversational lifestyle magazine inspired by the coffeehouse's traditional atmosphere. It was also a means of re-asserting Starbucks core values such as a feeling of romance, relaxation, and trust.

Starbucks' Missteps

Like many companies during the Internet boom, Starbucks over-reached to an extent in its rush to establish an elaborate Internet presence. In 1998, Starbucks began to develop an Internet strategy as another tool to increase sales and strengthen its brand image. Starbucks had already launched a direct-mail catalog program through which consumers, located anywhere in the United States, could order Starbucks coffee and other products. In 1999, Starbucks announced that profits for the current fiscal year would be 10 percent below expectations, due in part to the expensive internet start-up (roughly $4 million), higher labor costs, and a slow-starting Frappuccino supermarket launch.

That same summer, Starbucks made a bid to buy the kitchen and home-goods retailer Williams-Sonoma. Unfortunately for Starbucks, Williams-Sonoma chose to remain independent and rejected the bid. A month later, Starbucks did announce a $20 million investment in Living.com, a start-up that planned to sell non-branded furniture via the Internet.

Uncertain about the practicality of these plans and still reeling from the bad news concerning sales and profits, Wall Street hammered the Starbucks stock, resulting in a drop in share price of 28 percent in one day—a $2 billion loss in the company's market capitalization. Wall Street seemed to be condemning these plans, accusing Starbucks of losing focus and diluting earnings. Some traditional retail investors interpreted the announcement as an early signal that the company's core retail business was weakening, while investors regarded Starbucks' retail locations as excess physical overhead that would hamper its web presence.

In response to the negative reaction, Starbucks revised its web strategy. Instead, the company chose to invest in other net companies such as the Internet chat site TalkCity for $20 million and Cooking.com for $10 million The company stuck to its plan of opening a website for its coffee products and unveiled Starbucks.com in early 2000. These scaled-back web developments assuaged the fears of investors and Starbucks stock began climbing steadily in late 1999.

In 2000, sales of their lifestyle magazine *Joe* faltered and the project was axed less than year after its launch. In the aftermath of the Internet bubble, investments in Living.com, Cooking.com, and TalkCity all proved to be unsuccessful. Furthermore, citing higher costs for milk, as well as higher rent and health-insurance costs, the company was forced to raise prices by approximately 3 percent in August of 2000. The company also faced increased competition in the café business.

Increased Competition

It did not take long for other companies to try and duplicate the Starbucks experience. Whereas Starbucks stores had a hip, urban feel, some competitors tried to broaden this experience by creating a different atmosphere. Caribou Coffee was perhaps the most successful, designing their stores to resemble ski lodges and rustic mountain cabins. "Caribou gets you out of the urban environment and gets you in a different world for a short period of time. In many ways, Starbucks is an extension of the hustle and bustle of a city street,"[6] said Dennis Lombardi, Executive VP at WD Partners, a Columbus, Ohio-based retail design firm. As of 2006, Caribou Coffee, with over 30 locations in 13 states, was the distant number two coffeehouse brand to Starbucks. Gloria Jean's Coffee and the Coffee Beanery were smaller competitors in this segment.

Perhaps the greatest threat was from Dunkin' Donuts, who in 2006 had 4,400 locations in the United States and over 6,000 stores in 29 countries worldwide. "Espresso has become mainstream in America, and who does mainstream better than Dunkin' Donuts?"[7] asked Jon Luther, chief executive of Allied Domecq's (parent company of Dunkin' Donuts) restaurant division. Not only had Dunkin' Donuts introduced cappuccinos and lattes in many stores, but they had eliminated the need for baristas by purchasing machines that churned out quality cappuccinos in less than a minute. The company also offered Wi-Fi service at some locations, expanding its product line to include frozen coffee drinks, and tended to locate its stores in blue-collar communities, an area that Starbuck was just beginning to target. This combination of speed, consistency, and lower prices (up to 25 percent lower than Starbucks) was winning converts, as the company recorded worldwide sales of $3.6 billion in fiscal 2004.

With the total retail coffee sales in the United States of $4.2 billion in 2005, there was no shortage of competitors. Another threat to Starbucks came from fast food heavyweights such as McDonald's and Burger King. McDonald's changed its bean blend and equipment systemwide, and offered cappuccinos and lattes in some chains. Burger King tested its own premium blend and planned to offer it under the name *BK Joe*. Another competitor, Carl's Jr., launched a new Arabica bean roast, and Dairy Queen began offering a frozen/iced coffee in the summer of 2004.

AGGRESSIVE EXPANSION

In response to this competition, Starbucks got "back to basics" and focused on new markets. By the end of fiscal year 1998, Starbucks operated 26 stores in Japan, 11 in Singapore, 6 in Taiwan, 5 in the Philippines, and 1 in Thailand. Late 1998 and early 1999 saw the opening of Starbucks specialty coffee stores in Malaysia, New Zealand, and China. In 2001, Starbucks opened locations in Switzerland and Austria. The following year, Starbucks expanded its European presence into Spain, Germany, and Greece. By 2006, Starbucks was in 37 countries, including Argentina, Peru, Brazil, Turkey, Japan, Mexico, Jordan, India, and The Bahamas (see Exhibit 3 for store growth data). Starbucks also achieved further international expansion to the Middle East and new markets in the Pacific Rim.

Investors as well as consumers were clamoring for coffee. In June of 2000, the Hong Kong Stock Exchange added six NASDAQ stocks, of which Starbucks was the only non-tech stock. Starbucks expected that its presence in Asian stock markets would provide the company with more inroads into Asian commerce. By 2006, there were over 200 shops in China and Hong Kong and 150 locations in Taiwan.

Starbucks' longtime chairman and CEO Howard Schultz had his sights fixed firmly on the international market. In June 2000, he surrendered the title of CEO to then-president and COO Orin Smith. Schultz remained chairman of the company and assumed the new title of "Chief Global Strategist," a role that enabled him to focus on overseas growth and brand development. Schultz, who estimated that the global market for Starbucks was over 15,000 stores, was certain that Starbucks would continue to enjoy success in Asia. He stated that the growth overseas "will be a mirror image of what we did here (in North America)."[8] Smith remained CEO until 2005, when he was replaced by James Donald, former President of Starbucks North America.

Success Overseas

International success grew at a rapid pace. The company continued to open stores in established markets, while looking for new opportunities. By early 2003, there were a total of 1,532 overseas stores, accounting for 23 percent of total locations.

These stores were not immediately profitable, accounting for only 9 percent of sales. It was not until the end of 2003 that the company's international stores became profitable, narrowly squeezing out operating income of $5 million on net revenues of over $600 million.

Starbucks faced challenges with this rapid international growth. As of 2005, Japan boasted Starbucks' biggest foray outside the United States After initial success, the Japanese operation see-sawed between being in the black and red in subsequent years. All six Starbucks cafés in Israel shut down in 2003 due to a severe recession and security problems. Starbucks drinks in London were hurt by rivals with lower costs, while in Germany, markets in Frankfurt and Berlin were saturated by Starbucks-like coffee bars.

These setbacks did not deter Schultz or his plans to one day have over 15,000 international locations. Starbucks' goal was to have 6,500 locations in Asia, fueled in large part by growth in China. The company set aggressive goals for Europe, the Middle East, and Africa with a target of 6,000 stores. Schultz also planned to have 1,500 stores in Latin America, and double the number of outlets in Canada to 1,000.

STARBUCKS FIGHTS BACK

Schultz faced the challenges heading the company and outlined ambitious plans to extend the brand. He wanted Starbucks to be known for more than just offering high quality coffee in comfortable settings. Schultz planned to make Starbucks "the most recognized and respected brand in the world."[9]

The company began with strengthening its core product, coffee. Starbucks unveiled new Frappuccino flavors, including Chocolate Brownie, Orange Mocha Chip, and Strawberries & Crème, as well as a low-calorie line of drinks. By 2005, Frappuccino was the number one selling ready-to-drink coffee in the United States with $152 million in sales and held an 83 percent market share.[10] In 2002, Starbucks introduced the DoubleShot, a chilled espresso drink sold by grocery stores in 6.5 ounce cans. Three years later, DoubleShot was the number two selling ready-to-drink coffee in the United States with $25 million in sales and a 13 percent market share. In fact, 71 new RTD tea and coffee drinks were introduced throughout the industry in 2005 alone.[11]

That same year, the company launched the Chiantico, an indulgent drinking chocolate, in the hopes of selling more products that would sell during the afternoon and early evening hours. They also added new food products, like Reduced Fat Blueberry Coffee Cake and a Lemon Raspberry Loaf. In 2006, Starbucks introduced Blackberry Green Tea Frappuccino and Tazo Green Tea Latte in hopes of combining tea into their already popular coffee drinks.

Growth beyond Coffee

Starbucks started offering prepackaged sandwiches and other lunch items after realizing that only 10 percent of sales were made between noon and 2 pm. By 2005, they offered lunch items in 2,300 U.S. stores, with plans to expand the service to 70 percent of all stores. Starbucks also began testing a "warming program" in Seattle and Washington, D.C. This initiative required baristas to heat up breakfast sandwiches (e.g. sausage and egg English muffins) in an oven. This service expanded Starbucks' current breakfast offerings of bagels and pastries, but added complication to already busy baristas during the critical morning hours.

Starbucks began offering stored value cards in 2002 to make it easier for customers to purchase items. These cards offered customers a cash-free way to purchase their favorite Starbucks items and beverages (many of which cost close to $4.00). The cards were an instant hit, and Starbucks soon expanded the idea. The following year they introduced the Starbucks Card DuettoVisa, a first-of-its-kind payment card that blended a traditional credit card and the reloadable Starbucks Card into one. Within two months of its introduction, the Duetto Card was recognized by *BusinessWeek*, as one of the "Best Products of 2003."

As the Internet continued its explosive growth and permeated all aspects of daily life, Starbucks teamed with wireless service provider T-Mobile to provide Internet Hot Spots in Starbucks stores. During its first year, the company installed over 2,600 Hot Spots in its stores, and actively explored new ways to introduce technological innovations to encourage customers to stay longer and, hopefully, drink more coffee.

Expansion into Non-Traditional Areas

In an effort to reinvent one of the world's best-known brands, Starbucks purchased alternative music retailer Hear Music in 1999 for $8 million. Though Starbucks had been selling pre-packaged CDs for years, they used this acquisition to begin offering Hear Music Media Bars in select stores in 2004. Media Bars were kiosks that allowed customers to browse over 150,000 song titles, then choose their favorites and "burn" them to create their own custom CDs. Starbucks further leveraged its ownership of Hear Music with the addition of a Hear Music channel on XM Satellite Radio.

Starbucks invested cautiously in the digital music field. Although the cost per Media Bar was about $20,000 (and eventually installing these in 3,000 stores would cost $57 million), this represented a small portion of the $600 million Starbucks had scheduled for capital-expansion spending in 2005. However, with the recent explosion of iPod use, an increasing number of consumers were more comfortable getting their music in a digital format (such as MP3 files) than more traditional CDs.

Starbucks experimented with music in other ways, too. The company co-produced the late Ray Charles' *Genius Loves Company* with Concord Records. Featured prominently in more than 4,500 Starbucks locations, the album won eight Grammy awards and soared to the top of the Billboard R&B charts, all without radio play. This success with a traditional, already popular artist was followed with sheer marketing muscle in promoting Madeleine Peyroux, a relatively obscure torch singer on the independent Rounder Records, who put out her first album in 1996. Her latest, *Careless Love*, was released in September 2004 to little fanfare. In March 2005, Starbucks started prominently displaying it. Sales tripled in just one week, from 4,849 albums to 16,636, pushing the album to No. 81 on the *Billboard* Top 200.

Starbucks entered into an agreement with Jim Beam Brands to develop, manufacture, and market a Starbucks-branded coffee liqueur since nearly 50 percent of its loyal patrons consumed coffee liqueurs. Coffee-flavored liqueurs were a big piece of the estimated $4 billion to $5 billion U.S. cordial-and-liqueur market. A print ad campaign sporting the tagline, "The Art of Coffee comes to Cocktails," helped support the product, which was sold at liquor stores, not Starbucks locations. In an interesting twist, Starbucks' coffee liqueur squared off against the popular Kahlua brand, made by Allied Domecq (who was also the parent company of competitor Dunkin' Donuts). Since the introduction of their coffee liqueur, Starbucks had been removed from some socially conscious mutual funds that previously invested in the company.

In 2006, Starbucks entered the film business. The company partnered with Lions Gate, an independent film maker, to promote "Akeelah" a film about an 11-year old spelling bee whiz. Starbucks promoted the film in several ways. Customers received a free "Akeelah" spelling be word on every cup of coffee. The movie's soundtrack and DVD were sold in Starbucks locations. And, the company gave out free movie tickets to its baristas hoping to encourage them to promote the film through to the end customer. The company also planned to invest much more into the film industry in upcoming years and once reporter called Starbucks the "Oprah's Book Club of the independent filmmaking world."[12]

These new initiatives helped stores increase sales substantially. In 1999, an average Starbucks store posted $750,000 in sales. By 2004, this per store number had surged to $940,000. However, there was concern whether this same-store sales growth could continue. Analysts were especially concerned about market growth and saturation.

Continued Growth

Starbucks continued its ambitious international growth plans in 2004 and 2005, adding stores in France, Cyprus, Jordan, the Republic of Ireland and the Bahamas. In fiscal 2006, the company planned to open 1,800 stores—more than they had opened during the first 25 years of the company's history. To further differentiate itself from increased competition, Starbucks developed the Coffee Master certification program. Upon passing a series of tests on the intricacies and nuances of coffee, Starbucks employees earned the right to wear a distinctive black apron. The company's goal was to have at least one black apron-clad Coffee Master in every store. The company raised prices by another 3 percent in the fall of 2004. This did not appear to hurt the company; by 2005 Starbucks' stock had climbed over 3,500 percent since its 1992 IPO, and hit record numbers in 2006 (see Exhibit 4 for stock performance).

The question remained whether this rapid expansion in retail, product inventory, and strategic partnerships would harm Starbucks brand equity and run the risk of becoming a cookie-cutter chain. In an April 2005 interview, CEO James Donald addressed this very issue:

> "Our success comes down to the way we connect with our customers, our communities, our farms—with each other. We just had a four-day leadership conference. The theme was human connection. We didn't once talk about sales and profits. We talked about how we continue to grow and how we connect. You know, Howard [Schultz] has always said that we're not in the coffee business, serving people; we're in the people business, serving coffee.[13]

Starbucks' ability to grow without alienating large segments of their consumer base would hinge on the public's perception of the company.

CONCLUSION

Many viewed Starbucks' meteoric rise from a tiny local retailer to an international coffee powerhouse as one of the great success stories in American business in the last decade. Incredibly, Starbucks achieved its market leader position largely without aid from advertising campaigns (in 2004, only 1.3 percent of sales was spent on marketing). Instead, the company built the brand by relying on the quality of their products and services to induce free word-of-mouth "advertising" from customer to customer.

As Starbucks continued to push for new product innovations and business opportunities as a way to differentiate itself from its competitors and maintain its growth, the company ran the risk of straying too far from its original focus of spreading its passion for fine coffee. Even with $6.4 billion in sales in 2005 and a soaring stock in 2006, Schultz vowed to keep Starbucks "small" in terms of its close interactions with employees and customers. However, the ballooning size of the corporation suggested that the quality of Starbucks products and services, and the strength of the company's relationships with its most valued people, would need to be closely monitored. A larger, global Starbucks had to find the right balance in pursuing product-, people-, values- and sales-driven objectives.

DISCUSSION QUESTIONS

1. What were the keys for success for Starbucks in building the brand? What were its brand values? What were its sources of equity?
2. How would you evaluate Starbucks' growth strategy? Are there things you would do differently? How would you evaluate its partnerships (e.g. with United Airlines)? How do you know whether it is a "good" or "bad" partnership?
3. What does it take to make a world class global brand? Can Starbucks become one? What hurdles must its overcome? In terms of the American market, what do you see as Starbucks' biggest challenges?

4. Evaluate Starbucks' move into non-coffee areas like credit cards, music, and film. Are these natural extensions of the Starbucks brand, or has the company gone too far in creating a "lifestyle" brand? Where should Starbucks go next?

5. Do you agree with Starbucks' international expansion? Should the company continue its aggressive expansion plans? Are there markets where Starbucks cannot expand?

6. Who represents the biggest threat to Starbucks? Direct competitors in the coffee market, such as Dunkin' Donuts? Chains like McDonald's that are expanding their coffee quality? Panera Bread and other locations that might be the new "third place"?

7. How much are customers willing to pay for the *Starbucks Experience*? Can the company continue to raise prices on its coffees and drinks? Is there a market for $400+ coffee makers?

Exhibit 1: Starbucks Net Revenues
         ($ billions)

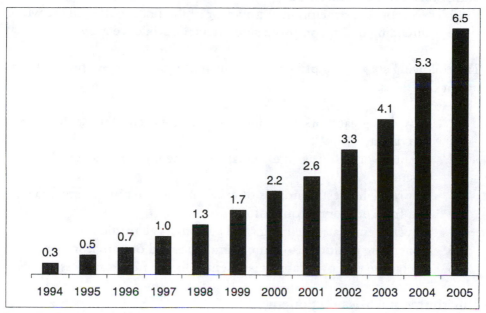

Source: Company Reports

Exhibit 2: Starbuck Mission Statement

Starbucks Mission Statement
Establish Starbucks as the premier purveyor of the finest coffee in the world while maintaining our uncompromising principles while we grow.

The following six guiding principles will help us measure the appropriateness of our decisions:

1. Provide a great work environment and treat each other with respect and dignity.
2. Embrace diversity as an essential component in the way we do business.
3. Apply the highest standards of excellence to the purchasing, roasting, and fresh delivery of our coffee.
4. Develop enthusiastically satisfied customers all of the time.
5. Contribute positively to our communities and our environment.
6. Recognize that profitability is essential to our future success.

Environmental Mission Statement
Starbucks is committed to a role of environmental leadership in all facets of our business.
We fulfill this mission by a commitment to:

1. Understanding of environmental issues and sharing information with our partners.
2. Developing innovative and flexible solutions to bring about change.
3. Striving to buy, sell, and use environmentally friendly products.
4. Recognizing that fiscal responsibility is essential to our environmental future.
5. Instilling environmental responsibility as a corporate value.
6. Measuring and monitoring our progress for each project.
7. Encouraging all partners to share in our mission.

Exhibit 3: U.S. and International Stores Open at Year End
(Company operated stores)

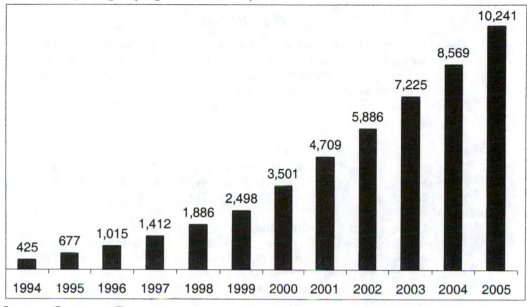

Source: Company Reports

Exhibit 4: Starbucks Weekly Closing Stock Price (through April 2006)

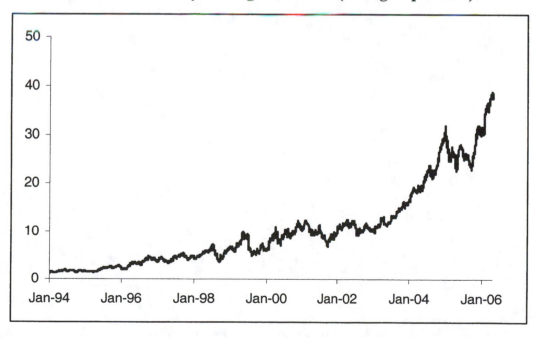

REFERENCES

1 The initial draft of this case was written by Peter Gilmore, Dartmouth '99 and Keith Richey with assistance from Emmanuelle Louis Hofer under the supervision of Professor Kevin Lane Keller as the basis for class discussion. Revisions and updates were later completed by Jonathan Michaels.

2 Howard Schultz. *Pour Your Heart Into It.* Hyperion: New York, 1997.

3 Ibid.

4 Ibid.

5 Ibid.

6 "Starbucks it isn't—and purposely so." *Advertising Age*, March 14, 2005, p. 12.

7 Deborah Ball. "Latte Versus Latte." The *Wall Street Journal*, February 10, 2004, p. B1.

8 Robert T. Nelson. "Now, Barista to the World." The *Seattle Times*, April 7, 2000, p. C1.

9 Starbucks Corporation Fiscal 2004 Annual Report, p.13

10 Information Resources Inc. Total food, drug and mass merchandise excluding Wal-Mart for 52 weeks ending December 25, 2005.

11 Mintel's global new product database. March 2006.

12 Jose Lourenco. "Starbucks stops making up words, teaches us new ones." The *Toronto Star*, April 25, 2006.

13 "Starbucks: The Next Generation." *Fortune*, April 4, 2005, p. 30.

SNAPPLE:
REVITALIZING A BRAND[1]

INTRODUCTION

In the 1990s, Snapple Corporation was one of the leading "New Age" beverage brands when the category was just beginning to take off. With the combination of a unique product, package design, and quirky advertising, the company grew from a regional underground favorite to a nationally recognized brand.

Snapple's rise in the beverage industry was crowned in 1994, when the Quaker Oats Company purchased Snapple for $1.7 billion. Quaker expected to make Snapple a major player in the industry, as it had done with Gatorade. However, the company was unable to capitalize on the brand's previous success. Snapple languished for a period of three years in the hands of Quaker management.

In 1997, Quaker sold Snapple to Triarc Beverage Group for $300 million. Triarc faced a number of challenges, including reversing the sales slide, revamping the distribution system, and creating new products that would enable growth. Most importantly, Triarc had to find a way to reconnect the brand with its consumers. Triarc successfully resurrected the Snapple brand, and in 2000 sold Snapple to Cadbury Schweppes for $1.45 billion. Cadbury Schweppes then faced the challenge of maintaining Snapple's brand strength in an increasingly competitive beverage environment.

THE EMERGENCE OF SNAPPLE

The roots of Snapple Corporation date back to 1972 in Brooklyn, New York when brothers-in-law, Leonard Marsh and Hyman Golden, left their window-washing business and teamed up with Marsh's childhood friend and health food store owner Arnold Greenberg to sell pure fruit juice as the "Unadulterated Food Products Co." In 1978, they created an apple soda that fizzled—so much so that several bottles exploded—inspiring the "snap" in the drink's eventual name. They bought the rights to the name from a man in Texas for what then seemed like a very expensive price of $500. Over time they established themselves as the "first company to produce a complete line of all-natural beverages," that were "Made from the Best Stuff on Earth."

In the 1980s, Snapple essentially created the non-carbonated segment of ready-to-drink beverages with its introduction of ready-to-drink fruit juices and iced teas. Snapple was also the first company to sell its drinks in single serving wide-mouthed glass bottles, rather than the ubiquitous aluminum cans. The company clad its bottles in unique, bright labeling and introduced a new process called "hot-packing" (where they filled bottles with 180° F liquid to sterilize the contents) that eliminated the need for preservatives and enabled it to extend its "all-natural" claims to its entire line of products. Its goal was to "make a natural product and make sure it tastes good, smells good, and looks good." Although Snapple remained a small niche brand throughout much of the decade, the strategy had begun to work. By the late 1980s, growing ranks of health-conscious consumers were snapping up Snapple products as an alternative to sodas. By 1991, Snapple emerged as a nationally recognized brand.

In the spring of 1992, Snapple management raised capital by selling a majority stake of the firm to Thomas H. Lee, a Boston-based investment firm, for $140 million. Marsh, Golden, and Greenberg maintained control of the company and continued to improve operations. In December of the same year, the company went public by selling 4 million shares of common stock at a price of $20. per share. The offering was oversubscribed and, by the day's end, the share price had risen 45 percent. A month later, Snapple shares traded at $34. and by the end of 1993, Snapple sales had exploded to $516 million, more than double its 1992 figures. The stock price had risen to five times its initial offering price and Snapple was a household name. Yet, operating costs were also on the rise. Sales, and general and administration expenses had grown from $22.7 to $59 million from 1992 to 1993, and operating margins had fallen 2.3 percent.

The Snapple Formula

Over time, Marsh, Golden, and Greenburg had developed a set of tactics that they believed propelled Snapple sales. First, they tried to differentiate the company from its competitors by continually offering customers new and exotic choices of ready-to-drink beverages. In 1993 alone, the company produced 52 different flavors (see Exhibit 1 for list of Snapple flavors). In addition to offering diverse flavors, the company concentrated on providing quality flavors in its beverages. For example, 95 percent of Snapple teas came from India and a small percentage came from Sri Lanka. The extensive offering of new and exotic flavors helped stimulate consumer interest and support sales. Not all of Snapple offerings, however, were successful. Within the tea segment, for example, decaffeinated and unsweetened teas consistently performed below management's expectations. Even so, the team was able to bring more blockbuster flavors to market than unsuccessful introductions.

Second, the team elected to focus its early marketing efforts on the East and West coasts, where demand for New Age beverages was highest. Early sales to Midwestern states were not as strong, leading some to believe that Snapple's quirky urban advertising alienated middle America. International sales accounted for just 1 percent of total revenues and, despite the fact that faster growth would require a significant amount of capital, management planned to aggressively push into Europe, Central and South America, and Asia.

Third, the company initially developed its own distribution channels, eschewing the traditional wholesaler supermarket model used by its larger, established competition. Instead, Snapple sold "up-and-down-the-street" channels like convenience outlets, sandwich shops, gas stations, and delicatessens through a system of independent distributors.

Fourth, in the high-growth, ready-to-drink beverage market, Snapple management positioned and priced its products at a significant premium. In 1993, Snapple charged $1.00 to $1.25 for a 16-ounce bottle, a 30 to 38 percent margin. When asked to justify the beverage's relatively high price, Snapple marketers responded that it was a premium product that was "available to anyone," as opposed to traditional luxury goods, such as a Porsche automobile, which were out-of-reach of the average consumer. But critics wondered whether the company could sustain such a high price premium, especially in the iced tea segment, which could easily be prepared at home. Consequently, many analysts believed that in order to successfully enter the supermarket business, Snapple management would have to reposition the brand and sell products in multi-packs, in cans, and at a lower price.

Snapple Brand Equity

By 1994, Snapple was experiencing tremendous growth. Jude Hammerle, Snapple's Director of Advertising and Promotion commented, "The velocity at which the brand is growing now is so monumental that you could get dizzy just thinking about that." Michael Bellas, the President of Beverage Marketing agreed, "Snapple has made us all believers."

Consumers loved Snapple. Fan clubs, testimonials, letter writing; some considered it a kind of Snapple cult. Snapple appeared on license plates and even became the middle name for a New Jersey baby boy. Consumer surveys suggested that the Snapple name was catchy and popular and engendered positive feelings in consumers. As Hammerle explained, "The name is really one of the most user-friendly, consumer-friendly names that you can ever find." The company's marketing targeted mostly teens, 18 to 30 year olds, and the "traditional iced tea consumer."

During the early 1990s, Snapple ran a series of very successful ad campaigns, and had a great deal of success advertising on national radio and television, using off-beat humor and consumer-composed jingles. One advertisement the company invited an art critic to analyze the Snapple label. Snapple also gained appeal through product placements in popular shows such as *Seinfeld*, movies such as *Sleepless in Seattle*, as well as official sponsorship of well-known celebrities such as Rush Limbaugh, Howard Stern, and Jennifer Capriati. Television commercials featured people such as New York's ex-Mayor Ed Koch defending his city and Snapple to a critical Kentucky farmer. Snapple also relied on "word-of-mouth" advertising and pursued unusual events throughout the country that Coke and Pepsi avoided, such as a Minnesotan Cherry Spitting and New Jersey Miss Crustacean contests.

The company's most successful ad campaign, however, starred Wendy "the Snapple Lady." Wendy Kaufman, a woman with a thick New York accent, was a company employee in the order department. She took it upon herself to personally answer incoming consumer letters and became the drink's unofficial spokeswoman. She rocketed to stardom after starring in the television commercials where she read letters from Snapple fans. Capitalizing on the growing trend toward testimonial advertising, the Wendy ads projected a "real people" image in unscripted and spontaneous commercials with real Snapple customers. Wendy gained national recognition through appearances in places such as the Oprah Winfrey Show. Snapple was now one of the leading brands in the exploding New Age beverage market, which had passed the fad stage and was a legitimate segment in the beverage industry.

THE NEW AGE BEVERAGE MARKET

For nearly two decades, the non-alcoholic beverage market had thrived. The soft drink sector reached a staggering $47 billion in retail sales in 1993 and dominated other ready-to-drink categories by a factor of nearly 50 to 1. Growth in the segment was expected to slow down to 2 or 3 percent per year so many of the large beverage companies looked into new categories to improve revenues.

During the late-1980s, a new trend—the New Age movement of the non-alcoholic beverage market—emerged and evolved in response to consumers' growing concerns over calories and artificial additives. By 1994, New Age ready-to-drink beverages broke down into eight distinct groups; Ready-to-drink tea (30 share), Sports beverages (23 share), PET (plastic) bottled water (16 share), Single-serve fruit beverages (15 share), All-natural soda (14 share), Sparkling flavored water (~1 share), Sparkling fruit beverages (~1 share), and Ready-to-drink Coffee (~1 share).

Market research about the New Age ready-to-drink segment suggested that customers generally selected beverages based on fashion, taste, and status related considerations. Consequently, distinctive flavors, quality ingredients, and clean labels were generally more important than price. Product, packaging, and promotion considerations—as they combined to form overall brand image—played a critical role in the consumers buying decision.

As of October 1993, between 75 percent and 80 percent of all U.S. households drank iced tea, placing the product third to soft drinks and beer in the beverage consumption rankings. As the New Age movement gained momentum, the ready-to-drink iced tea segment grew at an amazing rate of 189 percent as health-conscious consumers embraced iced tea, with fewer calories and additives, as an alternative to soda and beer. In response, several beverage companies began to stress the importance of the high-quality ingredients in their advertising. For example, Perrier/Celestial Seasonings, Crystal Geyser, and White Rock highlighted the quality of their respective brands of spring water, which were used in their ready-to-drink tea products.

New Competition

Although Snapple may have penetrated the ready-to-drink beverage market first and precipitated the New Age category few observers believed that it would continue to dominate the market for long.

With flat sales in the soda segment, Snapple had begun to attract the attention of beverage industry behemoths such as Coca-Cola and Pepsi. It was just a matter of time before new players entered the market. A key question would be whether newer, larger players would create momentum in the ready-to-drink market and carry Snapple along with it.

Pepsi, along with Unilever, became the first major brand to challenge Snapple. In 1992, the two companies announced a joint effort to sell Unilever's Lipton iced tea in a ready-to-drink package. The new Pepsi/Lipton partnership first offered the bottled Lipton Original, "the only ready-to-drink iced tea brewed from real tea leaves," followed by the canned Lipton Brisk. In 1993, the companies launched a $30 to $35 million advertising campaign featuring *Sports Illustrated* swimsuit edition cover model Vendela drinking Lipton in front of a fascinated audience of both men and women. The joint venture also launched an aggressive radio campaign targeting Snapple, attacking the company for its use of reconstituted tea powders.

At the same time, English beverage giant Tetley licensed the rights to manufacture and distribute all ready-to-drink products bearing the Tetley trademark to A&W. Tetley planned to invest $35 million to market a new round tea bag and saw opportunities to cross-market to hot tea drinkers. The Tetley/A&W combination's advertising introduced "Pearle," a sandwich shop waitress who couldn't understand why the bags were round. Tetley also included coupons for the ready-to-drink product with every box of round bag tea.

In 1994, Coca-Cola entered the New Age beverage market with the introduction of a psychedelic fruit drink, Fruitopia, which was marketed using a retro peace-and-love ad theme and the slogan "Fruitopia. For the mind, body and planet." The upstart brand totaled sales of $20.4 million in its first year on advertising spending of approximately $30 million. The new Fruitopia brand was able to piggyback on Coke's extensive distribution system, thus bypassing some of its competitors' logistical problems. Despite the hype surrounding Coke's launch of Fruitopia, sales for 1994 finished at only $60 million, far below the target of $400 million.

At the time, the ready-to-drink tea market was suffering for several reasons. First, slower growth rates naturally occurred as the sales base grew. Second, the three largest brands in the category could no longer count on domestic geographic expansion to increase sales. Third, fruit drinks were beginning to provide stiff competition (see Exhibit 2 for a partial list of Snapple's competitors).

Further complicating things was additional competition. Arizona Iced Tea entered the ready-to-drink iced tea market. Like Snapple, Arizona was founded by two New Yorkers, Don Vultaggio and John Ferolito. The two developed a canned iced tea that captured a nearly 17% percent market share and $2 billion in revenues in 1995, putting it squarely in competition with the larger players in the market. Priced similarly to Snapple, the new company also added a liquor-like 20-ounce bottle. Despite the fact that the company 1) gave its products practically no marketing support beyond the point-of-purchase, 2) was slow to develop a formal product development process, and 3) was plagued by lawsuits from numerous angry ex-distributors, Arizona moved into a strong position in the ready-to-drink category.

THE QUAKER OATS TAKEOVER

Despite the new competitors in the ready-to-drink tea market and plunging share prices in late 1994, Snapple executives remained bullish. However, Snapple's majority investors, Thomas H. Lee, quickly accepted Quaker Oats' proposed $1.7 billion acquisition deal—generating a gain of nearly $1 billion over a two-year period. All told, the $1.7 billion deal represented a multiple of about 17 times earnings, significantly more than the 10 or 11 times earnings yielded by other recent transactions in the beverage category or by comparable publicly traded companies. Some analysts believed that the deal was a good one. "There are some significant synergies," suggested Michael Bellas, president of New York-based Beverage

Marketing Corporation. "They are very professional, a big force on the horizon now. I'm sure that's being considered by both Atlanta [Coca-Cola] and Somers [Pepsi]."

Snapple Under Quaker Oats Management

New competitors aside, by 1995 many analysts felt that the market for New Age drinks was changing dramatically. Increasingly, the young, trendy consumers that had created the ready-to-drink category seemed to be getting bored and began to shift back to the more neutral flavors of colas and clear sodas.

Quaker Oats attempted to respond to these trends with new advertising and promotional tactics. Because Snapple was considered a brand whose popularity spread primarily by word of mouth, the company tried to be especially receptive to the consumer ideas. For example, it introduced a new flavor, Ralph's Cantaloupe Cocktail, when its namesake, Ralph Orafino, wrote to the company and requested a melon-flavored drink. Also, in August 1995, the company sponsored the "First Annual Snapple Convention" in Hempstead, New York for 3,000 of the drinks' most hardcore fans. The idea for this "Snapple love fest" came from the brand's self-proclaimed "#1 Fan," 6 year-old Jennifer Murry, who wrote to the company:

> Dear Snapple Woman,
> Shouldn't Snapple have some kind of special day or holiday or festival even?
> Because, you see people on TV, I mean, like the man that didn't believe
> Snapple was made of natural things or fruits. I think there should be a holiday
> or festival. Or a Snapple parade.

Quaker sent announcements for the convention to the quarter-million Snapple devotees who had felt strongly enough about the product to send personal letters to the company. In exchange for a $5.00 admission fee and 20 Snapple labels, Quaker offered the fans "36,000 square feet of taste tests, a Wendy look-alike contest, television commercials on video monitors, web surfing, a cooking demonstration, panel discussions featuring Wendy and the real-life 'stars' of Snapple TV spots, trivia contests, Snapple-inspired artwork and fashions, raffles, miniature golf, and carnival games. Plus, each attendee received two free bottles of Snapple."

Despite the apparent success of the convention, Quaker made several critical errors in its first major selling season after acquiring Snapple. In a world where refreshment drink sales skyrocket in the summer season, Quaker neither followed a regular advertising schedule for Snapple, nor introduced new products quickly enough. As a result, supermarket sales slipped. June sales of Snapple iced tea dropped 19 percent, fruit blends dropped 25 percent, and lemonades dropped 32 percent from the previous year.

Snapple's "healthy" reputation began to suffer, too. Jane Hurley of the Center for Science in the Public Interest—the same woman who exposed the nutrition fallacies of movie theatre popcorn and Chinese food—pointed out that Snapple drinks are mostly sweetened water, containing less than 10 percent fruit juice. "It's about the same as Hi-C, and no one ever called that a health drink. We're not saying to this stuff will hurt you. It's more of a rip-off than a health risk." Other critics noted that a bottle of Snapple iced tea contained more calories than a Coke.

Further complicating matters, Quaker had expected to use Snapple's extensive distribution network of 300 national distributors to push Gatorade into smaller retail outlets that Quaker had not traditionally used. The company discovered too late that the Snapple distribution systems were not compatible with its existing Gatorade system. Quaker responded by trying to transfer big supermarket accounts from Snapple distributors to Gatorade distributors and encouraging the Snapple distributors to push the up-and-down-the-street channels harder, which the Snapple distributors refused.

Quaker Attempts New Strategies

Quaker management responded with drastic changes. They installed new people in brand management positions, reduced the number of flavors offered from 50 to 35, reduced contract manufacturers, and tripled the ad budget. In addition, Quaker also made changes to the flavor line, including introducing seasonal products such as cider tea for Halloween. At the same time, the company continued the push into supermarkets with new packaging: 12-packs, 4-packs, and plastic 32- and 64-ounce bottles.

Quaker worked on a system to process orders faster and make the bottling plants more efficient. This move cut inventory in half and enabled deliveries to be made within two days, instead of 21 days. In addition, Snapple announced plans to place highly visible coolers in supermarkets, just like Coke and Pepsi, and introduce a diet line of drinks.

SNAPPLE SALES DECLINE

The efforts to save the summer of 1995 were too little, too late, and Coke and Pepsi aggressively promoted new iced tea and fruit juice campaigns. Despite spending more than $40 million for a national summertime sampling campaign, Snapple's sales dropped another 20 percent for the quarter. Supermarket tea sales were down 14 percent and juice sales fell 15 percent, prompting critics to question whether Quaker Oats had made a mistake in purchasing the company. Tom Pirko, President of Bevmark commented, "They bought the brand at a point it was past its zenith."

Despite the disappointing summer, Quaker Oats management continued to think otherwise. Margaret Stender, Quaker Oats' vice president of marketing enforced, "Snapple is on the verge of a comeback." Despite the company's apparent optimism, Lipton overtook Snapple in volume sales in the ready-to-drink tea category in 1995, although Snapple maintained its number one position in dollar sales due to its premium pricing strategy.

In 1996, Quaker attempted to move Snapple back toward more traditional marketing approaches. First, it introduced an inside-the-bottle-cap game promotion for 1996 and began a $40 million nationwide give-away campaign during the summer. Backed by a TV and radio ad campaign touting how Snapple was "spreading taste all over the place," extensive "sampling brigades" passed out free Snapple at beaches, parks, and on street corners. Consumers could also call a toll-free number to get coupons good for free bottles. Next, it launched a new advertising campaign to replace the "Wendy" ads. Those ads had aired for years and some key Quaker Oats staff believed that the ads were losing steam and that

Wendy's New York brashness might be hindering Snapple's acceptance in the Midwest. The company hired Spike Lee to direct several new spots, "Threedom Equals Freedom" and "We want to be No. 3," which announced that Snapple knew it was running in third place behind Coke and Pepsi. The company also revived "The Best Stuff on Earth" theme. Finally, Quaker terminated its "risky" associations with Rush Limbaugh and Howard Stern.

Quaker's trouble with Snapple continued, however. Although revenues in the new diet drink segment grew 23 percent in 1996 to nearly 12 percent of total sales, the company continued to struggle. "We have no evidence that [Quaker is] closer to solving Snapple's problems," said Naomi Ghez, food-stock analyst for Goldman, Sachs & Co. Others were more pointed in their comments. "They can't even give Snapple away right" noted *Brandweek*. "What the hell *is* Snapple? No one knows what it means any more," stated Alan Brew, a corporate brand consultant. In the first quarter of 1997, Snapple's market share in the iced tea category dropped another 4.7 points to 16.7 percent. Although it continued to retain its number one position in the juice drink category, the brand had lost 2 share points to its competition.

TRIARC ENTERS THE PICTURE

In 1997, Quaker sold Snapple to the Triarc Beverage Group for $300 million. Triarc was a subsidiary of the Triarc Companies, a holding company run by two buyout specialists, Nelson Peltz and Peter May. Formed in 1929, the Triarc Companies and its predecessor had focused on the specialty chemical, natural gas, and textiles industries. In recent years, the firm had begun to diversify by collecting assets in the food and beverage sectors. By 1996, it had acquired Mistic Brands, a producer of premium non-alcoholic beverages, Arby's Corporation, a national fast food franchise, and Royal Crown, a producer of soft drinks such RC Cola and Diet Rite Cola. Triarc Beverage Group CEO Michael Weinstein commented, "Well, we really think we bought…not a company, but a brand and not only the largest brand in the premium beverage category, but a brand that actually defines what the category is."

The sale was met with mixed reaction. John McMillin, a food industry analyst at Prudential Securities, stated: "It was a fire sale price…The bad news is the investment has been a disaster, the good news is they're trying to put it behind them." Michael Branca, a food industry analyst at Lehman Brothers, expressed a different view, stating, "Triarc's beverage management is highly respected in the beverage distribution business…Snapple could well be reborn under Triarc."

Triarc's Initial Moves with Snapple

While beverage industry analysts predicted that the Snapple brand was doomed for phase-out, Triarc was confident that it could restore Snapple to its pre-Quaker market share and status. At the time of Triarc's purchase of Snapple, consumers had more choices between ready-to-drink beverages than ever before. By mid-1997, the New Age market had undergone yet another shake-up. Pepsi stopped distributing fruit drinks from Ocean Spray and launched its own FruitWorks brand. Other new brands like Nantucket Nectars, a line of 100 percent juice drinks packaged in unique bottles, and Campbell Soup Co.'s V8 Splash, a carrot-based blend of fruit juices targeting younger consumers, had entered the market rapidly and threatened to squeeze out even more market share from Snapple. To breathe life back into Snapple, Triarc invested heavily in new product development and employed dynamic marketing strategies that would differentiate Snapple from competitors and recapture consumer's attention.

Amid much speculation, Weinstein, with the assistance of senior vice president of marketing Ken Gilbert, immediately began the process of rebuilding the brand. Triarc soon announced that it would apply the same marketing principles to Snapple that it used to turn around its successful Mistic beverage line: edgy advertising, strong distributor relationships, colorful labels, and focused street sales. Within weeks, Weinstein met with former Snapple spokeswoman Wendy Kaufman. "If we can just get the brand back to where it was, we've done a great job," said Weinstein. He admitted that bringing Wendy back would not turn Snapple around, but he felt it would signal the return of "speed, fun, innovation and quirkiness." The first set of Snapple ads under Triarc's direction featured Wendy's reappearance on a desert island and the labels of several of Snapple's products featuring Wendy's face to symbolize the return of Snapple to its core values. "Wendy this year is going to do lots of local appearances," said Steve Jarmon, vice president of communications. "We're getting her involved with grass-roots kinds of activities. She draws well."

New Products

One of Triarc's most significant moves to revive the brand was to invest greatly in new product development. Some of new products included:

Whipper Snapple Perhaps the most innovative and important development to emerge out of Triarc's product development efforts was the Whipper Snapple, a fruit smoothie beverage introduced in the summer of 1998. Whipper Snapple aimed at capitalizing on the growing popularity of juice bars and offered the first bottled fruit smoothie to hit the beverage market. Whipper Snapple was touted as a breakthrough product for Snapple because of its unique bottle design and eye-catching labeling, the product's creative name, and the variety of flavors offered including a lineup of "power smoothies" containing popular herbal ingredients such as bee pollen, gingko biloba, and wheat grass aimed at capturing health-conscious consumers.

Sweet Tea To create greater appeal of Snapple among Southerners, Snapple introduced its Sweet Tea product line, which added cane sugar and other sweeteners to traditional Snapple tea recipes to create a Snapple version of the popular Southern beverage. The development of variations of a lemonade iced tea competed with a similar beverage marketed by Nantucket Nectars was begun and expected to reach consumers by 1999.

Snapple Farms Triarc launched Snapple Farms, a 100 percent pure juice drink with the potential to enter the lucrative school lunch market. The fresh and natural approach of the Snapple Farms line was aimed at changing consumer impressions of Snapple as a sugary, unnatural beverage.

Snapple Hydro Snapple Hydro thirst quenchers were re-launched in April 1999 after an unsuccessful try in 1998 under the Refreshers brand name. The range was composed of several fruit juices and two real-brewed sun teas. Snapple Hydro had all the characteristics of a sport beverage: as with Gatorade, it contained sodium electrolytes, which enable the body to replenish the chemicals lost during exercise, and had less sugar than regular sodas. Hydro wanted to be seen as the ideal beverage for health-conscious consumers looking for easy-to-drink refreshment during leisure activities or simply when they were "on the go." Hydro relied on Snapple's keys of success: it offered all-natural ingredients and punchy fruit flavors in an innovative 20-ounce plastic bottle.

Snapple Elements In April 1999, Snapple launched Snapple Elements—a range of six-flavor herbal-enhanced fruit drinks and teas—positioned in the fast-growing Wellness Beverage Category along with SoBe. These new functional drinks were intended to offer more than refreshment. For example, Elements offered health-conscious consumers the benefits of guarana or gingko biloba, for energy and digestibility respectively, combined with the pleasure of great tasting fruit juice or tea. With product names such as Fire, Moon, Sun, or Earth and a "refresh your natural resources" positioning, the new Elements lineup was a means to enhance the healthy product side of Snapple's brand image.

Rejuvenating Snapple's Marketing

Many of Triarc's marketing efforts aimed to recapture the "feel" Snapple had before it was purchased by Quaker (i.e., using off-the-wall marketing techniques such as nationwide contests and unusual bottle labeling). The company once again established a sponsorship agreement with two controversial personalities: shock jock Howard Stern for Snapple and conservative talk show host Rush Limbaugh for Diet Snapple.

In addition to enlisting the help of Wendy Kaufman, "the Snapple Lady," in the brand's marketing program, Triarc sought the attention of consumers through imaginative nationwide promotion campaigns and contests. The "Win Nothing Instantly" contest was a popular 1998 marketing program in which Snapple consumers won unique cash prizes such as "free rent for a year" or "no car payments for six months." Subsequent promotion campaigns focused on using Snapple's packaging and labeling to emphasize the renewed quirkiness of the brand.

Triarc's marketing team hoped that these unusual marketing campaigns would restore "attitude" to the brand and give it the creative buzz it once benefited from while still a leading beverage brand earlier in the decade. As one Triarc executive explained, "This brand is not about marketing b.s., but about having fun, being quirky, having the best stuff—including real people." Recognizing the importance of packaging and labeling of its products to capture the attention of consumers, Snapple executives redesigned the theme of the brand's labels to reflect a woodcut motif to emphasize Snapple's purity. Triarc also began exploring new methods of labeling so as to maximize color quality and reduce the occurrence of label damage.

Triarc's innovative efforts paid off. Despite the continued fierce competitiveness of the beverage market, Triarc slowed Snapple's downslide by boosting sales across the board. In its first year operating Snapple, Triarc sold 100 million more bottles of Snapple than Quaker would have if Quaker's 22 percent first-half sales decline had continued. In fiscal 1998, Triarc increased annual sales for the first time since 1995. Sales of Snapple rose 8 percent in 1998 and contributed significantly to Triarc's 50 percent increase in premium beverage sales that year. "This is a fashion business," commented Havis Dawson of *Beverage World*. "Snapple is coming back into fashion because it's once again asking the question: What's new?"

TRIARC'S PLANS FOR FURTHER GROWTH

With the Snapple brand "back on its feet," Triarc now needed to implement new marketing plans to ensure its continued growth and prosperity. Snapple's marketing program for 1999 was a mixture of traditional and more innovative elements. Triarc's objectives were to re-assert the brand values that helped to build Snapple's success, as well as to keep the brand on a cutting edge and moving forward. Back-to-the-roots advertising campaigns and sponsorship programs, combined with the launch of Snapple's website and an innovative outdoor campaign, were also key points of Snapple's marketing program.

Television Advertising

In April 1999, advertising agency Deutsch N.Y. developed two new commercials advertising Snapple's core fruit juice and iced tea as part of a $27 million television and radio campaign. They both highlighted a strong product-focused message aimed at strengthening the key differentiating asset of Snapple's core products against lower-end competitors. The spots stuck to the premium and all-natural positioning of the brand and emphasized the fact that Snapple was made from real juice. The ads presented the "Little Fruits" characters—actors dressed as bananas, strawberries, lemons, and other Snapple ingredients. One ad played on the idea of Snapple as a "safe home" for "at-risk" fruit. As a narrator informed the audience, "At Snapple, we know the pressure facing young fruit today, and how easy it is to go bad," the ad showed some of the Little Fruits committing crimes against other fruit. These scenes were contrasted with footage of fruit playing music and playing in the grass at the safe home with narration stating, "That's why…we've created a place where good fruit can come and get even better." This product focus was presented in a quirky, off-kilter, not too adversarial tone, as summarized in the tagline, "The Best Stuff Is in Here." The ad was honored by *Adweek* magazine as one of the best ads of 1999.

The campaign included television, radio, outdoor media, and a new communication vehicle, which created impressions of the Snapple logo in the sand across U.S. beaches during the summer of 1999.

Sponsorships

In 1999, Snapple Iced Tea became the official iced tea of the New York Yankees, an appropriate match for the brand given Snapple's Brooklyn roots. A fully integrated marketing program enhanced the local significance and impact of this program. Apart from traditional vending and signage, the newly-launched Sun-Tea and Diet Sun-Tea brands were specially promoted, commercials were aired during the games, and a donation of Yankees home game tickets was organized through a charity. Triarc also signed on Olympic figure skating champion Tara Lipinski as a Snapple spokesperson, promoting the sponsorship with a humorous ad spoofing the association.

Web Site
Snapple launched Snapple.com in May 1999. Designed by SF Interactive, the site was intended to be an active part of Snapple's integrated marketing program. It provided an innovative vehicle to support on-going promotion programs, as well as to relive Snapple's advertising campaign or to unveil novelties. The tone of the website was designed to fit Snapple's brand character, enhancing the humorous side of the brand image and leveraging the graphic look and feel of Snapple equities.

Brand Performance
Following these new marketing efforts, sales of Snapple cases rose 14 percent during the second quarter of 1999. The "New Age" beverage category grew by 15 percent in 1999 and Snapple maintained the number one market share in the category. In 2000, Snapple's had a 40 percent market share and surpassed its 1999 sales numbers.

Snapple introduced its first brand extension in July 2000 in the form of four new candy products—Snapplets hard candy, Beans jelly beans, Fruits chewy candy, and Whirls gummies. The candies all bore the Snapple trademark, but were created and manufactured under license by Cody-Kramer Imports. During the development of these new promotions and products, Snapple's financial performance continued to improve. In the first six months of 2000, Snapple volume increased 27 percent compared with overall juice industry growth of only 11 percent. For that period, Snapple's revenues rose 7 percent from the same six months the previous year to $349.4 million.

Following this success, Triarc spun off the Snapple Beverage Group into its own business unit, which included Snapple, Mistic, Royal Crown, Diet Rite, Stewart's, and Nehi. Triarc Beverage Group CEO Michael Weinstein became the new Snapple Beverage Group CEO.

THE SALE OF SNAPPLE...AGAIN
In September 2000, Cadbury Schweppes announced plans to purchase Snapple Beverage Group for $1.45 billion (12 times the estimated EBITDA for Snapple Beverage Group). Triarc expected to gain $700 million from the sale. Careful to avoid making the same mistakes as Quaker Oats, Cadbury kept Snapple management intact, preserved the company's headquarters in Long Island, NY, and maintained the existing distribution system. Michael Weinstein remained CEO of the Snapple Beverage Group, which Cadbury administered separately from its Doctor Pepper/Seven Up unit. The acquisition of the Snapple Beverage Group gave Cadbury a 2 percent boost in its share of the overall (carbonated and non-carbonated) refreshment beverage market.

Cadbury had high hopes for synergies and cost benefits that could be gained from the purchase. The company identified nearly $500 million in cost saving opportunities that included savings in manufacturing and distribution, administration and systems, and raw material procurement. Cadbury also planned on significant potential revenue synergies by expanding Snapple distribution, while at the same time selling more Mott's, Dr. Pepper, and 7UP products through the extensive Snapple distribution system. The company even had plans to extend the Snapple brand to Cadbury's existing confections business.

The purchase of Snapple Beverage Group also made Cadbury a leader in non-carbonated premium New Age beverages, which according to Cadbury COO John Brock, "Put [Cadbury] in an outstanding position to compete."[2] Considering that Triarc bought Snapple from Quaker in 1997 for $300 million, its sale to Cadbury represented the final step in Snapple's turnaround in the hands of Triarc management.

Cadbury Schweppes Takes Over

Cadbury Schweppes was a major international company with origins stretching back over 200 years. Cadbury, based in the United Kingdom, had over 58,000 employees worldwide and a market capitalization of over $20 billion. The company was organized around five regional operating units: Americas Beverages, Americas Confectionary, Europe, Middle East, and Africa, Europe Beverages, and Asia Pacific (see Exhibit 3). The Americas Beverages group sold a broad range of beverages, including carbonated drinks, fruit juices, iced teas, and water. The biggest brands in this group were Dr. Pepper, Mott's, Snapple, 7UP, Hawaiian Punch, Sunkist, and A&W. Dr. Pepper was the most important carbonated soft drink brand and accounted for almost half of U.S. carbonate sales.

Cadbury had pursued an aggressive strategy of acquisitions since buying the Snapple Beverage Group. In 2003, the company purchased long-time Snapple rival Nantucket Nectars for an undisclosed sum. Also that year, Cadbury acquired Adams Confections for $4.2 billion, bringing the Halls, Trident, and Dentyne brands under Cadbury's control.

Competitive Environment

With an ever-increasing number of beverage categories (teas, juices, energy drinks, meal replacements, water, etc.), competition among beverage producers remained fierce. In 2002, *Beverage World* reported that 1,235 new beverage products were introduced in the United States alone. By November of 2003, only 250 of those products were still on the market. This was not a surprise to those in the industry—the failure rate for new beverage products had hovered at the 80 percent mark for years. In this environment, it was fully expected for Snapple to encounter significant competition. Many Snapple products, including Whipper Snapple, Snapple Farms, and Snapple Hydro, were either unsuccessful or discontinued to make room for new products (see Exhibit 4 for list of "Retired Flavors" and Exhibit 5 for growth estimates of Snapple revenues).

New Advertising

In 2001, Snapple added some "edge" to its advertising. The company retained the "Little Fruits" characters, and cast them in ads themed around reproduction and jail. One ad showed the fruit attending a sex-education seminar where the instructor read from "The Joys of Ripening." Footage of a lime studying a centerfold in *Peeled* (the fruit equivalent of *Playboy*), a raspberry and lemon discovered in a compromising position in a closet, and a banana and strawberry locked in an embrace along the shore of a beach plays before the ad concludes, "With fruit joined together, it's a very special thing—at Snapple." Another spot featuring a prison was titled "Where Bad Fruit Go."

In summer 2001, Snapple introduced a new energy beverage called Venom, designed to compete with the likes of Red Bull, Coca-Cola's KMX, and Anheuser-Busch's 180. Venom contained the equivalent caffeine of one cup of coffee and was flavored with a blend of citrus and juniper. Like other energy drinks, Venom was priced above $2.00 for a slender 8-ounce can. Venom initially received no advertising support.

In 2002, Cadbury developed a new advertising campaign to replace the "Little Fruits" spots, which had been running since 1998. Created by the ad agency Deutsch, this "Bottles Personified" series featured an anthropomorphized Snapple bottle in a number of real-life situations. The ads targeted many demographics, including 18–24 year-olds who wanted to be different, fun-seeking 12 year-olds, and core Snapple consumers in their 30s and 40s. The campaign also involved a promotion, called "What's your story?" that asked consumers to share humorous anecdotes from their lives. Winning entries were then "acted out" by animated Snapple bottles in nationally-televised commercials. These included a performance of a boy band made from dressed-up Snapple bottles, and a wild house party filled with Snapple bottle teens that comes to a halt when the parent Snapple bottles come home.

Snapple took the campaign one step further in the summer of 2002 by launching the Dye Hard Snapple Tour. This 13-city extravaganza included Snapple chugging contests, music, and a mobile barbershop that gave participants mullet-enabling hair extensions, gaudy dye jobs, and in some cases, Mohawk haircuts. The tour attracted audiences as large as 50,000 in some cities and huge media attention. By Snapple's account, the 14,000 mile tour generated more than 70 million PR impressions.

Other ads in the "Bottles Personified" campaign included wig-wearing Snapple bottles performing as a heavy metal band, bottles peeking in showers a la *Porky's*, and a King-Kong spoof, where a giant robot attacks a city, and stops only to pick up a lovely young woman (portrayed by a Diet Snapple Peach). One billboard ad caused some controversy in 2002. It showed two bottles with hair and Delta Omega Delta ball caps in a fraternity house looking smug over a prostrate pledge. A broken pledge paddle sits nearby. This ad prompted an e-mail campaign to Snapple headquarters, complaining that the ad, depicting violence, was targeted at teens. Overall, however, the campaign was effective; *Beverage Digest* reported that Snapple's volume rose 3.2 percent for the first nine months of 2003, while the category shrank 0.9 percent.

"Official" Beverage of New York City

Building off the 1999 announcement that Snapple was the official iced tea of the New York Yankees, Snapple and City of New York announced a five-year, $166 million vending and marketing agreement in 2003. The agreement made Snapple the exclusive provider (via vending machines) of water and fruit juices in the City's 1,200 schools. Proceeds from vending machines were used to support sports and physical education programs. Outside of schools, another agreement made Snapple the official iced tea, water, and chocolate drink (Yoo-hoo) for vending machines in the City.

There were some initial problems with the deal. New York agreed to sell 750,000 cases of Snapple in city buildings and parks during the first year. However, after seven months into the deal, only 26,000 cases had been sold.

Continuing Innovation at Snapple

While pursuing these other marketing efforts, Snapple continued to introduce new and exotic flavors and announce them in creative ways. In a 2002 tongue-in-cheek press release titled "Apricot and Orange Tie the Knot on Valentine's Day," the company wrote, "Snapple announces a fruit-ful union—the marriage of Ms. Apricot to Mr. Orange on Valentine's Day. The new couple, and unexpected pairing of Apricot and Orange, will go by the name of Snapricot Orange and will reside in Snapple's signature bottle." [3]

Snapple unveiled other new products around other special days. Just in time for April Fool's Day 2003, Snapple announced its new Kiwi Teawi Iced Tea. Sporting an upside-down label, Snapple encouraged consumers to "Flip your hat, turn your shirt backwards, and keep a bottle close by your side—if anyone asks why you're dressed so oddly, reply, 'The Kiwi in me did it'." [4] Just two weeks later, Snapple took advantage of early-April tax season anxiety by proclaiming, "Whether you're going crazy or handling the season in stride, Snapple hears your tax day needs and just in time for April 15th has created the new 'Go Bananas' juice drink." [5] In honor of its 2004 drink "What-A-Melon," Snapple offered a $25,000 prize and a year's supply of the drink to anyone who could break the world record for growing the world's largest watermelon.

Snapple entered the meal replacement market in 2003 with "Snapple-a-Day." Touting it as a "Delicious way to keep fit," Snapple-a-Day contained 24 essential minerals and vitamins as well as calcium, fiber, and protein. The product, squarely aimed at meal replacement stalwarts Slim-Fast and Ensure, was offered in a resealable plastic bottle that eliminated the metallic taste that Snapple claimed its competitors had, and allowed consumers to drink the beverage while "on the run." Snapple soon followed with a low-carb version in three different flavors.

In the summer of 2004 Snapple began licensing its name and flavors to the lip balm company Lotta Luv. Lotta Luv produced Snapple-flavored lip balms flavors such as Kiwi Teawi, Pink Lemonade, Go Bananas, and Fruit Punch. The products were sold in containers that resembled screw top Snapple bottle caps. Prices ranged from $2.50 to $5.00.

In 2005, Snapple launched Diet Lemonade Iced Tea and Diet Plum-A-Granate (plum and pomegranate-flavored) Iced Tea. These flavors were promoted as part of Snapple's "Return the Favor" series, where customers said nice things about Snapple and then Snapple finds people to say nice things about the customer. More importantly, these spots marked the return of Wendy Kaufman to Snapple's advertising efforts. She provided narration for the television, radio, and Internet ads.

In 2006, Snapple launched three new television spots under the "Baby Steps" series. "Revolving Door," "Recliner," and "Treadmill" all highlighted the benefits of the antioxidants that naturally were in Snapple's iced teas products. The three spots took on a humorous tone. In "Treadmill" an average looking guy in his early 30s held up a Diet Snapple and said to the camera, "Diet Snapple Iced Tea has antioxidants so it's better for me. Kind of makes me want to start doing other things that are better for me." Loud, triumphant music played as the man turned to the treadmill in his apartment and plugged it in. The music stopped suddenly and the man took a sip of his Snapple and walked out of the room. A Snapple voiceover explained, "Diet Snapple. A baby step to a better you."

That same year, Snapple introduced Snapple White Tea to help reverse its sliding market share in the tea category.[6] White Tea was made from young white tea leaves and produced a lighter flavor with fewer calories than Snapple's other tea flavors. Snapple launched three flavors—Green Apple, Nectarine, and Raspberry, and used the slogan, "The Lightest Tea on Earth." Jim Trebilcock, Snapple's senior vice president of brand management explained the strategy, "Antioxidants and nutritional benefits of tea are placing the spotlight on non-carbonated beverages. We want to bring this to Snapple drinkers."[7] Television commercials were planned to air in late 2006.

CONCLUSION

As the beverage landscape became increasingly competitive in the mid-2000s, Cadbury moved Mott's and Snapple into a combined facility outside New York City, which completed the integration of the North America Beverages operation into a unified entity. This move also further distanced Snapple from its roots as an independent upstart. Despite rising sales in 2005, which followed three years of declines, Snapple continued to lose share in the iced tea market (see Exhibit 6 for Snapple revenues).

Due to the increasingly competitive environment, many industry analysts believed that Cadbury would spin-off the Americas Beverage business, or the overall beverage business. When questioned on this point in December 2004, Todd Stitzer, Cadbury's CEO, said that Cadbury was committed to the beverage business for the foreseeable future. When pushed to give a more direct answer to the possibility of a spin-off, Stitzer replied, "I never say never."[8] Snapple, which had survived a series of corporate owners, would likely remain intact following another sale or spin-off. The brand was not performing as well as it had at its peak, however, and Cadbury hoped that additional consumers would be attracted by marketing activities conveying Snapple's independent spirit, while at the same time realizing efficiencies by combining Snapple with its other American beverage operations.

DISCUSSION QUESTIONS

1. How would you characterize Snapple's brand image and sources of brand equity? What are the strengths and weaknesses of the brand's existing personality and image?

2. Where did Quaker go wrong? What could it have done differently? Is Cadbury in danger of making the same mistakes as Quaker did?

3. How effective and appropriate do you think Triarc's marketing program was? How effective and appropriate do you think Cadbury's marketing program is? What changes, if any, would you recommend Cadbury make to Snapple marketing?

4. How has Snapple's sale to Cadbury affected Snapple's equity? Are there dangers of the brand's association with a large corporation?

5. What do you think Cadbury's next moves with Snapple should be? Should the company attempt to expand or reposition Snapple? Should Cadbury spin-off its Americas Beverages group?

Exhibit 1: List of Snapple Flavors in 2006

Teas	Lime Green Tea	Mint Tea
	Very Cherry Tea	Peach Tea
	Caffeine Free Lemon Tea	Raspberry Tea
	Lemon Tea	Kiwi Teawi
	Just Plain Tea Unsweetened	

Juices	Snapricot Orange	Mango Madness
	Snapple Apple	Orangeade
	Cranberry Raspberry	Raspberry Peach
	Fruit Punch	Summer Peach
	Kiwi Strawberry	Go Bananas
	What-a-Melon	

| Lemonade | Lemonade Iced Tea | Pink Lemonade |
| | Lemonade | Super Sour Lemonade |

Diet drinks	Lime Green Tea	Peach Tea
	Pink Lemonade	Raspberry Tea
	Cranberry Raspberry	Kiwi Strawberry
	Lemon Tea	Orange Carrot
	Snapple Apple	Lemonade Iced Tea
	Plum-a-Granate Iced Tea	

Snapple-a-Day		
	Strawberry Banana	Tropical Blend
	Peach	

Elements		
	Metal (orange)	Venom (citrus)
	Fire (dragonfruit)	Rain (agave cactus)
	Subzero (cherry)	Meteor (tangelo)

Exhibit 2: Selected Beverage Market Segments and a Partial List of Competitors

Segment	Competitor (parent company)
Teas	Nestea (Coca-Cola) Lipton (PepsiCo) Arizona (Arizona)
Juices	Minute Made, Hi-C, (Coca-Cola) VeryFine, Capri-Sun (Kraft) Tropicana, Dole (PepsiCo) Sunny Delight (Procter & Gamble) V8 (Campbell Soup) SoBe (PepsiCo)
Energy drinks	Red Bull Monster (Hansen) Adrenaline Rush, No Fear (SoBe) KMX (Coca-Cola) Amp (PepsiCo) Frappuccino, DoubleShot (PepsiCo/Starbucks) 180 (Anheuser-Busch)
Water	Dasani (Coca-Cola) Aquafina (PepsiCo) VitaminWater (Glaceau) Evian (Group Danone) Poland Spring (Nestle)
Meal replacements	Ensure (Abbott Laboratories) Slim-Fast (Unilever) Advantage Shakes (Atkins) Odwalla (Coca-Cola)

Exhibit 3:   Cadbury Schweppes' Operating Units and Operating Profits

(percentage of total 2005 revenues)

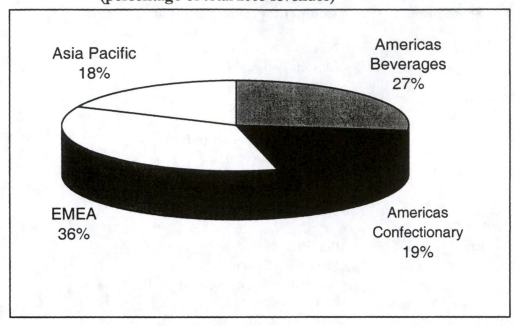

Source: Company reports

Exhibit 4: Snapple's "Retired Flavors" as of 2006

Snap-Up/Snapple Sport
Fruit Flavored	Lemon	Lemon Lime
Orange		

Snapple Refreshers
Lemon Sport	Mountain Grape	Orange Punch
Sport Punch	Strawberry Lemon	Strawberry Melon
Whipper Snapple		

Teas
Cactus Tea	Cider Tea	Cranberry Iced Tea
Diet Sun Tea	Ginseng Tea	Green Tea with Lemon
Lemon Sun Tea	Mango Iced Tea	Orange Iced Tea
Orange Jasmine	Passion Fruit Iced Tea	Peach Sun Tea
Strawberry Iced Tea	Sun Tea	Sweet Tea
Just Plain Tea Sweetened		

Juice drinks
Apple Cherry	Bali Blast	Grape Watermelon
Guava Mania	Papaya Colada	Samoan Splash
Strawberry	Ralph's Cantaloupe Cocktail	

100% Juice
Amazin' Grape	Apple Crisp	Apple 'N Cherry
Apricot Royale	Cranberry Grapefruit	Cranberry Royale
Dixie Peach	Grapefruit Juice	Papaya Holiday
Passion Supreme	Pineapple Juice	Pink Grapefruit
Raspberry Royale	Straight Grape	Strawberry Royale

Lemonades
Raspberry Lemonade	Strawberry Lemonade	Sun Lemonade

Sodas
Diet Lemon Lime	Ginger Ale	Jamaican Ginger Beer
Kiwi Peach	Passion Supreme	Peach Melba
Raspberry Royale	Strawberry	

Seltzers
Black Cherry	Lemon Lime	Original
Tangerine		

Exhibit 4 (cont.)

Diets

Diet Mango Madness   Diet White Grape   Diet Ruby Red

Exhibit 5: Growth of Estimated Snapple Beverage Group Revenues

Brand	1997/98	1998/99	1999/00	2000/01	2001/02
Elements Teas	–	–	-4.0%	-16.7%	-70.0%
Regular Teas	12.9%	1.9%	9.8%	12.0%	-12.4%
Snapple Teas	**12.9%**	**9.3%**	**8.9%**	**10.3%**	**-14.9%**
Elements Juices	–	–	92.0%	-12.2%	-18.0%
WhipperSnapple	–	-40.0%	-73.3%	-83.8%	-76.9%
Regular Juices	-15.1%	-2.3%	2.3%	11.0%	0.3%
Snapple Juices	**7.1%**	**3.7%**	**5.2%**	**2.5%**	**-3.9%**
All Other Snapple					
Mistic Teas	0.0%	-7.7%	-58.3%	-16.0%	-26.2%
Mistic Juices	-16.4%	-3.1%	-9.6%	-19.4%	-18.4%
Stewart's	16.0%	17.2%	14.7%	1.8%	15.6%
Orangina				5.2%	-5.2%
Yoo-hoo				4.0%	-3.4%
Nantucket Nectars				4.8%	17.4%
TOTAL	**4.3%**	**6.6%**	**3.3%**	**3.1%**	**-1.4%**

Source: Beverage Marketing Corp.

Exhibit 6: Snapple Beverage Group Revenues

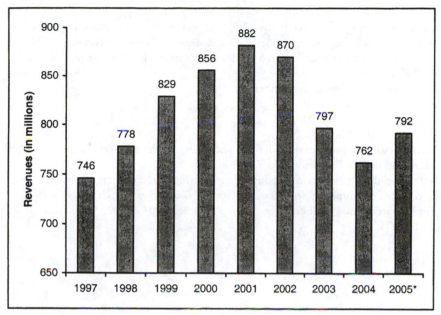

* Estimate
Source: Beverage Marketing Corp.

REFERENCES

1 This case was written by Eric Free (Fuqua '98), and was revised and updated by Jonathan Michaels and Lowey Bundy Sichol, under the supervision of Professor Kevin Lane Keller. Research assistance was provided by Peter Gilmore, Dartmouth '99, Emmanuelle Louis Hofer, and Keith Richey.

2 As quoted in Beverage Digest, September 18, 2000.

3 Snapple press release, January 30, 2002.

4 Snapple press release, March 20, 2003.

5 Snapple press release, April 6, 2003.

6 Information Resources Inc. Total food, drug, and mass merchandise (excluding Wal-Mart) for the 52 weeks ending December 25, 2005.

7 Jessie Male. "Drinks for everyone: options are multiplying in the beverage aisle, reflecting the wide range of consumer lifestyle choices. *Grocery Headquarters*. March 1, 2006.

8 Bernstein Research Call. "Cadbury Schweppes: Reiterated 2004 & 2005 Guidance." December 16, 2004.

ACCENTURE:
REBRANDING A GLOBAL BRAND[1]

INTRODUCTION

Andersen Consulting was established in 1989 when the consulting practice of the accounting firm Arthur Andersen separated to form an independent business unit. Andersen Consulting faced the extremely difficult task of positioning itself in the Information Technology market space while simultaneously forging an identity separate from its accounting heritage. The business challenge was to retain the positive aspects of the brand equity developed over decades at Arthur Andersen, yet break away from the limitations associated with an accounting brand. Notably, Andersen's consulting practice was generating almost $1 billion annually in revenue before its formal inception, yet it wasn't well known in the information technology marketplace. To those who did know the consultants, they were often thought of accountants, and not up to the task of delivering innovative technology solutions.

In order to bridge this gap, Andersen Consulting set a groundbreaking precedent by using sophisticated marketing strategies coupled with the professional services industry's first large-scale advertising campaign to promote its name, positioning, and brand image. Andersen Consulting's expertise in marketing and communications quickly set it apart from its consulting competitors, making a name for itself amidst a crowded competitive field ranging from hardware/software providers like IBM to strategy consulting firms like McKinsey. Over the next decade, Andersen Consulting grew from an accounting firm's offshoot into the world's largest management and technology consulting organization.

In part due to this success, the relationship between Arthur Andersen and Andersen Consulting became strained over time, leading Andersen Consulting to seek its independence as a separate company from Arthur Andersen. In August 2000, following a successful arbitration against Andersen Worldwide and Arthur Andersen, Andersen Consulting was granted its independence. The firm then faced a tremendous new challenge. As part of the ruling granting its independence, the license to use the Andersen Consulting name was to expire December 31, 2000. After spending an estimated $7 billion[2] building the Andersen Consulting brand over a decade, the company now had to find, implement, and introduce to the world a new name in a matter of months. Never before had a rebranding of such scope been implemented over so short a timeframe. Moreover, this rebranding also coincided with a new positioning that reflected the organization's further growth and broadened set of capabilities.

COMPANY HISTORY

In 1913, Northwestern University economics professor Arthur Andersen, then 28 years old, founded the accounting firm Arthur Andersen & Co. He envisioned an accounting firm that offered more than the standard certifications of corporate balance sheets. In his mind, a "thoroughly trained accountant [possessed] a sound understanding of the principles of economics, of finance and of organization."[3]

Arthur Andersen & Co. created an early version of the consulting unit when it formed the Administrative Accounting group in 1942. The Administrative Accounting practice was charged with developing accounting systems, methods, and procedures for Arthur Andersen clients. In the 1950s, Arthur Andersen began offering consulting services to companies wishing to implement information systems, and renamed the unit the Administrative Services Division. Consultants from the company programmed and installed the world's first business computer for General Electric in 1954. Demand for information systems rose, and by the 1970s the Administrative Services Division broadened the scope of its business beyond "the design and implementation of systems" to include "the conduct of studies to produce the information needed by management to direct the activities of its organization."[4]

In 1979, what was once the Administrative Services Division of Arthur Andersen became the Management Information Consulting Division (MICD). MICD performed a range of consulting services defined as "Information Business—providing information to people who run things."[5]

CONSULTING TAKES OFF

The consulting business boomed in the 1980s, particularly because a national recession forced companies to rethink their strategies—with the help of consultants—in order to stay competitive. As a result, MICD began generating significant profits for the accounting firm. Though MICD operated as a professional services firm, it functioned as a unit of Arthur Andersen. However, when MICD went to market, it went to market as Arthur Andersen, not as MICD. Consequently, MICD's identity was directly linked to Arthur Andersen. This link did not necessarily benefit MICD. The qualities typically associated with accounting firms, such as risk-aversion and conservatism, did not match the traits essential for a consulting organization—innovative, creative, dynamic, and strategic. As a result, Arthur Andersen's MICD division suffered low visibility and suffered from the perception that it was not a major player in the consulting market.

A 1982 recruiting image study conducted by Decision Research advised MICD that its recruiting efforts "must convince recruits that the Consulting Division is not primarily an accounting function." A 1984 study by Decision Research concluded that MICD's "image among non-clients [was] undifferentiated from the remainder of the Big 8 [accounting firms]."[6]

Image Initiative

To respond to this image crisis, MICD decided to embark on an "Image Initiative" in 1987 to generate awareness and to differentiate itself in the information technology services market space, as well as to distance itself from its accountancy heritage image. A critical component of the Image Initiative was the selection of a new name for MICD.

Relying on the benefits of sound market research, and the counsel of its marketing advisors, MICD chose the succinct "Andersen Consulting" name, thus providing separation from Arthur Andersen while at the same time benefiting from its equity. The name also created a clear positioning in the market space with the "consulting" descriptor. When the logo appeared in print, "Andersen Consulting" was followed by the subscript tagline "Arthur Andersen & Co., S.C." the firm therefore retained a link to Arthur Andersen. The association with Arthur Andersen lent credibility and name-recognition to the firm at first, but became a liability as Andersen Consulting encountered greater competition in the consulting market. An article in *The Economist* noted, "The 'safety-first' image so vital to accountancy began to hurt the consulting business, which competed in a market where a reputation for innovation was the key to success."[7]

ROLE OF MARKETING

The newly formed Andersen Consulting set a new standard for marketing a professional services company. It was widely credited for being the first professional services firm to advertise aggressively. The professional services category historically had formal rules that prevented advertising, but by 1989 this restriction was no longer in place. Still, most professional services firms chose not to advertise, feeling it was inappropriate or unprofessional. In a bold and unprecedented step, Andersen Consulting began marketing itself as an organization that helped companies apply technology to create business advantage. A small group of partners knew that marketing activities would be invaluable in Andersen Consulting's quest to forge an independent identity. Teresa Poggenpohl, partner and Director of Global Advertising and Brand Management explained that the group of partners "understood marketing in a strategic sense and had the courage to create the brand and invest in it" at a time when branding was not a priority for professional services firms.

Breakthrough Approaches

The Andersen Consulting brand was officially launched in 1989 with a New Year's campaign featuring a television commercial that stressed Andersen Consulting's technological expertise, positioning them as a leader in empowering organizations and individuals to effectively apply technology to their business advantage. The commercial also demonstrated the differentiation that Andersen Consulting sought with its clever tone and manner, thus personifying the organization as creative, driven, far-sighted, and innovative. As the camera panned a computer-animated cityscape where the 2000 New Year was being counted down, a voiceover intoned:

> One night, not too many years from now, some companies will have cause for celebration. They'll be the ones who used information and technology not merely as a way to compute, but as a way to compete. Andersen Consulting would like to help you be one of them.

The campaign also featured print advertising to complement the broadcast commercials. Andersen Consulting spent approximately $5 million in advertising during its first year, which at the time was a full 50 percent of all media expenditures for the entire consulting category. This level of expenditure, combined with the use of flighted media schedules (alternating periods of high advertising activity with

355

inactivity to create the illusion of a more ambitious advertising program), was highly unorthodox within the consulting industry. The vast majority of consulting companies favored business relationships, trade shows and credentials brochures to image advertising.

Andersen Consulting's break with tradition had been the subject of an internal debate, with many partners opposing what they regarded as a costly risk. Once the marketing program was in place, however, it turned out to be instrumental in Andersen Consulting's early success. Teresa Poggenpohl credited the early image work with being "the catalyst to get senior executive registration of the Andersen Consulting brand, serving as a critical door opener for partners and business development."[8] Complementing its extensive advertising program, the firm also initiated an aggressive and targeted media relations program. A team of media specialists within Andersen Consulting partnered with Burson-Marsteller, a leading public relations firm, to influence industry analysts, leading industry publications, and the tier-one business press to position Andersen Consulting as a thought leader in the market space.

Metrics to Drive Performance

Andersen Consulting sought consistency in its marketing activities. Market research was critical in obtaining valuable input from its key target audience, while also measuring the success of its initiatives. The partners continually demanded proof that the results of the
advertising warranted the expenditures. Because the advertising investment was drawn directly from the partners' potential profits, they needed assurance that their money was well spent. This led to the development of efficient and effective marketing techniques as well as metrics to gauge the effectiveness of the marketing.

From its inception, Andersen Consulting conducted extensive market research focusing on five factors: 1) marketplace awareness—the measure of brand awareness in each of the major countries across brand attributes, personality traits, and service offerings; 2) client satisfaction—the measure of Andersen Consulting's performance with its global client base; 3) buyer values—the measure of the key values of its global target audience to understand and stay ahead of market trends; 4) advertising copy testing—the pre- and post-testing measuring the effectiveness of all print, poster, and television advertising concepts; and (5) media monitoring—the measure of the number and type of media hits in the leading business and industry press. In 1988, Andersen Consulting initiated a tracking study of market awareness of its name. At that time, on an unaided basis only 6 percent of respondents nationally knew of Andersen Consulting as a systems integration consultancy, a number that would climb to 37 percent globally in five years. For comparison, IBM had 90 percent awareness.

ANDERSEN CONSULTING ADVANCES

The consulting business experienced tremendous growth in the 1980s, ballooning to an estimated $30 billion annual business globally in 1990 from just $3 billion in 1980. While a U.S. recession in the 1980s had driven growth, a similar recession in the early 1990s was not as beneficial to consulting firms. The latter downturn affected consulting firms more severely than the companies they counted on for revenue, partly because the business climate of the previous decade had fostered corporate distrust of consultancies. Additionally, corporations wanted changes implemented, not merely suggested, and not every consulting firm was able to execute the strategy it recommended. Numerous consulting firms posted losses for the first time in years, and many were forced to heed their own advice and downsize. Andersen Consulting grew, however, even as the consulting industry faltered. During its first few years as a separate business unit, Andersen Consulting emerged as one of the premier IT consultancies. In 1991, the company's revenues rose 20 percent to $2.26 billion. Andersen Consulting's revenues grew another 19 percent to $2.7 billion in 1992, a year when the IT consultancy segment grew by under 7 percent.

Developing Global Advertising

As the marketplace continued to evolve, Andersen Consulting anticipated and moved with it, taking a major step in global branding by developing a globally integrated advertising program in 1994. Prior to that year, Andersen Consulting advertising either originated in the United States for export to different international markets, or select markets created their own advertising campaigns. As the firm's business focus became more global, Andersen Consulting began developing an advertising program that projected globally consistent images and messages across all media and was powerful in all local markets. The firm conducted rigorous focus group testing in the United States, Europe, Japan, and Australia to determine which ad concepts would help Andersen Consulting achieve the desired image, positioning, and messaging. In part due to this diligent research approach, the company and its advertising agency, Young & Rubicam, earned many advertising awards over the years, including the *Wall Street Journal* top scoring advertising award and the *Business Week* Award for Excellence in Corporate Advertising.

For efficiency, and to ensure a highly targeted strategy for its global campaign, Andersen Consulting sought advertising paths that targeted key prospects and clients where they lived and worked, targeting business publications and business and news television programming. An example was the company's development of airport billboard advertising. Andersen Consulting was the first consulting company to embrace airports as a marketing opportunity in the mid-1990s. Its message stood out, with billboard style advertisements in prominent, high-traffic areas near airline executive lounges in over 30 airports worldwide. The airport advertising strategy complemented traditional print and television advertising, surrounding a captive audience of key prospects and clients where they lived and worked.

The firm's advertising appeared in 18 countries in 1994, up from just five the previous year. Another significant development for Andersen Consulting in 1994 was its international sports sponsorships strategy. That year the company became a sponsor for the Williams Formula One racing team. In 1994 Andersen Consulting also became the title sponsor of the then titled Andersen Consulting World Championship of Golf. This event evolved into its present day form as one component of the World Golf Championships entitled the Accenture Match Play Championship.

Measurable Results

In just half a decade, Andersen Consulting's marketing and communications program achieved noticeable results. Awareness in Europe increased approximately 75 percent in three years, while awareness in the United States increased from 6 percent to 50 percent. Additionally, between 1990 and 1993, total global awareness of Andersen Consulting grew from 32 percent to 79 percent. Awareness levels for the firm as a business reengineering services provider increased from 26 percent in 1993 to 43 percent in 1997. A study conducted in 1997 by industry analyst IDC found that Andersen Consulting and IBM enjoyed the greatest familiarity among technology buyers.

Andersen Consulting's status as an IT leader was a source of equity that aided the company in its growth during the early 1990s. Other associations for clients and prospects included "creative and innovative in developing applications," "visionary," and "leader." Thus, the firm was known not only for its technological capabilities, but also for its strategy consulting. In little over five years, with the help of effective advertising and a proven record for results, Andersen Consulting had earned a reputation as one of the premier consultancies in the world. By 1998, they were the market leader in four major categories in consumer rankings of consulting firms: 1) management and technology consulting, 2) operational strategy consulting, 3) systems integration, and 4) business reengineering.[9]

CONFLICTS WITH ARTHUR ANDERSEN

As Andersen Consulting continued to prosper, Arthur Andersen was also changing as an organization. A 1990 agreement allowed the accounting unit of the parent company Andersen Worldwide to establish a non-computer consulting practice for businesses with annual revenue under $175 million. The consultants and accountants agreed that each company would provide "separate, complementary services with minimal overlap"[10] in order to limit competitive crossover. As Arthur Andersen expanded its business capabilities over the next several years to include consulting services similar to those offered by Andersen Consulting, the distinction between the two companies was further eroded. This overlap created confusion in the marketplace.

Exploring Marketplace Confusion

Over time, Arthur Andersen also began using marketing as a tool to build business. In 1993, Andersen Consulting hired the OmniTech Consulting Group to research client and potential client perceptions of the confusing relationship between Arthur Andersen and Andersen Consulting. OmniTech concluded that by developing a willfully ambiguous advertising campaign, Arthur Andersen was attempting to leverage Andersen Consulting's brand image. A different study, also conducted by OmniTech, discovered that respondents were capable of differentiating the two brands to a satisfactory extent until Arthur Andersen advertisements were introduced to the group, at which point the differentiation lessened. Ultimately, OmniTech concluded "despite the favorable brand identity for Andersen Consulting, brand confusion is a major and growing issue for Andersen Consulting."[11]

Because this confusion resulted in loss of potential clients, Andersen Consulting kept a close watch on the issue after the OmniTech report. A domestic awareness tracking study from 1994 reported that 41 percent of senior-level executive respondents and 81 percent of CEOs surveyed expressed confusion about the relationship between Arthur Andersen and Andersen Consulting.

Arthur Andersen Business Consulting

Arthur Andersen combined several practices within the firm to create Arthur Andersen Business Consulting in 1994. Soon after its formation, Arthur Andersen Business Consulting targeted companies above the $175 million ceiling and offered computer-systems consulting. A research report from the Gartner Group remarked, "If this expansion of services by AA continues, we could see these two organizations becoming direct competitors. This would confuse clients and the market."[12] Adding to the confusion was the media, who at times referred to both Arthur Andersen Business Consulting and Andersen Consulting as "Arthur Andersen Consulting." Mistakes such as these were made in major publications like the *Wall Street Journal* and *Dow Jones News*, as well as in Associated Press articles.

Arthur Andersen commissioned a Global Reputation Study, which reported that Andersen Consulting enjoyed a stronger image than Arthur Andersen, and consequently Arthur Andersen benefited from confusion with Andersen Consulting. Further proof of this benefit to Arthur Andersen was evidenced by awareness tracking studies from 1994 and 1995 (see Exhibit 1). Not only did awareness levels for Arthur Andersen move consistently with Andersen Consulting levels, but the accounting unit also enjoyed relatively high levels of awareness for service categories in which the firm had little market presence. For example, Arthur Andersen achieved a high awareness score in the "strategy consulting" category despite the fact that the company had almost no corporate strategy practice.

CAPITALIZING ON SUCCESS

The mid-1990s was a time of great success for Andersen Consulting. From 1994 to 1997, consumer perceptions of Andersen Consulting improved considerably. The percentage that agreed that the firm was "creative" grew from 44 percent in 1994 to 58 percent in 1997 and the percentage of respondents who considered the firm a "leader" rose from 48 percent in 1994 to 68 percent in 1997. The firm's client retention percentage rose from 55 percent to 70 percent between 1993 and 1997. Andersen Consulting reaped financial successes as well. From 1993 to 1998, the firm's billings grew an average of 20 percent annually, reaching $8.2 billion in 1998. The firm's revenues continued to grow until they topped $11 billion in 2001.

"A-to-the-Power-of-C" Rebranding

In an effort to evolve and stay ahead of the marketplace, an 18-month comprehensive review of Andersen Consulting was undertaken in 1998. This analysis produced a revised positioning to reflect the move to an eCommerce business environment. Andersen Consulting also sought to extend and strengthen its brand image by updating the corporate logo. Previously, the company had removed the "Arthur Andersen & Co., S.C." tagline from its name and all related materials to emphasize the distinction and separation from Arthur Andersen. Now, the firm wished to overhaul its logo to reflect its new brand positioning and further distance it from Arthur Andersen in look and feel.

The new logo used the initials "AC" in a unique way, with a lower-case "c" resting above and to the right of the upper-case "A." This graphic identity was drawn from the exponential notation in mathematics, so the logo communicated "A" raised to the "c" power. Other aspects of the revised branding and logo included the concept of a "foundation line," which represented a firm business foundation and stability in a changing world, a 24-color palette demonstrating the company's range of capabilities for diverse application across all marketing and communications materials and a new musical "aural signature" for use in television, video, and multimedia applications.

To inform its global audience of its new image, Andersen Consulting committed to expanding and strengthening its global marketing efforts. Midway through 1998 (and continuing over the next two years), Andersen Consulting boosted its global marketing and communications commitment significantly, two-thirds of which was slated for use outside the U.S. The campaign included print and airport poster advertising in 30 countries. Half of the budget went towards corporate sponsorships, which included events such as a Van Gogh exhibit in Washington D.C. during the fall of 1998, the 1998 Andersen Consulting Match Play Championship, and Formula One auto racing.

SPLITTING FROM ARTHUR ANDERSEN

In mid-December 1997, Andersen Consulting sought to split from Arthur Andersen. Citing "breaches of contract and irreconcilable differences," Andersen Consulting filed arbitration with the International Court of Arbitration in Paris that would force the two business units to formally separate.

360

At issue were the annual payments Andersen Consulting had to yield to Arthur Andersen under the terms of their 1989 agreement and the expansion by Arthur Andersen as a direct competitor into IT consulting. When the two firms split in 1989, they agreed that the more profitable of the two would pay the other a portion of annual profits no greater than 15 percent. As the more profitable company, Andersen Consulting transferred over $450 million to Arthur Andersen from 1989 to 1997, with payments for 1997 totaling $173 million. By 1996, Arthur Andersen Business Consulting was offering a range of IT services and directly competing with Andersen Consulting for clients. That year, Arthur Andersen's chief executive Richard Measelle expressed his firm's intention of working with clients with sales of up to $2 billion, well above the $175 million limit established after the 1989 separation agreement. Measelle also declared technology would be a "core competency" of the company, and later restated Arthur Andersen's core objectives, "To pursue unconstrained growth; to provide consulting services, either directly or indirectly to all markets and to have the technology we need to compete."[13]

After several failed attempts by parent company Andersen Worldwide to reconcile the differences between the two competing business units, Andersen Consulting filed arbitration seeking official separation from Arthur Andersen. Arthur Andersen was willing to part with Andersen Consulting if the consulting firm paid upward of $14 billion in compensation for use of the Andersen name and use of technology developed by the accounting group. Andersen Consulting countered by demanding return of the transfer payments and seeking damages for Arthur Andersen's negative effect on the consulting firm's brand equity.

REPOSITIONING ANDERSEN CONSULTING

Measuring Brand Equity

As the arbitration process advanced, Andersen Consulting developed plans to reposition itself. Andersen Consulting had distinguished itself from its competition over the last several years, and the firm wished to capitalize on this momentum with a new brand positioning. To evaluate the value of the Andersen Consulting brand, the company undertook a brand equity measurement study. Using data collected by the research firm BPRI, the study compared public perceptions of Andersen Consulting with four competitors: IBM, Ernst & Young, McKinsey, and EDS. In terms of perceived capabilities, McKinsey emerged as the foremost business strategy services company while IBM led the IT services segment. Andersen Consulting however had a strong position in "both" business strategy and Information Technology services that enabled it to post very strong consideration scores, and ultimately lead on brand equity. An overall brand equity model was applied to rank the companies by assigning each company a score in each of four categories (image, awareness, consideration, preference) and averaging the scores. Andersen Consulting staked out a leadership position, achieving the highest score on the brand equity scale (see Exhibit 2).

A different study conducted by Harris Research ranked U.S. consulting firms using a different set of competitors. Compared with McKinsey, Booz Allen,

BCG, and A.T. Kearney, Andersen Consulting ranked first in the following categories: share of mind, value for money, uniqueness, and momentum. The study revealed that not only did Andersen Consulting possess favorable qualities and attributes that combined to provide strong overall brand equity, but the company also occupied a unique position in that it offered valued strategic business services and well-regarded IT solutions.

Based on results from both studies, Andersen Consulting leadership concluded that the company was "the company that combines strategic insight, vision and thought leadership with IT expertise in developing client solutions."[14] This unique combination of skills enabled Andersen Consulting to establish points of parity with technology and strategy firms, while at the same time achieving points of difference. For example, Andersen Consulting's technology capabilities were a point of parity that enabled the firm to compete for clients with IBM. Because clients viewed IBM as a technology consultant and not a business strategist, Andersen Consulting's reputation for insight and vision constituted a point of difference.

Developing a New Positioning

Over the years, Andersen Consulting had evolved its positioning to better meet the needs of its clients and marketplace opportunity (see Exhibit 3). In this sense, Andersen Consulting fostered a fluid and evolving positioning. This evolutionary model came not just from the demands of the marketplace. According to Jim Murphy, Andersen Consulting's Global Managing Director of Marketing & Communications, the business leadership of Andersen Consulting was "historically uneasy with the status quo. There is a hunger for pushing the next horizon."[15]

In the months before the arbitration decision, Andersen Consulting developed a new positioning that sought to formalize its position as a leader in the new economy. To distinguish Andersen Consulting from its competition, the firm developed a positioning platform that captured the company's vision and strategy—positioning it as a bridge builder helping companies close the gap from the old economy to the new. It also positioned the company as one who helped companies transform trends into business
opportunities using its deep global knowledge, its unique vantage point, and its breadth and depth of resources and relationships. Behind this idea of partnering with clients was Andersen Consulting's vision statement: "To help our clients create their future."

OFFICIAL SEPARATION FROM ARTHUR ANDERSEN

Arbitrator's Ruling

On August 7, 2000, the arbitration ruling from Columbian lawyer Dr. Guillermo Gamba released Andersen Consulting from any further obligation to Arthur Andersen or Andersen Worldwide—financial, professional, or otherwise. Although the arbitrator's decision required Andersen Consulting to forfeit the annual transfer payments the firm had placed in escrow since 1997 (totaling $530 million) in addition to the $300 million transfer payment for fiscal 1999, this payment was significantly less than the $14.5 billion asked for by the accounting firm. In justifying his decision to award separation to Andersen Consulting, Gamba faulted Andersen Worldwide for improperly supervising the two units since their separation in 1989.

In return for its independence, Andersen Consulting did have to make one concession. The license to use the Andersen Consulting name was to expire December 31, 2000. Coincidentally, the organization had begun to explore changing its name in advance of the arbitration decision. Many in the leadership team felt the label "consulting" was somewhat limiting to the future role of Andersen Consulting as an organization. Andersen Consulting had to now quickly create a new name, effectively transfer equity of the old name to the new one, raise awareness of the new name globally, decisively eliminate confusion between itself and Arthur Andersen, and reposition the firm in the marketplace to reflect its new vision and strategy. Never in history had such a large scale rebranding occurred in such a short time frame (see Exhibit 4). Within 147 days of the ruling, the company had to unveil a name that was trademarkable in 47 countries, effective and inoffensive in over 200 languages, corresponded with an available URL, and was acceptable to employees and clients.

THE REBRANDING AND REPOSITIONING PROCESS

Though the execution of the rebranding and repositioning process was a daunting task, Andersen Consulting executives embraced the opportunity to create a new image for the company. Joe Forehand, Managing Partner of CEO of Andersen Consulting, explained in a press release:

> We are a very different organization today than we were when we formed Andersen Consulting back in 1989, so adopting a new name and brand identity is a logical next step in our growth strategy.[16]

Andersen Consulting was well-prepared for a rebranding project of such scope because, just two years prior, the business had overhauled its visual identity as part of the "A-to-the-power-of-C" rebranding. In looking back, Jim Murphy referred to the 1999 rebranding as being "a rehearsal of a global brand change."

To carry out the global rebranding and repositioning, Andersen Consulting supplemented its annual $75 million marketing and communications budget with an additional $100 million. To create interest around the effort, Andersen Consulting topped the advertising agency Young & Rubicam to develop a teaser advertising campaign in support of the rebranding and repositioning effort. The homepage of the corporate website was also updated to reflect the upcoming rebranding and repositioning effort. The ads and corporate website featured a graphic of a partially "torn" Andersen Consulting logo, which revealed the message: "Renamed. Redefined. Reborn. 01.01.01."

Andersen Consulting had a strong reputation from which to launch the new brand. James Murphy felt that the target audience and general public would readily adopt the new name. "It's not like we don't have the credentials," said Murphy. "Now, we want to transfer the equity that we have built into that name and brand it to a new name."[17] The short amount of time Andersen Consulting had in which to execute the change was, in the minds of many inside the firm, the major challenge.

Finding a New Name

Led by Andersen Consulting's marketing and communications department, the search for a new name began immediately following the arbitrator's ruling. With the help of outside branding experts Landor Associates, as well as through an internal Andersen Consulting name-generation initiative dubbed "Brandstorming," thousands of name candidates were generated.

From these names, 550 candidates were selected to undergo research based on specific criteria: how well the name fit with the organization's strategy, how distinctive or unique it was, and the name's potential for longevity. The research entailed a preliminary round of trademark and URL availability research in the United States, where the majority of the company's business was generated. After this legal review, fifty-one names were still viable. These candidates were then subjected to more rigorous research, including native speaker review and linguistic analysis in 47 countries and against 200 languages, to screen for cultural sensitivities and ensure the name carried positive connotations in each market. The tight deadline compounded the already complex global trademark check.

In addition to time, another challenge was the recent increase in volume of registered Internet domain names. Registration had increased 46 percent over levels from the year 2000. From May to September 2000, the number of registered domains had nearly doubled to 17 million—practically one registration per second. As a result, when the 51 names were found to be available globally, the firm began purchasing the URLs for these name candidates in the United States. After the final name selection, Accenture would purchase the URLs in each country where it conducted business.

The overall name development and search for Accenture was unprecedented, not only because of the 81 days in which it was conducted, but also because of its scale and scope. For example, any external client or consumer research is typically limited, if conducted at all, during name searches. However, Andersen Consulting wanted to gain its clients' perspectives on the name candidates, so it tested the 51 name candidates across eight key markets with its senior executive target audience. The objective of the research was to gauge their overall reaction, the fit with the company's vision, and positioning and measure the name's uniqueness.

At the conclusion of this research, the name candidate list was down to 10 names, which were presented to Andersen Consulting's executive committee for final selection. The executive committee chose the name "Accenture," which had been submitted by consultant Kim Petersen, who worked in Andersen Consulting's Oslo office. The name rhymes with "adventure" and connoted "an accent on the future." Petersen explained his submission:

When trying to come up with a new name for the firm, I thought of things like bold growth, operational excellence and a great place to work. Accenture seemed to capture all those things.[18]

The executive committee selected the name Accenture because it clearly fit the firm's positioning and vision. In addition, they thought the name was catchy and distinctive. Because an employee created the name, the executives hoped it would build consensus within the firm and speed the adoption of the Accenture name.

Announcing Accenture

Following the specified launch schedule, Andersen Consulting announced its new name on October 26, 2000. The company held an internal global webcast to announce the Accenture name and to answer questions about the name change with its partners and employees. Managing Partner and CEO Joe Forehand commented on the new name at the time of the announcement:

> Accenture expresses what we have become as an organization as well as what we hope to be—a network of businesses that transcends the boundaries of traditional consulting and brings innovations that dramatically improve the way the world works and lives.[19]

External activities included an announcement press release, followed by a teleconference with leading media to launch the name to the marketplace. Until the official changeover on midnight of December 31, 2000, the firm retained the Andersen Consulting name and logo, and continued to globally heighten awareness and interest of the new name, through the "Renamed. Redefined. Reborn. 01.01.01" print, poster and television effort.

As a second step in the renaming process in mid-November, Andersen Consulting launched a new logo to visually represent Accenture. The logo consisted of the word "Accenture" written in lowercase letters, with a "greater-than" symbol above the letter "T" serving to accent the word. The greater-than symbol was included in the design as a means of symbolically pointing forward to the future. The lower case "a" was intended to demonstrate that Accenture was approachable and accessible. Once the logo was revealed, the challenging task of rebranding the organization really began.

ACCENTURE LAUNCH

On midnight, December 31, 2000, Andersen Consulting officially adopted the Accenture name. Accordingly, on January 1, the company's corporate website was changed from www.ac.com to www.accenture.com. Accompanying the announcement was a massive global marketing program designed to raise awareness of the new name. The program targeted senior executives at Accenture's clients and prospects, all Accenture Partners and employees, the media, leading industry analysts, potential recruits, and academia.

Internal Launch

Launching the new Accenture name internally was an equally important and daunting task. Accenture needed to execute a complete and monumental changeover throughout all levels of the organization and ensure that all employees and clients understood the new brand and the new positioning. This process was managed and realized by 55 teams of nearly 2,000 employees across the organization, as well as many more outside individuals and agencies. The new name had to be reflected by the company's 178 offices in 47 countries, by its 70,000 employees and their 7 million business cards, by its 1,200 proprietary software applications, and by all other documents (including signage and stationary) and 20,000 databases. To keep employees apprised of the rebranding and repositioning process, Accenture began distributing internal newsletters and e-mails, along with special issues of the internal magazine *Dialogue* beginning in August 2000. Throughout the process, Joe Forehand kept everyone informed from the arbitration announcement to the selection of the new name with periodic global webcasts.

On January 3, 2001, Joe Forehand welcomed the New Year and the new company, "Accenture," with a global webcast from Australia, the site of the Accenture Match Play Championship. Additionally, when employees returned to work after New Year's Day, they found Accenture launch packages which included a letter from Joe Forehand, a brand book that explained the new brand, and new positioning, and special launch-themed issues of *Dialogue* and *Dialogue Online*, the company's internal communications website and magazine. Throughout January, Accenture executed a series of open houses and celebratory events to recognize the new brand at local offices around the world.

External Launch Efforts: Phase One

Accenture planned a two-phased marketing strategy for introducing Accenture to its global audience. The aim of both phases was to surround the company's target audience—including 40,000 clients and prospects and Accenture's 70,000 employees, as well as 1.5 million recruits—with messages informing them about the new name and new positioning.

The first phase was a high impact launch on January 1, 2001 using extensive global advertising. In addition to continued media and analyst relations, the launch utilized television, print, poster, and Internet placements that linked the Accenture name with the New Year, a linkage that harkened back to Accenture's first ever advertisements from 1989. In the United States, Accenture television spots appeared during College Bowl games on New Year's Day. Accenture commercials also debuted at this time across other international markets. The campaign also included print and airport poster advertising. The ads were intended to introduce the new name and transfer equity from its former brand. Additionally, they positioned Accenture as offering a broad range of capabilities across consulting, technology, outsourcing, and alliances. By highlighting each of Accenture's core capabilities, the firm hoped to illustrate that it offered far more than just strategy or IT consulting. This repositioning recast Accenture as a company who could bridge boundaries to create the future—helping its clients bridge the gap from the old economy to the new.

An Accenture branded airship was introduced at the January 2001 Accenture Match Play Championship (formerly the Andersen Consulting Match Play Championship) event in Melbourne, Australia. Accenture utilized its sponsorships of other major global sporting events to achieve a high impact internationally. High-profile global advertising opportunities included the Formula 1 Racing Series, several European skiing events, the Six Nations Rugby tournament, the Asian PGA tour, the Accenture Dream Soccer Match in Japan, and the Italian Football Championship. By January 2001, television, print, Internet, and poster advertisements touting the Accenture name appeared in each of 47 different countries where the company did business. Between January and March, over 6,000 total television commercials spots aired in markets globally. This ad schedule was supplemented by over 1,000 global print ads.

The company utilized innovative print and billboard advertising in addition to television. In Australia, the company placed a "cover wrap" on the magazine *Business Review Weekly* and placed advertising on bus stops and park benches in Sydney's business district. The company adorned its Paris office building with gigantic Accenture branding, and several Air France buses bore the new logo. Andersen Consulting placed large-scale outdoor ads in Milan's Oberdan Square and Rome's Obelisk, and covered 10 taxis in London with Accenture signage.

In addition to the high profile advertising program, over 43,000 clients received a launch mailing which included creative packaging to announce the new name and positioning, a capabilities brochure outlining the companies service offerings, *Outlook* magazine (the company's thought leadership publication) and a letter from Joe Forehand. Furthermore, the Accenture Match Play Championship golf tournament hosted 450 clients and partners. The impact of the launch was noticeable in other ways. Traffic to Accenture.com was up 72 percent over a typical week with 27,700 visitors daily. Finally, the media touted the launch impact as the largest rebranding initiative ever undertaken by a professional services company—the "01.01.01" launch garnered approximately 120 news items globally in just the first two weeks alone.

External Launch Efforts: Phase Two

The second phase of the advertising program began in late January 2001 with high-profile television spots in the United States during the Super Bowl on January 28. Provocative print ads were also a part of the mix. The new series of ads presented the viewer (or reader) with a striking fact regarding the future in the form of an unexpected headline, followed by the phrase "Now it gets interesting." One print ad had a headline appearing as if torn from newsprint and reading "Bacteria Tested As a Digital Circuit: Use In Chips May Dwarf Silicon" was superimposed over a microscope-view of a bacteria colony. "Now it gets interesting" appeared between brackets under the newsprint headline. Jim Murphy explained the purpose of the ads:

Our goal was to make target audiences take notice of dramatic global changes in the marketplace in a way that positions Accenture as the organization that can help clients take advantage of these changes and turn them into opportunities.[20]

The advertisements were interactive as they were integrated with the corporate website where users could find out more information on how Accenture could help them capitalize on the marketplace opportunities identified in the ad. Although the Super Bowl television spots were not seen as typical for the broadcast, a study conducted by the Zyman Marketing Group pointed out their beneficial effects. Specifically, the study measured advertising effectiveness by tracking purchase intent before and after consumers viewed the ads. Accenture's "Bacteria" spot garnered a 77 percent increase in purchase intent, the most of any 2001 Super Bowl ad. Other Accenture spots—"Birthday Cake," "Sports Car," and "Surgery"— ranked third, eighth, and twelfth, respectively.

The ads had the desired effect of generating interest in the company. Traffic to Accenture.com increased dramatically in the days following the Super Bowl. On that Sunday, overall traffic to the website doubled. In the week that followed the broadcast, traffic to the advertising section of the website rose 2,100 percent. These television spots also aired during several major golf tournaments including The Players Championship in March and the United States Open in June.

RESULTS AND RESEARCH

After the launch, the company executed an evaluation of the rebranding and repositioning program as part of its global awareness tracking study with senior executives, its annual brand equity assessment, and its biannual recruitment awareness tracking study. At the end of 2001, one year after the launch of the new brand, the awareness for the Accenture name remained at, or above, previous levels for Andersen Consulting in most countries. Teresa Poggenpohl credited the advertising campaign with driving these levels, commenting "We would never have achieved this awareness so quickly on a global basis around the world…without advertising."[21]

The results of the advertising, marketing, and communications campaigns were impressive. The advertising effect on purchase consideration of Accenture's services increased 350 percent following the campaign. The brand equity of Accenture also increased by 11 percent. Awareness of Accenture's breadth and depth of services had achieved 96 percent of its previous level. Globally, awareness of Accenture as a provider of Management & Technology consulting services was 76 percent of the former Andersen Consulting levels.

The timing of Accenture's forced name change was fortuitous. As the new Accenture name achieved heightened and favorable recognition, its former parent company, Arthur Andersen, faced considerable legal scrutiny. In late 2001, the Securities and Exchange Commission launched an investigation into Enron and Arthur Andersen for possible irregular accounting and auditing procedures. Accenture published a press release in January 2002 to remind the public that Accenture and Arthur Andersen were separate entities and that all historical contractual ties between the two firms had been completely severed. In June 2002, Arthur Andersen was convicted of witness tampering and obstruction of justice for shredding documents related to its audits of Enron, which effectively put the firm out of business.[22]

Accenture IPO and Financial Results

In July 2001, Accenture offered shares of its stock in a $1.7 billion initial public offering. As a consequence of the IPO, Accenture believed it was better able to deliver a broader range of capabilities and solutions for its clients. The IPO climate at the time of the offering was not favorable, but Accenture outperformed many of the companies in its market space. By the end of the year, Accenture stock was up almost 80 percent from its IPO price of $14.50. Comparatively, competitor KPMG Consulting's stock closed down more than 20 percent on the year.

Refining the Positioning

The marketplace underwent dramatic changes as a result of the fallout from the dot-com crash and the general slowdown of the U.S. economy in 2001. Money evaporated from the venture capital pool. Companies looked for ways to cut costs as consumer spending declined. Businesses grew hesitant to turn to consulting companies for strategies that they could develop themselves. Derek Young, Accenture's Australia managing director, said at the time, "The days when you got paid to give advice are finished. Our client management now want outcomes and they want to tie your remuneration to the value you deliver."[23] To better serve its clients, Accenture now sought to "partner" with companies and help them execute their ideas. Accenture focused its energy toward developing an evolved positioning that better suited the marketplace and client demands.

In 2002, Accenture unveiled a new positioning to reflect its new role as a partner to aid execution of strategy, summarized succinctly by the tagline "Innovation Delivered." This tagline was supported by the statement, "From innovation to execution, Accenture helps accelerate your vision."

According to surveys conducted by the company, senior executives from a diverse group of industry sectors and countries identified "their ability to execute and deliver on their ideas" as the number one barrier to success. The respondents expressed a need for external assistance from consulting firms to help them bring their ideas to life. Furthermore, senior executives named Accenture as the only company positioned to provide this assistance. Additionally, the survey revealed that executives considered consulting companies as a source of validation for innovative ideas generated within a company. The new positioning and brand essence came from these findings.

Accenture stressed that the innovation could come from either the consulting firm or the client, as explained by CEO Joe Forehand:

> We don't want to back away from being seen as someone who brings the best consulting, innovation, and ideas to clients, but our clients are telling us they have a lot of smart people with good ideas, too. They just need execution. We are uniquely positioned to fit into this intersection

of business and technology capability to drive shareholder value for clients. . . . There's nobody in the industry that can be the best at everything across the whole spectrum of hardware, software, technology services and consulting. Our clients value [a company] that is an independent services organization that can make sure their interests are put first and foremost, but also one that has a network of alliance partners it can bring together.[24]

With this new positioning, the company targeted senior executives of global companies "with the ability to drive change in their organizations." The type of executive that Accenture targeted understood the importance of moving rapidly to capitalize on emerging opportunities in the ever-changing marketplace. This group of executives also recognized that the pursuit of competitive advantages sometimes required difficult decisions on their part. Accenture would ensure that such decisions were implemented successfully with the right execution, as described by the company's role with respect to its new positioning:

> [Accenture is a] catalyst to accelerate innovation to results. We spur ideas, put plans into action and help provoke significant change.

Accenture believed its global network of employees and alliance partners, as well as its breadth of services (e.g., Consulting, Technology, Outsourcing, Alliances), represented unparalleled resources to provide clients with innovative solutions. Further building on the "Innovation Delivered" idea, the Accenture signature had been updated to include the phrase "Innovation Delivered" to the existing Accenture logo. Going forward, the Accenture "Innovation Delivered" signature would serve as the company's primary logo, reinforcing how Accenture collaborated with its clients to bring ideas to life.

Bringing "Innovation Delivered" to Life: "I Am Your Idea" Advertising Campaign

The new Accenture global advertising campaign, "I am your idea," was launched on February 20, 2002, the first day of the 2002 Accenture Match Play Championship. The campaign provided a clever and unique perspective. The "I am your idea" ads spoke from the point of view of the idea itself, giving the idea its own voice and personality. In addition, the campaign drove the new "Innovation Delivered" positioning message by illustrating "whether it's your idea or Accenture's, we'll help you turn innovation into results." The advertisements were in response to the frustration cited by senior executives that great ideas may go unrealized.

A print ad from the campaign entitled "Highway" featured a highway scene in which the reader had to make a choice. A central sign above the highway read "I am your idea" with two additional signs underneath. One sign provided direction to a straight path and read "Use me," and another sign pointed toward a highway turn-off and read "Lose me." The copy read, "It's not how many ideas you have. It's how many you make happen. So whether it's your idea or Accenture's, we'll help you turn innovation into results. See how at Accenture.com." The advertising campaign appeared in 31 countries and was seen on leading business and television news programs and in leading business publications. It was also supported by airport posters and outdoor advertising.

ACCENTURE DRIVES ON

Global Growth

Accenture had truly become a global company. By 2004, the company, headquartered in Hamilton, Bermuda, operated 110 offices in 48 countries. It had grown into an organization that employed over 115,000 people and had 2,200 partners. Accenture provided services that included management consulting, technology services, and outsourcing. Accenture was organized around five operating groups: Communications and High Tech, Financial Services, Products, Resources, and Government. These operating groups were further broken down into 18 focused industry groups, providing Accenture's employees with a thorough understanding of specific industries and the associated business issues and applicable technologies (see Exhibit 5). Revenues had grown from $1.4 billion in 1989 to $13.6 billion in 2004 (see Exhibits 6–8), with over half of these revenues coming from international operations.

Accenture continued to land high-profile contracts, providing unique solutions to companies around the world. For example, New York City faced the challenge of having over 14 pages in its phone book just to list municipal services. Accenture teamed with the city and created a single "311" number for New Yorkers to access non-emergency services 24 hours a day. The result was that New York City residents had to dial only three digits to obtain the help they needed, all provided in 171 different languages. The company worked for BP Petrochemicals (a subsidiary of British Petroleum) to build a custom global positioning and monitoring system for BP's hazardous chemicals rail fleet. Web-based software allowed BP to monitor real-time information on the location, temperature, product conditions, and status of any shipment. Accenture signed a six-year contract with Barclays, one of the 10 largest banks in the world, in 2004. Accenture was to manage Barclay's IT applications development function related to its commercial and retail banking systems. At the time, this was the largest outsourcing deal ever signed by the Accenture Financial Services operating group.

Accenture was capitalizing on the growing global market. The global management and marketing consultancy market had an estimated value of nearly $140 billion in 2003, and was forecasted to grow to $160 billion by 2008.[25] The market was dominated by a small group of leading multinational companies, of which Accenture was a part, and recent consolidation had strengthened the position of these leading companies.

Competition Intensifies

Although Accenture had achieved considerable success, it still faced significant competition. A significant challenge came from International Business Machines (IBM). IBM had become one of the largest computer companies in the world by selling hardware and software to customers across the globe. The company had been transformed from a hardware company into an IT services company in the 1990s, and it solidified this position by purchasing Monday—the newly invented name of PricewaterhouseCoopers Consulting—in 2002 for $3.5 billion. Clients of IBM included Virgin Megastores, the Mayo Clinic, and Procter & Gamble. Revenues from IBM's Global Services division, which accounted for more than half of the company's total revenues, totaled $46 billion in 2004.

Publicly, Accenture expressed confidence in competing with IBM. Although Accenture could not match IBM's technical skills or research staff (IBM had over 330,000 employees in 2004), Accenture felt it had a significant lead and proven record in helping companies reach their business goals. "IBM is generally a technology company," said Joel Friedman, president of Accenture's Business Process Outsourcing unit. "I think our history of solving business problems and our industry knowledge gives us an enormous advantage."[26]

Aside from IBM, other firms competed in Accenture's core IT consulting area. Like IBM, HP entered the IT services business from a background in computer hardware. In 2005, HP's consulting and services business generated $16 billion in revenue. BearingPoint (formerly KPMG Consulting) was a business services company that provided management consulting and systems integration. BearingPoint reported revenues of $3.1 billion in 2003. Deloitte Consulting specialized in eBusiness consulting and offered services to businesses in health care, manufacturing, financial services, and energy. The company posted revenue of $3.2 billion in 2003. Accenture also experienced increased competition from firms based in India, such as Wipro, Tata Consultancy Services, and Infosys, which had significantly lower costs.

Government Contracts

One important area for Accenture was services performed for various U.S. government agencies, which accounted for about 15 percent of Accenture's revenue. Accenture worked with the Department of Agriculture to help them comply with the Government Paperwork Elimination and the Freedom to eFile acts. It was contracted by the Department of Defense in 2004 to implement a voting technology system that would allow military personnel stationed overseas to vote in U.S. elections by casting their ballots over the Internet. One of the biggest contracts with the government came in 2004 when Accenture won a $10 billion contract from the Department of Homeland Security to manage the information technology that tracks border entries and exits of non-U.S. citizens, verifies visitor identification, and supports visa and immigration compliance.

These contracts did not come without controversy. Many government officials questioned whether Accenture, a corporation that was officially operated out of Bermuda, should have received numerous government contracts in sensitive areas. Certain politicians were calling for the Department of Homeland Security contract to be reviewed and given to another firm.

Accenture faced further scrutiny in the debate over outsourcing. Business Process Outsourcing had become a significant source of the company's revenue and was increasingly being recommended to their clients. The political debate in the United States over outsourcing had intensified in recent years. With many Americans losing jobs to outsourcing overseas, politicians were considering legislation that would bar companies that shift jobs offshore from getting government contracts. Legislation to this effect would severely hurt Accenture and its future revenue stream.

High Performance. Delivered.

Accenture built upon the "Innovation Delivered" theme when it announced its new "High Performance Business" strategy in late 2003. According to the Accenture website, a high-performance business is one which:

> Balance[s] today's needs and tomorrow's opportunities. They consistently outperform their peers in revenue, profit growth and total return to shareholders. And they do so over a sustained time frame, across business cycles, industry disruptions and changes in CEO leadership.[27]

Accenture conducted research to determine characteristics of high performance, which apply across multiple industries and business functions, while also pinpointing industry-specific findings to reflect the fact that the drivers of value varied significantly by industry.

The company announced that it had signed professional golfer Tiger Woods to a multi-year agreement to represent the company and its new High Performance Business Strategy. The campaign included print, cable and network TV advertising in 27 countries, as well as display ads in airports. Ads aired during golf tournaments on ESPN and ABC, as well as on CNN and CNBC. Print ads were featured in the *New York Times*, *USA Today*, *Financial Times*, *Australian Financial Review*, and *Nikkei Business*, as well as global editions of the *Wall Street Journal*, *Fortune*, *Forbes*, and *The Economist*.

The majority of the ads positioned Woods in situations during golf matches that demanded optimum performance in stressful and competitive environments. One ad showed Woods with no shoes, standing in ankle keep water with his pants rolled up to his knees in order to attempt a challenging shot. The ad copy read, "High performers create their own opportunities. Go on. Be a Tiger." At the bottom of each ad, under the Accenture logo, were the words "High performance. Delivered." In describing their relationship with Tiger Woods, Joe Forehand remarked:

> Tiger Woods' strength, mastery, discipline, and relentless focus on winning are universally recognized qualities that mirror the characteristics of a high-performance business, making him the ideal representative for out market positioning. A high-performance business is one that optimizes its resources to achieve its objectives and consistently outperforms competitors. Tiger is the best at his game, and we want our clients to be the best at theirs.[28]

Corporate Sponsorship

Accenture continued its sponsorship of the BMW Williams Formula One Team and the Accenture Match Play Golf Championship, but the company looked to expand beyond these events and attempted to reach a broader audience. In 2002, it began sponsoring the Accenture Marathon in Buenos Aires, Argentina, and followed this with the Accenture Chicago Triathlon in 2003. Beyond sports, Accenture looked to strengthen its ties with cultural organizations around the world. The company continued its sponsorship of Sweden's National Museum of Fine Arts and the Rheingau Musik Festival in Germany. In Italy, Accenture worked with La Scala Opera House in Milan to conceive, design, and execute La Scala's official website. The Louvre Museum in France benefited from Accenture's expertise in project management and technological innovation. In 2004, Accenture announced that it had teamed with the Royal Shakespeare Company and was the exclusive "High Performance Business Partner" of the U.K. theater company. Back in the United States, Accenture acted as the management consulting and information technology services advisor to the National Museum of the American Indian.

Leadership Change

In September 2004, Joe Forehand stepped down as CEO (he remained Chairman of the company) and turned the reigns over to William Green, former Chief Operating Officer. Green inherited the High Performance Business strategy and set about to activate it. One of his first moves was to introduce a policy whereby many Accenture contracts contained incentives that were realized only if specific business targets were met. For instance, a contract with British travel agent Thomas Cook was structured such that Accenture's bonus depended on five metrics, including a cost-cutting one. In 2004, 30 percent of the company's contracts contained such incentives. Green also continued Accenture's push to win large multi-year contracts exceeding a billion dollars, which were potentially more profitable but also involved a greater level of risk due to their complexity. Accenture recruited aggressively to staff these and other contracts, hiring 20,000 people in 2004. During the first year of Green's tenure as CEO, Accenture's success continued apace, with revenues growing 13 percent to $15.1 billion while profits rose 36 percent to $690 million.

Green's ambition for Accenture was that it would develop products and services that were so useful to companies that they became necessary to compete. In explaining this ambition in an interview, he issued an implicit challenge to his company:

> How do you become the de facto standard for a set of products or services that an industry uses to operate? How do you become not optional?[29]

CONCLUSION

Following a decade of prosperity and growth, Accenture staked a new direction and forged a new identity at the turn of the twenty-first century. After successful arbitration against Andersen Worldwide and Arthur Andersen, the company was able to recast itself under a new name, coinciding with the launch of a new positioning. The rebranding and repositioning of Accenture was unprecedented in scope and timeframe—the largest rebranding initiative ever undertaken by a professional services firm was successfully implemented across 47 countries in just 147 days. Accenture launched this rebranding and repositioning to its global audience with a multi-phase global marketing campaign that began before the official changeover occurred on January 1, 2001. The challenge was daunting, but the objectives clear: reposition the company, transfer brand equity to Accenture, raise awareness of Accenture globally, and eliminate residual confusion with Arthur Andersen.

Accenture was successful in these efforts, as evidenced in their ranking in *BusinessWeek*'s "Best Global Brands." The company was recognized as the 50th strongest worldwide brand in 2004 (up from 52nd in 2003). Accenture received recognition in other areas as well. The *London Times* ranked the company number three in its listing of "Top 100 Graduate Employers". In the U.S., *Working Mother* magazine named Accenture to its list of "100 Best Companies for Working Mothers." Accenture was also named by *Black Collegian* magazine as one of the "Top 50 Diversity Employers." Accenture had done much to deserve these accolades, and it continued its impressive performance as a new CEO took over the company. Still, the future for Accenture was not free of challenges. One notable challenge was managing the risk inherent in fulfilling ever-bigger multi-billion dollar contracts. Another challenge was the intensified competition from both established firms such as IBM and newer Indian rivals such as Infosys. The company management would have to find solutions to these and other challenges if the company was to replicate the success it enjoyed during its first five years as Accenture.

DISCUSSION QUESTIONS

1. How would you characterize Andersen Consulting's brand equity in the late-1990s? What factors and decisions contributed to the building of this equity?
2. Compare the characteristics of Accenture's brand equity to those of Andersen Consulting. Do you think the rebranding and repositioning of the company successfully transferred the equity from the old name to the new one?
3. How much of a competitive threat is IBM? How should Accenture best compete with them?
4. Evaluate the effectiveness of Tiger Woods as a spokesman for the company. Is Accenture achieving its objectives with a celebrity spokesman?

Exhibit 1: Awareness Tracking: Andersen Consulting versus Arthur Andersen

1994 Unaided Awareness

	Business Re-Engineering	Strategy Consulting	Systems Integration	Organizational Change
Andersen Consulting	24%	18%	19%	10%
Arthur Andersen	27%	17%	18%	12%

1995 Unaided Awareness

	Business Re-Engineering	Strategy Consulting	Systems Integration	Organizational Change
Andersen Consulting	35%	32%	29%	23%
Arthur Andersen	31%	22%	25%	18%

Source: 1995 Global Awareness Tracking Study

Exhibit 2: Overall Brand Equity Index

	Image	Awareness	Consideration	Preference	Average
Andersen Consulting	6.5	10	9.1	5.8	7.9
McKinsey	7.2	8.4	9.2	6.4	7.8
IBM	5.3	4.9	3.6	1.2	3.8
Ernst & Young	3.8	3.2	5.3	1.9	3.6
EDS	1.9	0	1.6	0	0.7

Source: Brand Equity Measurement Initiative, Andersen Consulting, November 1999

Exhibit 3: Brand Positioning Evolution

Period	Positioning
1988–1991	Help Apply Technology to Business Advantage
1992	Empower to Reengineer for Business Advantage
1993	Empower to Change for Business Advantage
1994–1998	Continually Strengthen Performance to Achieve Goals
1998	Far-Reaching Change for Success
1999	Help Achieve Value at Speed in the New Economy
2000	Bridging Boundaries to Create the Future
2002	Innovation Delivered
2003	High Performance Delivered

Source: Positioning Platform, Andersen Consulting

Exhibit 4: Rebranding Launch Timeline

Aug 7 - 11	Aug 11 - Oct	Sept - Oct	Nov - Dec	Jan 1
PLANNING	**BRAND DEVELOP.**	**RESEARCH**	**EXECUTE NAME CHANGE**	**BRAND LAUNCH**
Arbitration Decision	Name Develop.	Market Testing	Logo	Advertising
Strategy Develop.	Visual Identity	Native Speaker Review	Dialogue Mag.	Direct Mktg.
Creative Brief	Brand Line & Descriptor Develop.	Linguistic Analysis	Prelude Ads	Accenture.com
		Final Recommend-ation	Media/Analyst Relations	Media/Analyst Relations
	Launch Plan Develop.			Int./Ext. Events
				Outlook Mag.
				Signage

**(Source: "The Rebranding and Repositioning of Andersen Consulting."
Andersen Consulting, October 2, 2000)**

Exhibit 5: Operating Groups and Industry Groups

Communications and High Tech	Financial Services	Products	Resources	Government
Industry Groups: - Communication - Electronics & High Tech - Media & Entertainment	*Industry Groups:* - Banking - Capital Markets - Insurance	*Industry Groups:* - Automotive - Health Services - Industrial Equipment - Pharmaceuticals & Medical - Retail & Consumer - Transportation	*Industry Groups:* - Chemicals - Energy - Forest Products - Metals & Mining - Utilities	*Industry Groups:* - Government

378

Exhibit 6: Revenues Before Reimbursements*

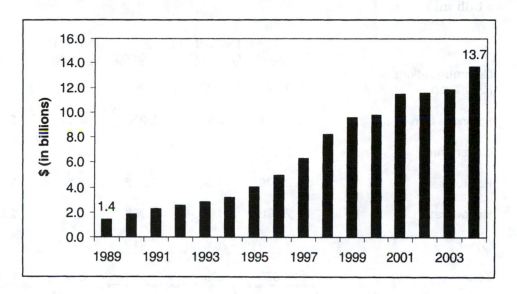

* This chart reflects revenues before reimbursements ("net revenues"). Reimbursements include travel and out-of-pocket expenses and third-party costs, such as the cost of hardware and software resales.

Source: Accenture Annual Report 2004

Exhibit 7: Revenues Before Reimbursement by Operating Group ($ in billions)

	2004	Percent Change	2003	Percent Change	2002
Communications & High Tech	$ 3,741	14%	$ 3,290	3%	$ 3,182
Financial Services	2,771	18%	2,355	0%	2,366
Government	1,995	26%	1,582	20%	1,316
Products	2,979	14%	2,613	-3%	2,696
Resources	2,178	11%	1,966	-2%	2,005
Other	9	-20%	12	20%	9
Total	$13,673	16%	$ 11,818	2%	$ 11,574

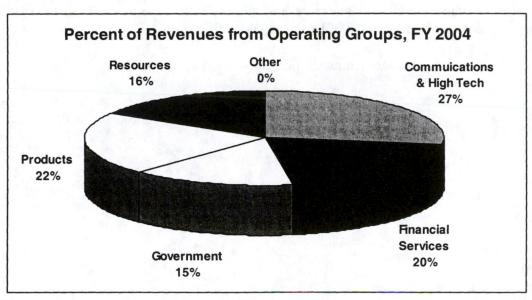

Percent of Revenues from Operating Groups, FY 2004

Resources 16%
Other 0%
Commuications & High Tech 27%
Products 22%
Government 15%
Financial Services 20%

Source: Accenture Annual Report 2004

Exhibit 8: Revenues Before Reimbursement by Geography
($ in billions)

	2004	Percent Change	2003	Percent Change	2002
Europe, Middle East, Africa	$ 6,572	23%	$ 5,353	8%	$ 4,963
Americas	6,133	8%	5,671	-3%	5,836
Asia Pacific	968	22%	794	2%	775
Total	$13,673	16%	$ 11,818	2%	$ 11,574

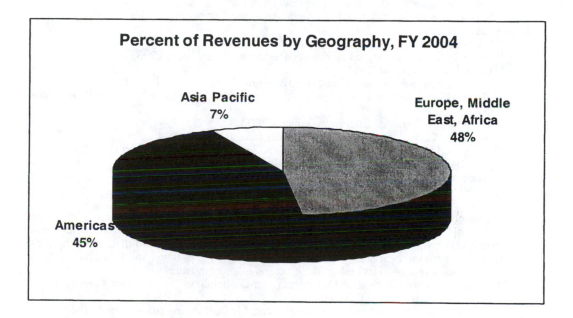

Source: Accenture Annual Report 2004

REFERENCES

[1] This case was made possible through the cooperation Accenture and Teresa Poggenpohl, Jim Murphy, Brian Harvey, and Chuck Teeter. Keith Richey prepared this case, which was revised and updated by Jonathan Michaels, under the supervision of Professor Kevin Lane Keller as the basis for class discussion.

[2] Andersen Consulting estimate, quoted in "Andersen Consulting Wins Independence." The *Wall Street Journal*, 2000.

[3] As quoted in "Our Founder." Arthur Andersen Press Release, 2000.

[4] As quoted in International Court of Arbitration decision, v. 2. July 28, 2000.

[5] As quoted in International Court of Arbitration decision, v. 2. July 28, 2000.

[6] "A Summary of the Buyer's Perspective." Decision Research, March 1998.

[7] "Civil War at Arthur Andersen." *The Economist*, August 17, 1991.

[8] Teresa Poggenpohl. Personal Interview. December 15, 2000.

[9] Kevin Lane Keller. Witness Statement. Andersen Consulting Business Unit Firms v. Arthur Andersen.

[10] "Arbitration Chronology." *AC.com*, 2000.

[11] "Brand Name and Corporate Imagery Research." OmniTech, 1993.

[12] Gartner Group report, 1995.

[13] As quoted in International Court of Arbitration decision, v. 2. July 28, 2000.

[14] "Brand Equity Measurement Initiative." Presentation, Andersen Consulting, November 1999.

[15] Jim Murphy. Personal Interview, January 2002.

[16] Andersen Consulting press release, October 26, 2000.

[17] As quoted in "Divorced Andersen Readies New Name." *B to B*, October 9, 2000.

[18] "Choosing the Name." Andersen Consulting Annual Report, 1999.

[19] Andersen Consulting press release, October 26, 2000.

[20] "So Now It Gets Interesting." *Accenture.com*, 2001.

[21] Teresa Poggenpohl. Personal Interview. January, 2002.

[22] This conviction was overturned in 2005 by the Supreme Court of the United States due to flaws in the jury instructions. By that time, however, Arthur Andersen had shrunk from over 85,000 worldwide employees to about 200 working on the legal matters facing the firm. The firm lost nearly all their clients when they were indicted and faced over 100 civil lawsuits related to its audits of Enron and other companies.

[23] Emma Connors. "Accent on Outsourcing for Global Giant." *Australian Financial Review*, January 23, 2002, p. 40.

[24] Cirillo, Rich. "No Ordinary Joe: Joe Forehand Is Positioning Accenture As the Prototypical IT Services. Firm." *VARBusiness*, January 21, 2002, p. 26.

[25] Datamonitor Industry Profile, Global Management and Marketing Consultancy, November 2004

[26] www.businessweek.com, "Beyond Blue," April 18, 2005.

[27] www.accenture.com

[28] Company new release, "Accenture Selects Tiger Woods to Launch High Performance Business Strategy." October 3, 2003.

[29] Spencer E. Ante, "Accenture's New High-Wire Act." *BusinessWeek*, November 15, 2004, p. 92.